TRAVELER

costa rica

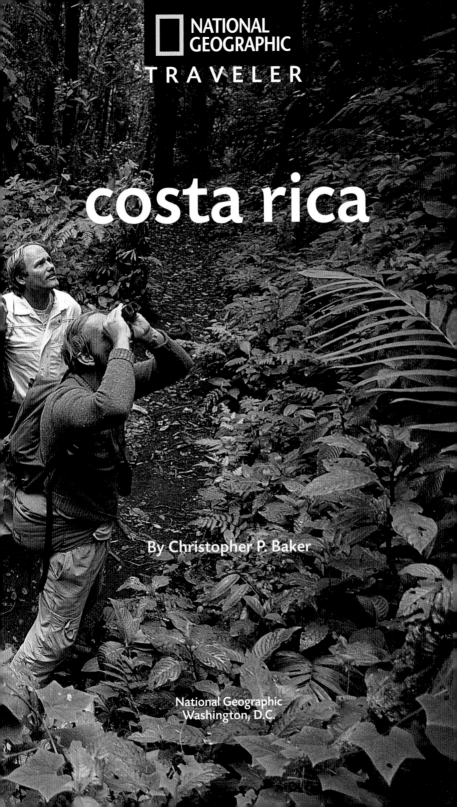

NATIONAL GEOGRAPHIC

T R A V E L E R

costa rica

By Christopher P. Baker

National Geographic
Washington, D.C.

F
1543.5
.S35
avg

CONTENTS

Pages 2–3: Birders thrill to Costa Rica's avian wonders.
Left: Intricate designs on an oxcart wheel

TRAVELING WITH EYES OPEN

Alert travelers go with a purpose and leave with a benefit. If you travel responsibly, you can help support wildlife conservation, historic preservation, and cultural enrichment in the places you visit. You can enrich your own travel experience as well.

To be a geo-savvy traveler:

- Recognize that your presence has an impact on the places you visit.

- Spend your time and money in ways that sustain local character. (Besides, it's more interesting that way.)

- Value the destination's natural and cultural heritage.

- Respect the local customs and traditions.

- Express appreciation to local people about things you find interesting and unique to the place: its nature and scenery, music and food, historic villages and buildings.

- Vote with your wallet: Support the people who support the place, patronizing businesses that make an effort to celebrate and protect what's special there. Seek out shops, local restaurants, inns, and tour operators who love their home—who love taking care of it and showing it off. Avoid businesses that detract from the character of the place.

- Enrich yourself, taking home memories and stories to tell, knowing that you have contributed to the preservation and enhancement of the destination.

That is the type of travel now called geotourism, is defined as "tourism that sustains or enhances the geographical character of a place—its environment, culture, aesthetics, heritage, and the well-being of its residents." To learn more, visit National Geographic's Center for Sustainable Destinations at *www. nationalgeographic.com/travel/sustainable.*

costa rica

ABOUT THE AUTHOR

Christopher P. Baker

After studying geography at the University of London and Latin American studies at the University of Liverpool, author Christopher P. Baker settled in California and established a career as a travel writer, photographer, and lecturer, with a special focus on the Caribbean and Latin America. He has written numerous guidebooks about the Bahamas, California, Jamaica, Puerto Rico, and elsewhere, and is acknowledged as an authority on travel to Cuba. For National Geographic, he has also written the *National Geographic Traveler: Cuba* and *National Geographic Traveler: Dominican Republic,* as well as the award-winning *Mi Moto Fidel: Motorcycling Through Castro's Cuba.* He also writes regularly for such publications as *Caribbean Travel & Life, Maxim, The Robb Report,* and *National Geographic Traveler* magazine. He has been featured on the National Geographic Channel and NPR, and currently lectures on National Geographic Expeditions' Costa Rica and Panama Canal cruise-tours. In 2005, the Caribbean Tourism Organization named him Travel Journalist of the Year. He promotes his work through his website: www.travelguidebooks.com.

Charting Your Trip

Abundantly blessed by Mother Nature, Costa Rica—a world leader in ecotourism—enthralls for its scenic beauty and tropical wildlife. Wilderness lodges throughout the country immerse you deep in the animal and avian world, placing you in close proximity to monkeys, jaguars, marine turtles, and birds by the score.

Money Matters

The national currency is the *colón*. U.S. currency, however, is widely accepted. Most stores, shops, restaurants, and tour companies take dollars. One tip: Bring lots of single dollar bills, for tips, streetside souvenirs, and other small purchases, as change for larger bills may be hard to come by.

If you do use colones, know that exchange rates are notoriously fickle; check the rate before leaving for your trip, but expect some fluctuation upon arrival.

Travelers checks are difficult to cash, due to widespread fraud. Credit cards are widely accepted.

Many banks have ATMs that work with U.S. bank cards, usually with a small usage charge.

The diversity of terrains also astounds. You can explore a lowland rain forest or snorkel a coral reef in the morning and steep in the mist-shrouded cloud forest or hike the rim of a steaming volcano in the afternoon. Active travelers rave about the dizzying options offered by this small-size nation. Sportfishing. Mountain biking. White-water rafting. Horseback riding. Even golf! Your options are seemingly endless.

How to Visit in One Week

Despite so many options, it's easy to plan an itinerary that condenses the crème de la crème. A week-long visit should begin in San José, the capital city, where rental cars, buses, and planes are all readily available for your touring needs. Although it lacks the colonial structures of many other Central American cities, San José's Teatro Nacional is a neoclassical gem, and several superb museums honor the pre-Columbian cultures. The city's key sites can all be seen in one day.

San José makes a great base for visiting the surrounding Central Highlands, where there's plenty to keep you busy. De rigeur sights include Poás volcano, a little more than

Pre-Columbian gold feline-shaped pendant made between A.D. 700 and 1550

an hour by road northwest of San José, where you can drive to the summit and peer down into the steaming depths. While here, you'll want to visit La Paz Waterfall Garden, 5 miles (8 km) to the east, with superb exhibits on butterflies, hummingbirds, snakes, and frogs, as well as rigorous hikes to the waterfalls. The drive from San José to Poás takes you through coffee country. En route, stop at Café Britt for a fun-filled tour that explains coffee culture, from the plantation to the cup.

Next, consider two days exploring the Monteverde region—about 100 miles (160 km) west of Poás via a cliff-hanging, pot-holed road—where options are boundless. Start with a hike in the world-famous Monteverde Cloud Forest Biological Reserve, considered ground zero for birders keen to spot a resplendent quetzal. A zipline ride on the Sky Tram adds an adrenalin rush to your forest exploration. And you'll want to check out the area's many fine restaurants, plus its quirky nature exhibits, including Bat Jungle, the Serpentarium, and the Jewels of the Rain Forest Bio-Art Exhibition, which displays thousands of colorful arachnids and insects.

To close out your week's adventure, drive to Volcán Arenal—Costa Rica's most active volcano—a circuitous three-hour trip from Monteverde around Laguna de Arenal. Even if the clouds dampen the view of the volcano, there's fabulous hiking on trails at the base, horseback riding, and even helicopter rides—plus steaming hot springs in which to soak.

If you're eager to visit the beach during your week's stay, bypass Arenal and head southeast from Monteverde to the coast. Any of the country's stellar Pacific beaches will beckon—fine locations include Jacó and Parque Nacional Manuel Antonio (about three and four hours southeast of Monteverde, respectively).

If You Have More Time
Costa Rica's biggest draw, undoubtedly, is wildlife viewing. You'll see monkeys, iguanas, and a ranbow of birds everywhere, but dozens of national parks and private wildlife reserves offer

NOT TO BE MISSED:

Tipping Tips
In Costa Rica, tipping is used to reward good service, rather than given automatically. Most restaurants add a 10 percent service charge to the bill; there's no obligation to pay extra except for exceptional service. On group tours, tip guides $1 per person per day; $5 daily per person is an appropriate fee for private tour guides. Tip bellboys $0.50 per bag. Chambermaids are often overlooked—$1 per day is plenty. Note that taxi drivers don't normally expect tips, and should never receive a tip if they display aggressive or disrespectful driving.

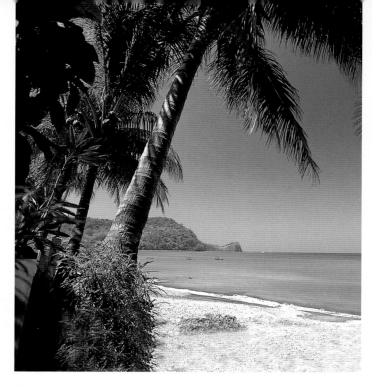

Playa Ajuga near Tárcoles

unparalleled opportunities for spying a Noah's Ark worth of wildlife species. Corcovado (on the Osa Peninsula southeast of the capital, a nine-hour drive or a short flight away) and Tortuguero (150 miles/240 km by road and canal northeast of San José on the Caribbean), for example, both offer genuine wilderness experiences and a chance to experience Costa Rica's incredible natural diversity, while beaches up and down the Caribbean and Pacific shores promise virtually guaranteed viewing of marine turtles nesting and hatching.

Birding is also world-class throughout the country, with more than 850 species recorded to date. In addition to quetzal-spotting in Monteverde, birders flock to Caño Negro wildlife refuge (about 50 miles/80 km north of Arenal) for waterbirds by the thousands, and Carara National Park (a three-hour drive west of San José) to see rare scarlet macaws.

For exploring more off-the-beaten-path zones, the southwestern Pacific coast of Nicoya, in the western reaches of the country, offers challenges by 4WD (if fording rivers is your idea of fun). Also, remote parts of both the Northern Lowlands and the Osa Peninsula beyond Corcovado are being opened up, permitting access to pristine

What to Take

Costa Rica has a tropical climate, so dress accordingly. Expect hot days with warm evenings, except in mountain areas where nights can be chilly. Avoid bright colors if you want to get close to wildlife. Informal wear is fine nearly everywhere, but you might want a more elegant outfit for smarter restaurants in San José.

You'll want comfortable shoes for hiking, but be prepared to get them wet (bring a spare pair). Also bring insect repellent, sunglasses, sunscreen, and a hat or cap to ward off the tropical sun.

areas teeming with wildlife. And the Talamanca mountains, knifing southeast from San José, are a rugged new frontier where indigenous communities on both the Caribbean and Pacific sides are now opening up to tourism.

Active Pursuits

Costa Rica is also famous for surfing, and surfers come from far and wide for its diamond-dust beaches and thrilling breakers. Beaches up and down the Pacific coast (especially Jacó) have great surfing, and instruction is available everywhere. Puerto Viejo, on the Caribbean, is also a fine option.

Costa Rica has few coral reefs, but scuba diving is nonetheless superb, with large pelagics (including manta rays and sharks) being the biggest draw. Drake Bay, on the Osa Peninsula, and Playas del Coco in northern Nicoya are the main centers, but experienced divers will want to try Isla Cocos, 300 miles (485 km) off the Pacific coast.

White-water rafting in Costa Rica is also top shelf, with rivers such as the Central Highland's Pacuare and the Reventazón drawing aficionados to their rapids as they cascade Caribbean-bound.

Sportfishing gives anglers rod-bending fights to remember. Seeking tarpon or snook? Then head to Parismina or Barra del Colorado, on the Caribbean. On the Pacific, sportfishing vessels set out principally from Playas del Coco, Tamarindo, Playa Herradura (near Jacó), Quepos, and Golfito. ∎

Renting a Car

Renting a car is a fabulous way to get around Costa Rica, but it comes with some warnings.

Roads throughout the country are poor. Local drivers can be reckless. Stray cattle, pedestrians in the road, and potholes are additional hazards.

Don't leave anything in your car, for fear of theft. Don't pay tickets on the spot; take care of them with the rental company.

Insurance is mandatory, and most rental companies refuse to honor insurance issued abroad. Drive the speed limit, be on your guard, and you'll be fine.

Wet or Dry? Best Times to Visit Costa Rica

The nation has distinct wet (May–Nov.) and dry (Dec.–April) seasons, and weather is predictable throughout the year. Dry season is considered the best time for touring, as sunny skies are the norm. It's also high season, when many hotels are full, rental cars are booked, and rates for both are high. However, Costa Rica also has a dozen distinct climatic zones, with many microclimates and regional variations. Along the Caribbean and the Pacific southwest, there is a good chance of rainfall year-round. And while temperatures throughout the country vary little year-round, Guanacaste and northern Nicoya broil in spring.

The wet season sees a drop in visitors and in hotel and car rental rates. The Costa Rican Tourism Institute (ICT) promotes this time of year as "green season" with good reason: The country is lush from all the rains. In much of the country, rainfall is typically an afternoon affair, often limited to short-lived downpours. However, the Caribbean, Pacific southwest, and northern lowlands often see day after day of heavy rains. And exploring such off-the-beaten-track corners as southwest Nicoya and the Osa Peninsula can be tough going.

Note that Costa Ricans call the summer wet season *invierno* (winter) and the winter dry season *verano* (summer).

History & Culture

Pre-Columbian Indians used gold to create elaborate ornaments. Opposite: The Holy Grail of tropical birds, the quetzal

Costa Rica Today

Common clichés about Costa Rica paint a canvas in tropical hues. The background is of glorious emerald, teeming with colorful wildlife: rainbow-hued scarlet macaws, electric blue morpho butterflies the size of saucers, and the iridescent green Holy Grail of neotropical birds, the quetzal.

The settings are also familiar: sweeping rain forest, rugged mountains, fire-spitting volcanoes, and lonesome beaches stretching along jungle-lined shores. All of these images fulfill the stereotype of Costa Rica as a Lilliputian country proffering virginal nature on a Brobdingnagian scale.

These familiar impressions are real, and made easier to confirm by the nation's size: about the same as West Virginia or Nova Scotia and only slightly larger than Switzerland. Costa Rica has the advantage of being small enough to explore end to end in a matter of

Dominoes is an all-male pastime in Costa Rica's macho society.

days. A more slothful pace lets you discover the full kaleidoscope of wilderness wonders. The diversity of terrain is remarkable, and the landscape changes as if on a revolving hinge.

The Central Highlands are ringed by mountains flanked by row upon row of glossy green coffee bushes. Guanacaste is cowboy country and provides a strong sense of the past, while the Nicoya Peninsula beckons with diamond-dust beaches where turtles come ashore to lay eggs. The Caribbean appeals for a distinct culture rooted in a Jamaican heritage. No less compelling is the rugged Pacific coast, popular with surfers. The lagoons of the Northern Lowlands boil with tarpon, and the remote Talamanca massif is an unexplored world where jaguars still roam free.

Virtually everywhere you will encounter wildlife: Costa Rica boasts 5 percent of all the known species on Earth, including more butterfly species than are found in all of Africa. Seeing the wildlife is easy. About 25 percent of the country is protected in wildlife reserves or national parks. Local entrepreneurs have been inventive in finding ways to make wildlife viewing easy. The country

> **Costa Ricans are proud of a distinct identity that owes much to this country's relative prosperity and stability.**

boasts scores of serpentariums, butterfly farms, and elevated walkways through the rain forest canopy. You could spend a lifetime *oohing* and *aahing* over the exotic flora and fauna.

Costa Rica, the most homogeneous society in Central America, is set apart from its neighbors by its lack of indigenous culture. Visitors will find no Teotihuacans, Tuxmels, or Tikals, although Monumento Nacional Guayabo continues to be excavated from the jungle and promises to elevate Costa Rica's archaeological standing. As capital cities go, San José is small fry, but it boasts art museums and some phenomenal gold and jade museums. It has improved vastly in recent years, with a vibrant nightlife that makes even the most city-wise sophisticates sit up and take notice.

Costa Rica has blossomed as a popular destination for active pursuits, from angling to white-water rafting. It's also become recognized as one of the world's leading ecotourism destinations. In fact, Costa Rica helped define the notion of ecotourism due to good stewardship of the nation's 12 distinct ecological zones. Today, more than 190 national parks, wildlife refuges, and other protected entities lure nature lovers seeking a wish-list of tropical treats: a birding trip in the Central Highlands, an aquatic jungle journey in Parque Nacional Tortuguero, a crocodile safari on the Tárcoles River, whale-watching south of Uvita, and perhaps even a stint volunteering to help save endangered species, such as leatherback turtles or scarlet and great green macaws.

Ticos

Costa Ricans—*los Costarricenses,* or *Ticos*—are unique on the isthmus. They know it, and are proud of a distinct identity that owes much to this country's relative prosperity and stability in a region beset by poverty and turmoil. Tenaciously proud of their country, Ticos cling to tradition.

Costa Rica's original inhabitants were the roughly 100,000 indigenous peoples organized in disparate tribes. Most of them rapidly succumbed to disease and the ruthless ways of 16th-century Spanish conquistadors and were reduced to subsistence status. Whereas in neighboring countries Spaniards intermixed with the native peoples, producing a large mixed blood population, Costa Rica, largely devoid of an indigenous base, has remained primarily European.

The early Spanish colonialists came in search of gold and, frustrated in that quest, settled the Central Valley. Starting in the 18th century, they were joined by other European immigrants, notably Germans and Swiss peasant farmers who began to arrive in larger numbers in the 19th century—along with Italians—as the boom in coffee took hold. Widely dispersed in the countryside, they were quickly assimilated into the mainstream Spanish-speaking Tico culture. On the Caribbean, African slaves had intermarried with Native Americans as early as the 16th century, resulting in mixed-blood Moskitos. Beginning in the 1870s, about 11,000 English-speaking Jamaicans also came as contract labor; they put down roots in the Caribbean Lowlands and have managed to affirm their own colorful Afro-Caribbean identities. "White" highlanders looked down (literally and figuratively) upon their darker brethren; it was only in 1949 that blacks were granted citizenship and legally permitted to travel to and take jobs in the highlands.

> **The peaceable Costa Rican way is based on compromise and a desire to please, using charm, humor, and, often, avoidance.**

In recent decades, there has been a large influx of North Americans (around 40,000) seeking to retire in the sun, predominantly around Escazú, Santa Ana, and Alajuela. In addition, Nicaraguans and other Central American immigrants (around 750,000, about 18 percent of Costa Rica's population of 4.2 million) have arrived in the wake of warfare in their own countries, causing some resentment among Costa Ricans. Easily recognized by their dark skin and Native American features, Nicaraguan refugees are treated with a general contempt by their color- and class-conscious host culture. Most recently, Europeans of every nationality have begun to arrive; these newest residents have primarily settled around the Pacific and Caribbean beaches.

What Makes Ticos Tick: The evolution of *criollo* (locally born) society differed markedly from that of neighboring lands, characterized by feudal land ownership and serfdom. In Costa Rica, the neglected settlers tilled their own lands and were equalized as peasant farmers, called *hermanticos* (little brothers), the name given to fellow citizens by the ruling cliques, who shared hardships and destitution. (In 1719, the governor of Costa Rica complained that he, too, had to till his own land). In time, they became known by the diminutive: *Tico*. Cut off from most outside influence by the forbidding terrain, they began to develop distinct traits—not least *ticismos*, a unique vocabulary and slang, and a profound aversion to conflict. The peaceable Costa Rican way is based on compromise and a desire to please, known as *quedar bien* (to be appealing), using charm, humor, and, often, avoidance.

An indicator of geological youth, volcanoes provide a dramatic backdrop to Costa Rica.

These sometimes surface-thin courtesies are endearing. But the temporizing Ticos know that promises should never be taken as such. Regional blood runs thick. Frustration and resentment get bottled up and find their outlets in this otherwise pacific society in drunkenness, lunacy on the roads, and surreptitious acts of revenge.

Although Tico society is not fraught with the tensions of neighboring nations, Costa Rica is far from egalitarian. It is riddled with elitist ways. "Whiteness" is considered an ideal, and many urbanites and members of the San José–based social elite look down on *campesinos* (peasants). Nonetheless, while 51 percent of the population is urban, the vast majority of Ticos retain ties to the land; Costa Rica has the highest rural population density in Latin America. The vast majority of rural folk live a simple life, tending coffee

Sarongs for sale on the beach at Parque Nacional Manuel Antonio, on Costa Rica's Pacific coast.

and cows in the highlands or as *sabaneros* (cowboys) in Guanacaste, where everyday life evokes the cowboy spirit. Tico society is far from urbane: The only true city is San José, the capital, which has burgeoned in recent years. Most other towns are regional market centers with their own subtle charm.

Standards of Living: Costa Rica's annual per capita income in 2007 was about $5,200, and its standard of living is exemplary in a region racked by destitution and disease. Both life expectancy and infant mortality are on a par with developed nations. The population enjoys free, albeit much-burdened, public education, and decent, though inefficient, health care, paid for by none-too-progressive taxation. The telecommunications system is the equal of anywhere in Latin America. The average Tico lives thriftily in a modest-size home with a small garden patch. But the regional disparities are great; the average income in the Northern Lowlands is less than 20 percent of the national average. About 20 percent of the population are *marginados* (disadvantaged groups) who live in humbling poverty, usually in wood-and-adobe huts in the countryside or on the fringes of the towns, in slum shacks hammered together from corrugated metal sheets and refuse.

Indigenous Peoples Today: Costa Rica has around 40,000 indigenous people in a population of 4.2 million; about 1 percent of the total. The Indigenous Bill of 1977 guaranteed the eight indigenous tribes rights to self-government on their lands in which the government held title in trust. Today they live a reclusive, marginalized existence and are widely dispersed on 12 indigenous reserves in the Talamancas and the rugged mountains of the Pacific Southwest. Only in 1992 did the indigenous peoples receive citizenship, and they were permitted to vote for the first time only in 1994.

While the campesino views himself as a pioneer and the forest as a resource to be conquered, indigenous people see themselves as custodians of the forest and its inter-related inhabitants. Native Americans live in simple homesteads scattered around the reservations, much of it low-quality land. The men hunt in the forests; grow bananas, beans, citrus fruits, coca, and corn; and drink home-brewed *chica* (beer made of yucca or corn). The communities struggle to preserve vital elements of their traditional culture. Most wear Western clothes and speak Spanish—few know their native languages. Alcoholism and other social problems are rife. Their cultural integrity is further eroded by the efforts of missionaries working to break down their traditional religious beliefs.

> The only true city in Costa Rica is San José, the capital. Most other towns are regional market centers with their own subtle charm.

Politically disempowered, these groups are suspicious of outsiders and feel intensely dissatisfied by the National Commission for Indigenous Affairs (CONA), which has responsibility for their welfare. Despite the passage of laws intended to safeguard their heritage, the government continues to issue rights to powerful mining and logging entities that whittle away at the Native Americans' land. While not subject to the systematic persecution of Guatemala's indigenous peoples, Costa Rica's Native Americans suffer ongoing rights violations. Yet the past few decades have brought attempts to provide greater self-sufficiency, including the establishment of the first Native American bank in 1994. Acknowledgment and appreciation of indigenous cultures has grown in recent years.

The Bribrí, who inhabit the mountains inland of the southern Caribbean, welcome visitors on a limited basis. Other groups are turning to tourism as interest in indigenous culture revives, although a permit is required from CONA to enter some reserves. A revival in crafts is nascent; women of the Boruca and other tribes of the Pacific Southwest still dress in traditional garments. Among the Chorotega of Nicoya, a renaissance of pride finds its outlet in faithfully reproduced ceramics made by the villagers of Guaitíl.

Government & Politics

The 1949 constitution defines Costa Rica as a democratic republic run by an elected president and a 19-member cabinet, called the Council of Government. A president must be a secular citizen and traditionally could only serve one term (as of 2003, a president may serve two terms). Power rests with the Legislative Assembly, composed of 57 elected members *(diputados)* representing the country's seven provinces. Voting is compulsory for citizens aged 18–70 (though there are no consequences for those who choose not to vote). Elections are held on the first Sunday in February, every four years, and are overseen by a Special Electoral Tribunal whose members are elected by the Supreme Court judges and serve staggered six-year terms. Diputados are elected by proportional representation, with seats allocated according to the number of votes for each party. They serve four-year terms and may not be elected for consecutive terms. There is no higher chamber of review. The legislature's right to veto presidential decisions is a source of friction that occasionally results in rule by presidential decree. The Assembly sits in a handsome Moorish building overlooking the Plaza de la Democracia, in San José.

Costa Rica is divided into seven provinces: Alajuela, Cartago, Guanacaste, Heredia, Limón, Puntarenas, and San José. Each is run by a governor appointed by the president, while municipal councils run the day-to-day affairs of 421 *distritos* (districts) that make up the province's 81 *cantones* (counties).

Parties & Personalities: Costa Rica traditionally alternates presidents every election, switching back and forth between candidates for the two great rival parties: the National Liberation Party (PLN) and Social Christian Unity Party (PUSC); victors, however, rarely win by more than 2 or 3 percent. The left-leaning PLN inclines toward welfare-state liberalism. The PUSC is made up of progressive conservatives who support business interests. The PLN traditionally holds a majority in the Legislative Assembly. Both parties are clannish.

Though party affiliations are defended fiercely, this loyalty has more to do with personal interest than philosophical sentiment. Costa Rica's political process is mired in crony-ism, and favors and contracts are dispensed liberally by the victorious side. Bribery and corruption are rife in a country whose politics have been dominated since independence by a small number of families. President Abel Pacheco (b. 1933) and his three predecessors have all been tainted by corruption scandals, and two—Miguel Ángel Rodríguez and Rafael Ángel Calderón—were jailed.

Top Ten Local Phrases

¿Al chile?	Seriously?
Con toda la pata	Perfect, fantastic
¡Guacala!	Disgusting!
¡Lo duda!	You said it!
¡Pura vida!	"Pure life," used as a greeting or as "Cool!" or "Perfect!"
¡Que polo!	Pathetic! How lame!
¡Salado!	Tough luck!
Tico/Tica	A Costa Rican male/female
Tiquicia	Costa Rica
Tuanis	A greeting meaning "fantastic" or "great."

Public employees—25 percent of the workforce—form the country's most powerful interest group; the well-paid bureaucracy is a crippling burden on the economy. Says one Ticoism, "The government is a cash cow with a thousand teats and everyone wants a teat to suck." The interminable bureaucratic process has given rise to a whole class of workers called *despachantes*, who tackle the bureaucracy on behalf of others.

Cattle are the lifeblood of Costa Rica's seasonally dry northwest region.

Pride in Neutrality: Costa Rica declared neutrality in 1949 and has no armed forces. A heavily armed National Guard looks after the nation's security, backed by various specialized paramilitary police units. Pride in neutrality is reflected in the Ticos' passive psyche. They are not easily aroused to strong emotion or political passions about issues: "Don Pepe" Figueres (1906–1990), leader of the 1948 revolution, accused them of being as "domesticated as sheep." Issues either get resolved by consensus, or, frequently, get shelved to avoid conflict and thus fester unresolved. Harmony is more highly valued than discord, even at the cost of irresolution.

Post-independence politics has been marked by liberalism and stability. The country has had its fair share of *caudillos* (dictatorial leaders), but most redeemed themselves as proponents of progressive reform, and only three presidents have been military men. Ticos pride themselves on the "cleanliness" of their political process. Election day is a national holiday, which Ticos turn into a grand fiesta. Elections are not marred by the violence and mayhem that has traditionally accompanied polling in neighboring countries (during elections, control of the police force reverts to the Special Electoral Tribunal to protect constitutional guarantees). Costa Rica's mainstream media is conservative. ■

Food & Drink

Costa Rica boasts fine dining, concentrated overwhelmingly in San José, where the restaurant scene plays all the notes on the international scale. Beyond the capital city, however, Ticos are timid diners whose affinities are closely attached to homey peasant fare.

The ubiquitous staple of rice and black beans—*gallo pinto*—forms the backbone of local cuisines, or *comida típica*. Even breakfast, typically gallo pinto with scrambled eggs, isn't exempt from this rule. Served with fried plantains (Costa Ricans are fond of fried foods) and a basic salad of tomatoes and cabbage, gallo pinto becomes a cheap *casado,* or set special, sometimes served with *sopa negra,* a bean broth. Roast pork is the main meat staple. Both it and chicken are often roasted over coffee wood *(a la leña)* which gives a smoky flavor. Many restaurants serve

Campesino cooking is the heart of local fare.

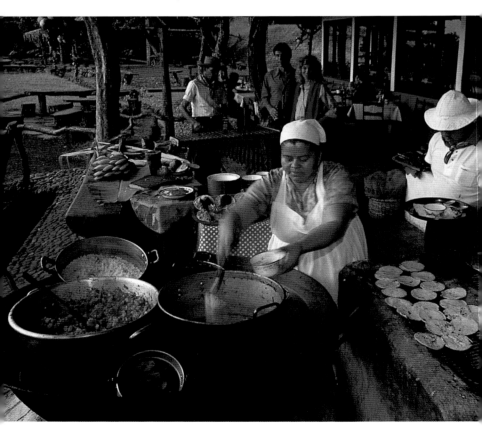

steaks *(lomito).* Chewy is the rule, and rarely do beef dishes come up to par for North American tastes, although *lomito encebollado,* steak marinated with local Linzano sauce, is often delicious. Seafoods are relatively scarce away from the coasts, though shrimp and lobster dishes are widely available. In San José the fish of choice is *corvina* (sea bass), usually fried with garlic *(ajo).* At seaside resorts you'll also find dolphin fish *(dorado),* swordfish, and snapper *(pargo),* almost always fried and served with white rice.

Corn finds its way into tortillas and corn pancakes called *chorreados,* and *tamales,* stuffed cornmeal pastries wrapped and baked in corn leaf. Jalapeños and other hot spices are rarely used. Nor are vegetables, though over-boiled carrots and greens are served, and other vegetables find their way into soups and stews, such as *olla de carne,* a meat and vegetable stew of potato, corn, yucca, and gourds. The favored vegetable is plantain (a relative of the banana) served fried with almost any meal.

The ubiquitous staple of rice and black beans—*gallo pinto*—forms the backbone of local cuisines, or *comida típica.*

The Caribbean coast has its own unique flavor, one steeped in spices and coconut milk. Nowhere else in Costa Rica will you find salted codfish on the breakfast menu.

Everywhere, roadside stalls are cornucopias of tropical fruits: mangoes, melons, papayas, pineapples, and many you may not have heard of, such as the *carambeloa* (starfruit), *marañon* (cashew fruit), and *pejibayes* (like tiny coconuts), all of which find their way into *frescas,* fruit blended with ice, water, or milk, and sugar. Milk is used in cheeses such as the mild white *queso blanco,* which frequently finds its way into desserts. *Tres leches,* a three-layered custard flan, is the national dessert. It is best followed by espresso, drunk thick and sugared. *Café con leche* is coffee served in a 50:50 ratio with hot milk.

Other dishes to try include:

Arregladas: greasy puff pastries filled with beef, chicken, or cheese.

Dulche de leche: a boiled milk and sugar syrup.

Empañada: turnovers filled with beans, meat, and potatoes.

Palmito: soft heart of the *pejibaye* palm (not the fruit of the same name), popular in salads.

Costa Ricans are beer drinkers, and local lager-style brews (e.g., Imperial and Bavaria) are perfectly suited to the tropical climate. *Bocas*—snacks such as *ceviche* (marinated and spiced seafood) and thirst-inducing deep-fried *chicharrones* (pork rinds)—are usually served in bars. Wine is not popular, and imported wines, generally found in upscale restaurants, are expensive. The working man's drink is a potent, clear white spirit called *guaro,* worth trying once. Local liquors are best avoided, although coffee liqueurs make good souvenirs. ∎

Costa Rican History

When conquistadors first stepped ashore to subjugate the isthmus of Central America and claim it for Spain, the region was already a complex mosaic of cultures. The term "Costa Rica" first entered the European lexicon in 1522 when Captain Gil González Davila (died 1526) set out from Panama with a colonizing fleet to settle the region then known as Veragua.

González and his men found Indian dignitaries adorned with gold, for which the conquistador coined the term "Rich Coast." Compared to its northern neighbors, however, the land was relatively sparsely populated; perhaps no more than 100,000 inhabitants occupied the densely forested and mountainous region at the time of first European contact.

First Peoples

Little is known of the potpourri of indigenous people, who belonged to as many as 25 distinct and antagonistic groups that followed their own ways of life. The earliest occupants arrived from the north around 10,000 B.C., rather late in the day of human advancement following the first crossing by Hominoids of the Bering Strait around 60,000 B.C. Although these peoples came under the influence of the high civilizations of the Andes and Mesoamerica, the region remained a buffer zone and one whose meager population never evolved either the complex sociopolitical structures nor the monumental architecture of societies to the north and south. The peoples never unified to form a kingdom but remained under chieftains (caciques) who ruled over competing areas and whose names were adopted by the Spanish for each tribe.

> González and his men found Indian dignitaries adorned with gold, for which the conquistador coined the term "Rich Coast."

People of the Northwest: The most developed group were the Chorotega, who occupied today's Guanacaste following their arrival in the region around A.D. 500, displacing earlier and much simpler societies about which little is known. The Chorotega were influenced by the more advanced cultures of Mexico and Guatemala, initially the Olmec, and later by the Aztec and Maya, who dispersed south, imposing their culture on less advanced peoples. The name chorotega means "people who escaped." The details are shrouded in mystery.

The Chorotega lived in longhouses of wood and thatch inhabited by entire clans and centered on stone plazas where religious and civic ceremonies were held. The Chorotega constructed irrigation ditches and evolved an advanced agricultural society based predominantly on corn. They also cultivated cotton that they wove into dyed clothing. Among Costa Rica's indigenous peoples, only the Chorotega had a calendar and a written language, both of Mayan origin. They spoke Nahua, an Aztec tongue, and shared in common with their northern ancestors a rigid hierarchical system that included nobility

Lighting a votive candle, an adherent affirms her Catholic faith, which lies at the core of Costa Rica's culture.

and slavery, and a religious system based on bloodletting that included virgin sacrifice every full moon. The Chorotega were also noted for their distinctive ceramics, including phallic figurines, and anthropomorphic motifs of jaguars, frogs, and snakes in striking black, white, and red colors. They also traded for jade with their northern neighbors and worked it into exquisite figurines using a string-saw technique.

Highland Cultures: The Corobicís, who lived in small bands as hunter-gatherers and farmers, were the predominant group of the Central Highlands (Meseta Central). They traded gold with lowland tribes and became superb goldsmiths, leaving a legacy of beautiful amulets and statuettes depicting sacred idols, such as frogs. Although most groups lived in stockaded villages called *palenques,* the Corobicís built the only pre-Columbian town of note to have been discovered in Costa Rica: Guayabo, at the base of Volcán Turrialba. The settlement, which featured cobbled streets *(calzadas),* burial mounds, aqueducts, and stone cisterns, dates from around A.D. 1000 and may have had a population of 1,000 people. It was mysteriously abandoned about A.D. 1400.

The Cabécar and Guaymí inhabited the Talamancas farther south and lived primarily as hunter-gatherers. Shamans were important in these societies, which lived in harmony with their environment and revered the jaguar.

Coastal Tribes: The Boruca, Chibcha, and Diquis in the southwest, and the Bribrí, Caribes, and KéKöLdi on the Caribbean shore, drew their influences from South American cultures. They were semi-nomadic hunters and fishermen and supplemented the bounty of forest and sea with yucca, squash, and tubers. The preeminent group, the Diquis of the Pacific Southwest, shared with the Chorotega a tradition of ritual sacrifice and slavery.

About 1000 B.C., the Diquis began crafting lithic spheres called *bolas,* often of immense size, perhaps for religious purposes. A major change in the culture occurred between A.D. 500 and A.D. 800 as a result of contact with the seafaring peoples of Colombia or Peru. At about this time, the Diquis began fashioning gold figurines and soon became skilled goldsmiths, making use of gold from the Península de Osa. It appears that there was little cultural exchange between these mainly matriarchal groups, who remained in a state of internecine warfare. Both men and women of the Boruca were warriors.

Destruction of Local Culture

First Europeans: The first European to reach Costa Rica was Christopher Columbus, on September 18, 1502, on his fourth voyage to the New World. He was followed by

Europeans Thwarted

Christopher Columbus, the first European to reach Costa Rica, in 1502, recorded signs of vast wealth in the region he called "The Garden." The first attempt at colonization, in 1506, however, proved disastrous. Ferdinand of Spain appointed Diego de Nicuesa as governor of Veragua and financed an expedition to settle the Caribbean coast and discover the source of the Indian gold. The governor foundered off the coast of Panama and he and his troops were forced to hack their way north through the jungle. They were soon repelled by the ferocity of local tribes, sweltering swamps, and diseases—a fate that also awaited Gil González in 1522. In 1524, Francisco Fernández de Córdoba established the first colony on the Pacific coast, at Bruselas, but its inhabitants, too, succumbed. New attempts were made, but the *arrivistes* failed miserably, driven one and all to despair and decimation by the cruel hardships of the New World.

Diego de Nicuesa (see sidebar above), who made an attempt to colonize. Despite many further attempts, the Spaniards were never able to establish permanent settlements in eastern Costa Rica. After 1513, when Vasco Nuñez de Balboa (1475–1517) discovered the Pacific Ocean, the Spaniards focused their explorations along that shore. Pacific native populations came under Spanish control in the 1520s. The Spaniards were not on a holy mission: The conquistadors had set out in search of gold and silver. In 1532 Pizarro found it in Peru and, a decade later, Cortes discovered the vast silver veins of Mexico. The Spanish found no source of gold in Costa Rica, so they plundered the gold reserves of the indigenous peoples, then began to enslave them to work in the foreign mines. Victims of the Spaniards' ruthless forays, the once noble indigenous populations of Costa Rica began their decline.

In 1543 the Captaincy-General of Guatemala was created, incorporating all the lands from the Isthmus of Tehuantepec, in the Yucatán, to the swampy lowlands of southern Panama. Most of Costa Rica's indigenous peoples had by then been conquered, though the region languished as the Spanish consolidated their hold farther north. In 1562 conquistador Juan Vásquez de Coronado (1523–1565) was appointed governor of Costa Rica. He established a settlement in the cool highlands and named it El Guarco (later Cartago)—Costa Rica's first capital. Although Coronado was a relatively benign conquistador, during ensuing decades, large land grants (*encomiendas*) were issued to Spanish soldiers. Thus, they received rights of vassalage over the indigenous peoples, who withered under forced labor. European diseases—smallpox, measles, tuberculosis—against which the

Vasco Nuñez de Balboa, the first European to see the Pacific

locals had no resistance hastened their demise (the Great Pandemic of 1610–1660 cut through the population like a scythe). The survivors fled to the interior mountains.

Spanish settlers found themselves without labor to work the rich soils. Therefore, conditions were lacking for the development of the feudal system imposed by the Spaniards elsewhere in the New World, which were based on large haciendas worked by slave labor. An exception was lowland Greater Nicoya (today's Guanacaste), which was administered as part of Nicaragua and where cattle haciendas evolved, worked by enslaved Chorotega. Without gold, which had already been stolen and shipped to Spain, or other items of value for trade with the homeland, Costa Rica's settlers were forced to sow their own lands for a livelihood. The region became a backwater full of poor farmers foiled in their hopes of becoming nobles.

Settlement: Settlements were meager and modest. When Volcán Irazú erupted in 1723, destroying Cartago, the lowly capital consisted of a single church and a few score houses made of adobe.

By the early 18th century, however, Costa Rica had evolved a viable agricultural base and the population expanded. Other towns began to take shape: in 1717, Heredia; in 1737, San José; and in 1782, Alajuela. The population remained far removed from central authority and evolved free of the rigid social and color distinctions that developed in neighboring countries, where miscegenation between Spaniard and Indian produced large mixed blood (mestizo) populations. In Costa Rica, intermixing of the races was limited, and this resulted in large numbers of poor white farmers and the absence of a resentful mestizo class subject to the abuses of the established white aristocracy.

On the Caribbean Lowlands, a separate cultural scene had evolved. English, Dutch, and French pirates and merchantmen had for three centuries raided and traded along the shores of the "Spanish Main." Piracy had driven the Spanish to close their port at Puerto Limón in 1665, choking legal trade and fostering a rise in smuggling and the evolution of English-run ports for precious hardwoods beyond the limits of Spanish authority.

The Cinderella colony received little official attention. Never having felt the stern hand of colonial rule, its inhabitants remained aloof from the bitter independence movement sweeping through Spain's American empire by the close of the 18th century.

Independence & Wealth

When independence for Central America came on September 15, 1821, on the coattails of Mexico, it took a full month for the news to reach Costa Rica, where a provisional council elected to accede to the new nation of Mexico.

Time of Turmoil: It was a time of confusion. Throughout the isthmus, battles raged between disparate interests competing to shape national boundaries. In 1823 the four provinces of Guatemala, El Salvador, Honduras, and Nicaragua formed a federation—the United Provinces of Central America—with its capital in Guatemala City and autonomy for individual states (Panama became a part of Colombia).

....

By 1830 high-grade coffee was already the nation's prime export.

....

The decision sparked a brief civil war in Costa Rica: The conservative leaders of Cartago and Heredia favored maintaining alignment with Mexico; the more progressive gentry of Alajuela and San José were federalists. On April 5, 1823, tensions boiled over into a battle at Ochomongo in which the federalists were victorious. Costa Rica then joined the United Provinces.

It was a poor fit. Central America descended into a cycle of civil wars and rule by repressive caudillos (strongmen leaders) representing the interests of elites. In Costa Rica, however, institutional rule had never been consolidated and the gains of economic prosperity were shared among a relatively classless society. Democratic institutions emerged that permitted resolution of social tensions through reform.

Consolidation & Coffee: In 1824 Costa Rica named teacher Juan Mora Fernández (1784–1854) its first head of state. He established a trend for progressive, liberal political leadership that would characterize the nation as it evolved apart from its reactionary neighbors. Internal rivalry resurfaced in 1835 when forces from the three subordinate towns attacked San José, which won the War of the League and consolidated its status as Costa Rica's capital city. Tensions within the United Provinces resulted in

The railroad's arrival in the 1800s boosted the fortunes of the banana industry. By the end of that century, Costa Rica produced more bananas than anywhere else in the world.

its dissolution in 1839, one year after Costa Rica's benevolent dictator Braulio Carrillo (1800–1845)—best known for establishing civil legal codes and an orderly public administration—had withdrawn from the federation and declared independence.

At the time, coffee drinking was all the rage in Europe. Costa Rica's pattern of rural smallholdings, combined with conditions of climate and terrain in the Meseta Central, proved conducive to coffee cultivation. Mora and Carrillo had sponsored this cultivation by issuing land grants, luring European immigrants who brought fashionable liberal ideals. By 1830 high-grade coffee—*grano de oro* (grain of gold)—was already the nation's prime export. Coffee income was used to prettify San José with neoclassical buildings. Earnings were spread throughout the farming community, but the immensely profitable coffee trade coalesced in the hands of a few coffee barons—*cafeteleros*—who began to dominate the political scene. In 1849 they ousted the nation's enlightened first president, José María Castro (1818–1892), replacing him with one of their own, Juan Rafael Mora (1814–1860).

Invasion & Militarism: Mora served two terms marked by economic prosperity. His second was highlighted by an unlikely invasion. U.S. President James Buchanan wanted to build a canal across Nicaragua, whose government was charging what to the U.S. government appeared an exorbitant fee. Backed by Buchanan, a brash Tennessean named William Walker (1824–1860) landed in Nicaragua in June 1855 with a band of mercenaries. He toppled the government, established himself as president, and in November 1856, invaded Guanacaste. President Mora was victorious over Walker's motley toughs at La Casona (in today's Parque Nacional Santa Rosa). Walker fled to Rivas in Nicaragua, where a Costa Rican drummer boy called Juan Santamaría gave his life torching the fort where Walker was hiding, earning a posthumous distinction as a national hero.

The war ushered in a period of militarism as politically ambitious cafeteleros used self-styled generals to attain power. In 1870, General Tomás Guardia (1831–1882) seized power as a reformer. He established a viable central government, tamed the cafeteleros and their military cronies, used coffee-tax revenues to fund civic construction, and promoted a railroad linking San José with the Atlantic to facilitate the transshipment of coffee. The railroad, built against almighty odds at the cost of 4,000 lives (mostly imported Chinese and Jamaican labor) and completed in 1890, was the accomplishment of Minor Keith (1848–1929), a determined North American who also started the United Fruit Company (see sidebar below).

Democracy Affirmed: President Bernardo Soto (1854–1931) stood for reelection in 1889. The nation's first honest election with popular participation produced an upset victory for Soto's opponent. When Soto refused to step down, the people took to the streets and enforced their decision. The democratic process was still tenuous and marred by presidents who whittled away at the constitution or exiled rivals to extend their rule. The army remained in its barracks— until 1917, when President Alfredo González Flores (1877–1962) proposed a system of progressive taxation and the cafeteleros prompted Minister of War Federico Tinoco (1868–1931) to seize power. Tinoco was a bullying dictator who suspended the constitution. But Costa Rica's educated populace would no longer accept oligarchic caudillos. Tinoco was ousted peacefully by a demonstration led by women and high-school students, ushering in another period of peaceful liberal leaders. Democracy had been affirmed.

United Fruit Company

Minor Keith, a North American living in Costa Rica to manage railroad construction, began in 1873 planting bananas along the train route, and later, on concessions wrangled from the government. By 1899 Costa Rica was the world's leading banana producer. That year, Keith's company merged with Boston Fruit to become United Fruit Company. By 1930 the company was the largest employer in Central America. Company ownership has since changed, but bananas are still a major export of Costa Rica—the second largest exporter of bananas in the world.

Civil War & Reform

Old-style paternalism had failed to alleviate the social ills of the relatively prosperous nation. Many people lived in destitution, a situation worsened by the Great Depression in the wake of the Wall Street crash of 1929, and by the stranglehold that the United Fruit Company—by now a powerful force—held over its workers, fueling a virulent four-year strike initiated in 1934 against "Big Fruit." A series of illegal labor strikes paralyzed Costa Rica. Change was needed.

Calderón Sets the Stage: It came in 1940s, when Rafael Angel Calderón Guardia (1900–1970) became president and promulgated a series of much needed reforms that included progressive taxation, a social security system, and a Labor Code that established workers' rights. Calderón, a deeply religious man, earned the ire of the rural-based upper classes, including cafeteleros of German descent who resented government seizure of their land when Costa Rica declared war on Nazi Germany. Calderón's massive public- spending programs coincided with a stymied economy that combined to produce rapid inflation, whittling away his support with the poor. When the 1944 election came around, he wed himself to an unholy alliance with the Communists and Catholic Church. The triumvirate formed the Social Christian Unity Party (PUSC). Meanwhile, labor leaders made an unlikely pact with the business and rural elites and, joined by urban intellectuals, formed the Social Democratic Party.

Calderón's handpicked successor, Teodoro Picado (1900–1960), served an uneventful four-year term (1944–1948). In 1948 Calderón stood again for election. Tensions were rife; violence broke out on the streets. Unexpectedly, a third-party contender, Otilio Ulante (1891–1973), won the election. Calderón claimed fraud. That night, the building holding the ballots burned. The Calderonista congress annulled the election. On March 10, 1948, Costa Rica erupted in civil war. The ensuing events are mired in mythology.

War of National Liberation: José María Figueres (1906–1990), an ambitious revolutionary, later affectionately known as "Don Pepe," had been planning a coup for years. Exiled to Mexico in 1942 for his firebrand ways, he was permitted to return in 1944, but immediately launched a bid for the violent overthrow of the government. He founded a ragtag army—the National Liberation Armed Forces—that trained at his mountain farm in Santa María de Dota. The election debacle was a godsend. Figueres' insurrectionists swept down from the mountain and quickly took Cartago and Puerto Limón. The ill-trained government army of 500 men was armed by Nicaragua's right-wing Somoza regime and included machete-wielding banana workers. For 40 days the two forces skirmished, leaving more than 2,000 (mostly civilians) dead. As Figueres' forces prepared to strike at San José, the government's paltry standing army surrendered.

Figueres established the grandiloquently named Founding Junta of the Second Republic. Calderón was exiled, while many of his followers were executed along with leading leftists and labor leaders. Then Figueres surprised everyone by disbanding the army and declaring neutrality. He saw himself as a crusader against communism and corruption. He banned the Communists, drew up a new constitution, and launched a whirlwind of social reform. He abrogated Costa Rica's apartheid laws, gave women the vote, nationalized the banks and insurance companies, and established presidential term limits and an independent body—the Electoral Tribunal—to oversee future elections. Then he handed power to Otilio Ulate as had been agreed and stepped down. "Don Pepe" was hailed as a national hero and went on to

José María "Don Pepe" Figueres, "savior of the nation," visits his lumber mill in 1980. He disbanded the army in the late 1940s.

win two terms as president (1953–1957 and 1970–1974) as leader of the PLN, which he founded in 1951. Figueres earned the wrath of his long-time enemy, Nicaraguan dictator "Tacho" Somoza. Their two nations had a brief skirmish in 1955, when Nicaraguan troops attacked Guanacaste, meeting a pathetic demise at La Casona.

Modern Times
Immediate post-civil war politics were marked by political stability and economic prosperity. PLN governments followed conservative, pro-business agendas, while the

welfare state was vastly expanded by the Social Democrats, until it reached every sector of society and subsidies consumed 40 percent of the national budget. By the 1970s, 25 percent of the workforce was employed by the state. Economic stagnation set in. A massive currency devaluation added to woes caused by crippling inflation and by the devastating fall in worldwide prices of coffee, bananas, and sugar, Costa Rica's three largest exports. The economic crisis was worsened by the Nicaraguan crisis, which consumed the region for one long, dark decade.

War & Peace: During the 1970s, Nicaragua's Sandinista National Liberation Front (FSLN) launched a war to topple the right-wing Somoza regime. The government of Costa Rican President Rodrigo Carazo (b. 1926) permitted the Sandinistas to set up shop in Costa Rica. When Somoza's air force struck across the border, Carazo tried to close the Sandinistas' camps, but also cut diplomatic relations with Nicaragua and seized the Somoza family's estates in Guanacaste.

On July 19, 1979, the tables turned. The Sandinistas swept into Managua. Right-wing Somoza supporters flooded Costa Rica and found support with wealthy ranchers in Guanacaste. The exiles coalesced to form the Nicaraguan Democratic Front (FDN), better known as the Contras. Costa Rica's new president, Luís Alberto Monge Álvarez (b. 1925), struggled to remain neutral, but the economy was a shambles and the United States was pressuring Monge to commit to the Contras. Soon the CIA was building airstrips and supply bases close to the Nicaraguan border, and U.S. military specialists were militarizing the Costa Rican police forces. The Sandinista air force was bombing Contra bases, and paramilitary groups—supported by right-wingers in Monge's government (1982–1986)—were committing acts of domestic terrorism meant to implicate the Sandinistas. Costa Rica was edging dangerously away from neutrality.

In February 1986, a liberal economic lawyer named Oscar Arias Sánchez (b. 1940) became president. He kicked out the Contras and worked ceaselessly for peace in the

President Oscar Arias Sánchez at the Summit of Central and South American countries in 2008

isthmus (El Salvador and Guatemala were also wracked by internal strife). In February 1987, Arias presented a peace plan. The Reagan administration tried to nix it. But the five Central American presidents signed up. Arias earned the Nobel Prize. In a speech to the U.S. Congress, he announced that the Costa Rican people "are convinced that the risks we run in the struggle for peace will always be less than the irreparable cost of war."

Putting the House in Order: The war destabilized Costa Rica. Around 250,000 Nicaraguan refugees had flooded in, draining scarce resources. International confidence had also suffered, resulting in capital flight and a 60 percent drop in trade. The country was bankrupt.

Throughout the 1960s, 1970s, and 1980s, Costa Rica had funded its development through massive loans. In September 1981, Costa Rica became the first country in the world to default on its loans, causing a banking crisis throughout the Americas. By 1989, with a five-billion-dollar national debt, Costa Rica had the dubious distinction of being the world's largest per capita debtor. A stiff dose of economic austerity was needed to put Costa Rica back on course.

In February 1990, Rafael Angel Calderón Fournier (b. 1949), a conservative lawyer and son of the reforming president, was inaugurated on the 50th anniversary of his father's inauguration. He initiated measures to curb Costa Rica's massive deficit and debt. Calderón was succeeded by José María Figueres (b. 1954), son of the elder Calderón's nemesis. Under pressure from the International Monetary Fund and World Bank, Figueres continued the austerity program, which was painful for a people used to handouts. With inflation rampant, 100,000 people took to the streets in 1995—the largest demonstration ever in Costa Rica. In July 1996, Hurricane César devastated the region. A summit of Central American leaders in May 1997 provided a ray of sunshine: President Bill Clinton attended, the first U.S. president to visit Costa Rica since John F. Kennedy in 1963.

> **"The risks we run in the struggle for peace will always be less than the irreparable cost of war."**
>
> —PRESIDENT OSCAR ARIAS SÁNCHEZ, *1987*

A series of government scandals tainted Figueres' administration. He was replaced in February 1998 by wealthy businessman Miguel Angel Rodríguez, whose bid for the presidency in 1994 unearthed his own involvement in a tainted-beef scandal. Dr. Abel Pacheco of the center right Social Christian Unity Party was elected president in 2002. His government was considered corrupt and inept and he was replaced in 2006 by Oscar Arias Sánchez, in the country's first ever re-election of a former president.

Corruption, nepotism, and crime are major concerns. Burglary and petty theft are endemic and, since Manuel Noriega's ouster in Panama in 1989, Costa Rica has developed a reputation as a drug transshipment center. Despite these problems, the country has managed to avoid sinking into the turmoil that surrounds it, drawing tourists in increasing numbers (tourism is Costa Rica's largest source of foreign income, generating 1.9 billion dollars from 1.9 million tourists in 2007). Big-name hotels have sprouted on waterfront property, adding a touch of resort life to a destination known primarily for more rugged attractions, notably stupendous scenery, active adventures, exotic flora, and wonderful wildlife.

The country has also proved attractive to high-tech investors, as well as foreign retirees, who are lured by clean air, relative prosperity, and the appeals of a stunningly scenic land of a happy medium. In 2007, residential tourism surpassed nature as the stated reason most people visited Costa Rica. ∎

Land & Landscape

Mountains dominate Costa Rica, a pocket-size prodigy that packs a potpourri of other terrains, landscapes, and climates into its 19,652 square miles (50,900 sq km). Nowhere is the country more than 175 miles (280 km) wide, and nowhere more than 300 miles (480 km) north to south—totaling an area equal to three ten-thousandths of the world's land area.

Yet Costa Rica seems to contain the entire world within its small compass, whisking the surprised visitor allegorically on a world tour, from cool Swiss alpine forest to steamy Amazonian lowland jungle. A glance at a map explains why. Costa Rica lies at the thread-thin southern end of the Central American isthmus separating two dramatically disparate continents. It is also a land between seas: The Caribbean Sea and Pacific Ocean are separated by a mountain backbone that is still being pushed skyward by awesome tectonic forces that erupt in volcanoes and earthquakes.

A majority of the population lives in the Central Highlands, most within towns that cluster on a temperate plateau, the Meseta Central, that lies within a few hours' drive of beach and ocean. Though the country lies wholly within the tropics, vast extremes of elevation and relief spawn a profusion of climates and microclimates. The result is a spectacular amalgam of vegetation and wildlife. Costa Rica, a meeting point for the biota of North and South America, is crowded with exotic flora and fauna.

Wilderness Guides

When it comes to spotting wildlife and learning about Costa Rica's flora and fauna, a naturalist guide is essential. Countless visitors report that touring with a naturalist was the highlight of their trip. The amazing interpretive ability of the finest guides includes an eagle-eyed ability to spot and identify wildlife that the untrained eye will surely miss. The best guides have had a lifetime of experience in the field and have built solid reputations. Many are specialists in birds, botany, or herpetology. Most are freelancers and can be hired through such companies as Costa Rica Expeditions (see p. 260).

The Volatile Earth

Costa Rica lies at a critical juncture where four of the Earth's crustal plates converge and crumple. These plates, interconnected pieces resembling a cracked eggshell, are powered in their jostling movement by currents deep within the Earth's molten core and wrestle one another until one gives way. Costa Rica sits atop the Caribbean plate. Its arch contestant is the Pacific's Cocos plate, which shoves against it from the east and nosedives beneath it, sparking cataclysmic earthquakes and fueling volcanoes that spew out magma (molten rock) produced by the stupendous friction. The Costa Rican landmass is relatively young—only around three million years ago was it thrust upward from beneath the sea by the Cocos' dynamic burrowing. The tectonic movement has further fractured the Earth along fault lines. Megaquakes frequently rattle the country, such as the 7.4 shocker that struck on April 22, 1991, heaving the Caribbean shoreline upward and leaving coral reefs high and dry.

Gazing into the active crater of Volcán Poás is an awesome experience.

Volcanic Vertebrae

Costa Rica's lush green shawl drapes itself over a spine of volcanoes that march south from the Nicaraguan border, studding the landscape with perfect cones that look as if they've fallen from their own postcards. These volcanoes are part of the 9,000-mile (14,500 km) chain of mountains that runs along the western edge of the Americas from Alaska to Tierra del Fuego. Of the 42 active volcanoes in Central America, Costa Rica has 7. These are found in three distinct ranges, or *cordilleras*, arrayed northwest to southeast: the Cordillera de Guanacaste, the Cordillera de Tilarán, and the Cordillera Central, the latter a string of four volcanoes—Poás, Barva, Irazú, and Turrialba—that encircle the Meseta Central. Set between the Guanacaste and Tilarán chains is windswept Lake Arenal.

....

Both Volcanes Poás and Irazú recently awoke from their slumbers and periodically boil over.

....

Many of Costa Rica's threatening giants are ephemerally user-friendly: At two of them, Poás and Irazú, visitors can drive to the crater rims and peer into the bubbling bowels. Both Poás and Irazú recently awoke from their slumbers and periodically boil over in small but intense eruptions. At restless Poás, a mini-volcano is being birthed within a mile-wide caldera—the largest collapsed crater in the Western Hemisphere. On Rincón de la Vieja and Miravalles, in Guanacaste, steaming vents have been harnessed for geothermal electricity. The most sensational sight is youthful Volcán Arenal, an archetypal cone that thrills visitors with almost daily eruptions (a Hollywood favorite, it starred in 1995 in Michael Crichton's *Congo*). On upper slopes, mists veil cloud forest, as at Monteverde which encompasses eight ecological zones.

Meseta Central

Around two-thirds of Costa Rica's population lives in the Meseta Central, a huge scalloped valley that basks in eternal springtime in the heart of the temperate Central Highlands at an average elevation of 5,000 feet (1,524 m) above sea level. The plateau measures 50 miles (80 km) across and 25 miles (40 km) north-south and nestles beneath the gentle volcanic slopes of the Cordillera Central to the north and the dauntingly sheer, forest-clad slopes of the Talamancas. It is divided in two by a low range of hills, the Cerro de la Carpintera. San José and its nouveau-riche suburbs dominate the larger and more populous level valley to the west of the hills, where most of the nation's major towns are found; the smaller Cartago Valley slopes gently eastward before falling steeply through the valley of the Río Reventazón—very popular with white-water rafters—to the Caribbean Lowlands.

The climate is idyllic. Sunshine pours down year-round (temperatures average a balmy 74° F/23° C), combining with reliable and modest rainfall and rich volcanic soils to metamorphose the Meseta into the rich breadbasket of the nation. Sugarcane dominates the valley floor, rippling in the constant light breeze like folds of green silk. The lower slopes are intensely farmed for coffee, with dairy farms, horticultural gardens and strawberry patches situated on the cooler, higher slopes that gradually merge into lush montane forests where eco-minded visitors can hike through cloud forests on the flanks of mist-shrouded volcanoes.

Talamanca Massif

Massive, dauntingly rugged, the Talamancas induce humility. They dominate the southern half of the country and consist of a chain of mountains extending along a northwest-southeast axis from the Meseta Central into Panama. Here are Costa Rica's highest peaks. Rising to 12,526 feet (3,818 m) atop Cerro Chirripó, the Talamancas separate the Caribbean from the Pacific. These great *cerros,* or peaks, are folded in serrated pleats with vast valleys nestling in between. Moisture-laden winds racing in from the east dump their cargo and bruised clouds swirl ominously about windswept summits so cold that trees cower. Towering and sodden, they have been little explored although crosshatched by pathways known only to Indians who live in remote reserves on the lower slopes. A plush cloak of greenery covers the rugged peaks. Much of the velveteen jungle is protected within Parque Internacional La Amistad—a refuge for endangered wildlife. The montane forest merges with cloud forest on higher slopes, where stunted dwarf forests meld into *páramo,* high mountain grasslands.

Pacific Northwest

Costa Rica's dry quarter defies the image of Costa Rica the green. Humpbacked, floppy-eared Zebu cattle munch savannas that shimmer gold in the searing sun, and cowboys register a poignant effect on the landscape. The region, lowland Guanacaste, averages less than 20 inches (50 cm) of rain per year—this in the lee of volcanoes whose sodden eastern slopes soak up as many feet. Rivers that form oases for wildlife spill down from the curving slopes and loop through the parched lowlands of the Tempisque basin to merge in watery Parque Nacional Palo Verde, a spectacular haven for birdlife. Patches of rare dry forest burst into Monet-colored blossom year-round. Mere morsels of the great forests that were felled for cattle following Spanish settlement, these remnant tracts are easily explored at Parque Nacional Santa Rosa, where La Casona evokes Costa

Visitors get a bird's-eye view of Monteverde's rain forest canopy.

Rica's turbulent past relations with Nicaragua. A chain of sleepy and historic cowboy towns—Liberia, Cañas, and Bagaces—speckle the Inter-American Highway, while Puntarenas, a motley port city extending along a thread-thin peninsula, is a gateway to the Nicoya Peninsula by ferry across the Golfo de Nicoya. The peninsula is lined on its Pacific coast with stunning beaches swept by surf and warm currents that bring ashore marine turtles. The country's only white-sand beaches are here—draws for a bevy of upscale resorts and golf courses whose emergence in recent years have lent a new cachet to the region. The warm waters of the Gulf of Papagayo teem with gamefish, yet another angle on adventure, centered on the sportfishing resort of Playa Tamarindo. And spelunkers can explore the limestone caverns at Parque Nacional Barra Honda.

Pacific Southwest

This zone is made up of valley, mountain, and coast. To the east, the Río General, which is popular with white-water rafters, powers out of the Talamancas. The river has carved a broad trough—the Valle de El General—that is an important center for fruit plantations south of San Isidro. The valley was brought into the mainstream only in the 1950s, when the Inter-American Highway linked it with San José and Panama, drawing immigrants, including Italians whose influence is paramount in the hilltop town of San Vito, in the southerly Valle de Coto Brus. A narrow range of mountains between valley and warm fecund sea rises precipitously in the north to create a narrow littoral quilted by palm plantations and, farther

south, a coastal plain covered in bananas. Beaches are backed by jungles where birds flash their bright colors and monkeys cavort in the trees, as at Parque Nacional Manuel Antonio, a tiny emerald where coral reefs and diamond-dust beaches enclose a rare swath of humid forest teeming with wildlife. Rainfall increases to the south, reaching a peak on the overwhelmingly green Osa Peninsula. Osa's Parque Nacional Corcovado is a sodden refuge for jaguars, scarlet macaws, and hardy hikers. Nutrient-rich offshore waters draw humpback whales to the Bahía de Coronado, and game fish to the Golfo Dulce. Here, sportfishermen are lured to funky Golfito, an old United Fruit Company town that now attempts to attract business with its duty-free zone. Laid-back Zancudo is among the scores of beaches favored by surfers. Uninhabited Isla Caño, 10 miles (16 km) offshore, boasts pre-Columbian remains. And Isla del Coco, about 300 miles (480 km) southwest of Costa Rica and part of the Galápagos chain, offers superb scuba diving.

The Northern *&* Caribbean Lowlands

Lush forests extend across the vast *llanuras*—flatlands—of northern and eastern Costa Rica like a damp carpet. The undulating plains are drained by countless rivers that

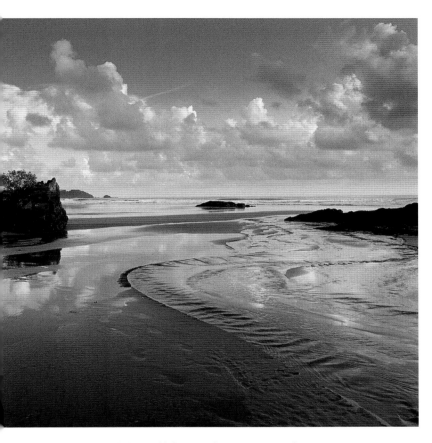

A chromatic sunset gilds the roughly hewn Pacific coast at Dominical.

cascade down from the mountains and flow into the Río San Juan, forming the Nicaraguan border. Other rivers drain into Refugio Nacional de Vida Silvestre Caño Negro, teeming with feisty gamefish, crocodiles, and birdlife. Much of the forest has been felled during recent decades for cattle, and international fruit companies are tightening their grip, pushing citrus and banana plantations up against the remaining forest. Tortuguero and Barra del Colorado, two ramshackle Caribbean hamlets, where the Río San Juan meets the sea, are sportfishing centers. Parque Nacional Tortuguero and Refugio Nacional de Vida Silvestre Barra del Colorado are channel-laced forest reserves where wildlife is viewed from canoes. The Caribbean coast sashays south from Barra to the Río Sixaola and the Panama border. The shore is lined by gray-sand beaches hemmed in by the sea and by the crowding Talamancas. Puerto Limón, a disheveled port, is the only town of significance, while the villages of Cahuita and Puerto Viejo preserve Afro-Carib culture, drawing surfers and younger counterculture vacationers. The Northern Lowlands are served by the Ciudad Quesada and by Fortuna, gateway to Parque Nacional Volcán Arenal and Tabacón Hot Springs. ■

A Conservation Ethic

Despite spiraling population growth and unsustainable economic practices —logging, ranching, large-scale commercial agriculture—that have diminished Costa Rica's forest cover by 60 percent during the past 400 years, the nation has set aside 28 percent of its land in national parks and reserves, a larger percentage than any other country on Earth.

The parks and reserves are grouped into 11 Regional Conservation Areas (RCAs) that create corridors for migratory wildlife by linking adjacent national parks. Every major ecosystem is represented, safeguarding natural treasures for ecotravelers to enjoy.

Diminishing Forests

To the casual visitor, Costa Rica looks like an endless lush swath of green. In fact, forest destruction has occurred at a frightening rate, much of it illicitly by loggers driven by immense profits in hardwoods. Where trees fall, rains cause wholesale erosion. The effect of lost forest is felt throughout the biological kingdom, where the survival of countless species (including jaguars, tapirs, and macaws) is at risk.

More than 95 percent of the lowland dry forests were felled during the colonial era to make way for cattle ranches. The 1960s and 1970s were particularly devastating to the rain forests of the Northern Lowlands, as vast tracts were felled to raise beef for the U.S. market. Fruit companies continue to whittle away at lowland rain forests, and squatters edge up against protected forests, which they destroy with slash-and-burn agriculture.

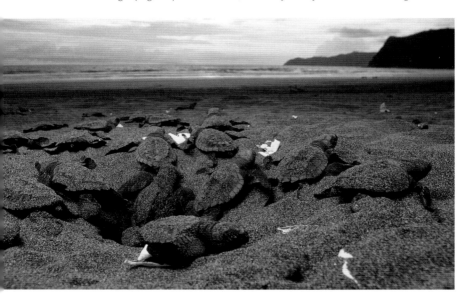

Newly hatched olive Ridley turtles make a dash to the sea. Only about one percent will survive to adulthood.

Nonetheless, the rate of deforestation slowed during the past decade and, in fact, has been reversed.

Saving What Remains

Costa Rica is at the forefront of attempts to create sustainable revenue from tropical forests, and boasts 34 national parks and more than 160 wildlife refuges, biological reserves, and marine parks, grouped into the 11 RCAs. Ecotourism is a boon; more private reserves are being opened to public visitation. A conservation ethic has taken hold among the local population, many of whom have traditionally seen the forest as an economic resource to be culled. In the modern world, Costa Rica's forests must earn their keep to survive. Harvesting ornamental plants and raising tree-dwelling iguanas for meat are among the schemes introduced by dozens of conservation organizations within Costa Rica to give local communities a vested interest in preservation. International bodies such as the Nature Conservancy, World Wide Fund for Nature, and U.S. Agency for International Development now sponsor creative forest management projects such as "debt for nature" swaps, where Costa Rica "swaps" part of its national debt (duly discounted) for a guarantee to safeguard a specific amount of forest. Scores of private reserves have been established in recent years dedicated to restoring native ecosystems, which take many hundreds of years to replenish themselves. As a result of all these efforts, the percentage of forested land had increased to 51 percent of the nation in 2005.

Back from the Grave

It's not often that an animal that has been classified as extinct is rediscovered alive. But recently, the brown and metallic green tree frog, which hadn't been seen in Costa Rica's Monteverde Cloud Forest Reserve since the 1980s, when the amphibian population crashed probably due to climate change and fungal infection, was spotted high atop a moss-covered tree branch by British zoologist Andrew Gray. Taking a nocturnal hike deep in Monteverde's hinterlands, Gray, an expert in frog voices, heard the frog chirping and didn't recognize its species. Climbing the branch, he was astounded to discover a lone *Isthomhyla rivularis*. He took several photos and released the frog to the wild, with the intent of returning to set up a breeding program. This exciting discovery has given scientists hope that other species considered to be extinct may still survive.

A Mixed Report Card

Protection requires a balancing act. Some national parks are being degraded by too many feet, while hotels squeeze parks, such as Manuel Antonio, against the sea. Although the scale has tipped toward greater integrity and enforcement in recent years, lack of funding and poor management bedevil the beleaguered National Park Service and the Forestry Department, which are tainted by corruption. In addition, entrenched political interests have a toehold in fighting conservation, and illegal logging and hunting continue with the connivance of NPS personnel.

The situation has been complicated by the emergence of large-scale luxury resorts concentrated in dry northwest Nicoya, where new golf courses are draining the aquifers. The temptation to build bigger was resisted for many years, but the Calderón administration (1990–1994) abandoned ecological principles established during preceding governments, paving the way for wanton disregard for protective laws. ∎

The Lush Environment

Nature lovers speak in hyperboles, using terms like "nirvana" for the Garden of Eden called Costa Rica. Though it lies strictly within the tropics, between 8 and 11 degrees north of the Equator, the country claims 12 distinct ecological zones, spanning tidal mangroves and dry deciduous forest to tropical rain forest and even subalpine grassland, called *páramo*, atop the windswept heights of the Talamanca massif.

Costa Rica offers some surprises: Cactuses stud desert-dry pockets of the northwest, where hardy Zebu cattle range parched savanna bordering wetlands where crocodiles bask on mudbanks, motionless as logs. This is a veritable hothouse of biodiversity. Acre for acre, Costa Rica is as species rich as anywhere else on Earth. Around 5 percent of all known Species on Earth slither, skip, or swoop through the varied habitats, including one-tenth of all known birds species. The extraordinary biodiversity stems from Costa Rica's position at the juncture of two major continents; over eons, life-forms from both have migrated across the narrow land bridge and adapted to constantly varied local relief and climate. In this arena of intense competition they have diversified remarkably to survive. No wonder travelers who are tired of just seeing pictures of jaguars, quetzals, and three-toed sloths flock here like migrating macaws.

Hothouse Diversity

In the tropics, temperatures are relatively constant, for the sun shines directly overhead throughout the year, while drenching downpours and an annual rainfall in excess of 100 inches (250 cm) maintain a constant high humidity that fosters the luxuriant growth. Lush to the point of saturation, Costa Rica is a botanical breeding ground of stupendous proportion. Its 800 or so species of ferns, for example, far outnumber those found in the whole of North America. Costa Rica is particularly rich in orchid species; about 1,400 have been identified so far. Orchids are found from sea level to the heights of Cerro Chirripó, with flowers ranging from less than 1 millimeter across to pendulous petals spanning 20 inches (50 cm). The greatest diversity is associated with rain forests, where orchids steep in year-round moisture. Around 90 percent of orchid species are epiphytes, or "air plants" (plants that root on other plants but are not parasitic), which thrive in the compost deposited on the limbs by decayed forebears and draw moisture by dangling their roots in the air. Whole colonies of epiphytes live atop the massive boughs, which often resemble vast galleries. Other epiphytes include bromeliads, which have evolved tightly wrapped leaves that act as miniature cisterns, trapping water and leaf litter that decays and donates its nutrients to the plant. Costa Rica has more than 2,000 species of bromeliads, which reach awesome sizes—some species measure as much as 4 feet (1.2 m) across.

> **Costa Rica is particularly rich in orchid species; about 1,400 have been identified so far.**

A red-eyed tree frog epitomizes the beauty of Costa Rica's miraculous fauna.

Ecological Zones

Costa Rica's landscapes are classified into 12 ecological "life zones," identified in 1947 by internationally renowned tropical forest biologist Leslie R. Holdridge (1907–1999). Each zone is characterized by a distinct terrain, climate, and life-forms. While the canvas is overwhelmingly green, Costa Rica's ecological zones include dry deciduous forest and subalpine grasslands. Various gradations exist in between.

Mangroves & Wetlands: Costa Rica's variegated coastline is rimmed by mangrove colonies, groups of halophytic plants (able to survive with their roots in salt water) that thrive on the land formed from silt carried by the slow-flowing rivers. Five species of mangroves grow at the juncture of land and sea, notably along the coast of Golfo de Nicoya (particularly the mouth of the Río Tempisque), the delta of the Río Terraba, the shores of Golfo Dulce, and in the lagoons of Tortuguero and Gandoca-Manzanillo, where variant mangrove ecosystems— *jollilos* and *orey,* respectively—have evolved. The trees' humble appearance disguises an intricate environment protecting vast numbers of wild creatures—not least, crocodiles—from human encroachment. Migratory waterfowl, wading birds, and small mammals abound in the shallows and tidal creeks, feeding on the amphipods, crabs, marine worms, mussels, and other organisms that thrive on the decayed vegetation amid the dense roots. Bacteria rework decaying leaf litter into detritus that feeds a legion of marine species that are consumed in turn by larger creatures.

> ### EXPERIENCE:
> ### Exploring the Canopy
>
> **Arenal Hanging Bridges** (tel 2479-9686, www.hangingbridges.com) has *colgantes* (suspension bridges) slung between treetops and across canyons, offering eye-to-eye views with the wildlife. **Corcovado Tent Camp** (tel 2257-0766, www.costaricaexpeditions.com) lets you sleep (or maybe not!) in a tent on a canopy platform 120 feet (36.6 m) above the forest floor. It gives a whole new definition to "night life." **Rain Forest Aerial Tram** (tel 2257-5961, www.rainforesttram.com) slices silently through the forest canopy. You ride in an open-air gondola, accompanied by your own guide, on a 1.6-mile (2.6 km) circuit.

Inland, Costa Rica's two prime wetland ecosystems are Caño Negro, in the Northern Lowlands, and Palo Verde, at the mouth of the Río Tempisque. Both are congenial to aquatic birds and shelter a variety of migratory birds and other creatures—crocodiles, monkeys, deer, peccaries, coatis, ocelots—that is the equal of any other environment in Costa Rica. The wetlands flood in the rainy season and contract to mudflats in the dry season. Streams and rivers wind among these vast aquatic systems, connecting channels and broad lagoons that draw tens of thousands of waterfowl and other exotic birds.

Rain Forests: Rain forests are among the most complex ecosystems on Earth. More than 50 percent of *all* known living species on the planet can be found in tropical rain forests, in a band 10 degrees north and south of the Equator. Biologists recognize at least 13 distinct types of rain forest, based on differences in altitude, rainfall, and soil conditions. Thus, the same latitude in Costa Rica may be marked by tropical evergreen rain forest on the Caribbean coast and seasonally dry evergreen forest on the Pacific shore, though both share near-constant, stifling humidity and heat, and a profusion of plant life. All rain forests receive more than 100 inches (250 cm) of rainfall per year; lowland rain forests may receive up to 300 inches (750 cm)! Premontane wet forest is found at higher elevations, as in rain-soaked Braulio Carrillo and Tapantí National Parks, where conditions are cooler. Pockets of mist-soaked tropical montane rain forest, or cloud forest, swathe the mountains at elevations around 4,000 feet (1,220 m), where branches drip with mosses and epiphytes thrive in the humidity. At the highest elevations, as atop Poás and Irazú Volcanoes, stunted trees cower before wind-driven rains.

The true lowland rain forests that smother the *llanuras*—flatlands—of the Atlantic lowlands, the Osa Peninsula, and the eastern flanks of the Talamancas are of Gothic proportion, with trees soaring 100 feet (30 m) or more before merging like a crowd of giant umbrellas. Their mushroom-shaped crowns form a green canopy so dense that you might imagine yourself able to walk across it. The canopy is shaded by mammoth trees—emergents, such as the kapok *(Ceiba pentandra)*—that soar past their neighbors like great Corinthian columns. Height is paramount in the competitive search for light. Most trees have long, straight limbless trunks with branching not occurring until 60 or more feet (18 m) above ground. These branches

The tightly wrapped leaves of bromeliads act as cisterns, providing nutrients from trapped and decaying insects.

form an understory. Some emergents tower as much as 100 feet (30 m) above the canopy. The lowland rain forest is a multilayered labyrinth (see illustration pp. 180–181).

The canopy is subject to the passage of clouds, wind, and storms and has a separate climate than the forest understory and the shrub-covered floor below. Rainfall may take many minutes to reach the ground, if at all. Similarly, only about 10 percent of sunlight reaches the ground, where the vegetation is consequently sparse. Saplings of many high canopy species stop growing once they reach about 10 feet (30 m) in height, then wait until a tree falls before erupting into explosive growth with the sudden burst of sunlight. Forest floor species have adapted crafty techniques to make the most of the subaqueous light. In clearings, plants put out broad leaves to soak up the sun, such as the "poor man's umbrella" *(sombrilla de pobre)*, whose leaves like elephant ears make perfect cover in downpours.

Whereas in temperate zones, forests may have "neighborhoods" of one or two tree species, in rain forests hundreds of species intermingle—from cecropia trees favored by sloths to towering mahoganies favored by loggers. One tree may host around one hundred other species of smaller plants, such as ferns, vines, and bromeliads. In the hot and humid tropics, plants grow and reproduce year-round. Dead leaves decompose and nutrients are quickly recycled and sucked back up to the forest canopy and reabsorbed, unlike in temperate zones where tissue breakdown is slow and nutrient-rich humus builds up a thick layer of soil. Since tropical soils are thin, most tree species have adapted and spread their roots wide for balance and maximum nutrient uptake; the emergents, unsecured by the intertwined canopy, have evolved great flanges, like rocket fins, to overcome their inherent instability. Vines twine up their hosts, often reaching several hundred feet in length as they coil along branches and between trees, knitting the canopy together. The strangler fig, however, germinates in the canopy and sends down tendril roots, which anchor to the forest floor and send up nutrients. As the roots envelop the host tree, they suffocate it until it dies and decomposes, providing sustenance and leaving a cylindrical, freestanding fig.

Wildlife Viewing

Most wildlife in Costa Rica is well camouflaged or shy, and viewing it usually requires great patience. Often animals and birds may be present, but the untrained eye can't see them. The more still and quiet you are, the more species will reveal themselves. Wear khakis and colors that blend with the background. Binoculars are essential. It pays to educate yourself about local ecology and the particular species you're eager to see. Bring a good field guide to identify individual species or tracks. Above all, hire a reputable guide (see p. 34).

Dry Forests: On the eve of Columbus's landfall, the lowlands of the Pacific Northwest were swathed in dry deciduous forest, which covered a greater expanse than did Central America's rain forests. These forests evolved in the five-month seasonal drought that befalls Guanacaste in November, when the trees shed their leaves to conserve water. Trees in dry forest rarely rise more than 40 feet (12 m) and are relatively sparsely distributed, making wildlife viewing easy; anteaters, monkeys, and scarlet macaws are numerous. The open-crowned canopy rises above a secondary layer of trees with smaller crowns, and thorny scrub and grass at ground layer. Often all the members of a single species burst into bloom on the same day before dropping their petals like colored confetti: jacaranda in purple, the *poró* in bright orange, and the *corteza amarillo*—Guanacaste's state flower—in yellow. Trees blossom one after another in a strict cycle: the rose pink *pouí* in January, for example, followed by the pastel pink *tabebuia rosea* in March and the vermilion *malinche* in April. When the rains return in April or May, the dry forest buds afresh.

During the colonial era, the Spanish destroyed vast areas of forest for cattle, decimating dry forests from Panama to Mexico. In Costa Rica, only some 200 square miles (520 sq km)—about 2 percent—of the original dry forest cover remained in a threadbare patchwork in Guanacaste and Santa Rosa National Parks and the Tempisque Basin. Reforestation projects have begun to reverse the decline.

Tropical Menagerie

Costa Rica is a cornucopia of botanical and zoological treasures. The National Institute of Biodiversity, which is attempting to identify every plant and animal species in the country, estimates there are at least one million species. Anteaters, coatis, iguanas, monkeys, birds by the hundreds, and insects in tens of thousands, are colorful as creatures in a Rousseau painting and often can be seen within an arm's length. Yet only the rare visitor is fortunate enough to see an elusive jaguar on the prowl.

Mammals: Costa Rica claims only around 200 species of mammals, of which half are bats—including vampire bats and a giant fishing bat which scoops up fish with its claws while on the wing. Most mammal species are shy and rarely seen by the casual visitor. The cats are well represented, notably by jaguars, ocelots, pumas, and extremely rare margays and oncillas—both spotted like cheetahs—and dark brown

Support group: Buttress roots of a ficus tree at Hacienda Barú

jaguarundis. Superb climbers, cats can sometimes be seen racing up tree trunks to chase down rodents and monkeys scampering along the high branches. All six cat species are both endangered and elusive.

Far more easily seen are the four species of neotropical monkeys found in all lowland and mid-elevation habitats. Descendants of Old World monkeys that migrated across the Bering land bridge eons ago, the New World species are noted for their long prehensile tails. The large, leaf-eating black howler monkey is the most common species—and the most noticeable: The males frighten tourists with their loud roars, announcing their territorial fiefdoms, particularly at dawn and dusk. The small, omnivorous, black-and-white-faced capuchin monkeys are also easily spotted playing among the branches, notably at Parque Nacional Manuel Antonio, where their presence is guaranteed. The diminutive, orange-hued squirrel monkey *(titi),* though endangered, is gregarious, and groups of 40 or so family members are not unusual. By contrast, the long-limbed, copper-colored spider monkey is a solitary critter that faces severe deprivations from loss of habitat.

Living high up in the treetops and sleeping an average of 18 hours a day, sloths (see sidebar p. 49) are perhaps the slowest animal of the forest.

Two species of raccoon *(mapache)* are found in Costa Rica: The white-faced northern raccoon is found throughout the lowlands, while its dark-faced, crab-eating cousin confines itself to habitats along the Pacific coast. One of the most frequently seen mammals is the coati *(pizote),* which can be easily identified by its panda-like ringed eyes, brown coat, and ringed tail, which the animal craftily uses to thwart predators: When attacked, it rears up, stuffs its tail between its legs and waves it in front of its face, so that predators will attack the tail and get slashed in the eyes in return. Smaller, nocturnal, tree-climbing cousins in the raccoon family are the olingo, cacomistle, and kinkajou.

In addition to two squirrel species and around 40 species of rats and mice, Costa Rica claims two neotropical rodents of note. The large, brown agouti *(guatusa)* is a dainty forest-dwelling creature that resembles a large tailless squirrel with long, slender legs. Different subspecies have evolved with both darker and lighter coloration as adaptations to either wet or dry forest habitats. The agouti and its nocturnal cousin, the paca *(tepezcuintle),* which resembles a large guinea pig, are traditionally hunted by campesinos for meat and are now endangered. The timid tapir *(danta),* a distant relative of the elephant, also once roamed far and wide but has been brought to the point of extinction by hunting. Intrepid hikers may find these trunk-snouted animals high in the mountains, drinking at volcanic lakes, and in remote sections of Corcovado and the Talamancas.

Other mammals include Costa Rica's three species of anteaters, which subsist solely on a diet of ants, scooped up with a long sticky tongue; and two species of armor-plated armadillos. Coyotes and foxes abound, as do rabbits, and two species of opossums represent the marsupials (mammals whose embryonic offspring are reared in an external pouch). Peccaries *(sainos),* fearsome wild pigs, roam in herds and grub up roots and other foods from beneath the topsoil. Although normally shy around humans, aggressive males

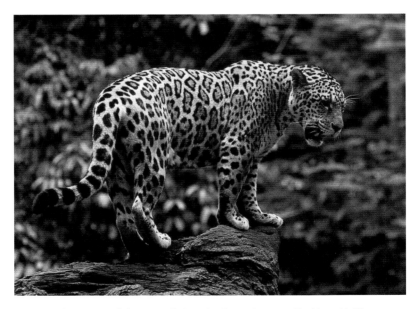

The jaguar symbolizes not only Costa Rica but environmental health worldwide.

have been known to attack people. Several kinds of skunk are also common, including the fierce badger-like grison; and the sleek, chocolate brown tayra, a 3-foot-long (0.9 m) giant that hunts rodents and small deer and can be found in both lowland and highland habitats. Sloths abound throughout the country (see sidebar, opposite). Manatees—endangered marine herbivores that resemble tuskless walruses and have a spatulate tail in lieu of flippers—inhabit the watery recluses of Parque Nacional Tortuguero and Refugio Nacional de Vida Silvestre Gandoca-Manzanillo, where a rare dolphin endemic to the region, the *tucuxí,* inhabits the lagoons. Otters are commonly seen in lowland rivers, notably in the waterways of Tortuguero and the adjacent Refugio Nacional de Vida Silvestre Barra del Colorado.

Amphibians & Reptiles: Amphibians and reptiles thrive in the hot, damp tropics. Costa Rica claims around 160 species of the former and 220 or so reptile species, of which 162 are snakes, though only 22 species are poisonous.

Frogs abound, including gaily colored poison-dart frogs (dendrobatids) hopping among the forest litter in their Day-glo livery—red as lipstick and blue as the morning sky—meant to scare predators. About 20 species of Costa Rican frogs produce deadly toxins. Frog and toad populations have declined precipitously in recent years. The golden toad, a diminutive wonder discovered at Monteverde only in 1964, is already considered extinct. Many frogs have adapted to life away from large bodies of water; some have evolved suction-cup feet and taken to a life in the trees, where they lay their eggs in the cisterns of bromeliads.

While snakes are ubiquitous, most are fairly small, like the chunk-headed snake, and feed on birds, small rodents, and lizards. Others, such as the commonly seen boas, can grow up to 10 feet (3 m) in length. Pythons are often spotted along riverbanks, glowing yellow or iridescent green, snoozing in sensuous coils on a branch. The viper family includes the burnished brown fer-de-lance *(terciopelo)*, waiting with jaws of death for passing fodder. This aggressive giant accounts for three-quarters of all snakebites in Costa Rica, and almost all snakebite deaths. Most other fatalities are due to the brightly banded coral snakes, which have a distinct venom (all other snakes produce the same venom).

Costa Rica's river estuaries and lowland waterways are favored by American crocodiles *(cocodrilos)*, which reach lengths of up to 15 feet (4.5 m). Their diminutive cousins, caimans, rarely grow beyond 6 feet (1.8 m). Crocodiles have suffered mightily from hunting during four centuries. Protected since the 1970s, they are making a comeback, particularly in the Río Tárcoles and Refugio Nacional de Vida Silvestre Caño Negro.

The tree-dwelling iguana inhabits both wet and dry lowland forest and can grow to 3 feet (0.9 m) in length. Cloaked in scaly armor, it presents a fearsome appearance but is quite harmless to humans. The spiny-tailed iguana is green, though males turn orange during the November–December mating season; the smaller ctenosaur is dun colored. The dozens of smaller lizard species include the Jesus Christ lizard, a resident of the Pacific Lowlands, named for its ability to run across water on its hind legs.

Many visitors come to Costa Rica hoping to see marine turtles laying their eggs, which is easily done at beaches on both the Caribbean and Pacific coasts. The females of five species of turtle come ashore here at various times throughout the year. The green turtle is most easily seen at Tortuguero. Leatherback turtles, the largest reptiles on Earth (they can weigh up to a ton/907 kg), nest at Playa Grande in Nicoya. Most exhilarating are the synchronized nestings *(arribadas)* at Refugio Nacional de Vida Silvestre Ostional, where tens of thousands of olive Ridley turtles swarm ashore during full moons from July to December.

Sloths

Sloths *(perozosos)* are commonly seen moving in treetops at a pace close to rigor mortis using their powerful arms and curved claws. Costa Rica has two species: the three-toed sloth and the smaller, nocturnal Hoffman's two-toed sloth. These leaf-eaters have huge stomachs to process large quantities of fairly indigestible food, which can remain in their stomach for up to one week. Their metabolic rate is correspondingly slow; the animal even garners heat from direct sunlight, much like cold-blooded reptiles. Sloths typically spend 18 hours a day sleeping and digesting their meals. They do not wash much, and their shaggy fur is tinted green by algae and inhabited by bugs.

Insects: Costa Rica's insect fauna is incalculably rich—from the microscopic flower mite, which hitches a ride inside the hummingbird's nostril, to giants such as the 3-inch-long (7.5 cm) rhinoceros beetle, so named for its horn. Tens of thousands of species await identification. The kingdom comes into its own at night, when moths and beetles take wing and the forests resound with a cacophonous chirruping and croaking.

Guanacaste is particularly rich; when seasonal rains strike, the insect fauna explodes. More than one thousand species of butterflies—one-quarter of the world's total—flit about the country. The undisputed king is the saucer-size, electric blue morpho. Subspecies differ in coloration according to locale; one rain-forest-canopy species is iridescent red. When threatened, the 6-inch (15 cm) owl butterfly (*Caligo memnon*) flashes its underwing coloration, which resembles a pair of owl eyes.

....

Leaf-cutter ants farm mushrooms underground using mulch chewed from leaves.

....

Of the thousands of species of ants, the most intriguing are the leaf-cutters, which farm mushrooms underground using mulch chewed from leaves stripped from trees. Costa Rica even has army ants, fearsome colonies that number in the millions and sweep through the countryside, terrorizing and devouring any living thing in their path.

Birds, Birds, Birds! Remarkably, one-tenth of all known bird species in the world inhabit this little patch of land. Of the 850 or so species found here, at least 600 are permanent residents, including 51 species of hummingbirds found throughout the nation in cloaks of shimmering cerulean blue, green, purple, and red.

Costa Rica has 16 species of parrots, from diminutive green parakeets to giant scarlet macaws, which are easily seen at Corcovado, Manuel Antonio, and Carará National Parks. The smaller, predominantly green Buffon's macaw is found only around Tortuguero and the Northeastern Lowlands. Both species are endangered due to habitat loss. Several private institutions have active breeding programs that release macaws back to the wild.

Another dazzler is the quetzal, the crown jewel of the cloud forest and the sole reason that many visitors flock to Costa Rica. This pigeon-size beauty—one of ten species of trogons in Costa Rica—boasts iridescent emerald feathers. The male woos potential mates with a blood red chest and a sweeping, forked tail up to 24 inches (60 cm) long. At Monteverde in the spring, the birds descend to lower altitudes and perform acrobatic midair mating displays. Visitors should listen for their mournful two-note whistle. That eerie metallic *bonk* resounding through the cloud forests is the call of the three-wattled bellbird.

Keel-billed and chestnut-mandibled toucans, with banana-like beaks, are common. Their sharp-beaked cousins, the toucanets and aracaris, are no less flamboyant. A favorite of birders is the motmot, which has a racquet-like tail and lives in a hole in the ground. Tanagers, exotically colored in flame reds and sky blues, are represented by 50 species. There are 78 species of flycatchers, 52 species of warblers, and 22 species of wrens. Some 50 species of raptors feed on everything from crabs and fish to monkeys—a favorite of the harpy eagle, reduced to remote parts of Corcovado and the Talamancas. Four species of vultures (*zopilotes*) pick at carrion; count yourself lucky to spot the mighty king vulture.

White cattle egrets are seen in pastures and along riverbanks. The remaining 25 species of waders include herons; three species of ibis; storks, such as the massive jabiru; and the roseate spoonbill, now confined to the safety of Caño Negro and Palo Verde. Costa Rica's wetlands, directly beneath the Pacific migratory flyway, attract waterfowl—coots, ducks, grebes, teal—in such numbers that their wings sometimes mimic the roar of a jet engine. Marine birds include cormorants, anhingas, and boobies. In Bahía Salinas and Golfo de Nicoya, the mangroves prove ideal nesting sites for frigatebirds. Ironically, the national bird of Costa Rica is the somewhat drab robin, locally known as the *yiguirro*. When the male sings during the spring mating season, local lore says he is calling the rains.

Marine Life: The tropical waters of both of Costa Rica's coasts allow scuba divers to swim with whale sharks, manta rays, and groupers, and anglers can cast lures for the billfish that cruise the offshore waters. The Golfo de Papagayo and Golfo Dulce are particularly rich in game fish, such as dolphin fish, marlin, tuna, and wahoo. The top draw for experienced divers is Isla del Coco, where hammerhead sharks school in unsurpassed numbers. Off Manuel Antonio and in Bahía Ballena, an extravaganza of fish play amid the coral, while stingrays flap over the ocean bottom. Smaller coral reefs exist off Gandoca-Manzanillo and Cahuita in the Caribbean, and off Isla del Caño. Humpback whales gather seasonally to feed and mate in the warm, nutrient-rich waters of Bahía Ballena, providing exhilarating encounters for whale-watchers. ∎

EXPERIENCE: Birding at Its Best

Wherever you are in the country, the birding is sure to astound. With so many dedicated wilderness lodges, and so many distinct ecological zones, you have many choices. Still, some specific locales offer birding par excellence. Here are a few of the best places to find some of the more than 850 species found in Costa Rica.

Bosque de Paz *(tel 2234-6676, wwwbosquedepaz .com; see p. 77),* on the northern foothills of the Cordillera Central, boasts at least 330 species in its 988-acre (400 ha) cloud-forest reserve. Tours offer a chance to see the black guan, resplendent quetzal, and three-wattled bellbird. **Finca Eddie Serrano** *(tel 8381-8456),* off the Pan-American Hwy. south of Cartago, is perhaps the best site in Costa Rica for viewing quetzals—a virtu-ally guaranteed experience. Self-guided and guided hikes are offered.

Parque Nacional Palo Verde *(tel 2671-1290, www .sinaccr.net; see p. 112)* protects the floodplains and marshes of the Río Tempisque estuary, plus 15 distinct habitats, including dry forest. Roseate spoon-bills and scarlet macaws are among the highlights. **Parque Nacional Tortuguero** *(tel 2257-0766, www.costaricaexpedi tions.com; see p. 223)* grants a unique perspective as you cruise the waterways in search of toucans and green macaws. Forest walls lining the open waterways are like a gallery for 300 bird species. Costa Rica Ex-peditions is recommended for guided tours.

Selva Verde *(tel 2766-6800, www.selvaverde.com; see p. 209),* a private re-serve protecting 474 acres (192 ha) of northern low-land rain forest, abounds in bird-life. It specializes in guided birding trips, offered from the lodge.

Companies specializing in birding tours include **Cheeseman's Ecology Safaris** *(408/2867-1371, www.cheesemans.com)* and **Field Guides** *(512/2263-7295, www.fieldguides.com).*

The Cultural Scene

Costa Rica's modern National Symphony Orchestra rises to the standard of its stunning venue: the Teatro Nacional (National Theater) in San José. But otherwise, Costa Rica is relatively culturally underdeveloped, and the nation has sought in vain for a pre-Columbian legacy to stimulate a modern renaissance.

The sterility can be explained by Costa Rica's benign colonial history, because social tensions have always been a spark for vibrant cultural expression. This peaceful nation thereafter suffered from a creative paucity, with the exception of a few native crafts.

The nation has long been dismissed as a cultural backwater. The entire cultural scene, including dance and theater, was for a long time moved by the national sense of a brotherhood of lowly, country-based Ticos. For example, visual art struggled to break out of the traditional confines of portraying idyllic rural scenes.

In recent years, however, Costa Rica has developed a new confidence as artists have cast aside rigid norms. The nation's young, up-and-coming artists and wood-carvers are following the examples of American artists-in-residence, whose success owes much to their freedom from the constraints of a campesino-based national identity and spirit.

In performing arts, too, dance and theater companies have broken away from their traditional bonds, especially in the realm of contemporary dance.

Visual Arts

Until recent years, there was little energy to Costa Rican art, which has lacked the passionate, visceral, socially engaged formats of other Latin nations. Artists struggled for decades to Houdini out of a straitjacket of stylized Costa Rican landscape that developed in the late 1920s based on depictions of campesino life. The so-called Group of New Sensibility was influenced by the French Impressionists and headed by Teodorico Quirós (1897–1977). The movement's legacy remains preeminent today in paintings, including miniatures, showing adobe dwellings and cobbled rural villages, usually with a volcano for backdrop. The school evolved in Escazú and neighboring Santa Ana, southwest of San José, which remain an informal artists' enclave.

Costa Rica's crop of current young artists displays an eclectic world vision.

This art of *casitas* (little houses) was derided by the next generation of artists, who by the 1950s were experimenting in abstract styles. Modernist and en vogue contemporary styles have since found their way into a more mature artistic expression, and Costa Rica's current crop of young artists displays an eclectic world vision. In recent years, artists such as Isidro Con Wong (b. 1931), have won international acclaim. Wong's works—described as "magic realism"—fetch up to $35,000 on the world market. Rafa Fernández (b. 1935) is another magic realist, specializing in erotic female images. And Zapote's Rolando Castellón (b. 1937) is known for his 3-D art.

Plastic Arts

Sculpture has never been a strong suit in Costa Rica, although the pre-Columbian influence can be seen in a tradition of jewelry work and an outpouring of splendid gold and silver adornment. Contemporary jewelry styles owe much to traditional indigenous forms, such as animist figurines.

The nation's most famous sculptural piece dates back to 1936, when sculptor Francisco Zuñiga (1912–1998) unveiled a stone carving of a mother suckling her child. The piece, called "Maternity," can be seen today outside San José's Maternidad Caritas maternity clinic. It was ridiculed by local critics who derided it as looking more like a cow than a woman, causing Zuñigo to leave for Mexico. His "Evelia con Batan" stands at the entrance

The ceiling of the Teatro Nacional's lobby depicts an idyllic scene from the 19th-century heyday of coffee.

to San José's Centro Nacional de Artes y Cultura, and the modernist sculpture garden at the Museo de Arte Contemporaneo has several of his works.

Tourism has sparked a revolution in crafts, notably in wood carvings inspired primarily by Escazú's Barry Biesanz (b. 1948). Sarchí, however, is the undisputed center of crafts. Here, Costa Rica's cliché wooden oxcarts called *carretas* are still made and decorated in floral motifs, including miniatures intended as garden ornaments or as domestic liquor carts for the home. Sarchí is also the main center for other craft items and traditional wooden furniture hewn from hardwoods including mahogany, lignum vitae, and rosewood.

Santa Ana is famed for its earthenware. And at Guaitíl, in Nicoya, a renaissance in Chorotega pride finds its outlet in much-sought-after pottery. Members of the Boruca tribe make traditional musical instruments, wooden masks, and handwoven textiles.

Literature

Unlike other Latin American cultures, the dispassionate Ticos are not a particularly literate people, despite a high literacy level. Only a fistful of writers make a living from the profession, which is dominated by parochial themes. Costa Rica's literary style is insipid and the country has yet to produce a writer of international note.

Injustice and social turmoil are the grist for great literature and Costa Rica has lacked both; the singular literary work to gain broad recognition is *Mamita Yunai*, a story decrying the injustices wrought by the United Fruit Company upon Costa Rica's banana workers, by Carlos Luis Fallas (1912–1996). Likewise, the acclaimed *El Eco de los Pasos* by Julieta Pinto (b. 1922) had the 1948 civil war as its theme. The works represented in a lone anthology of literary works by 20th-century Costa Rican authors, *Costa Rica: A Traveler's Literary Companion,* are prosaic and anemic. Cocorí, a little cartoon character by José Joaquín Gutiérrez (1918-2000), played on the stereotypical idiosyncrasies of Ticos.

Music & Dance

Costa Rica is the southernmost of the *marimba* countries—those owing much to the Africa-derived xylophone that forms the base of native music throughout Central America. It is no surprise then that Guanacaste, where the native tradition remains strongest, provides the impetus for traditional music and dance, typified by the national dance: the *punto guanacaste,* a toe-and-heel stomp for couples. Pre-Columbian instruments, such as the *quijongo* (a gourd amplifier attached to a string bow) are still used to accompany the Spanish guitar. Traditional dancing is based on the stylized Spanish *paseo,* with men and women alternately circling each other, accompanied by much *"yip-yipping"* and tossing of hats and scarves. It is now mostly performed at tourist venues by such groups as Fantasía Folklórica.

The traditional Latin *peña,* where intellectuals gather and share poems and music, is strong among the educated middle class. On the classical front, however, Costa Rica has been neither an inspirational locale nor a breeding ground for composers and instrumentalists. The Teatro Nacional hosts the National Symphony Orchestra, formed in 1970, which draws middle-class *Josefinos* (residents of San José) during the April–November season. Several minor classical and choral groups also perform.

Theater

Ticos enjoy theater so much that the country boasts more theaters per capita than any other country in the world. This enthusiasm dates from the turn of the 20th century, when drama became part of the school curriculum and an influx of South American playwrights boosted theatrical fortunes. San José's tiny theaters offer a mix of comedy, mime, and avant-garde, drawing the residents of San José every night except Mondays. The nation's oldest theatrical group, the Little Theater Group, performs in English.

Younger Ticos have forsaken traditional music and dance for the modern dance hall. Latin rhythms draw them to discos featuring hip-swiveling merengue, cumbia, and salsa. On the Caribbean coast, where musical influences derive from Jamaica, Bob Marley is king. Reggae, a modern phenomenon, has displaced traditional musical forms such as the *sinkit* and *cuadrille,* colonial island carryovers based on banjo and drum.

Jazz has gained in popularity in recent years and finds its major outlet in the annual International Festival of Music each August. A national style has emerged–a bravura, macho style with trumpeters playing the highest possible notes and pianists going as fast as they can go. The Southern Caribbean Music Festival in February also offers jazz side by side with reggae and classical music. ∎

A capital city with a provincial feel, plenty of small museums, pocket-size plazas, and intriguing edifices from the halcyon days of coffee

San José

A mountain backdrop silhouettes the city.

San José

Perched among a crescent of mountains, San José enjoys an enviable setting in the heart of the Meseta Central at 3,773 feet (1,150 m). The compact city of around 300,000 enjoys what *National Geographic* dubbed one of the three best climates in the world, with temperatures that hover around 70°F (21°C) daily year-round.

Rainfall is mostly short-lived showers and occasional downpours, May to October. Pleasantly small-scale as Central American capitals go, San José clings to a provincial feel despite sprawling suburbs that now claim 1.3 million residents—one-third of the nation's total. San José can never be called colonial quaint. The city was founded as late as 1737 and has relatively few colonial architectural glories. The main commercial boulevards are little strips of America, with neon signs blaring the offerings of fast-food outlets, car dealerships, strip clubs, and shopping malls. The city—which is made up of a set of distinct districts called barrios—has not entirely shaken off its village feel, however. In many ways it remains a working-class city where social life is based around the local *pulpería*, or corner store.

Coffee Culture

Throughout its first century of existence, San José endured as a humble village of simple adobe structures. But its position in the heart of the fertile valley was advantageous, and by the 1820s it had grown to equal the then capital Cartago in size. In 1823 the city seized the standard after a brief civil war and became the capital. San José prospered as coffee took hold on the surrounding slopes; plazas, parks, and fine public buildings rose up. The city's nouveau-riche *cafeteleros* (coffee-trading barons), who looked to Europe for inspiration, adopted the French-inspired New Orleans and Port-au-Prince (Haiti) style for their new homes.

The years following World War II saw rapid growth, and the city's infrastructure has been hard-pressed ever since to keep pace

with the changes. Beyond the touristed core, central San José is a chaos of ugly modern buildings, decrepit sidewalks, open sewers, and potholed streets. Crowds elbow their way along streets that teem with overflowing markets, lottery sellers, and sidewalk vendors. Pedestrians are forced to fend off a noisily honking armada of buses, trucks, motorcycles, and taxis that belch out fumes. Friendly, efficient tourist police patrol the city center, although petty theft is still common and muggings occur; visitors are advised to leave valuables in their hotel safe.

NOT TO BE MISSED:

The pre-Columbian gold in the Museo de Oro Precolombino **58**

A concert at the neoclassical Teatro Nacional **58–59**

The jewelry collection at the Museo de Jade Marco Fidel Tristán **61**

A stroll around Parque Nacional **62**

A walking tour of Barrio Amón **64–65**

Browsing and eating local fare at the Mercado Central **66**

Architectural Renewal

Nonetheless, San José has an undeniable charm and many visitors grow fond of *chepe*, as the city is colloquially known. Most sites of interest lie within a few blocks of the Plaza de la Cultura. On weekends the heavy traffic thins and Josefinos, the residents of San José, stroll the pedestrian-only Avenida Central and the half dozen plazas shaded by mauve jacarandas. In recent years, the Ministry of Culture has put a polish on the previously run-down plazas and the fistful of notable edifices, such as the Catedral Metropólitano.

Most tourists find that San José can be fully explored in two days, after which you will be ready to escape to the country. Coffee fields edge up against the city, so the countryside is close at hand. San José provides a splendid base for day trips throughout the Central Highlands, either by rental car or organized excursion.

Popular destinations from the capital include the Butterfly Farm, Café Britt Coffee Plantation Tour, Poás Volcano, Orosí, the Rainforest Aerial Tram, La Paz Waterfall Garden, and the artisans' center, Sarchí. ■

The City Core

Although San José offers suburban temptations, the city's main sights of interest are concentrated in a compact core laid out in a grid, which makes exploring easy. Use Avenida Central as an axis to find major nodes of interest sprinkled handily along its route. A good place to start is Plaza de la Cultura, not least for the main visitor information bureau accessed on the east side.

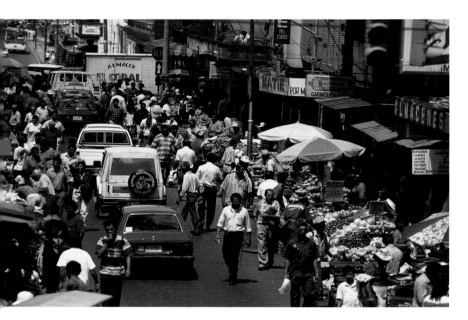

San José's downtown streets pulse like veins of the city.

San José

🅜 Map pp. 56–57

Visitor Information

✉ Calle 5, Ave. Central/2

☎ 2222-1090

Museo de Oro Precolombino

🅜 See map p. 57

✉ Calle 5, Ave. Central

☎ 2243-4202

🕐 Closed Mon.

💲 $$

Plaza de la Cultura

The nondescript Plaza de la Cultura is the center around which life in San José whirls. Hemmed by Calles 3 and 5, it lies at the heart of a pedestrian-only shopping zone extending seven blocks along Avenida Central. The plaza is a gathering spot for young people, and jugglers and musicians entertain the crowds who gather here on weekends. A clock tower and fountain stand at the junction of Avenida Central and Calle 3.

On the east side of the plaza, on Calle 5, steps lead to the subterranean **Museo de Oro Precolombino,** the gold museum, which is best explored using the audio-taped self-guided tour. Some 2,000 pieces of pre-Columbian gold jewelry, as well as life-size figures adorned in gold glitter under spotlights. The collections of the adjoining **Museo Numismático** *(for visitor information, see Museo de Oro Precolombino),* include coinage dating back three centuries.

On the south side is the neoclassic **Teatro Nacional,** the jewel in Costa Rica's architectural crown. It owes its origins to a fit of local pique when operatic prima donna Adelina Patti (1843–1919) bypassed Costa Rica during a Central American tour in 1890. The ruling clique promptly voted

INSIDER TIP:

Nature in the heart of the city? The National Museum has a walk-through butterfly garden under shrouds, plus a "passion flower" garden, new in May 2008.

—CHRISTOPHER P. BAKER
National Geographic author

a tax on coffee exports to pay for the construction of a theater in the style of the Paris Opera House. The resulting edifice was sumptuous enough to tempt the Paris Opera to perform *Faust* at the inauguration in October 1897. Statues of the Muses of Dance, Music, and Fame decorate the Renaissance facade. Beyond the pink marble foyer, the intermezzo has a colorful mural of an idyllic coffee harvest, while in the lavish triple-tiered auditorium nude deities prance across the ceiling.

The theater and the landmark **Gran Hotel** (see p. 242) open onto tiny **Plaza Mora Fernández,** where marimba bands frequently perform. The hotel lobby has a 24-hour casino fronted by the bal-

cony of the **Café 1830,** a popular spot for watching life pass by.

Parque Central

This bustling plaza draws Ticos to converse and flirt beneath the guanacaste trees and bandstand, where concerts are given on Sundays. The city's blue-domed **Catedral Metropólitano,** erected in 1871 in an austere Greek Orthodox style, looms to the east. The cathedral replaces an original structure toppled by an earthquake in 1821 and boasts an ornate altarpiece. Attached is the rugged and mellowed **La Curia** *(closed to the public),* the Archbishop's

Teatro Nacional
- Map p. 57
- Ave. 2, Calle 3
- 2221-9417
- Closed Sun.
- $

www.teatro nacional.go.cr

Know the Way in San José?

Avenidas (avenues) run east-west in San Jose. They ascend in odd numbers north of Avenida Central, and in even numbers south of it. *Calles* (streets) run north-south; they ascend in odd numbers east of Calle Central, and in even numbers west of it. Street addresses and numbers are rarely used. Instead, general addresses are given: Avenida 1 between Calles 6 and 8, would be written as "Avenida 1, Calles 6/8." Often addresses are stated in relation to a well-known landmark, such as "100 meters east and 200 meters south of Coca-Cola," a reference to a bus depot that is still referred to by a defunct bottling factory.

EXPERIENCE: Where the Music's At

San José has a nightlife hot enough to boil a pot of *gallo pinto*. Whether you're seeking mellow jazz or sizzling salsa, there's a wide choice of venues. Here are some of the best:

El Cuartel de la Boca del Monte *(Ave. 1, Calles 21/23, Barrio La California, tel 2221-0327)* This dressy, bohemian, brick-lined nightspot is popular with students and the well-heeled alike. It packs in the crowds for live music on Mon., Wed., and Fri. A late-night venue, it has a vast cocktail list and serves meals, too.
El Tobogán *(Calle Blancos, off Guápiles Hwy., 660 feet/200 m north and*

330 feet/100 m east of La República, tel 2223-8920, closed Mon.–Thurs.) With a cavernous dance floor beneath soaring thatch, this is perhaps the city's most popular dance spot on weekends for spicy-hot merengue and salsa. Live bands perform.
Jazz Café *(Ave. Central, San Pedro, tel 2253-8933, www.jazzcafecostarica .com)* Though small, this red-brick building is Costa Rica's premier jazz venue.

International stars such as Chucho Valdés and The Yellowjackets often perform alongside the nation's own accomplished musicians.
Shakespeare Bar *(Ave. 2, Calle 28, tel 2258-6787)* A laid-back basement bar adjoining the Sala Garbo and Laurence Olivier Theater. It's perfect for pre- or post-theater cocktails and it hosts live blues, folk, jazz, and R&B.

Palace, built in 1887. To the left of the cathedral entrance stands a marble modernist monument, *Homenaje a Juan Pablo II* (Homage to John Paul II), erected in September 2006.

Parque Central's north fringe is Avenida 2, the city's busy main thoroughfare, dominated by the neoclassical facade of the **Teatro Mélico Salazar** *(tel 2222-5424, www.teatro melico.go.cr)*, built in the 1920s and named for Costa Rican tenor Melico Salazar (1887–1950). The marble lobby is supported by Corinthian columns that extend into the delightful café. The theater is

A pre-Columbian gold figurine

occasionally used for classical and folklore-related concerts.

Parque Morazán

Situated between Avenidas 3 and 5 and Calles 5 and 9, this small park is highlighted by the domed Temple of Music and makes a quiet retreat. Named for Central American federalist Francisco Morazán (1800–1845), the park features statues and busts of Latin American notables, including the South American liberator Simón Bolívar (1783–1830).

The area to the south forms a mini red-light district serving the tourist trade. Many visitors choose to pop into **Key Largo** to sample the bordello flavor that belies the beauty of the turn-of-the-20th-century mansion, which features exquisite stained-glass work as well as a metal crest crowning the roof.

Parque Morazán is bordered to the east by tree-shaded **Parque España,** featuring busts of conquistador Juan Vásquez de Coronado and Queen Isabella of Spain (1830–1904). Songbirds roost in the densely packed trees. To the northwest is the green **Edificio Metálico** *(private)* made in Belgium of prefabricated metal and shipped to Costa Rica in 1892. Now a school, it took four years to weld together.

To the north is the National Insurance Company (INS) Building. To the glass-fronted building's left is the **Museo de Jade Marco Fidel Tristán** *(Ave. 7, Calles 9/11, tel 2287-6034, www.ins-cr.com, closed Sat.–Sun., $)*. You'll find a superb collection of pre-Columbian jade jewelry and carvings, plus ceramics and stone *metates,* stools used for grinding corn with a pestle.

Plaza de la Democracia

San José's largest square, 400 yards (365 m) east of Plaza de la Cultura, is a lugubrious affair laid out in 1989 for the Hemispheric Summit. It is centered around a small waterfall and a bronze statue of "Don Pepe" Figueres. It is well worth taking time to browse and shop for homespun crafts and Guatemalan textiles in the tiny market that sits at the foot of the sloping plaza.

To the east, the castle-like, ocher-colored Bellavista Fortress overshadows the plaza. Riddled with bullet holes from the 1948 civil war, like a vision from *Beau Geste.* Today the fortress is home

to the **Museo Nacional de Costa Rica,** which traces the nation's historical and cultural development using exhibits illustrating topics that range from religion to geology and archaeology. A room dedicated to pre-Columbian gold and jade is the highlight.

On the plaza's southwest corner, the **Museo Para la Paz** is dedicated to the cause of peace and displays former president Oscar Arias' Nobel Peace Prize.

Museo Nacional de Costa Rica

San José swirls around the vortex of Parque Central and its simple cathedral.

The seat of Costa Rica's government is a handsome whitewashed building off the plaza, on Calle 15. The Moorish-style **Palacio Nacional,** which houses the Legislative Assembly, began life in 1912 as the would-be home of presidential candidate Máximo Fernández (1858–1933). He lost the election, but then magnanimously offered his house to the victor, Alfredo Gonzalez Flores.

Museo Nacional de Costa Rica

🅰 See map p. 57

✉ Bellavista Fortress, Calle 17, Ave. Central/2

☎ 2221-4429 2257-1433

🕐 Closed Mon.

💲 $

www.museo costarica.go.cr

Museo Para la Paz

🅰 See map p. 57

✉ Ave. 2, Calle 13

☎ 2223-4646

🕐 Closed Sat.–Sun.

www.arias.or.cr/ museo.html

Centro Nacional de la Cultura

⚠ See map p. 57
✉ Ave. 3, Calles 15/17
☎ 2255-3638
🕐 Closed Sun.–Mon.

Museo de Formas, Espacios & Sonidos

⚠ See map p. 57
✉ Ave. 3, Calle 21
☎ 2222-9462
🕐 Closed Sat.–Sun.
💲 $

Parque Nacional

All levels of society take to San José's largest inner-city park—at the east side of downtown—at lunchtime and on weekends, when it is pleasant to stroll beneath shade trees and palms that vibrate with birdsong.

The white marble **Monumento Nacional** proclaims the victory of the Central American nations in 1856 over William Walker and his *filibusteros* (mercenaries). It was cast in the Rodin studios in Paris and stands atop a granite pedestal with bas-reliefs. Costa Rica's national hero, the drummer boy Juan Santamaría, stands in effigy at the park's southwest corner. Go see the monuments during the day, because it is best to avoid the park at night.

The **Biblioteca Nacional** (tel 2221-2436, closed Sat.–Sun.), the nation's main library, lords over the park to the northwest, on Avenida 3.

Across the street is the **Centro Nacional de la Cultural,** containing the **Museo de Arte y Diseño Contemporaneo.** This museum features collections of art from throughout Latin America. The gallery is housed in a former liquor factory dating from 1887, which is also home to two theaters and the office of the Ministerio de Cultura.

INSIDER TIP:

When leaving your car unattended, look for a "watchman" wearing a reflective vest. For a few hundred colones, he'll keep an eye on it.

—ELLIANA SPIEGEL
National Geographic contributor

The **Museo de Formas, Espacios y Sonidos** (Museum of Forms, Space, and Sounds) is housed in the ornate Atlantic train station built in 1907 on the northeast corner. Three salons offer interactive displays. The eclectic displays include scale models of the old station and other important historical sites, plus instruction in the plastic arts. The museum is due to move to an unspecified new location to make room for a new presidential office. ■

Beating Pickpockets at Their Game

Thieves seek easy targets. Here are a few common-sense precautions that can help you avoid becoming a victim.

- Wear your shirt over your fanny-pack; make sure the clasp isn't exposed.
- Use a zippable purse; keep it locked, and wear it around your neck.
- Carry money and documents in a money belt worn inside the waistband of your skirt or pants.

- Make photocopies of your important documents. Leave the originals in the hotel safe.
- Don't carry your camera loosely on your shoulder; sling it around your neck.
- Leave your jewelry at home and your valuables in the hotel safe.
- Stick to well-lit main streets, especially after dark.
- Educate yourself on problem areas, and avoid them.

Parque Sábana & Nearby

West of downtown, Avenida Central opens up into a wide boulevard, Paseo Colón, sloping gently uphill to Parque Sábana de Metropólitano. Paseo Colón epitomizes the modern mayhem of San José with its billboards, supercharged neon advertisements, and pandemonium of honking traffic culminating, eventually, in the pacific counterpoint of leafy Sábana.

Parque Sábana is a bucolic retreat situated in the heart of the city.

A stroll along Paseo Colón puts you in touch with San José's busy main artery. Step south along Calle 24, where after 440 yards (400 m) you will arrive at the **Cementerio de Obreros,** on the south side of Avenida 10. Here the wealthy of past decades vied for immortality on a grand scale. This exercise in pious excess makes for intriguing browsing among the flamboyant mausoleums, vaults, and tombs embellished with angels, griffins, cherubs, and other ornamentation.

The west end of Paseo Colón bumps up against **Parque Sábana de Metropólitano,** with grassy expanses, tree-lined jogging trails, and a miscellany of sports facilities. The bucolic, yet disheveled, retreat

overlays the old airport, and the former terminal is today the **Museo de Arte Costarricense,** displaying many of the nation's finest artworks, ranging from pre-Columbian artifacts through robust contemporary pieces, including a superb collection of wooden sculptures and woodcuts. To the rear, the **Jardín de Esculturas** displays pre-Columbian and contemporary sculptures, including those by such leading artists as Francisco Zuñiga.

Tucked off the southwest corner of Parque Sábana is the **Museo de Ciencias Naturales La Salle,** which spans the natural-science world with more than 22,500 exhibits. A dinosaur exhibit in the foyer features life-size T-rex, Torosaurus, and Utahraptors. ■

Museo de Arte Costarricense

- 🅰 See map inside back cover
- ✉ Calle 42 & Paseo Colón
- ☎ 2222-7155
- 🕐 Closed Mon.
- 💲 $ (free Sun.)

www. musarco.go.cr

Museo de Ciencias Naturales La Salle

- 🅰 See map inside back cover
- ✉ 100 yards (91 m) W of Colegio La Salle, Calle Lang
- ☎ 2232-1306
- 🕐 Closed Sat.–Sun.
- 💲 $

www.lasalle.edu.cr/museo

A Walk Around Barrios Otoya & Amón

This walk explores two contiguous barrios—Barrio Otoya to the east and Amón to the west—that form the city's historic district, replete with Victorian-era mansions squeezed into narrow one-way streets in a hilly area north of Avenida 7.

The quaint Casa Amarilla now houses the Ministry of Foreign Affairs.

The neighborhood contains much of the city's finest domestic architecture, built by *cafeteleros* inspired by the French style of New Orleans and Martinique. Many of these mansions once faced demolition. The area has been popularized in recent years by the wealthy class, including hotel owners, who have conjured beautiful mansions into homey inns. A few of the streets are steep, but the ambling is peacefully pleasant.

Begin the walk at the **Legación de México** ❶, a splendidly restored neoclassical stone gem 50 yards (45 m) northeast of Parque España, on the edge of Barrio Otoya. Immediately west, pause to admire the stuccoed facade of the **Casa Amarilla** ❷ the Yellow House, (closed to public), an 18th-century neobaroque edifice bequeathed to Costa Rica by Andrew Carnegie to serve as the Pan-American Court of Justice. Later the Residencia Presidencial and then the Asemblia Legislativa, it now houses the Ministry of Foreign Affairs. The ceiba tree

that looms over the west side was planted by President John F. Kennedy in 1963.

After visiting the **Museo de Jade Marco Fidel Tristán** (see p. 61), turn up Calle 11, which snakes uphill to Avenida 9. Turn left and walk downhill one block past the **Hemingway Inn** to Calle 9, then peek inside the **Hotel Don Carlos** ❸ (see p. 242), an exemplary wooden home, blending art deco and neoclassical elements with colonial-style grillwork. Built as the residence of President Tomás Guardia, it is run by art connoisseur Don Carlos Balser and brims with pre-Columbian treasures and Sarchí oxcarts. An exquisite ceramic in the lobby shows a quintessential bucolic scene—a theme that continues along Avenida 7 as you go downhill past walls inlaid with hand-painted tiles depicting coffee pickers and the like.

One block west, to your right at the corner of Calle 7, in Barrio Amón, is **La Casa Verde de Amón** ❹, which is intriguing for its antique details and a soaring lounge with a stained-glass atrium *(tragaluz)*. This stately mansion is made of red pine imported from New Orleans in exchange for a shipment of coffee. It received a UNESCO award in 1994 for the restoration that retains the Victorian claw-foot tubs, four-poster beds, and even a centenarian grand piano.

Victorian Flavor

Continue west along Avenida 9, lined with low-slung aristocratic wooden houses in Caribbean Victorian vernacular, with detailed wainscoting and extensive decorative touches. At Calle 5, to your right, note **Le Chambord,** another splendid home, and farther along Avenida 9, **Casa Morisca,** with Moorish influences. Turn right at Calle 3 and right again onto Avenida 11. At the corner of Calle 3 on the west side of the street, you will pass the **Castillo del Moro ❺,** colloquially called the Bishop's Castle after Archbishop Don Carlos Humberto Rodríguez, for whom it was built in 1925. The crenelated structure was inspired by Moorish design, with such extravagant touches as hand-painted tiles adorning a dome, keyhole windows, and intricate plaster decoration. On the east side is the **Britannia Hotel ❻** (see p. 241), which was built in 1910 and is one of several neo-Victorian mansions hereabouts to metamorphose into hotels.

Follow Avenida 11 east to the entrance to **Parque Zoológico Simón Bolívar ❼** *(tel 2256-0012, $),* just east of Calle 7. The zoo, with many of its tiny cages dating from 1916, is appalling by contemporary standards. You will get a good sense of Costa Rica's wildlife though.

Return to Avenida 9 via Calle 7, stopping at **TeoréTica,** an avant-garde art space in a restored mansion. Then, climb east 150 yards (137 m) up Avenida 9 and turn left on Calle 11 to admire the statue of a *campesino* on the patio of the mansion at No. 980.

To end your walk, follow Avenida 9 to Calle 15, where **Café Mundo ❽** serves cappuccinos and other beverages in one of the city's most beautiful restored houses.

NOT TO BE MISSED:

Casa Amarilla • Hotel Don Carlos • Café Mundo

- Also see area map pp. 56–57
- ▶ Legación de México
- ↔ 1.25 miles (2 km)
- ⏱ 90 minutes
- ▶ Café Mundo

More Places to Visit in San José

Centro Costarricense de Ciencias y Cultura

The turreted "castle," a former penitentiary, is now the Costa Rican Science and Cultural Center. The **Galería Nacional** displays avant-garde works of art in the converted jail cells. Its **Museo de Niños,** Children's Museum, spans themes ranging from astronomy to communication. A state-of-the-art theater, the **Auditorio Nacional,** has performances. www.museocr.com   🅰 Map p. 56   ✉ Calle 4, 100 yards (90 m) N of Ave. 9   ☎ 2238-4929,   🕐 Closed Mon.   💲 $

Edificio Correos

Built in 1917 with an ornate green facade, the Postal Building is one of San José's most dramatic structures. It functions as the nation's central post office and as the **Museo Postal, Telegráfico y Filatélico** (second floor). This

---

EXPERIENCE: Fun with the Family

To keep the kids happy in San José:

Fossil Land *(1.2 miles/2 km E of Patarrá, on SE outskirts of San José, tel 2276-6060, www.fossillandcr.com)* This adventure park thrills adolescents with paintball, ATV rides, and mountain cycling. Younger kids can enjoy a fossil trail, horseback rides, and confidence-building hikes with waterfall scrambles. **Museo de Niños** *(Calle 4, Ave. 9, tel 2238-4929; see this page)* The Children's Museum offers all manner of educational, interactive exhibits covering sciences, technology, the natural world, and human society. **Pueblo Antiguo** *(1.2 miles/2 km NW of Hospitál México, La Uruca, tel 2290-3035; see this page)* Recreations of a 19th-century farmstead, town plaza, and coastal port provide a fun-filled educational experience.

---

museum has a collection of early telegraphic and telephonic equipment, as well as a philatelic display. The Edificio Correos faces a plaza with a statue of Juan Mora Fernández, the nation's first president (1824–1828).
🅰 Map p. 57   ✉ Calle 2, Ave. 1/3   ☎ 2223-9766   🕐 Closed Sat.–Sun.   💲 $

Mercado Central

There is no more truly Costa Rican experience in San José than visiting this market built in 1880. Crowds manuever through alleyways lined with artisans' stalls, cobblers, fishmongers, florists, fruitsellers, and trinket sellers. Dine at one of the tiny sodas, which offer traditional meals for a pittance.
🅰 Map p. 56   ✉ Ave. Central, Calles 6/8   ☎ 2295-6104   🕐 Closed Sun.

Pueblo Antiguo

This theme park, a mixture of Colonial Williamsburg and Disney World, re-creates an idyllic past, with urban, rural, and coastal sections staffed by ticos in period costume. Children can help milkmaids fill their pails. Horse-drawn carriages ply the streets of the make-believe village. Marimba bands perform and folk troupes re-create historical scenes. Craft shops and restaurants complete the experience. Pueblo Antiguo is part of Parque Diversiones, a fairground with roller coasters, bumper cars, waterslides, and other rides. www.parquediversiones.com/pueblo.htm
🅰 Map pp. 56–57   ✉ 1.2 miles (2 km) NW of Hospital México   ☎ 2290-3035   💲 $$$$$ (4-hour tour)

Spirogyra

Immerse yourself in a lepidopteran world in the 420-square-yard (350 sq m) netted butterfly garden, home to more than 30 species. www.infocostarica.com/butterfly   🅰 Map p. 57   ✉ 100 yards (91 m) E & 150 yards (137 m) S of Centro Comercial El Pueblo
☎ 2222-2937   💲 $$

A mountain-rimmed region with colonial antiquities, butterfly farms, bubbling volcanoes, and cloud forests roamed by wildlife

Central Highlands

Traditional oxcart wheel

Central Highlands

Beauty lies around every bend in the sublime, temperate Central Highlands, a region of forest- and coffee-cloaked mountains cradling a broad fertile valley—the Meseta Central—some 40 miles (64 km) long by 20 miles (32 km) wide.

Touring is facilitated by roads that span the Inter-American Highway and spiderweb even the highest slope. No place is too remote to find lodgings ranging from rustic mountain hostelries to modern architectural stunners.

Many visitors explore the Central Highlands for the sheer pleasure of varying vistas, which grow more dramatic with altitude. You have no need for your own wheels—organized excursions are offered from San José—but a

rental car provides the flexibility to stop for snapshots and serendipitous treats. Everything of interest is within a three-hour drive of San José, although many of the narrow roads are appallingly potholed and deteriorate in places into rutted tracks that your vehicle ascends only with wheezing difficulty.

The intermontane Meseta Central—central plateau—is roughly wedge shaped: broad to the west and narrower to the east, averaging in

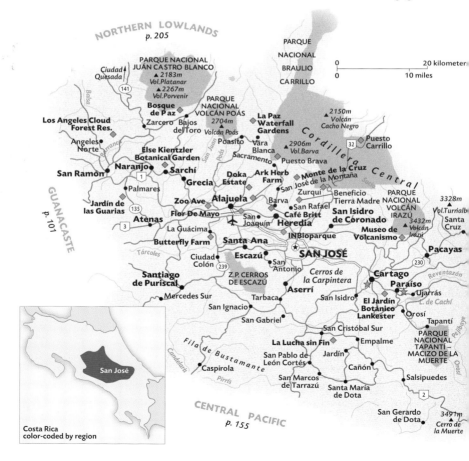

Costa Rica
color-coded by region

elevation around 3,000 feet (914 m). The Meseta Central is bisected by the Cerros de la Carpintera, a relatively low, north-south mountain range rising immediately east of the capital city. To the south are the Talamancas, dauntingly rugged and cut through with valleys that invite exploration. To the north, a series of volcanoes—notably Poás, Barva, Irazú, and Turrialba—form the Cordillera Central. The range reaches its apex at 11,260 feet (3,432 m) atop Irazú, which still fumes, although most days you can climb to the top to look into the burbling bowels.

You can also thrill to the sparkling highland sunshine and crystal clear air. The lower flanks are cloaked in coffee bushes—the sine qua non of the highland economy—shaded by *erythrina* trees and aligned in trim rows. At cooler heights, coffee gives way to dairy farms, strawberry patches, and *viveros* (flower farms) where tropical flowers grow under black cloth. To the east, Irazú's lower slopes are quilted in "market gardens" growing potatoes and carrots. Corn, sugarcane, coffee, and macadamia plantations dominate the fertile valley floors. On the upper slopes, mists swirl through pines and oaks festooned with mosses and epiphytes typical of conditions atop the continental divide—perfect for spotting quetzals and three-wattled bellbirds.

THE CARIBBEAN
p. 219

SOUTH CENTRAL
p. 189

NOT TO BE MISSED:

Bird-watching at Zoo Ave Wildlife Conservation Park   75

Viewing wildlife at Bosque de Paz   77

The topiary park at Zarcero   78–79

Learning about coffee culture at Café Britt   83

A drive up Volcán Poás   84

Cartago's Basílica de Nuestra Señora de los Ángeles   88

A walk through La Paz Waterfall Gardens   98

The region has always been a breadbasket. Pre-Columbian people tilled the soil and thrived. Although they were swiftly decimated following the arrival of the Spanish, their legacy remains in stone at Monumento Nacional Guayabo. The broad-leaved forests that originally covered the land were cleared during colonial times by yeoman farmers. The quintessential highland vignette remains the farmer wearing rubber boots and a machete, leading an ox-drawn cart or a herd of cows down the road. Church spires pinpoint scores of rural villages lined with colorful wood-and-adobe houses with neat trimmed lawns. The plateau shelters about 70 percent of Costa Rica's population, concentrated in three historic cities—Alajuela, Heredia, and San José (see pp. 55–66).

To the east sits Cartago, the original capital city, commanding the Reventazón Valley at a lower elevation than the main valley, which narrows eastward and falls ever more steeply as the Cordillera Central and Talamancas crimp together. The eastern, windward slopes of the mountains are rain sodden. Tapantí and Braulio Carrillo National Parks are lush forests echoing with birdsong; hikers might even spot pumas and tapirs. The Butterfly Farm, Zoo Ave Wildlife Conservation Park, and a dozen other roadside venues offer wildlife viewing for less intrepid souls. Cloud forests close to the mountain crests prove exhilarating for hikers hoping to glimpse quetzals. ■

Escazú & Santa Ana

The soaring hills southwest of San José are a dramatic setting for hip Escazú, which combines Old World charm and contemporary chic. This bewitching town is beloved by expatriates and wealthy Ticos alike for its luxury living, trendy restaurants and nightclubs, and well-stocked shopping plazas. Escazú is only 3 miles (4.8 km) west of Parque Sábana and central San José.

Barry Biesanz conjures one of his magical wooden creations on a lathe.

Escazú
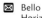 Map p. 68

Biesanz Woodworks
✉ Bello Horizonte, 2 blocks S of Bello Horizonte school (Business sign reads "Obras de Madera Design")
☎ 2289-4337
🕐 Weekends open by appt. only

www.biesanz.com

Though Escazú is linked to the capital by the Próspero Fernández Expressway, it retains a beguiling *campesino* spirit and has an array of B&Bs. Santa Ana, 5 miles (8 km) west, has a more reclusive, old-fashioned appeal.

Triptych Town

Escazú sprawls haphazardly up the northern slopes of its namesake mountain, **Cerro Escazú.** At the base of the hills, near the freeway, is trendy, modern **San Rafael de Escazú,** with deluxe villas and condominiums, restaurants, the **Costa Rica Country Club** *(members only),* and upscale shopping areas such as the **Multiplaza** (see p. 258), Costa Rica's largest mall. Incongruously in San Rafael's midst is a grassy plaza with a gleaming

white colonial-style church built in the 1930s. The hip restaurants and nightclubs draw crowds at night. The tony suburb of **Bello Horizonte,** northwest of San Rafael, is a center for charming country inns plus **Biesanz Woodworks,** where carvers conjure masterly hardwood bowls and boxes under the genius-level guidance of Barry Biesanz.

Calle León Cortes, the main road, leads a mile (1.6 km) uphill to **San Miguel de Escazú,** the tranquil heart of Escazú laid out around its own colonial-era square. This is the original town and one of the oldest settlements in the nation, dating back to at least 1711 when a chapel was built as a nucleus for an adobe hamlet. Many of the red-tile-roofed homes are extant; likewise the red-domed 1799 church commanding the square and fringed at its base by a strip of blue to ward off witches. Don't be surprised to see cattle or ox-drawn carts laden with coffee beans being led through the streets.

Calle 1 snakes sharply upward 2 miles (3.2 km) to the smaller community of **San Antonio de Escazú,** where rolling clouds swirl around the church. Every second Sunday in March, the square is the focus for an annual fiesta, the **Día de Boyeros,** when traditional gaily colored oxcarts *(carretas)* parade in honor of the *boyeros* (oxcart drivers), and young girls and women put on traditional garb.

Santa Ana

The Carretera Próspero Fernández sweeps west beyond Escazú and drops to Santa Ana, in a vale whose warm microclimate has fostered flower farms and apiaries. This town of simple adobe-and-wooden homes is also a center for ceramics.

Three miles (5 km) southwest of Cuidad Colón, **Hacienda de Rodeo** (tel 2249-1013) offers equestrian lessons and tours. Trails lead to the forest adjoining the **Universidad de Paz** (tel 2205-9000, www.upeace.org), dedicated to fostering world harmony. Its botanical garden is filled with statues of famous pacifists. An adjoining park with lake hosts the **Monument for Disarmament, Work & Peace.**

INSIDER TIP:

Tipping in Costa Rica is up to your own discretion. Waiters earn a wage. Many people in touristy areas do tip, so waiters there have learned to expect one—but don't feel obligated.

—BEN HORTON
National Geographic field researcher

Sylvan & Sybaritic Retreats

To enjoy the incredible vistas take to the steep coffee-clad hills above San Antonio de Escazú, where at upper heights mists swirl through the native

---

Of Brooms & Brujas

Some 60 witches are said to live in Escazú, the *bruja* (witch) capital of Costa Rica. "Any woman who lives in Escazú long enough eventually becomes a bruja," claims Doña Estrella, a town matriarch and self-acknowledged kindhearted witch in a town where they are openly accepted.

Yet evil spirits are said to abound here, too. Among them is La Zegua, a maiden whose enchanting beauty belies her true nature: Men who make love to her discover that she has turned into a horse. And many older residents still believe that the Río Tiribi is haunted, and that the evil monkey Mico Malo attacks those who dare to cross the Los Anonos bridge at night.

Local musician Lencho Salazar relates the legends of the brujas.

Cerros de Escazú

✉ El Cedral, San Antonio de Escazú

☎ 2228-0183

---

forests of the **Cerros de Escazú,** a protected zone good for hiking. With a keen eye you might spot sloths, monkeys, or even pumas amid the dense forests dripping with Spanish moss.

Indulge the sybarite in you with a spa treatment at **White House Hotel** (see p. 244), overlooking San Antonio with views across the Meseta Central. This Greek Revival hotel features a Garden Spa offering treatments from aromatherapy to massage. ■

A World of Butterflies

At times the Costa Rican countryside resembles a storm of sweetpeas as butterflies float by in endlessly colorful streams. The nation has around 1,250 species, more than the whole of Africa and one in ten of all known species worldwide. Most of these winged insects are as beautiful as the denizens of an exotic harem—from *Riondinidae* with metallic gold wings to the electric blue morphos, the neon narcissi of the butterfly world.

Camouflaged as poisonous thorns, this caterpillar is creative in its defense.

Color with a Purpose

There is nothing common about the morpho, colloquially called *celeste común,* which ranges from sea level to 4,500 feet (1,370 m) and zigzags through the forest with a great loping gait along flyways that follow the route of others, like cars on a highway. The 50 or so species range from satiny red to the teals of a Maxfield Parrish sea. The bluest of all morpho species are found on the Caribbean coast.

Unlike most butterflies, the morpho does not owe its coloration to pigmentation. Morphos are brown, but their scales have a complex structure that absorbs all colors of the spectrum except blue, making them appear that color. The morpho's dun-colored underwings are uninspired, but when it takes off it displays its iridescent upper wings like a flashing sign. The exotic flash serves as a dinner bell to flycatchers and jacamars, for whom the morpho is a favored tidbit.

There are also other purposes to bright coloration. Take the Heliconids, a family whose chromatic schemata—normally black speckled in red, white, and yellow—advertise their foul taste: As caterpillars, they gorge on leaves containing cyanide. The strategy works so well that edible species mimic Heliconids by adopting their liveries. Slight variations in coloration serve as flags so that potential suitors can distinguish their perfect partners from among the subspecies. The females of some Heliconid subspecies release pheromones while in the

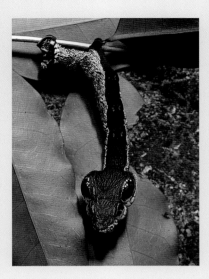

A caterpillar disguised as a snake's head confuses would-be predators.

chrysalis, drawing male butterflies to mate with them before they emerge.

Many species of Lepidoptera migrate to mate. With the onset of rainy season around May, the countryside is a never-ending ballet as millions of insects flutter from lowland to highland. The iridescent green-and-black *Uranidae* flaps its way between Mexico and Bolivia, a distance of 34 degrees latitude. The *Uranidae* is often mistaken for the swallowtail butterfly, which it mimics. Butterflies are experts at guile. One species of moth even imitates a wasp! Even caterpillars are expert tacticians. The larvae of the giant swallowtail *(Papilio cresphontes)* appear to be bird droppings and give off an appropriate stench. Another resembles the head of a viper.

A Mime Troupe

Some species blend with their backgrounds, such as the cream owl butterfly *(Caligo memnon),* whose wings

Right: The iridesecent blue morpho butterfly

up to 6 inches (15 cm) wide provide superb camouflage. While the upper wings are an attractive blue-gray, the undersides are mottled brown and gray and have yellow "eyes" complete with black pupils and white spots resembling reflected sunlight, so realistic that when opened they look like the face of a wide-eyed owl. They are relatively static by day, but with dusk they take to the air and flit about the forest in search of rotting fruit. The cream owl butterfly is found at elevations up to 3,500 feet (1,070 m), especially on the Pacific side.

The devilish *caligo* caterpillar can grow to 5 inches (13 cm) long; it has horns on its head and a forked tail. Caterpillars exist to eat and grow. "Butterfly larvae are a mouth with chewing mandibles and a long body to house a long gut," says P. J. DeVries, author of *Butterflies of Costa Rica.* Lacking jaws, butterflies use a proboscis to feed on juices—nectar, decaying fruit, or decomposed carrion.

Population densities vary by habitat and seasonality, but all habitats have significant increases in populations in June and July. In general, you will see more butterflies on sunny days. At least one species of butterfly is nocturnal, though most are diurnal and more active by morning.

To learn about butterfly ecology, visit a butterfly "farm," most of which are live exhibits. There are more than a dozen in the country. The Butterfly Farm (see p. 75) at La Guácima, near San José, is the largest butterfly breeding center in the Western Hemisphere.

Alajuela & Around

Alajuela, a small regional town founded in 1676, lies at the base of Volcán Poás a mile (1.6 km) north of the Juan Santamaría International Airport and 13 miles (21 km) northwest of San José. Although hardly a calling card in its own right, it is a splendid base for exploring Poás, and there are several key sites tucked amid the waves of coffee that wash against the town on all sides.

Juan Santamaría's statue in his eponymous park

Alajuela
 Map p. 68

Museo Cultural y Histórico Juan Santamaría
☎ 2441-4775
🕐 Closed Mon.
💲 $

www.museojuan
santamaria.go.cr

Alajuela, Costa Rica's second city, is colloquially called the City of the Mangoes for the trees that shade **Parque Central.** It's officially the Plaza de General Tomás Guardia; local wags call it Park of the Dead Doves for the old men who gather to gossip and watch pretty girls pass by.

The body of ex-president Guardia is buried in the simple metal-domed cathedral, dating from 1863, on the park's east side. The main attraction is the **Museo Cultural y Histórico Juan Santamaría**, to the northwest in the old city jail. Its meager collection relates the William Walker saga in 1856 in which Juan Santamaría, Alajuela's drummer-boy hero, gave his life (see p. 29). Cultural programs are offered in a screening room; you can request an English-language video about the saga. A statue of the young hero stands in the **Parque Juan Santamaría** at the corner of Calle 2 and Avenida 2.

The town bustles on Saturday, when you should visit the compact **Mercado Central,** where all manner of produce is sold within the tight, shaded warren.

The soccer team, La Liga, is a source of local pride. You can catch a game on weekends at Avenida 7 and Calle 13.

Toward Volcán Poás

North of Alajuela, the land rises incrementally toward the forested summit of Volcán Poás. The drive is superbly scenic as you wend up through coffee fields hugging the convex slope. Higher up, the coffee fields are replaced by strawberries and ornamental plants grown under black shade nets, while Holstein dairy cattle munch contentedly on green pastures. Log fires scent the crisp air, drawing you to eat at rustic restaurants that serve traditional peasant fare, such as

EXPERIENCE: Saving Macaws

Once abundant in Costa Rica's lowland tropical forests, green macaw and scarlet macaw populations have been reduced by deforestation and poaching for the pet trade. Two decades ago, only two areas on the Pacific side of the country had viable populations. Since then, efforts by private foundations to breed and reestablish macaw populations in the wild have had tremendous success.

Flor de Mayo *(tel 2441-2658, www.hatchedtoflyfree.org; see below)* breeds scarlet and green macaws for release into the wild. Volunteers are needed to help care for the birds. **Tiskita Scarlet Macaw**

Restoration Project *(tel 2296 8125, www.tiskita-lodge.co.cr)*, near Pavones, releases scarlet macaws into primary forest and has established a free flying flock of more than 30 birds. Volunteers observe

their progress and gather seeds to feed caged birds. **Zoo Ave** *(tel 2433-8989, www.zooave.org; see below)* hires volunteers for its Centro de Reproducción de Animales, where macaws are bred for release.

roast pork or chicken. At **Poasito** you can continue north to Parque Nacional Volcán Poás (see p. 84) or east to Vara Blanca and the Catarata La Paz (see p. 98).

Animal Worlds

You'll be enthralled by **Flor De Mayo,** a 7-acre (2.8 ha) breeding center for endangered green and scarlet macaws, at Río Segundo de Alajuela, 2 miles (3.2 km) southeast of Alajuela. Richard and Margot Frisius, founders of the Amigos de las Aves foundation, breed these majestic birds for release into the wild to counter the devastation wrought by habitat loss and poaching. The visitor center offers a prelude to watching the young birds career across the vast flyway.

Scarlet macaws are also bred at **Zoo Ave Wildlife Conservation Park,** situated in La Garita, west of Alajuela. This 142-acre (57 ha) zoo is a haven for more than one hundred species of birds, including quetzals, curassows, cranes, and toucans. Re-creations of natural

habitats are home to all four species of native monkeys, as well as crocodiles and other beasts. Injured and confiscated wildlife are tended at a rescue center *(closed to the public)*.

Another must-see is the **Butterfly Farm** at La Guácima, about 2 miles (3.2 km) south of the airport. Around 30,000 pupae are bred and exported each year to zoos around the world—the offspring of some 60 native species of butterflies that flap freely through a lush world secured by netting. A video and the farm's erudite guides enlighten visitors about the complex relationships between the insects and their host plants, and about butterfly life cycles from egg to adult. You can witness the metamorphosis as a butterfly wriggles free of its chrysalis.

Two miles (3.2 km) north of La Guácima, **Rancho San Miguel** *(tel 2438-0849, e-mail: ranchosanmiguel@ice.go.cr)* offers a chance to ride Andalusian horses. The highlight is the thrice-weekly show, when the beautiful horses perform. ∎

Flor De Mayo
- Map p. 68
- Río Segundo de Alajuela
- 2441-2658
- By appt.
- Donation

www.hatchedto flyfree.org

Zoo Ave Wildlife Conservation Park
- Map p. 68
- Dulce Nombre, 2 miles (3.2 km) E of the Inter-American Hwy.
- 2433-8989
- $$

www.zooave.org

Butterfly Farm
- Map p. 68
- 400 yards (360 m) S of Los Reyes Country Club, La Guácima
- 2438-0400

www.butterfly farm .co.cr

The Western Slopes

The classic touring circuit takes in the western Highlands, coffee and dairy country par excellence laced with small artisan and market towns lining the Inter-American Highway and Highway 3. Those two parallel routes weave through the region, ascending gradually toward the western rim before beginning their plummeting descents to the Pacific and the Northern Lowlands. The vistas over the Central Valley are stupendous.

Farmers markets are the social loci of highland towns.

Grecia

 Map p. 68

World of Snakes

✉ 0.5 mile
(0.8 km) E of
Grecia

☎ 2494-3700

Grecia

This compact market center, founded only in 1864, is known for its twin-spired **metal church,** which was imported from Belgium in 1897 and now commands the palm-shaded main plaza. The somewhat dour rust-red exterior of the edifice belies the handsome wooden interior, which features pendulous glass chandeliers and a soaring marble altar—a fanciful confection in stone.

Be sure, too, to stop in at **World of Snakes** on the old Alajuela road, where more than 300 live snakes are exhibited in glass-fronted cages. The Austrian owners breed snakes for sale and use educational labeling and guided tours to shatter commonly held negative stereotypes about snakes, replacing them with a healthy respect for these eco-logically vital reptiles. A "petting" program encourages children to handle nonvenomous snakes.

Sarchí

A staple on the beaten tourist path, this agricultural town—divided into Sarchí Norte (the main town) and Sarchí Sur (the artisan center) about 0.6 mile (1 km) farther east—is also renowned as Costa Rica's center of crafts and fine furniture despite being firmly in the grip of commercialism. The main road is lined with souvenir stores selling leather and wooden items—from handsome bowls of lignum vitae (wood of life) and classic wood-and-leather rockers to miniature hand-painted oxcarts, Sarchí's hallmark and also a national symbol.

You can see oxcarts being made and adorned at **Fábrica de Carretas Joaquín Chaverrí** *(tel 2454-4411)* in Sarchí Sur. Although many artisans now produce tawdry kitsch, others remain true to tradition. Recently opened after two decades in preparation, the **Else Kientzler Botanical Gardens** spans 7 acres (2.8 ha); trails—including one for the blind—wind through specialty gardens displaying more than 2,000 species of plants. Kids will love the maze.

The rambling town is cusped by coffee-clad vales. The photogenic appeal of this magnificent setting is enhanced by the town's quintessential floral motif adorning whitewashed adobe buildings and the blush pink **church** in the main square of Sarchí Norte. The church has an impressive vaulted ceiling.

Try to visit Sarchí during the first week of February for the town's lively fiesta.

Bosque de Paz & Around

North of Sarchí is a narrow winding road that climbs up the western flank of Volcán Poás and, beyond the cloud-shrouded saddle between Poás and Volcán Platanar (7,162 feet/2,183 m), plummets precariously down to **Bajos del Toro,** a scenic Shangri-la secreted in its own valley. This remote farming community provides access to the 960-acre (390 ha) Bosque de Paz, a private nature reserve whose mountainous rain-soaked terrain is a veritable Noah's Ark of safeguarded wildlife. Trails offer an opportunity to spot scores of rare birds such as curassows and black guans. Big cats, which give people a wide berth, prowl through the lush forests in search of brocket deer and primates, including howler monkeys, capuchins, and the endangered spider monkeys.

The reserve lies at the foot of **Parque Nacional Juan Castro Blanco,** a 35,230-acre (14,260 ha) swath created in 1995 to protect the precious montane rain forest and cloud forests of Volcán

---

Shopping with a Conscience

Be aware that many craft and souvenir items sold in Costa Rica are made from endangered flora or fauna. Buying such items contributes to their demise. Trade in endangered products is illegal and such items may be confiscated by U.S. Customs. Avoid jewelry made from turtle shell or coral; furs of ocelots or other animals; and items made from macaw or quetzal feathers. Only buy tropical hardwood products if they are made from fallen timber.

Sarchí
- Map p. 68

Else Kientzler Botanical Gardens
- Map p. 68
- 0.6 mile (1 km) N of Sarchí
- ☎ 2454-2070
- $ $$$
- www.elsekientzler garden.com

Bosque de Paz
- Map p. 68
- Bajos del Toro, 7 miles (11 km) N of Sarchí
- ☎ 2234-6676
- By appt.
- $ Call for details
- www.bosquede paz.com

Parque Nacional Juan Castro Blanco
- Map p. 68
- Bajos del Toro, 8 miles (13 km) N of Sarchí
- ☎ 2460-7600
- $ $$

San Ramón

⚑ Map p. 68

Jardín de Las Guarias

⚑ Map p. 68

✉ Cocaleca, 1 mile (1.6 km) S of Palmares

☎ 2452-0091

🕐 Call for details

💲 $

Platanar. The park is cut through by trails but otherwise has no facilities—perfect for hardy hikers.

Naranjo & Around

The countryside west of Sarchí appeals mainly for its uplifting vistas. Three miles (4.8 km) west of Sarchí is Naranjo, an important market town sitting astride Highway 3 and alluring for its comely church supported by Corinthian columns. Next comes the regional center of **San Ramón,** 7 miles (11.2 km) farther, on the western rim of the Meseta Central and gateway to Puntarenas and Guanacaste. The town's Saturday **farmers market** *(feria de agricultor)* is well worth a stop. So, too, is the centenarian metal church, which was made in Germany, shipped to Costa Rica, and welded together in situ.

The church in Grecia is made of steel plates.

INSIDER TIP:

Buy a ripe guanabana; the fruit is five pounds of sweet heaven. Quite possibly the most unshippable fruit in the world, it's not something you can easily get at home.

—JOHN LONGINO
National Geographic field researcher

The Inter-American Highway skirts San Ramón, which sits immediately to the north, and **Palmares,** a mile (1.6 km) to the south. Palmares is renowned for its colorful mid-January fiesta, which features rodeo-style bullfights and all the fun of the fair. Also here is the largest orchid collection in the country, consisting of some 40,000 blooms, can be enjoyed at **Jardín de las Guarias,** the private garden of Javier Solórzaro Murillo, at Cocaleca, a mile (1.6 km) south of Palmares.

Atop the Cordillera

You could be forgiven for imagining that you are in Switzerland as you drive along Highway 141 between Naranjo and **Ciudad Quesada** (see p. 212), a center of the local dairy industry that clings to the mountainside. The mountains fall away to the Northern Lowlands via a breathtaking switchback.

Midway between Naranjo and Ciudad Quesada is **Zarcero,** a pretty village whose simple church is fronted by a leafy arbor running through a **topiary park** that resembles a circus. The gardener responsible, Evange-listo Blanco, wields his pruning shears like an artist's paintbrush, conjuring up such smile-inducing spectacles as an elephant with light bulbs for eyes and a cat riding a motorcycle atop a hedge. All around the area, black-and-white Holstein cattle chomp on emerald green alpine meadows and even many of the farmsteads hint at Swiss provenance.

From San Ramón, lonesome Highway 702 climbs north up the mountain slopes and 12 miles (19 km) above the town, where it begins its looping drop to the Northern Lowlands. You'll want to stop at the **Valle Escondido Lodge** (tel 2231-0906), a vivero (flower farm) suspended in a cleft of the valley that offers hiking and horseback rides into the surrounding cloud forest. The **San Lorenzo Canopy Tour** is here as well. The lodge's restaurant has stunning views over the cascading valley.

For a fuller immersion, detour to the **Los Angeles Cloud Forest Reserve,** a private 2,000-acre (810 ha) reserve ranging from 2,100 feet (640 m) to 5,400 feet (1,650 m) in elevation. A steel cable 600 feet (182 m) long is slung between the treetops to grant a bird's-eye view of wildlife on a **canopy tour.** The property, part of an expansive dairy farm owned by ex-president Rodrigo Corazón, also offers horseback riding. Adjoining to the east, the **El Silencio de Los Angeles Reserve** has more than 200 bird species, plus monkeys and cats such as ocelots, which await visitors on guided hikes from the enchanting **Villa-blanca Cloudforest Lodge**

(see p. 245). Perched on the very edge of the continental divide, the hotel offers beautiful cottages with wood-burning fireplaces.

Atenas & Around

The charming town of Atenas on Hwy. 3, 8 miles (13 km) south of Palmares, has a truly sublime climate. The town plaza boasts an exquisite church and is

Cultural Faux Pas to Avoid

- Don't grip too tightly when shaking hands.
- Don't insult Costa Rican culture. Ticos are proud of their country.
- Don't behave like a know-it-all. Modesty is appreciated.
- Do maintain personal hygiene. Ticos appreciate cleanliness.
- Don't use piropos, impolite "compliments" meant to woo women.
- Don't attempt to draw the easygoing Ticos into arguments.

surrounded by venerable wooden homes. The **Monumento a Los Boyeros,** located on the east side of town, commemorates the days when Atenas was a major stop on the camino de carretas, the old coffee route to Puntarenas.

For a breathtaking view over coffee fields toward the Gulf of Nicoya, take a break to sample the coffees at **Mirador del Cafetal** on Hwy. 3, 5 miles (8 km) west of Atenas. ∎

Los Angeles Cloud Forest Reserve
- Map p. 68
- 5 miles (8 km) E of Angeles Norte
- 2461-0643
- $$

El Silencio de Los Angeles Reserve
- Off Hwy. 142, 6 miles (9.7 km) N of San Ramón
- 2461-3000
- $$$
- www.villablanca-costarica.com

Grano de Oro

Costa Ricans call coffee *grano de oro*—the grain of gold—with good reason. The humble bean lifted the nation out of obscurity two centuries ago, bringing wealth to countless subsistence farmers and to the country as a whole. The slopes and steep vales of the Meseta Central are patterned in endless rows of dark green corduroy.

A coffee grower harvests beans on his marginal riverside plot.

Coffee bushes, native to Ethiopia, came to Costa Rica from Jamaica in 1779; they turned out to be Costa Rica's economic salvation. The rise of coffee in Central America coincided with the demise of slavery in the Caribbean, which threw the islands' industry into chaos. Jamaica—at that time the world's largest coffee producer—was quickly displaced by Costa Rica, whose climate and rich volcanic soils proved perfect for coffee cultivation.

Ideal Conditions

The coffee plant grows best in well-drained soils at elevations of 2,500 to 3,500 feet (760–1,070 m), with nearly constant temperatures between 59 and 82°F (15–28°C) and a distinct wet and dry season. The Meseta Central met these conditions as well as anywhere in the world. On the Central Highlands a particular combination of aspect, slope, soil type, and climactic conditions combined to produce a distinctly flavored coffee—mellow and aromatic, with a hint of acidity—that international coffee connoisseurs soon acclaimed as one of the best in the world. Economically, a dry season aided the Costa Rican harvest; it was also propitious for the transportation of the beans down the mountains via mule train to the port of Puntarenas, whence a three-month journey via Cape Horn delivered the beans to java-thirsty Europe.

For Costa Rica's subsistence farmers, the coffee was a commercial godsend—and one on which no taxes were levied. Soon everyone was growing the grano de oro (in the early 1800s there was even a law that required every Tico household to grow coffee bushes in its yard), which by 1829 had established itself as the nation's numero uno income earner.

Small farmers dominated production and took their fair share of wealth. But the real profits lay in the processing and trade, which quickly coalesced into relatively few hands. Costa Rica gained its first social and political elite—the *cafeteleros* (coffee barons). Even today there are only 95 coffee mills *(beneficios)* in the country, although some 80,000 producers grow coffee on approximately 270,000 acres (110,000 ha).

From Seed to Bean

The seeds are planted in nurseries and nourished until, as yearlings, they are planted in rows that follow the contours of the mountain slopes under shade trees or tousled bananas, which fix nitrogen in the soil. Shaded coffee bushes are more productive. The glossy green bushes will begin fruiting by their fourth year (carefully tended, a coffee bush will bear fruit for up to 40 years). At the onset of the rainy season, their tiny white blossoms scent the air with a jasmine-like fragrance. The beans are surrounded by lush green berries that turn blood red by the seasonal harvest in November.

The handpicked beans are shipped to beneficios, where the fleshy outer layers are removed to expose the beans, which are blow-dried or spread out in the sun in the traditional manner. The leathery skins are then stripped away; the beans are roasted, sorted, vacuum sealed, and finally shipped to market.

Coffee remained the nation's prime source of income until 1991, when world coffee prices plummeted and the grano de oro was toppled from its pedestal by both bananas and tourism, causing economic distress in the industry. Coffee's fortunes have continued to decline; production has fallen from 2.5 million bags in 1997 to 1.88 million in 2007. Still, coffee producers attain higher productivity per acre in Costa Rica than anywhere else in the world. Ideal conditions are enhanced by the propagation of high-yielding plants and intensive production techniques. The highest quality coffee grows at higher elevations, where beans take longer to mature and are more robust and aromatic, with less caffeine.

EXPERIENCE: Learn About Coffee Culture

Coffee isn't simply an agricultural product of economic importance to Costa Rica. Its importance to the historical evolution of the modern nation is such that traditions associated with coffee production are the sine qua non of Tico culture. The following venues will help you appreciate the intricacies of its production and its hallowed place in the national psyche.

Beneficio Coopedota *(tel 2541-2828, www .dotacoffee.com)*, near San José, roasts the beans grown by scores of small-scale producers in the Tarrazú district. Tours are given during harvest. **Beneficio Tierra Madre** *(tel 2277-1600, www.beneficiotierramdre .com; see p. 83)*, in San Rafael, Heredia, a historic high-mountain coffee farm and mill, still processes coffee beans in age-old fashion and welcomes visitors by appointment. **Café Britt** *(tel 2260-2748, www.coffeetour.com; see p. 83)* near Barva, Heredia, is renowned for amusing multimedia tours, led by guides in period costume, which educate about the importance of coffee in Costa Rican culture. **Doka Estate** *(tel 2449-* 5152, www.dokaestate.com; see p. 98)*, on the slopes of Volcán Poás, offers organized tours with folkloric shows to teach about coffee production, roasting, and culture. **Finca Rosa Blanca** *(tel 2269-9392, www .fincarosablanca.com)*, at Santa Barbara de Heredia, offers tours of the coffee plantation at this deluxe boutique hotel.

Heredia & Volcán Barva

The pull of Heredia and its beautiful surroundings defies gravity, luring you inexorably up the slopes of Volcán Barva, where emerald pastures give way to pine and merge into the mystical cloud forests that shroud the uppermost slopes of Parque Nacional Braulio Carrillo. On weekends, Josefinos also head north, seeking cozy cottages warmed by log-burning hearths and rustic restaurants where simple fare is cooked over coffee-wood fires.

The grotto within the 1867 Basilica de Barva draws those seeking miracle cures.

Heredia
- Map p. 68

Casa de la Cultura
- Ave. Central, Calle Central, Heredia
- 2260-1619

INBioparque
- 1.5 miles (2.4 km) SW of Santo Domingo de Heredia
- 2507-8107
- Closed Mon.
- $$
- www.inbio parque.com

Heredia

This former coffee capital of Costa Rica, 7 miles (11.2 km) northwest of San José, dates from 1706 and is affectionately called City of the Flowers. At its core is the **Parque Central** dominated by the venerable **Basílica de la Immaculada Concepción,** erected in 1797 and featuring bells imported from Cuzco, Peru. The handsome tree-shaded plaza proffers a panoply of historic attractions, including the circular brick fortress, **El Fortín,** erected by president Alfredo González Flores (1914–1917). Note that the gun slits open outward, so that bullets ricochet into the fortress—a military heresy that

speaks volumes for Costa Rica's innocence in such matters. Flores lived across Calle Central in what is now the **Casa de la Cultura,** a small museum and art gallery.

On the east side of town is the **Universidad Nacional,** with its surrounding area bustling with coffee shops. West of town, the bougainvillea-lined suburb of **San Joaquín de las Flores** is famous for its traditional Easter Parade.

Near **Santo Domingo de Heredia,** southeast of town, is **INBioparque,** the headquarters of the Instituto Nacional de Biodiversidad. Housing millions of species of flora and fauna, this educational facility also has static and interactive exhibitions on tropical ecology. Trails go through a butterfly garden and re-creations of habitats.

Barva

Exquisite and endearing, this historic village 1.5 miles (2.4 km) north of Heredia lures visitors to its narrow streets lined with old adobe homes adorned with grill windows and terra-cotta roofs. At its heart is the **Iglesia de San Bartolomé de Barva,** built in 1867.

About 2 miles (3.2 km) northwest in Santa Barbara de Heredia, **Ark Herb Farm** (tel 2239-2111, www.arkherbfarm.com, $) spreads over 20 acres (8 ha) with hundreds of species of medicinal and culinary herbs raised for export. Trails weave among the herb beds, shrubbery, and fruit orchards. Guided tours are offered.

INSIDER TIP:

For a wide range of generous *bocas*—Costa Rican tapas—try Bar y Marisquería El Róbalo, in Heredia's southeastern suburb of Santo Domingo.

—MICHAEL H. GRAYUM
National Geographic field researcher

To see an example of adobe construction and learn about campesino culture at the turn of the 19th century, pop into the **Museo de la Cultura Popular,** housed in the former home of Alfredo González Flores at **Santa Lucía de Barva,** midway between Heredia and Barva.

Barva is surrounded by coffee, much of it belonging to the estates of **Café Britt,** Costa Rica's preeminent producer of export-quality coffee. Café Britt offers a highly recommended tour that features a multimedia presentation and includes the roasting plant and tasting room where visitors learn the fine art of coffee discernment. Actors in traditional garb blend the tale of an evolving love story, the nation's development, and the evolution of coffee. Nearby, the **Beneficio Tierra Madre** coffee farm (and mill) is adorned with murals celebrating the "golden bean" and welcomes visitors.

Volcán Barva

On weekends and holidays, Josefinos hit the slopes of Volcán Barva, where exclusive mountain regions such as **San José de la Montaña** and the **Reserva Monte de la Cruz** offer cabins amid the pines. Temperatures grow chillier as roads climb past alpine meadows and forests draped with orchids, ferns, and Spanish moss. It is easy to imagine yourself in the Tyrol, a notion enhanced by the prevalent Tyrolean architecture.

The finest example of the transplanted Alps is above **San Rafael de Heredia** at the **Hotel Chalet Tirol** (see p. 245), which looks like a set from *The Sound of Music.* The hotel has a superb French restaurant and in summer hosts the **International Music Festival,** with classical concerts in the Salzburg Theater.

Hiking at these upper heights is stupendous. Trails lead through cloud forest reserves such as that of **Cerro Dantas Wildlife Biological Center** (tel 2274-1997), which has an ecological center, educational trails, and guided hikes. ■

Barva
▲ Map p. 68

Museo de la Cultura Popular
✉ Carretera 126, 1.5 miles (2.4 km) NW of Heredia
☎ 2260-1619
$ $

Café Britt
▲ Map p. 68
✉ Carretera 126, 1.25 miles (2 km)NW of Heredia
☎ 2260-2748
$ $
www.coffeetour.com

Beneficio Tierra Madre
▲ Map p. 68
✉ San Rafael de Heredia
☎ 2277-1600
$ $$
www.beneficio tierramadre.com

Parque Nacional Volcán Poás

The most developed of the country's national parks protects the most dramatic of the region's volcanoes, which rises above the northwest Meseta Central. On clear days you can see both the Caribbean Sea and the Pacific Ocean from its summit. Peering down into the crater may evoke the same sensations that virgins of pre-Columbian times felt moments before they were tossed in as sacrificial lambs to the gods.

The steaming innards of Poás put you on edge.

**Parque
Nacional
Volcán Poás**
- Map p. 68
- 2482-2165
- $$

www.sinac.go.cr

The 13,838-acre (5,600 ha) Parque Nacional Volcán Poás is centered on the eponymous 8,871-foot-high (2,704 m) volcano, whose main crater collapsed eons ago to form a mile-wide (1.6 km) caldera. You can drive all the way to the summit. A 300-yard (275 m) walk from the parking lot leads to the viewing terrace 600 feet (183 m) above the cauldron, where fumaroles hiss, a sulfurous pool bubbles, and smoke is disgorged from a 300-foot-high (90 m) mini-volcano that has been thrown up in recent decades. At times, the sulfur fumes become so acidic that the park must be closed.

The feisty giant, still intermittently active, entered its most recent volatile phase in the early 1990s. The main crater burbles and belches persistently; occasionally it spews violently, frightening the farming communities on its slopes.

Poás also has two minor craters, both extinct, snoozing beneath lush green blankets. One, **Botos,** has a jade-colored lake reached via the **Botos Trail.** The cloud forest surrounding the lake can be accessed via the **El Canto de los Aves** trail. The forests resound with the songs of sooty robins and toucanets, as well as the two-note whistle of resplendent quetzals. Fiery-throated hummingbirds flit past, and you'll also see the endemic Poás squirrel.

Arrive early to beat the clouds that blanket the chill heights by midmorning. Bring warm clothing to shield yourself from the wind whistling over the Continental Divide. As the most visited park in the country, Poás is popular on weekends with Ticos who disdain the wondrous silence. If possible, visit midweek.

In the visitor center, a scale model of Poás and exhibits explain the processes at work. Audiovisual presentations are given on Sundays. The 23-mile (37 km) drive from Alajuela, featuring a summit road that winds like a coiled python, is half the fun; for those without transportation, excursions leave daily from San José. Check times and prices with tour operators. ■

Parque Nacional Braulio Carrillo

Rugged to the point of being almost impenetrable, Parque Nacional Braulio Carrillo protects a precious watershed on the windward side of the Cordillera Central—a massive tract of pristine wilderness spanning five life zones less than a 40-minute drive from the metropolis of San José.

Braulio Carrillo is a 108,970-acre (44,100 ha) swath of endless dark green cloaking the flanks of **Volcán Barva** (9,534 feet/2,906 m) and **Volcán Cacho Negro** (7,053 feet/2,150 m). It ranges from windswept cloud forest at higher elevations to lowland rain forest in the soggy Northern Lowlands barely 100 feet (30 m) above sea level. Given the park's size and elevation range, temperatures differ markedly, though rainfall is a near constant and nowhere less than 10 feet (3 m) per year.

INSIDER TIP:

Be sure to stop at the bridge over Río Sucio in Braulio Carrillo and see where a bright red river (caused by weird geology off the northern flanks of Volcán Irazú) joins a clear water river.

—JOHN LONGINO
National Geographic field researcher

Hiking the rugged trails guarantees seeing wildlife, including more than 500 species of birds, from quetzals to toucans, and almost 150 mammal species, including jaguars, monkeys, peccaries, pumas,

Rain Forest Railway

Few carnival rides are as thrilling as the 90-minute, mile-long (1.6 km) excursion through the forest canopy aboard this open-air aerial tram, in a private tropical wet forest reserve abutting Braulio Carrillo. The trip reveals details of everyday life in the tree-tops, where 75 percent of all rain forest species dwell. You can view monkeys eye to eye while dangling as high as 200 feet (60 m) above the forest floor.

and *tepezcuintles* (or pacas)—a giant rodent that's the park's mascot. Permission is required for camping.

The park is easily accessed by Highway 32, the Guápiles Highway, whose construction in 1978 led to the park's creation. **Zurquí Ranger Station,** on the highway 13 miles (21 km) northeast of San José, has an information center, but the trails here are closed. The main access is from the lowlands at the **Puesto Carrillo Ranger Station,** on the Guápiles Highway. You can also access with a rugged four-wheel-drive from the west, and from the south via the **Puesto Brava Ranger Station,** above Sacramento. ∎

Parque Nacional Braulio Carrillo

🅜 Map p. 68
✉ Hwy. 32, 14 miles (22.5 km) NE of San José
☎ 2233-4533, ext. 25
💲 $$

Rain Forest Aerial Tram

🅜 Map p. 205
✉ Rara Avis, Hwy. 32, 30 miles (48.3 km) NE of San José
☎ 2257-5961
💲 $$$$$
www.rainforest tram.com

Orosí Valley Drive

Southeast of Paraíso, 5 miles (8 km) east of Cartago, Highway 224 drops sharply into a Shangri-la canyon edged to the south by the dauntingly forested flanks of the Talamanca mountains. The rivers that drain the vale have been dammed to form Lago de Cachí, around which the road loops. This tour makes a circle that begins and ends in Paraíso, passing two precious colonial churches and many intriguing stops en route.

Ujarrás' ancient church

At the main square in **Paraíso**, turn south off the main highway—Highway 10—and follow the looping road 1.5 miles (2.4 km) to the **Mirador Orosí ❶**, offering views over the valley and set in a park run by the ICT (Instituto Costarricense de Turismo). Shortly beyond, the road begins to slalom the ski-ramp route into the canyon. At the foot you're instantly immersed in coffee, with shiny-leaved bushes to all sides.

The road wends through the coffee fields and beyond the **Río Aguacaliente** deposits you in the picturesque village of **Orosí ❷** (visitor information, tel 2533-3333), backed by forested hills. On your right you pass the **Iglesia de San José de Orosí,** a charming little church built in 1743 whose thick adobe walls and beamed roof have withstood many an earthquake. Its ascetic interior, with a terra-cotta floor and wooden gilt altar, was recently restored. Adjoining is a small **Museo de Arte Religioso** (tel 2533-3051, closed Mon.) containing religious art, chalices, and other ecclesiastical icons plus colonial furniture.

Photography is not permitted.

Continue four blocks south and one east to the hillside **Balnearios Termales Orosí** (tel 2533-2156, closed Tues.), offering relaxing bathing in well-maintained thermal mineral pools, which abound in the valley. Just south of the village you'll pass the **Beneficio Orlich** (tel 2533-3535, closed Sat.–Sun.) coffee-processing plant. The plant sits at a junction for Parque Nacional Tapantí Macizo de la Muerte (see p. 98). Turn left and cross the **Río Grande de Orosí** via a narrow suspension bridge. On the far bank is the **Hotel/Restaurante Río Paloma** (tel 2533-3128), specializing in dishes of local trout.

Turn left immediately beyond the river and trace its course along a deteriorated section of road. After about 4 miles (6.4 km) pick up the pavement again as the road swings along the southern shore of **Lago de Cachí ❸**, which attracts waterfowl. The lake was created in the 1960s when the Río Reventazón was dammed for hydroelectricity. It is becoming popular for fishing and boating offered at **La Casona del Cafetal** (tel 2533-3280), a lakeside coffee farm that also offers hiking and horseback riding and a restaurant with marvelous views.

Continue east less than 1 mile (1.6 km) to the rough-hewn **Casa El Soñador ❹** (House of the Dreamer, tel 2577-1983), a wooden-and-bamboo structure adorned with primitivist carvings—the whimsical creations of the late Macedonio Quesada, whose sons continue the tradition of conjuring twisted coffee-tree stumps into carvings. Two miles (3.2 km) farther, the road turns west and crosses the **Presa de Cachí ❺** (Cachí Dam), pointing you back to Paraíso. After about 5 miles (8 km) you'll see signs for **Ujarrás ❻**, renowned for its ruined church—**Iglesia de Nuestra Señora**

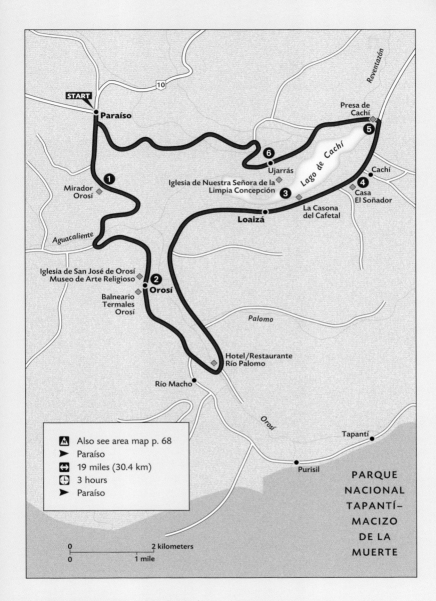

START
Paraíso

10

1 Mirador
   Orosí

Aguacaliente

Iglesia de San José de Orosí
Museo de Arte Religioso

2 Orosí

Balneario
Termales
Orosí

Río Macho

Iglesia de Nuestra Señora de la
Limpia Concepción

3

Loaizá

La Casona
del Cafetal

Lago de Cachí

6 Ujarrás

Presa de
Cachí
5

Cachí
4
Casa
El Soñador

Reventazón

Palomo

Hotel/Restaurante
Río Palomo

Orosí

Tapantí

Purisil

PARQUE
NACIONAL
TAPANTÍ–
MACIZO
DE LA
MUERTE

Also see area map p. 68
Paraíso
19 miles (30.4 km)
3 hours
Paraíso

0   2 kilometers
0   1 mile

de la Limpia Concepción—on the fringe of
the lake. The church dates from 1681 but was
abandoned in 1833 when the valley flooded.
Today it sits amid lawns fronted by giddily
colorful flowers. It is the setting every third
Sunday in April for a pilgrimage from Paraíso,
which awaits at the top of a scenic climb.

NOT TO BE MISSED:

**Iglesia de San José de Orosí
• Casa El Soñador • Ruins
at Ujarrás**

Cartago

Although Cartago, the nation's erstwhile capital and today its second largest city, offers meager attractions, a fistful of first-class sites lie nearby, the surrounding countryside is enrichingly scenic, and the city is a starting point for stupendous drives up Volcán Irazú, through the Orosi Valley, and along the mountain ridge that leads south to Cerro de la Muerte.

The interior of Cartago's basilica soars to a decagonal roof enclosed in a cupola.

Cartago
🅰 Map p. 68
Visitor Information
✉ Cartago
   Chamber of
   Commerce,
   30 yards
   (27 m) E of
   Las Ruinas de
   Cartago
☎ 2591-4785
🕐 Closed Sun.

Cartago, Costa Rica's oldest settlement, was founded in 1563 by conquistador Juan Vásquez de Coronado and remained the nation's capital until 1823, when it lost the Battle of Ochomongo to San José. It is hardly a beautiful city and long ago ceased to wear its history on its sleeve. Most of the colonial edifices have literally fallen victims to earthquakes (most recently in 1910), and nearby Volcán Irazú frequently spews ash on the city.

The parochial city, at the eastern base of the Cerros de la Carpintera, 16 miles (26 km) east of San José, retains its role as religious capital, symbolically represented by the ruins of **Iglesia de la Parroquia,** in a tree-shaded plaza at Avenida 2 and Calle 2. The nation's preeminent church, the gray-and-white **Basílica de Nuestra Señora de los Ángeles** (tel 2551-0465), stands foursquare in the main square at Avenida 2 and Calle 14. It was built of steel with a concrete stucco surface in 1929 in Byzantine style following the collapse of its precursor in 1926. The stunning interior of glistening hardwoods boasts exquisite stained glass. A steady stream of supplicants kneel and pray to **La Negrita,** the nation's

INSIDER TIP:

Learn from the locals; many times the little *sodas* on the side of the road are the best spots to grab a cheap bite to eat.

—BEN HORTON
National Geographic field researcher

mulatta (mixed-blood) patron saint to whom local superstition ascribes miraculous cures. She resides in an 8-inch-high (20 cm) effigy set in a gold-encrusted shrine above the main altar. In the basement, to the rear, the **Cripta de la Piedra** shrine is a veritable mini-museum of *promesas,* or votive offerings, left by worshippers as thanks for prayers granted. In the southeast corner, supposedly curative waters seep from a tiny cavern.

El Jardín Botánico Lankester

This 27-acre (11 ha) garden at **Paraíso,** 5 miles (8 km) east of Cartago, protects an invaluable collection of neotropical flora that is one of the largest in the Americas, including its pride and joy—more than 700 species of orchids. The gardens also abound with palms and bromeliads, effusive as a Pisarro painting, drawing butterflies and birds by the thousands. Peak blooming is in springtime.

Established in the 1940s, the gardens are named for their founder, Charles H. Lankester

La Negrita Pilgrimage

Pilgrims from Costa Rica and Central America descend on Cartago and the Basílica de Nuestra Señora de los Ángeles each August 2 for the Procesión de los Milagros (Procession of the Miracles). Penitents set out at dawn from San José to pray to La Negrita. Some carry large wooden crosses on their backs; others crawl on their knees. Lepers and mendicants plead for charitable donations while the townsfolk do a thriving business selling votive candles and flowers. The occasion is both colorful and emotional.

(1879–1969), an English orchiddologist and naturalist who worked to collate a representative corpus of Central American flora. Through the joint efforts of the American Orchid Society and the Stanley Smith Horticultural Trust, the garden was donated to the University of Costa Rica in 1973. ∎

El Jardín Botánico Lankester

🅰 Map p. 68
✉ Hwy. 1, Paraíso
☎ 2552-3247
$ $$

www.jardinbotanico lankesterorg

Parque Nacional Volcán Irazú

Volcán Irazú looms over both Cartago and the Reventazón Valley, rising to the north as steadily as the line created by a logarithmic equation. For anyone with a head for heights, a drive to the top offers sublime rewards. On clear days, the view takes in the shimmering waters of both the Caribbean and the Pacific.

Volcán Irazú and the larger of its two craters are breathtaking in scale.

Parque Nacional Volcán Irazú

- Map p. 68
- 22 miles (35 km) NE of Cartago
- 2200-5025
- $$

Volcán Irazú (11,260 feet/ 3,432 m) is an active volcano and made international news on March 13, 1963, when it erupted the day that President John F. Kennedy arrived in Costa Rica for an official visit. A resulting mudslide left highland dwellers ankle-deep in volcanic mud, obliterating the coffee crop but enriching the countryside for years to come. Irazú's last major hiccup was in 1996. In more benign moods, the giant welcomes visitors.

The volcano is the centerpiece of its namesake national park, created in 1955 and encompassing 5,705 acres (2,300 ha) of primary forest, including cloud forest. A 22-mile (35 km) drive from Cartago leads to the barren, windswept summit. As you climb upward, the views grow ever more panoramic until it is all you can do to keep your eye on the serpentine road. On the lower flanks you'll pass through trim little farming communities, like colorful pointillist dots on the emerald green canvas. Although dairy farming is predominant, the area is Costa Rica's main center for market gardening: the indecently rich slopes are a patchwork of fields growing vegetables such as carrots, potatoes, and legumes.

The volcano has twin craters. The smaller of the two, the 300-foot (91 m) deep **Diego de la Haya** Crater, cradles a mineral-rich lake that changes hue from jade green to blood red. Fumaroles steam in the larger crater, which yawns 900 feet (275 m) deep.

It is foggy and chilly up here most of the time. Bring a sweater and jacket to brave the wind that beats down the vegetation, such as stunted dwarf oaks that cling low to the ground. Don't be put off from below by the clouds swirling near the summit, for it is quite possible to climb above the clouds and emerge in the sunlight, giving you views of the crater with the clouds far below.

For your own safety, stick to the marked trails. Out of respect for the fragile ecosystems, refrain from following the illicit paths that have been trampled by visitors who

INSIDER TIP:

Because the clouds normally thicken as the day progresses, mornings are usually the best time to visit Volcán Irazú.

—CHRISTOPHER P. BAKER
National Geographic author

chose to ignore the signs warning not to approach the dangerously unstable rims of the craters.

Mountain rabbits, squirrel, and even armadillos and coyotes can be seen scurrying across the ashy plains, while birds such as the ruddy nuthatch, night sparrow, and masked woodpecker swoop by within arm's length.

The ranger station is 1.25 miles (2 km) below the summit, where facilities include picnic benches and a mobile *soda* that serves snacks. Take warm, rainproof clothing to guard against inclement weather. Also, plan on stopping at the **Restaurante Nochebuena** (*tel 2503-8013, www.nochebuena.org, $*) for hearty fare. Here, the **Museo Vulcanológico** (*$*) provides a fascinating educational overview of vulcanism and Irazú. ∎

Volcano Safety

Volcanoes are unpredictable and potentially lethal. A few precautions are in order when exploring. First, sign in with the rangers before setting off. Stay on assigned trails, and heed all warning signs. Do not venture into restricted areas nor get too close to fumaroles, mud pools, or vents; they can explode without warning, and the ground around them is often just a thin crust that can easily give way. Volcán Arenal is highly active, and hiking is restricted to designated "safety zones" around the base. On Irazú, Turrialba, and Rincón de la Vieja Volcanoes, trails lead into the active craters; resist any temptation to stroll off the trails to peer over the unstable rims. Take sturdy shoes and a rainproof jacket, plus a flashlight and sufficient water and food for longer hikes in case you get lost.

Valle de Reventazón

Draining Lake Cachí, the Río Reventazón falls through a narrow valley, tumbling ever more steeply to the east as the land steps down toward the Caribbean Lowlands. Hemmed between the Talamancas and the slopes of Volcán Turrialba, the area's charms are often overlooked.

Remote hamlet near Turrialba

Turrialba

🅽 Map p. 69

CATIE

🅽 Map p.69

✉ Hwy. 10, 2.5 miles (4 km) E of Turrialba

☎ 2556-6081

www.catie.ac.cr

At its heart lies **Turrialba,** a somewhat nondescript town in a broad valley swaddled in citrus, macadamia, and sugarcane plantations. Once a major waystation on the old highway between San José and the Caribbean, it has been left high and dry since the completion of the Guápiles Highway in 1987 and the subsequent demise of the Atlantic Railroad in 1991. It's now best known as the launching point for white-water rafting trips.

Worth a visit is **CATIE** (Centro Agronómico Tropical de Investigación y Enseñanza), a 2,150-acre (870 ha) research center devoted to the investigation of tropical agriculture and husbandry. Plants here have been culled from around the globe. Visitors can witness the results of breeding experiments with animals and crops. Trails offer superb birding. Visits are by prior arrangement, though some tour operators offer excursions from San José.

Nearby is **Hacienda Atirro,** a coffee, macadamia, and sugarcane farm that can be explored on horseback. Tours can be arranged from **Casa Turire** (see p. 246), a sublime hotel that also serves as a water-sports center for **Lago Angostura.** This 633-acre (256 ha) lake was created by

(see p. 246)

INSIDER TIP:

Because of Costa Rica's proximity to the Equator, the sun sets at roughly 6 p.m. year-round and the sky grows dark at a fast rate. Don't get stuck in the dark.

—ELLIANA SPIEGEL
National Geographic contributor

Proyecto Hidroeléctrico Angostura, a controversial project completed in 2000 that tapped the Río Reventazón (Exploding River) for energy by building the country's largest dam and hydroelectric plant. The lake now draws waterfowl, and much of the surrounding land is being rehabilitated to create wildlife habitats and natural forest, providing an ecological link with the forests of the Talamancas.

Turrialba is a base for rafting on the **Río Reventazón,** which plunges through a remote canyon and is considered a classic whitewater run. It is also the place to arrange excursions to **Volcán Turrialba** (10,919 feet/3,328 m), a dormant giant reached with four-wheel drive via Santa Cruz or

Santa Teresa. You can hike up to the summit, which boasts three craters and cloud forest; stay at the rustic **Volcán Turrialba Lodge** *(tel 2273-4335, www.volcanturrialba lodge.com).*

Monumento Nacional Guayabo

The nation's most important archaeological site pales beside the great Mexican and Guatemalan ruins, yet nonetheless is impressive for its setting amid the jungle at the base of Volcán Turrialba.

The settlement, which may have housed up to one thousand

Casa Turire

🏔 Map p. 69
✉ Highway 225, 8 miles (13 km) SE of Turrialba
☎ 2531-1111
www.hotelcasa turire.com

EXPERIENCE:
The Fun of 4WD

If the Indiana Jones within is hankering to explore Costa Rica, a four-wheel-drive (4WD) vehicle is a must. They can be rented at almost any rental car agency. Access to much of the country is via badly potholed, rock-strewn, and/or unpaved roads. Dusty in dry season, they turn to a bouillabaisse in the wet season, when fording rivers can add to the challenge. Even paved roads quickly wash out in the rainy season. In some areas, landslides are common.

Exploration by 4WD can be fun, turning touring into a true adventure. You get to explore remote parts of the country totally inaccessible by sedan, test your driving skills under conditions that would challenge a goat, and enjoy the thrill of feeling like a true pioneer. Even in 4WD vehicles, however, you have to know when to quit.

people, was occupied between 1000 B.C. and A.D. 1400, when it was mysteriously abandoned. The monument covers 540 acres (218 ha), mostly tropical wet

Mountain Ridge Drive

To travel this 45-mile (72 km) route between Cartago and the Cerro de la Muerte opens up some of the most spectacular vistas in the entire country. The rich profusion of scenic views—not to mention a chance to escape the heat of the lowlands atop the Talamancas—makes amends for the poorly engineered road.

Linking the valleys of the Meseta Central and El General, this section of the Inter-American Highway (Hwy. 2) exposes visitors to the highest mountains accessible by road, to dwarf forests, and to cloud forest reserves where a quetzal sighting is nearly guaranteed.

The Inter-American Highway was built in the 1950s to link the nations of the Central American isthmus. Remarkably, for most of its length the nation's main artery is an unlighted, shoulderless, narrow two-laner. Exercise extreme caution: Grades are steep, and the twisting road is subject to fog. Slide areas, potholes, and big-rig trucks are common. Three-lane passing zones may allow uphill traffic to pass slower vehicles. Pass with care, though, as downhill traffic often rips down this lane. Set out early in the morning to beat the clouds and to ensure that you'll be safely back in the valley before dusk. Note: In the rainy season (May–Nov.) clouds settle over the mountains, obscuring the beautiful panoramas.

Two miles (3.2 km) south of Cartago at **San Isidro ❶**, you begin to climb. The winding road rises to **Vara de Roble ❷**, where Highway 222 falls south to Santa María de Dota. The views down the mountain are sublime—and they grow more so as you ascend another 2 miles (3.2 km), to **Empalme ❸**, your last chance to buy gas. Orchards and lime green pastures cling to the slopes, forested with pines and oaks. Road side trout farms offer fishing and horseback rides.

Continue to the Km 58 marker, where the yellow church of **Cañón ❹** is a good place to admire the breathtaking vista. You are now atop the crest of the Continental Divide. Settlements thin as you continue up through the **Reserva Forestal Río Macho** and the **Iyöla Amí Cloud Forest Reserve,** which protect rare, 500-year-old cipresillo oaks and aguacatillos, a favorite

food of quetzals. At the Km 76 marker is the **Casa Refugio de Ojo de Agua ❺**, a refuge hut—now a meager museum—used by traders before a road over the mountains existed.

The road levels out near the Km 80 marker, where a side road spirals sharply westward into the valley of the **Río Savegre.** The rocky road drops 2,100 feet (640 m) in 9 miles (14.5 km), depositing you in the hamlet of **San Gerardo de Dota ❻**, tucked into a valley fulsome with orchards, trout-filled streams, and a large quetzal population. The **Savegre Biological Reserve** (tel 2740-1028, www.savegre.co.cr) welcomes visitors curious about these elusive birds; it also offers hikes and horseback riding. Midway between the highway and San Gerardo de Dota, stop at **Dantica Cloud Forest Lodge & Gallery** (see p. 246). This spectacular modernist lodge is a good access point for a brief hike in **Parque Nacional Los Quetzales,** created in 2005 to protect a cloud forest habitat of quetzals.

Return to the main road and continue south to Km 85, where a 1-mile (1.6 km) path leads to the windswept summit of **Cerro de la Muerte** (11,450 feet/3,491 m) ❼. The Mountain of Death is named for the many campesinos who froze to death hauling produce over it to San José. Above the tree line, shrubs skulk close to the ground; the peak is covered by bogs and páramo grasses. The road continues 2 miles (3.2 km) to a truck stop, **Las Torres ❽**, whence it begins its dizzying descent into the Valle de El General.

NOT TO BE MISSED:

Cañón church • Dantica Cloud Forest Reserve & Gallery
• Casa Refugio de Ojo de Agua

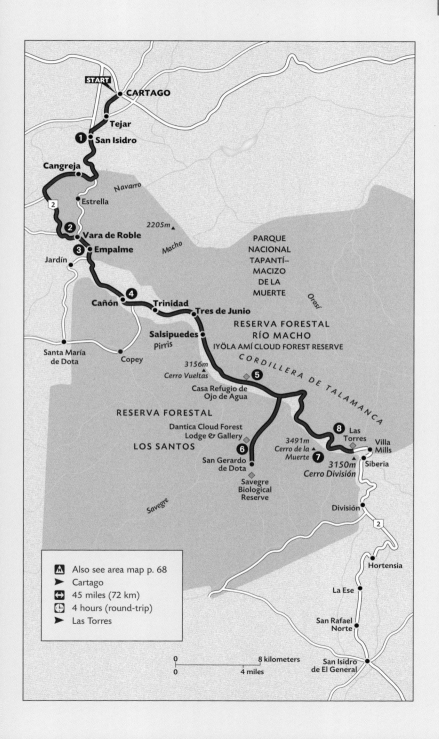

START
CARTAGO

Tejar
① **San Isidro**

Cangreja

Navarro

② **Estrella**

Macho

2205m

② **Vara de Roble**
③ **Empalme**

Jardín

PARQUE NACIONAL TAPANTÍ– MACIZO DE LA MUERTE

④ **Cañón** **Trinidad**
Tres de Junio

Orosí

RESERVA FORESTAL RÍO MACHO

Salsipuedes
Pirris

IYÖLA AMÍ CLOUD FOREST RESERVE

Santa María de Dota

Copey

3156m
Cerro Vueltas ⑤

CORDILLERA DE TALAMANCA

Casa Refugio de Ojo de Agua

RESERVA FORESTAL

Dantica Cloud Forest Lodge & Gallery

⑧ **Las Torres**
Villa Mills

LOS SANTOS

⑥
San Gerardo de Dota

3491m
Cerro de la Muerte ▲ ⑦

3150m
Cerro División

Siberia

Savegre Biological Reserve

Savegre

División

2

Hortensia

La Ese

San Rafael Norte

🅰 Also see area map p. 68
▶ Cartago
↔ 45 miles (72 km)
🕐 4 hours (round-trip)
▶ Las Torres

0   8 kilometers
0   4 miles

San Isidro de El General

Monumento Nacional Guayabo

🔺 Map p. 69

✉ 12 miles (19.3 km) N of Turrialba

☎ 2559-1220

🕐 Closed Mon.

💲 $$

www.sinac.go.cr

forest, which is gradually being peeled back to reveal a vast cobbled pavement (calzada). Trails lead to a lookout point above the excavated village featuring stone

INSIDER TIP:

Go out in the forest at night; it's a whole different world. Use a headlamp, not a flashlight. You see eyeshine better with a headlamp, and it frees your hands to slap mosquitoes.

—JOHN LONGINO
National Geographic field researcher

cisterns, working aqueducts, and circular terraces (montículos) on which conical bamboo structures were built. A self-guided walk leads down from the ranger station past petroglyphs and around the montículos, where lizards scuttle amid the bleached ruins.

The surrounding forests are rich in fauna and superb for birding: Oropendolas and aricaris are particularly numerous.

Into the Talamancas

East of the Río Reventazón, Highway 232 cuts into the flanks of the Talamanca mountains, deteriorating all the while until about 20 miles (32 km) east of Turrialba, beyond the hamlet of **Moravia del Chirripó,** you arrive at the threshold of **Reserva Indígena Chirripó,** a remote indigenous reserve that makes a

good base for expeditions into the dauntingly rugged **Parque Internacional La Amistad** (see pp. 198–199), a haven for wildlife extending south into Panama. The reserve receives few visitors and it is a good idea to go with a guide, which can be hired in Moravia del Chirripó.

At **Tuís,** midway between Turrialba and Moravia, a rugged

Quetzals

The resplendent trogon, better known as the quetzal, is an exotic and elusive species that draws many birders to Costa Rica. Its iridescent emerald plumage is so luxuriant that Mayans worshipped it as a god called Quetzalcoatl, or the Plumed Serpent. The endangered pigeon-size bird is common at elevations of 3,500 feet (1,070 m) associated with cloud forests. The male boasts a chest of brilliant crimson and trailing tail feathers, put to good use in its mating displays. The quetzal prefers the avocado-like fruit of the *aguacatillo*, which it plucks from below in mid-flight.

dirt road leads north 10 miles (16 km) to the remote hamlet of **Bajo Pacuare,** the traditional starting point for rafting trips on the **Río Pacuare.** Reservations for rafting should be made in advance with a local tour company such as Costa Rica Expeditions or Ríos Tropicales (see p. 260). ∎

Route of the Saints

Named for the villages that speckle the ridges south of San José, this off-the-beaten-track region offers superlative vistas as the roads rise and dip over forested highlands. It makes a fabulous day-long trip as you savor the calm poetry of green glens and felicitous silence broken only by the braying of a mule or the distant chiming of a church bell.

Situated on the northern face of the **Cerro de Escazú** mountains, **Aserrí,** 7 miles (11.2 km) south of San José on Highway 209, has a fine church, but it is better known for its rustic roadside restaurants that serve campesino fare and offer mesmerizing views across the Meseta Central toward the distant volcanoes. Beyond **Tarbaca,** Highway 222 drops eastward toward the whitewashed village of **San Gabriel;** at dusk it glistens like hammered gold from the sunlight slanting in from the west.

INSIDER TIP:

Buy the *Costa Rican Nature Atlas-Guidebook* before exploring the Route of the Saints, as the convoluted road system in this area can befuddle.

—CHRISTOPHER P. BAKER
National Geographic author

A quetzal feeds its chick.

East of **San Cristóbal Sur** is **La Lucha Sin Fin** (The Endless Struggle; *closed to the public),* the farm where "Don Pepe" Figueres trained his army for the 1948 revolution. Now a museum, it has trails and a **hemp-rope factory** *(tel 2544-1410)* to visit. The **Fila de Bustamente** rises south of San Cristóbal, and the slopes green with coffee surround the pretty villages of **San Pablo de León Cortés** and **San Marcos de Tarrazú,** which has a domed hilltop church sheathed in white light like a celestial glow. Finally you reach **Santa María de Dota,** where the road swings north up the mountain to the Inter-American Highway, offering stupendous views. The town boasts the **Monumento Liberación Nacional,** commemorating the 1948 revolution. ■

More Places to Visit in the Central Highlands

Doka Estate

For an authentic "Coffee 101" experience, head to this working coffee farm and beneficio (coffee-processing mill) on the slopes of Volcán Poás. Guided educational tours, taking place several times a day, take visitors into the fields and roasting facilities to learn about harvesting, processing, and roasting of coffee. The tour ends in the tasting rooms with a sampling of the estate's eight different roasts of coffee. The Vargas family has owned the 4,000-acre (1,600 ha) estate since 1929, although the beneficio dates from 1893. It is the oldest working water-powered mill in the entire country.
www.dokaestate.com 🅰 Map p. 68 ✉ San Luis de Sabanilla de Alajuela, 7 miles (11.3 km) N of Alajuela ☎ 2449-6623 💲 $$$$

La Paz Waterfall Gardens

Named for the Catarata La Paz (peace waterfall), this private nature reserve offers well-maintained trails that lead to a series of waterfalls, overhung by suspension bridges. You can actually walk behind the La Paz cataract (rainwear is provided). The falls are a series of cascades that tumble in tiers for some 3,000 feet (915 m) down the eastern flank of Volcán Poás, culminating in the narrow namesake falls. A visitor center and local nature guides explain rain forest and cloud forest ecology. A serpentarium (snakes), ranarium (frogs), giant butterfly garden, hummingbird garden, and trout ponds all entertain. See what life was like in Costa Rica one hundred years ago at the Casita de la Paz, a re-creation of a traditional farmstead A restaurant serves típica (traditional) fare. Accommodations are offered at the Peace Lodge.
www.waterfallgardens.com 🅰 Map p. 68 ✉ Hwy. 126, 5 miles (8 km) N of Varablanca and 23 miles (37 km) N of Alajuela ☎ 2482-2720 💲 $$$$

Museo de las Carretas

At Costa Rica's small Oxcart and Rural Life Museum, the traditional motif of the oxcart, both decorative and functional, is shown in a venerable adobe home in Desamparados, a working-class suburb on the southern outskirts of San José. Artifacts from traditional peasant life are on display, along with oxcarts from many different decades.
✉ Hwy. 209, 2 miles (3.2 km) S of San José ☎ 2259-7042 🕐 Closed Mon. 💲 $

Parque Nacional Tapantí-Macizo de la Muerte

This 15,024-acre (6,080 ha) national park covers mountainous territory ranging from 3,600 feet–8,832 feet (1,100 m–2,692 m) and protects the pre-montane and montane rain forest blanketing the precipitous northern slopes of the Talamancas. Trees such as giant mahoganies, Spanish cedar, and ficus thrive in the persistent rains, which average 300 inches (75 cm) a year, feeding numerous pummeling waterfalls. The park teems with wildlife, including anteaters, jaguars, monkeys, ocelots, otters, poison dart frogs, tapirs, and almost 300 bird species, including quetzals, which are often seen near the ranger station. The park is easily accessed using well-marked trails.
www.sinaccr.net 🅰 Map p. 68 ✉ 23 miles (37 km) SE of Cartago ☎ 2551-2970 💲 $$

Parque Vibarona

Giant boas hiss like teakettles as you step into their cages at this family-run serpentarium. More snakes, some of them deadly venomous, reside in glass cages. You can see the snakes being fed live tidbits. Trails lead into the adjacent pre-montane wet forest.
🅰 Map p. 69 ✉ Hwy. 10, at Chitaría, 15 miles (24 km) E of Turrialba ☎ 2538-1510 💲 $

Cowboy country with dramatic landscapes—from dry deciduous woodlands to mist-shrouded cloud forests—and a unique culture derived from its Chorotega Heritage

Guanacaste

Guanacaste tree

Guanacaste

Guanacaste is one of the country's premier attractions, drawing visitors to its untamed splendors. It is bounded on the east by volcanoes forming the Cordillera de Guanacaste and Cordillera de Tilarán. The vast alluvial plain below the mountains' steep flanks is drained into the Golfo de Nicoya by the Río Tempisempe—the nation's longest river.

The province is named for the *guanacaste* tree—the national tree—also called the ear pod tree. This unmistakable giant is as broad as it is high; branches spread low to the ground, providing a shady retreat for all manner of creatures. Guanacaste is Costa Rica's dry quarter. During summer (Nov.–April), the sun beats down relentlessly and no rain falls. The lowlands' dry deciduous forests and savannas bring forth bright blooms beloved by insects.

Historically the region developed apart from the rest of the nation, as befits its distinct physical nature. As part of Nicaragua, a province within the Captaincy General of Guatemala during the Spanish colonial era, the land was cleared at an early stage and developed into huge cattle haciendas worked by enslaved Chorotega, the most vibrant indigenous tribe of its day. A cowboy culture still clings to the reins and although the Chorotega culture was virtually annihilated, the Native American influence is clearly seen in the broad, bronze-skinned faces of Guanacastecans. The region was legally united with the rest of Costa Rica only in 1858 and has always felt strong affinities with Nicaragua.

You can savor the magnificent scenery without leaving the Inter-American Highway; national parks and wildlife reserves line the north-south route. Branch roads, many unpaved, probe east and west, leading to such varied treats as misty Reserva Biológica del Bosque Nuboso de Monteverde; bubbling mud pools on Volcán Miravalles; the wetlands of Palo Verde, where you can hunt crocodiles and roseate spoonbills from a boat with a camera; and fish-filled Laguna de Arenal, set like a jewel between the two cordilleras.

Cattle ranches invite visitors to saddle up. Mountain biking is popular. And hiking—be it backpacking into the upland wilds or tamer tramping on wildlife trails at Monteverde and Santa Rosa—truly puts you in the landscape. Waterborne options range from windsurfing on Laguna de Arenal and Bahía Salinas to river rafting trips.

The highway threads its way from one dusty colonial town to another, where *sabaneros* (cowboys)

gather for annual fiestas held in *retornos de toros* (bullrings). Horsemen preen and show off their steeds' fancy footwork at *topes*—lively horse parades—while every macho male leaps into the bullring to play tag with a snorting *toro*.

The national costume, music, dance, and fare originate in Guanacaste, where Costa Rica's cultural traditions are kept alive. Tourism has blossomed in recent years, thanks partly to the opening of the nation's second international airport west of Liberia. ∎

Costa Rica
color-coded by region

★ San José

NICARAGUA

Santa Cecilia
Haciendas
Brasilia
1487m
Volcán Orosí
1659m
Cerro Cacao
San José
4
Dos Ríos
164
1806m
Volcán Rincón de la Vieja
uebrada rande
1916m
Volcán S. María
Canalete
P. 205
Pital
PARQUE NACIONAL RINCÓN DE LA VIEJA
Aguas Claras
2028m
Volcán Miravalles
Santa María
Guayabo
Curubandé
añas Dulces
Centro Turístico Yökö
ZONA PROTECTORA MIRAVALLES
Bijagua
San Jorge
La Fortuna
Las Hornillas Volcano Activity Center
1916m
Volcán Tenorio
Cereceda
Liberia
21
Salitral
PARQUE NACIONAL VOLCÁN TENORIO
L. de Coter
Africa Mía
Pijije
Bagaces
6
Tierras Morenas
Nuevo Arenal
Arenal Hanging Bridges
RESERVA BIOLÓGICA LOMAS DE BARBUDAL
142
Tilarán
Laguna de Sangregado
Tabacón Resort
1633m
Volcán Arenal
Montenego
Arenal Observatory Lodge
El Castillo
1100m
Volcán Chato
REFUGIO DE VIDA SILVESTRE DR. LUCAS RODRÍGUEZ CABALLERO
Cañas
Arenal Rain Forest Reserve
Rancho Margot
PARQUE NACIONAL VOLCÁN ARENAL
Hacienda Palo Verde
Bebedero
San Miguel
Reserva Santa Elena
RESERVA BIOLÓGICA DEL BOSQUE NUBOSO DE MONTEVERDE
BOSQUE ETERNO DE LOS NIÑOS
NICOYA
p. 131
PARQUE NACIONAL PALO VERDE
Las Juntas de Abangares
145
Santa Elena
CENTRAL HIGHLANDS
Solimar
Palma
Limonal
Ecolodge San Luis & Research Station
San Buenaventura
18
Pueblo Nuevo
Colorado
Arizona
Guacimal
p. 68
Abangaritos
Manzanillo
Pájaros
Finca Daniel Adventure Park
Unión
Peñas Blancas
Refugio Nacional de Vida Silvestre La Ensenada
1
San Gerardo
Rancho Grande
Miramar
Reserva Biológica Isla Pájaros
Parque Megafauna Monteverde
144
San Isidro
Chomes
Santa Rosa
Pitahaya
Esparza
1
Barranca
Jesús María
Mahogany Park
Barranca
Puntarenas
Caldera
San Mateo
Orotina
San Pablo de Turrubares
Punta Caldera
Z.P. TIVIVES
PARQUE TROPICAL TURUBARI

0 _____ 30 kilometers
0 _____ 15 miles

CENTRAL PACIFIC
p. 155

NORTHERN LOWLANDS P. 205

Puntarenas & Costa Pájaros

Three miles (5 km) long but barely five blocks wide, the anomalous sea-girt city of Puntarenas is somewhat of an ugly duckling. Jutting into the Golfo de Nicoya at the tip of a pencil-thin peninsula, it makes an ideal springboard for maritime leaps to Nicoya by ferry or for day-long forays to Isla Tortuga. The mangrove-rimmed gulf shores lure binocular-laden birders, while inland the grasslands and tropical moist forest can be explored via canopy tours and even an aerial tram.

Rickety wharves are part of the funky charm of Puntarenas.

Puntarenas

📍 Map p. 101

Visitor information

✉ Puntarenas Chamber of Commerce, 1st floor, Oficina INC, Blvd. Casa de la Cultura

☎ 2661-2980

Puntarenas, 75 miles (120 km) west of San José, traces its lineage back to 1524, when conquistador Francisco Fernández de Córdova (1490–1526) founded an ill-fated settlement here. In time it grew to be the nation's major port for coffee export, but a gradual demise set in after the completion of the Atlantic Railroad in 1890. For a while, the town had a viable conch-pearl fleet and drew Josefinos to bathe at its *balnearios*

(swimming pools). Josefinos of modest means still flock to the brown-sand beach that runs unbroken for 7 miles (11 km) from **Boca de Barranca** to the tip of the spit.

Cruise ships call at the new cruise dock in Puntarenas but most passengers bypass the town. Still, if it's funky charm you are seeking, you will find plenty in the weathered wooden homes and in decrepit fishing boats tethered to equally decrepit piers. Ongoing development aims at beautifying the forlorn city. The small **Museo Histórico Maritino,** in the 19th-century jail, traces the city's history with displays spanning pre-Columbian times to the building of the Atlantic Railroad, as well as the coffee industry. The jail was a family residence and later served as the military command post and Casa de la Cultura. The **Paseo de las Turistas** boulevard makes an intriguing walk along the gulf shore. The north of the spit faces a mangrove-lined estuary that is a great spot to see roseate spoonbills.

Costa Pájaros

Pelicans—herons—frigatebirds—ibises. Bird-watching is the name of the game along the "bird coast," the inner gulf shoreline which stretches north from Puntarenas up to the mouth of the Río Tempisque. Small crocodiles called caimans also lurk in the dense reeds and mangroves. To get a look at them, head to **Refugio Nacional de Vida Silvestre La Enseñada,** which encompasses 940 acres (380 ha) of lagoons, creeks, and forest in the midst of a cattle and salt farm. A short way offshore, brown pelicans and other seabirds have colonized a rocky islet that is protected as **Reserva Biológica Isla Pájaros.** Only biologists may go ashore here, but you can view it from a boat.

The Hinterland

Inland from Puntarenas lies **Orotina,** a town known for its ceramics and fruit stalls that line

Highway 3. Orotina is gripped in a pincer by the **Río Jesús María** and **Río Cuarros,** which spill into the Gulf of Tivives. This wetland ecosystem supports crocodiles, monkeys, and all sorts of fabulous birds. Many of these species can be seen at the nearby **Mahogany Park,** where you can flit between the soaring trees on a zipline cable.

At San Juan de Mata, 4 miles (6.4 km) east of Orotina, **Parque Tropical Turubari** is an adventure theme park that sprawls across almost 500 acres (200 ha). The scenery ranges from tropical

Chorotega Pottery

In towns like Orotina and in every gift shop, pottery is sold with geometric and animal motifs emblematic of Costa Rica. Most of it comes from the village of Guaitíl, in Nicoya, where Chorotega indigenous people make vases, plates, and pots in traditional fashion by hand. Most pieces are ocher colored, with motifs in black, white and orange. Three-legged vases in the stylized form of cows are popular.

garden to primary forest. Some of the highlights in the park are a butterfly farm, a canopy tour, an aerial tram, and horseback riding. For an added kick, the "Sensational Cable" whisks you down a steep-angled zipline as you dangle prone in a harness, arms widespread, like a bird. ∎

Museo Histórico Maritino

- ✉ Ave. Central, Calles 5/7, Puntarenas
- ☎ 2661-5036
- 💲 $
- 🕐 Closed Mon.

www.museocostarica .com

Refugio Nacional de Vida Silvestre La Enseñada

- 🅰 Map p. 101
- ✉ 1.5 miles (2.4 km) S of Abangaritos, off Hwy. 132, 11 miles (17.7 km) W of Hwy. 1
- ☎ 2289-6655

www.laensenada.net

Mahogany Park

- 🅰 Map p. 101
- ✉ 10 miles (16 km) E of Orotina
- ☎ 2257-5149
- 💲 $$

www.canopytour .com

Parque Tropical Turubari

- 🅰 Map p. 101
- ✉ Turrubares, 4 miles (6.4 km) E of Orotina
- ☎ 2250-0705
- 💲 $$–$$$$

www.turubari.com

Inter-American Highway Drive

Highway 1, Costa Rica's umbilical cord to its neighboring states, sweeps through Guanacaste like a Roman imperial highway, linking historic cowboy towns. This section of the Inter-American Highway is magnificent, with the scenery gathering northward like a series of Hollywood stage sets making irresistible compositions for your camera.

Linking San José with Nicaragua, the road leads to sublime vistas of savanna ranged by *sabaneros*, with cattle against a backdrop of cloud-crowned volcanoes to the east. Side roads lead to national parks and wildlife reserves, but the beauty of the surrounding countryside—and the ugly quality of the road—may make you miss your turnoff.

The route described is a 128-mile (205 km) journey with only five traffic lights. The highway is mostly a fast two-laner; arrow-straight stretches unwind for miles, tempting motorists to speed. Don't do it! Traffic cops sit beneath shade trees, training their radar guns on unwary speedsters. Other caveats: Some potholes are big enough to swallow a cow; oncoming cars tend to swerve into your lane at inopportune moments; and behemoth, hell-bent trucks hurtle up and down the highway.

Begin in **Barranca ❶**, at the interchange of Highway 1 and Highway 27, the junction for Puntarenas (west), Jacó (south), and San José (east). This heavily trafficked southern section is a bit of a roller coaster and gives a foretaste of the beauty that lies ahead, with the western slopes of the Cordillera Tilarán pressing upon the road. After 4 miles (6.4 km), at **Santa Rosa ❷**, you will pass the turn-

off for Miramar and Refugio Nacional de Vida Silvestre Peñas Blancas. The road continues to dip and rise beyond **San Gerardo ❸**, where it becomes pinched between the hillsides of **Río Lagarto** valley, with long glades of trees leaning over the road like kissing lovers. The long grade descends to an iron-framed bridge over the river, 16 miles (26 km) north of Barranca. The turnoff for Monteverde is here, 100 yards (90 m) south of the bridge, poorly marked and well hidden. Slow down well before the bridge in either direction: *Túmulos*—road bumps—lie across the road and should *not* be hit at high speed.

Eight miles (13 km) farther along turn off for **Las Juntas de Abangares ❹**,

NOT TO BE MISSED:

Centro de Rescate Las Pumas
• Liberia • Parque Nacional
Santa Rosa

Also see area map p. 101

Barranca

128 miles (205 km)

3–8 hours, depending on stops

Bahía Salinas

Lago de
Nicaragua

Hotel Borinquen
Mountain Resort
Thermae
& Spa

1806m
Volcán Rincón
de la Vieja

C O R D I L L E R A

P.N. RINCÓN
DE LA VIEJA

Buena Vista
Mountain Lodge
& Adventure
Center

2028m
Volcán
Miravalles

1916m
Volcán Tenorio

Liberia

D E   G U A N A C A S T E

Tenorio

Corobicí

Laguna   de   Arenal

Liberia

8

Salto

Salto

Africa
Mía

Bagaces

7

Montenegro

Centro de
Rescate Las
Pumas

Tilarán

Corobicí

Piedras

Cañas

6

Santa
Elena

Monteverde

San
Miguel

Cañas

C O R D I L L E R A   D E   T I L A R Á N

PARQUE
NACIONAL
PALO
VERDE

Tempisque

Lajas

4

5

Las Juntas
de Abangares

Bebedero

Limonal

18

Arizona

1

Lagarto

Guacimal

Aranjuez

REFUGIO
SILVESTRE
DE PEÑAS
BLANCAS

Miramar

3

San Gerardo

Rancho
Grande

2

Santa
Rosa

San
Isidro

START

Golfo de Nicoya

1

Puntarenas

Barranca

0 _____ 20 kilometers
0 _____ 10 miles

Fancy hubcaps become status symbols in a culture fixated on social position.

a somewhat self-consciously attractive village strong on history tucked into the folds of the mountains, 4 miles (6.5 km) northeast of Highway 1. The town is famed for a gold rush that began in 1884 when nuggets were found in these hills, and *oreros*–miners–flocked from the four corners of the world to seek their fortunes. A patined bronze statue in their honor stands in a triangular plaza on the northeast side of town. A pint-size old steam train, *María Cristina,* sits in the main plaza.

Highway 1 edges north along the foothills, with the parched golden grasslands of the **Llanos San Pedro** to the west grazed by hardy humped cattle, ashen colored and well muscled, standing fixedly in the magnesium light like bovine figures on a Cretan urn. Rounded hillocks dot the plain. Deciduous trees speckle the scene in a palette of pastels: yellow *cortexa amarilla,* scarlet *poró,* and bright orange *spathodea,* locally known as the Jesús Cristo tree because it blooms blood red at Easter. You will notice the heat building as you move north,

with the warm air parting ahead of you like an unfolding blanket.

Beyond **Limonal** ❺, where Highway 18 peels off westward for the Río Tempisque ferry and the Península de Nicoya, continue straight 13 miles (21 km) to whitewashed **Cañas** ❻ *(tel 2669-0042),* a cowboy town par excellence and the gateway to Parque Nacional Palo Verde, Tilarán and Laguna de Arenal. On the far side of town is **Centro de Rescate Las Pumas** *(tel 2669-6044),* where Costa Rica's six species of cats—cougars, jaguars, jaguarundis, margays, ocelots, and "tiger" cats—prowl safely behind chain-link fences. The zoo takes in orphaned and injured cats and others confiscated from private owners and hunters. A stone's throw north, the highway crosses the 25-mile-long (40 km) **Río Corobicí.** Fed by dam-controlled runoff from Laguna de Arenal, it flows even in the midst of drought, and is popular for float trips—which are good for birding and for seeing howlers monkeying around above in the branches of stately mahoganies and ceiba trees. Rafting the river with **Safaris Corobicí** (*tel 2669-6091, www.nicoya.com*) takes several hours, and if time is short you can watch from the veranda of the roadside **Restaurante Rincón Corobicí** (see p. 246).

Beyond Cañas the road opens up, swinging northwest and ganing distance from the **Cordillera de Guanacaste** so that three volcanoes—Tenorio, Miravalles, and Rincón de la Vieja—are in glorious view, rather like a procession of monarchs. The sky is usually an exhilarating clear, deep blue; clouds pour up over the mountains from the Caribbean before burning off under the searing heat of the sun.

Continue north to **Bagaces ❼**, where Parque Nacional Palo Verde is signed to the west. The park is administered along with other regional parks and reserves as the **Area Conservación Tempisque** (see p. 112) whose administrative office is beside Highway 1, opposite the Palo Verde junction. Bagaces, which is also the gateway to Zona Protectora Miravalles, is intriguing for its old adobe houses. More appealing by far is **Liberia ❽**, 15 miles (24 km) farther north, the capital city of Guanacaste and another cowboy town known as the Ciudad Blanca (White City) for its dazzling white buildings. If low on gas, you should fill up at one of four stations at the junction with Highway 21 (which takes you to the airport and Nicoya).

Into Cattle Country

The final 33 miles (53 km) steal the show, with breathtaking landscapes seen fleetingly through gaps in the deciduous trees that flare with seasonal blooms. You are now in the heart of cattle country, hot as Hades in summer when a searing breeze rustles the grasslands that carpet the billowing flatlands, like a gently undulating sea of chartreuse. **Volcán Rincón de la Vieja** (5,925 feet/1,806 m) looms massively to the east, tempting you to tackle the blindingly white roads of exposed ignimbrite that lead to cattle haciendas where horseback rides are offered, and to the ranger stations that are gateways for hiking in Parque Nacional Rincón de la Vieja.

For an intriguing side trip, 11 miles (17.7 km) north of Liberia turn northeast from the highway. After 8 miles (13 km), you'll arrive at **Hotel Borinquen Mountain Resort Thermae & Spa** (see p. 248), a spa facility built around bubbling mud ponds good for rejuvenating thermal treatments. Monkeys abound in the surrounding forest. Nearby, the **Buena Vista Mountain Lodge & Adventure Center** (*tel 2690-1414, www.buenavistalodgecr. com*) is a ranch that offers horseback rides, a 0.6-mile-long (1 km) canopy tour, and a 1,312-foot (400 m) waterslide, plus occasional rodeos. Rustic yet charming cabins are available, and *típico* meals can be savored.

Farther north are the steep spires of **Cerro Cacao** (5,443 feet/1,659 m) and **Volcán Orosí** (4,879 feet/1,487 m) piercing the eastern sky. They both are accessed from **Potrerillos**, 15 miles (24 km) north of Liberia, with a police checkpoint at the junction. The two volcanoes are encompassed within **Parque Nacional Guanacaste** (see p. 126), a 208,800-acre (84,500 ha) expanse that spans the highway and tethers several disparate ecologically independent parks and reserves, including **Parque Nacional Santa Rosa** (see p. 127), accessed from Highway 1 about 5 miles (8 km) farther north and a must-see on any tourist's list. Wildlife viewing in Santa Rosa is staggering; more than one hundred mammal species include coatis, jaguars, ocelots, tamanduas, and three species of monkeys, plus a rainbow assortment of birds, all easily seen in the sparse dry forests. The park wears Costa Rica's history on its sleeve, too, at an old farmstead called **La Casona,** now a museum dedicated to the battle fought here in 1856.

From here, the traffic thins and it is a joy to zip along with the sun pouring down its warm rays, mantling the tousled palms and low-slung guanacaste trees in pools of sunlight and shadow. At last you reach **La Cruz ❾**, a sleepy town 14 miles (22 km) from the Nicaraguan border. A left turn at the town plaza in La Cruz leads 100 yards (91.4 m) to a vantage point over **Bahía Salinas** with great views.

Monteverde

The jewel in the crown of cloud forest reserves, Monteverde (officially the Reserva Biológica del Bosque Nuboso de Monteverde) is generously blessed with bucolic beauty. Its immense popularity has spawned contiguous forest reserves and a gamut of nature attractions that combine with Monteverde's world renown to draw tens of thousands of visitors annually.

Mist cloaks the ridge-top forests.

Monteverde
🅜 Map p. 101

Monteverde Institute Community Art Center
✉ Monteverde
☎ 2645-5053
www.mvinstitute.org

Serpentario Monteverde
✉ 400 yards (360 m) E of Santa Elena
☎ 2645-6002
💲 $$
www.snaketour.com

The community that translates as "green mountain" squats upon a plateau 3,500 feet (1,065 m) above sea level near the crest of the Cordillera de Tilarán; a vertiginous, bone-shaking road leads up to it from the Inter-American Highway. The setting is idyllically pastoral, with incandescent light intensifying the emerald greens of the mountain pastures grazed by black-and-white Holstein cattle. Ethereal mists swirl overhead and the crisp alpine climate is a constant interplay of drizzle and warming sunshine.

The heart of things is the village of **Santa Elena.** There is no village of Monteverde as such. Instead, this community of farmsteads sprawls upon the hillside that rises east of Santa Elena, accessed by paths that branch off the steep dirt road leading to Monteverde's cloud forest reserve. The community was founded in 1951 by Quakers who fled the draft in the United States and chose Costa Rica because it was neutral. *Cuaquerismo* (Quakerism) is still the bedrock of the local culture. Visitors are welcome to attend the Wednesday morning assemblies in the Friends' Meeting House.

The Quaker settlers have been at the forefront of conservation since Monteverde's inception: The kernel of today's world-famous cloud forest reserve was founded in

1972 jointly by the community and by scientists seeking to protect the watershed and the unique species it shelters. The contiguous communities have also been leaders in efforts to educate local children. The Centro de Educación Creativa, a local school for grades 1 to 12, has an environmentally based curriculum. The **Monteverde Cloud Forest Ecological Center** (tel 2645-5390) in Santa Elena and the **Monteverde Conservation League** (tel 2645-5003) work to educate youngsters in ecology, and train youths as naturalist guides to help move Tico families away from destructive practices and toward tourism-related income derived from conserving their green heritage.

Art is also vibrant here. Venues such as **El Sapo Dorado** (see p. 248) put on live musical performances. The **Monteverde Institute Community Art Center** has workshops with themes from basketry to wood turning from January to August with local craftspersons.

The Long & Winding Road

A narrow, serpentine road leads 3 miles (4.8 km) uphill, eastward from Santa Elena to the entrance to the Reserva Biológica del Bosque Nuboso de Monteverde (see pp. 110–111). The route—a quagmire in the wet season and cloudy with dust during rare dry spells—is lined with attractions, plus roughly 20 wooden mountain lodges with roaring log fires, to add to the alpine ambience.

To learn about amphibians and reptiles that can be encountered in the reserves, visit **Serpentario Monteverde** to see chameleons, poison-arrow frogs, and more than 20 species of snakes, including the fearsome fer-de-lance—safely behind glass. More than 500 orchid species are displayed at **Orquídeas de Monteverde,** an exquisite garden specializing in miniatures such as *Playstele jungermanniodes,* the world's smallest flower, best seen with the aid of a magnifying glass (thoughtfully supplied). And the **Ranario de Monteverde** (100 yards/90 m N of Monteverde Lodge, 2645-6320, $) is a herpetarium displaying frogs and other amphibians.

More than 500 species of butterflies flit about these hillsides and forests. More than 40 species are at **Monteverde Nature Center & Butterfly Gardens,** where North

La Lechería

Monteverde's original Quaker settlers established "the cheese factory" in 1953 to produce Gouda cheese. Twenty types of cheeses are now made, including Monte Rico, the local best seller. The original herd of 50 Jersey cows is today supplemented by milk from local farmers.

American biologist Jim Wolfe oversees a huge netted garden and two greenhouses that re-create three distinct natural habitats. The "Garden of the Butterflies" features an educational nature center, library, and weather center as well as exhibits of other colorful insects. Visit early- to mid-morning.

The first of its kind when it opened in 2006, **Bat Jungle** dispels common fearful notions about bats

Orquídeas de Monteverde
- ✉ 100 yards (90 m) S of Santa Elena bus station
- ☎ 2645-5308
- 💲 $$

Monteverde Nature Center & Butterfly Gardens
- ✉ 400 yards (360 m) W of Hotel Heliconia, Santa Elena
- ☎ 2645-5512
- 💲 $$

La Lechería
- ✉ 2.5 miles (4 km) E of Santa Elena on the road to Monteverde
- ☎ 2645-5436
- 🕐 Tours Mon.–Sat. 9 a.m. & 2 p.m.
- **www.monteverde.net**

Bat Jungle
- ✉ In front of Hotel El Bosque, Santa Elena
- ☎ 2645-6566
- 💲 $$
- **http://rwcarlson .googlepages.com**

**Reserva
Biológica del
Bosque Nuboso
de Monteverde**

Map p. 101

6 miles (10 km)
E of Santa Elena

2645-5122

$$

www.cct.or.cr

with exciting interactive exhibits that educate on the mammals' ecology and their critical importance to local ecosystems. Live bats swoop around behind a glass wall inside a re-created nocturnal habitat.

You can admire and purchase fine artwork at the **Hummingbird Gallery** (see p. 258), named for the scores of rufus-tailed, violet

slopes. The diversity of flora is astounding—from dwarf cloud forest atop the mountains to bamboo forests and even swamp forest in poorly drained areas. Zoological treasures include more than one hundred mammal species, all five species of cats, plus howler and capuchin monkeys, deer, and sloths. The

The Sky Walk provides a perfect vantage point for viewing wildlife in Reserva Bosque Nuboso Santa Elena.

saber-winged, and fiery-throated hummingbirds that zip in to feed on the patio of the gallery, where nature slide shows are given.

Reserva Biológica del Bosque Nuboso de Monteverde

This internationally acclaimed reserve straddles the Continental Divide. Its upper-elevation forests are cloaked year-round in swirling mists formed by humid Caribbean trade winds condensing as they are forced up and over the ridge crest. The reserve encompasses 25,730 acres (10,400 ha), covering eight distinct life zones on both the Caribbean and Pacific

400 species of birds here include 30 species of hummingbirds and the endangered three-wattled bellbird (named for the worm-like wattles that hang from its beak). About one hundred breeding pairs of quetzals also nest within the reserve, migrating to lower levels during the spring mating season.

The reserve is run by the Tropical Science Center of Costa Rica, which regulates visitor numbers and maintains the boardwalks that lead into the reserve. More rugged trails punch down the Caribbean slopes into true wilderness, spilling out in the Northern Lowlands. You can rent rubber boots to ease exploration. Guided nature hikes are offered, and well-versed nature guides can be hired.

Other Reserves

The **Reserva Bosque Nuboso Santa Elena,** which is owned and administered by the Santa Elena community, protects 1,440 acres (580 ha) abutting Reserva Biológica del Bosque Nuboso de Monteverde to the northwest. It has most of the same species as the larger reserve, plus endangered spider monkeys, which are absent at the Monteverde reserve. You can hike well-maintained trails or take to the air on a **Sky Walk** and follow half a mile (0.8 km) of "pathways" and suspension bridges through the treetops, while the **Original Canopy Tour** (tel 2645-5243, www.canopytour.com, $$$$) lets you glide through the treetops in a harness attached to a pulley.

The **Bosque Eterno de los Niños,** to the east and south of the Monteverde reserve, has grown to more than 50,000 acres (20,200 ha). Funded by children around the world and administered by the Monteverde Conservation League, it encompasses a similar range of terrain and flora and fauna to Santa Elena. Trails and facilities for visitors are minimal.

Sendero Bajo del Tigre (Jaguar Canyon Trail) grants access to a 44-acre (18 ha) portion of the reserve and features a forest habitat that's distinct in the region. It is especially good for seeing quetzals in springtime. There is an arboretum and self-guided interpretive trail, and kids will en-

joy the **Children's Nature Center,** with both live and static exhibits.

Nearby, the **Finca Ecológica Wildlife Refuge** is a 40-acre (16 ha) private reserve where trails grant access to montane moist forest and where coatis, capuchin monkeys, sloths, and countless bird species are easily seen with a guide.

Four miles (6.5 km) of trails crisscross the **Paradise for Bellbirds** (tel 2284-8590), another private reserve between Santa Elena and Monteverde, and renowned for its large population of three-wattled bellbirds, whose distinctive call—a metallic bonk—sounds hauntingly

---

Golden Toads

In 1967, an endemic species of vermilion toad was discovered in the Monteverde cloud forest, helping to spark the preserve's creation. Only the inch-long (2.5 cm) males are gold; the much larger females are black, speckled with vermilion and yellow. The last sighting was in 1988. This sudden demise has struck amphibious species worldwide.

---

through the forests. **Selvatura,** abutting the Reserva Bosque Nuboso Santa Elena, grants a similar entrée to a wildlife-rich world with treetop walkways, a zipline canopy tour, and guided nature hikes along forest trails. In the education center, the **Jewels of the Rain Forest Bio-Art Exhibition** features dramatic displays of arachnids and insects, comprising the largest such private collection in the world. ∎

Reserva Bosque Nuboso Santa Elena

- 🅰 Map p. 101
- ✉ 4.5 miles (7 km) NE of Santa Elena
- ☎ 2645-5390
- 💲 $$
- www.reserva santaelena.org

Sky Walk

- ✉ 1 mile (1.6 km) NE of Santa Elena
- ☎ 2645-5238
- 💲 $$$$$
- www.skywalk.co.cr

Bosque Eterno de los Niños

- 🅰 Map p. 101
- ✉ 2 miles (3.2 km) E of Santa Elena
- ☎ 2645-5003
- 💲 $$
- www.acmrcr.org

Finca Ecológica Wildlife Refuge

- ✉ 300 yards (274 m) W of Hotel Heliconia
- ☎ 2645-5869
- 💲 $$

Selvatura

- ✉ 4 miles (6.4 km) NE of Santa Elena
- ☎ 2645-5929
- 💲 $$$
- www.selvatura.com

Parque Nacional Palo Verde

Birders flock to rugged and remote Palo Verde, a marvelous repository of avian fauna at the mouth of the Río Tempisque, named for the green-barked *palo verde*, or horseshoe bean tree. Combining wet and dry ecosystems, it supports not only vast flocks of waterfowl but crocodiles and mammals that are easily seen in the sparse vegetation. ■

Parque Nacional Palo Verde
- 🅰 Map p. 101
- ✉ 18 miles (29 km) SW of Bagaces
- ☎ 2671-1290
- 💲 $$

A snowy cattle egret

Area Conservación Tempisque
- ☎ 2659-9194 or 2671-1290
- 💲 $

www.sinaccr.net

Organization for Tropical Studies
- ☎ 2240-6696
- 💲 Tours from $$$$

www.ots.ac.cr

The 32,266-acre (13,057 ha) park encompasses 15 distinct habitats, from mangroves, grassland, and scrubland to tropical dry forest. Along with the Refugio de Vida Silvestre Dr. Rafael Lucas Rodríguez Caballero and the Reserva Biológica Lomas de Barbudal, which abut it to the north, and Parque Nacional Barra Honda to the southwest, it forms the **Area Conservación Tempisque.** This vast arena of limestone ridges, marshes, and seasonally wet floodplains is best explored in the dry season (Nov.–April), when the drought-resistant trees shed their leaves and thirsty wildlife congregates at water holes.

Fed by the Río Tempisque and its mangrove-lined tributaries, this oasis in the heart of the Tempisque Basin forms an aquatic haven for birds—more than 300 species of neotropical birds roost or nest here. After the rainy season, the alluvial plains flood, and roughly 250,000 migratory ducks, geese, and other waterfowl winter alongside their native cousins. **Isla de Pájaros** has particularly prolific and unusual birdlife, including rarely seen great curassows. You also might see anhingas, white ibises, and the world's largest stork, the jabiru. Palo Verde also boasts the only permanent colony of scarlet macaws to inhabit a dry environment.

Trails lead to depressions that fill with water to become freshwater lagoons where birds and mammals gather at dawn and dusk. The park headquarters is situated in the old **Hacienda Palo Verde,** which is surrounded by mango trees that draw coatis, monkeys, peccaries, and white-tailed deer to feast. Anteaters and armadillos abound. Crocodiles—motionless as logs—rest on the muddy banks. There are modest

INSIDER TIP:

In the dry season, with the lack of foliage, wildlife is easy to spot. Early morning is always the best time to catch a glimpse.

—BEN HORTON
National Geographic field researcher

archaeological sites within the park, some in caverns gouged from limestone cliffs.

Local companies arrange guided natural history tours, as does the **Organization for Tropical Studies** *(tel 2661-4717),* which maintains a biological field station here. It's impossible to explore in the wet season other than by boat. Boats leave from Puerto Humo, on the riverbank 17 miles (27 km) east of Nicoya township on the Península de Nicoya. ■

Dry Forest Reserves

Costa Rican naturalists have worked hard to preserve the last vestiges of the dry forests that were so much a part of the environment in pre-Columbian days. Their chief success has been the establishment and maintenance of the Reserva Biológica Lomas de Barbudal, where the native woodland habitat supports a thriving range of wildlife.

Palo Verde adjoins two contiguous wilderness regions. To the north is the remote, infrequently visited 18,172-acre (7,353 ha) **Refugio de Vida Silvestre Dr. Rafael Lucas Rodríguez Caballero** (administered jointly with Lomas de Barbudal), which offers the same array of wetland and dry habitats and their associated wildlife. The refuge extends north to **Reserva Biológica Lomas de Barbudal,** enshrining 5,631 acres (2,279 ha) and protecting precious remnants of the dry deciduous forest that once encompassed most of the Tempisque Basin. The Río Cabuyo flows through the "bearded hills" reserve, named for the mosses that drape from tree branches, feeding lush riparian forest and drawing wildlife to its banks. There is a small **information center** and **museum** at the entrance beside the river. Nature trails lead from here to swimming holes.

Many endangered tropical hardwoods thrive here: the cannonball tree, mahogany, Panama redwood, rosewood, and sandbox, whose tart fruit is favored by scarlet macaws visiting from Palo Verde. Yellow-naped parrots and chicken-like great curassows, popularly hunted by *campesinos* for food, are among the many other bird species commonly seen, as are monkeys and a host of other mammalian frugivores that gorge on the seasonal fruits. The

A fire prevention ranger surveys the forest from a watchtower.

three parks form a vital migratory route for wildlife and are renowned for their huge insect populations, including hundreds of moth species and more than 250 bee species, pollinators for the flowering trees, which burst into often synchronized blooms in the midst of drought. ■

INSIDER TIP:

The Lomas de Barbudal reserve is best known for its long-term studies of bees and capuchin monkeys, but it is also an excellent place to observe birds and other animals, particularly in the dry season.

—SUSAN PERRY
National Geographic field researcher

Reserva Biológica Lomas de Barbudal

🅰 Map p. 101
✉ 4 miles (6.4 km) SW of Pijije (Km 221) on Inter-American Hwy.
☎ 2671-1290 (Bagaces office)
💲 $

Around Laguna de Arenal

Fringed by emerald mountains, Laguna de Arenal is a svelte platinum gem of entrancing beauty, enticing camera-toting visitors seeking pleasure in its picture-postcard appeal and proving the adage that a fine jewel is made complete by its setting.

Tropical flowers make a colorful frame for picture-perfect Laguna de Arenal.

Costa Rica's largest inland body of water occupies a depression that forms a gap between the Cordillera de Guanacaste and Cordillera de Tilarán. The lake, which covers 48 square miles (124 sq km), lies to the east of the Continental Divide at an elevation of 1,798 feet (548 m) above sea level. It is topped by mountains shimmering every shade of green in the clear light. To the south and west, carpets of green pasture unfurl down to the cobalt waters. To the north, primary tropical wet forest clambers up the steep slopes, dark and foreboding and raucous with the screeching of monkeys and birds. To the east, reflected in the silvery lake is the black, smoking peak of Volcán Arenal, brooding ominously between fits of pique.

Although the natural depression dates back about two million years, the lake was created by engineers in 1973 when **Presa Sangregado,** a 290-foot-long, 190-foot-high dam (88 m by 58 m), was built at the eastern egress, where the Río Arenal begins its cascade through a narrow gorge dropping down to the Northern Lowlands. The 20-mile-long, 3-mile-wide (32 km by 5 km) lake inundated several pre-Columbian sites plus the sole settlement in the valley. It is caressed by near-constant winds that whip up from the Caribbean and become compressed as they push through the gap. The howling winds, which can reach 60 mph (96 kph) in winter are beloved by windsurfers. They also drive the wind-turbines that have been erected atop the continental divide. Anglers, too, find their lures in *machaca*, mojarra, feisty *guapote*, or rainbow bass that give a good run on the end of a line. The **Rain Goddess** (see p. 260) now offers multiday fishing trips.

Laguna de Arenal lies 18 miles (29 km) east of Highway 1 on well-paved Highway 142, which leads via the trim agricultural town of **Tilarán** (on the western flank of the Continental Divide) to the lake around which it curls clockwise. The windswept western shore makes a perfect venue for the **Tilawa Viento Surf Center** (see p. 262) and **Tico Wind Surf Center** (see p. 262) from which active outdoorsy types set out to skim over the waves on their boards. For a diversion follow the signs to **Lago de Coter**, 3 miles (5 km) north of Laguna de Arenal. This much smaller body of water has been adopted as its own by the **Eco-Lodge** *(tel 2440-6768, www.ecolodgecostarica.com),* offering outdoor activities together with a small butterfly farm.

Capping the north shore is the small town of **Nuevo Arenal,** created in 1973 when its precursor was drowned with the lake's creation. This side of the lake is otherwise uninhabited except by the lakeside lodges spawned by the tourism boom. Immediately east of the town, the forested slopes crowd in with a murky closeness

and the pavement gives out, growing more deteriorated with every mile; often the narrowing causeway is blocked entirely by mud sluiced down from the rain-sodden hillsides. However, some stupendous vistas are thrown in as a reward for perseverance.

To catch your breath, stop in at **Toad Hall** (see p. 247), a café and general store where, ensconced in a hammock on the hillside veranda, you can savor divine desserts which are served as accompaniments to the incredible views. ■

A Tropical Eden

Explore nature's Eden via the sky tram at the **Arenal Rain Forest Reserve,** on the forested slopes southeast of the lake. A tram whisks visitors to a mountainside platform for stupendous views of the volcano and lake; for an adrenaline-charged return to Earth, try a zipline tour across the canyon.

Nearby, El Castillo hosts the **Butterfly Conservancy** *(tel 2306-7390, $$),* with a netted butterfly garden and fascinating insect displays; and the **Jardín Ecológico y Serpientes** *(tel 2358-6773, $$),* displaying snakes, lizards, and poison-arrow frogs. **Rancho Margot** offers a medley of wildlife and wilderness experiences. This organic farm doubles as an animal rescue center and offers kayaking, plus hiking and horseback rides into its rain forest reserve.

Arenal Rain Forest Reserve
🅰 Map p. 101
✉ 14 miles (22 km) SE of La Fortuna

Costa Rica Sky Adventures/ Sky Tram
☎ 479-9944
💲 $$$$$ (reservations required)
www.skytrek.com

Rancho Margot
🅰 Map p. 101
✉ 1 mile (1.6 km) W of El Castillo
☎ 2302-7318
💲 $
www.ranchomargot.org

Parque Nacional Volcán Arenal

Costa Rica's most dramatic attraction is known for the regularity of its eruptions, providing grandstand views of its fiery fury. The surrounding area offers soothing hot springs and fabulous hiking.

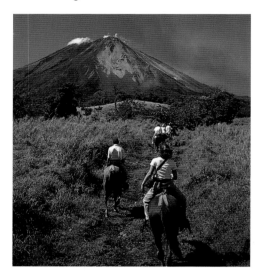

Exploring the flanks of Volcán Arenal by horseback

Parque Nacional Volcán Arenal

🏔 Map p. 101

✉ Hwy. 142,
   10 miles (16 km)
   W of Fortuna

☎ 2461-8499

💲 $$

www.sinaccr.net

The quintessential cone of Volcán Arenal (5,389 feet/1,643 m) is the focus of this national park, one of 16 protected reserves that make up the Arenal Conservation Area, which spans 12 life zones (see p. 42). The 26,690-acre (10,800 ha) park boasts two volcanoes; Volcán Arenal's minor sibling is **Volcán Chato** (3,609 feet/1,100 m), a dormant cone with a pea green lagoon within its collapsed crater.

Arenal began to emerge about one thousand years ago, pushing up like a great molehill. Understandably, pre-Columbian Indians considered it to be sacred. It barely hiccuped during the colonial era, then on July 29, 1968, a fateful earthquake awakened the slumbering giant, which exploded, decimating the nearby town of Tabacón. The volcano has simmered ever since and barely a day goes by without a minor eruption; there are usually smoking rocks rolling down the slopes. It is especially spectacular at night, when the pyrotechnics appear like giant fireworks and red-hot lava oozes down the steep slopes. Visitors are never assured of seeing an eruption, however, as clouds frequently obscure the summit. The best times are from around midnight to dawn and in dry season.

You can buy an interpretive mapguide at the ranger station, which lies 1 mile (1.6 km) south of Highway 142, 2 miles (3.2 km) east of Laguna de Arenal and 10 miles (16 km) west of La Fortuna (see p. 213), in the Northern Lowlands. Five separate trails lead to washes of lava fossilized by the sun. The **Arenal Observatory Lodge**, on the slopes of Volcán Chato, offers spectacular views, plus a museum on volcanology. You can also stay here (see p. 247).

The waters of **Río Tabacón** provide hot springs best enjoyed at **Tabacón Resort** *(tel 2460-2020, www.tabacon.com),* 1.5 miles (2.4 km) east of the park entrance, where mineral pools and a warm waterfall have been laid out amid gardens. Nearby, **Arenal Hanging Bridges** *(tel 2253-5080)* has a series of suspension bridges through the rain forest canopy and trails in the 618-acre (250 ha) forest reserve. ∎

Volcán Tenorio & Zona Protectora Miravalles

The twin volcanoes Tenorio and Miravalles lie within a few minutes drive of the Inter-American Highway, yet are a world away in their brawny, thick-forested, aloof appeal.

Mantled in savanna on the lower western slopes, montane rain forest at mid-elevations, and by cloud forest above, these contiguous volcanoes offer a pristine, wildlife-rich world seen by few tourists. Arrive prepared for the steep trails and you will be rewarded. Monkeys—howlers and white-faced capuchins—abound,

Mud pools gurgle up at both Tenorio and Miravalles.

INSIDER TIP:

The Llanos de Cortes waterfall on the Río Portrero makes for great swimming. Follow signs on the left of the road, beginning ten minutes past Bagaces as you drive from Cañas to Liberia.

—SUSAN PERRY
National Geographic field researcher

as do agoutis, pacas, and sloths. Visitors are as likely to see ocelots, cougars, or jaguars here as anywhere else in the country.

You'll reach **Parque Nacional Volcán Tenorio** from the Inter-American Highway north of Cañas via Highway 6, which dips and rises for 21 miles (34 km) northeastward to Bijagua, nestled between the volcanoes. **Heliconia Ecolodge** *(tel 2470-0115, www.losheliconias.org)* makes a perfect base for exploring

Volcán Tenorio. The arduous **Lago Las Dantas Trail** deposits you atop the volcano at 6,256 feet (1,916 m), where tapirs *(dantas)* reliably show up at dusk to sip at the crater lake. Another trail leads to a waterfall of the **Río Celeste** and on to mud pools and fumaroles.

The best way to reach Zona Protectora Miravalles is from Bagaces by Highway 164, arching over the volcano's western haunch. Miravalles (6,653 feet/2,028 m) is known for its fumaroles, sulfur springs, and mud pots, easily seen at **Las Hornillas,** where the Costa Rican Institute of Electricity harnesses superheated vapor for geothermal energy. To bathe in the thermal waters, head to **Centro Turístico Yökö.** Nearby, **Las Hornillas Volcano Activity Center** *(tel 2839-9769, www.lashornillas.com)* has trails through an active crater, plus therapeutic mud baths. ∎

Parque Nacional Volcán Tenorio

- Map p. 101
- 21 miles (34 km) NE of Inter-American Hwy. off Hwy. 6
- 2466-5982
- $$

Zona Protectora Miravalles

- Map p. 101
- 23 miles (37 km) NE of Inter-American Hwy. off Hwy. 164
- 2671-1290
- $$

Centro Turístico Yökö

- Map p. 101
- 2.5 miles (4 km) S of Guyabo, Hwy. 164
- 2673-0410
- $

Volcanoes

Volcanoes are the primary vents in the Earth's crust through which hot molten rock—magma—wells up from the mantle of liquid rock beneath the crust. There are more than 600 active volcanoes in the world today. Costa Rica has 7—another 60 are dormant or extinct—making it one of the most volcanically active areas of the world.

Volcanoes are associated with the movement of rigid sections of the earth's crust, or lithospheric plates, that ride atop the asthenosphere (mantle) made of hot, plastic rock—a process called plate tectonics proposed by the German geophysicist Alfred Wegener in 1915 and adopted by earth scientists in the 1960s. The major and minor plates pull apart or press against one another. Convection currents rise from deep within the Earth's interior, much like a pot of boiling water, to fuel the process, bringing

Cocos plate

molten material to the surface and forming necklaces of fire along the fractured joint lines.

There are two types of volcanoes. Basaltic formations, such as those of Hawaii and Iceland, are normally associated with rifts in the Earth's crust, as in mid-ocean ridges, where the plates are pulled apart by convection. The runny magma tends to pour steadily from the volcano. Costa Rica's volcanoes are andesitic types, taking their name

Caribbean plate

Subduction trench

Pyroclastic
flow

Magma
chamber

Molten lava pours down Volcán Arenal,
adding color to the tropical night.

from the Andes Mountains and
typical of coastal ranges worldwide.
They occur where two or more plates are
thrust together, forcing the thicker continental
plate to ride over the ocean plate, which is absorb
ed back into the mantle. The friction created
melts the rocks as one plate grinds beneath the
other under enormous pressure, producing molten magma. Silica-rich magma is stiff and viscous
and results in high, steep-sided, cone-shaped
volcanoes that typically rise 100 miles (160 km)
or so inland from the subduction trench.

Unlike basaltic volcanoes, these andesitic
volcanoes are usually highly explosive. Once a
volcano has been primed, the violence of an
explosion depends on the relative content of
water and silica, and the shape of the conduit.
Water, which seeps into magma chambers
through the ground and via subduction zones,
provides the explosive potential of steam.

Hikers negotiate a volcanic block
cascade at the base of Volcán Arenal.

Viscous, silica-rich magma prevents the steam from rising to the surface so that the pressure builds like a pressure-cooker. Silica-rich magma also tends to clog quickly, plugging the vent like a cork in a champagne bottle. When a dome is plugged by solidified lava, the magma becomes supersaturated with pressurized steam until the volcano is at a breaking point; it then ruptures explosively at its weakest spot. Sometimes the explosion may occur via a fissure to the side. When blasted laterally from the volcano, the lava appears as a *nouée ardente* (glowing cloud), a superheated avalanche of steam, red-hot ash, and poison gases that can roar downhill with the force of a thermonuclear explosion.

Vegetation for many miles around is often bowed down by blankets of hot mineral-rich ashes that eventually are transformed into fertile soils. The vast quantities of dust and energy released sometimes spawn great clouds above the volcano charged with lightning and triggering tremendous storms that dump torrential rain.

At other times, the walls protecting a crater lake may rupture and the waters cascade downhill, turning into a *lahore*–a massive avalanche of mud up to 100 feet (30 m) deep and laden with trees, boulders, and other debris, as destructive in its power as a runaway locomotive.

Volcanoes can lie dormant for centuries before awakening with a series of mutterings that grow gradually stronger and more ominous. There may initially be emissions of sulfurous gas, followed by puffs of steam, a series of small earth tremors, and clouds of ash. Then—*BOOM!* The mountain detonates either all at once or in an ongoing series of thunderous explosions that may end in a cataclysmic detonation. In lush tropical settings such as Costa Rica, such pronounced eruptions often set off stampedes of wildlife, so that any settlements in their path of flight become overrun with ants, centipedes, and a variety of venomous snakes.

Several volcanoes, such as Miravalles and Rincón de la Vieja, are associated with features such as the fumaroles and boiling mud pools that occur where rainwater seeps into the porous ground above the volcano's magma chambers. The water in the permeable ground thus becomes superheated from below like a giant boiler, with water temperatures reaching 5,000°F (2,760°C). Rising back to the surface, the water begins to boil as pressure is released, emerging in great vents of steam or bubbling mud pools, or mingling with cool groundwater to form hot springs, like those at Tabacón on the flanks of Volcán Arenal.

Sign of an active giant: Arenal puffs clouds of smoke and ash on a daily basis.

Liberia

Striking for its simple adobe architecture, this whitewashed provincial capital resounds to the clip-clop of hooves, providing an intriguing sun-bleached way station beneath the gaze of Volcán Rincón de la Vieja and handily situated as a springboard for Parque Nacional Santa Rosa and the Península de Nicoya.

Liberia is without a doubt the most colonial of Costa Rican cities, redolent with its own unique charm that owes much to its historic core of red-tile-roofed buildings made of ignimbrite, a diatomaceous rock as white as burning magnesium for which Liberia is known colloquially as the Ciudad Blanca, or White City. Many venerable old homes feature *puertas del sol,* corner entranceways with doors on two sides as an effective air-vent system.

Situated at the heart of Guanacaste and cattle country, Liberia is wholeheartedly a cow-boy town and plays host to several lively fiestas, when townsfolk dress up in traditional garb for the parades, mariachis serenade, and rodeos provide entertainment. The liveliest fiesta is the **Día de Guanacaste,** on July 25, which is a celebration of Guanacaste's independence from Nicaragua in 1812. The festive spirit is resurrected in early September for **Semana Cultural.**

The town sprawls eastward from the Inter-American Highway and is accessed along a broad tree-shaded boulevard, Avenida Central, which features a life-size bronze cowboy statue, the **Monumento Sabanero** *(Calle 10).* The avenue slopes gently past the peaceful tree-shaded main plaza *(bet. Calles 2 & Central),* which

The venerable Iglesia La Agonía attests to the antiquity of Liberia, the charming provincial capital of Guanacaste.

EXPERIENCE:
Local Fiestas

Costa Rica's annual calendar is a whirligig of fiestas. Almost every town has its *fiestas patronales* (patron saint's day), typically featuring a traditional rodeo and *tope* (display of horse-riding skills), fireworks, a beauty pageant, and traditional music and dance. Religious *feriados* (holidays) and processions are held during Easter Holy Week *(Holy Thurs.–Easter Sun.).* And the nation's indigenous communities hold their own unique and colorful festivals that incorporate Catholic and pre-Columbian traditions. The **Instituto Costariccense de Turismo** website has a complete listing of events: *www.visitcostarica.com.*

A fiesta worth catching takes place in Liberia every July 25, when Día de Guanacaste celebrates Guanacaste's independence from Nicaragua with a rodeo, bullfights, and folkloric dancing.

All comers can jump into the ring to prove their bravado before a raging *toro*.

Liberia

⚐ Map p. 101

Visitor Information

✉ Ave. 6 & Calle 1

☎ 2666-1606

🕐 Closed Sun.

💲 $

Hacienda La Chácara

✉ 3 miles (5 km) W of Liberia

☎ 2350-1627

🕐 Closed Sun.

💲 $$$$$

www.hacienda lachacara.com

features a historic church. The old town hall, or *ayuntamiento*, locally called the **Gobernación,** is topped by a fluttering Guanacastecan flag. The plaza ends at the **Iglesia La**

Rodeo

Costa Rica's cowboy *(sabanero)* culture has been part of the traditional Guanacastecan way of life for centuries. Just as in North America's Wild West, breaking wild broncos was a part of the daily routine, while riding bulls served to prove a sabanero's manhood—a tradition kept alive at *fiestas cívicas*, where *recorridos de toros* (bull rodeos) are everyone's favorite part of the entertainment. The sabaneros ride the enraged bulls bareback and display their rope-handling skills, accompanied by much whooping and hollering.

Agonía *(Calle 11, tel 2666-0107),* an enchanting church dating from 1854, which is simply adorned within. Time your visit for mid-afternoon—the only time the church is open—when women gather daily for the rosary. Be sure to stop in, too, at the **Casa de la Cultura** *(Ave. 6 & Calle 1, tel 2666-0135, closed Mon.).* This charming example of typical Guanacastecan colonial architecture houses both the regional tourist information office and the **Museo de Sabaneros,** in which weathered saddles and other memorabilia pay homage to local cowboy culture.

The old city jail, one block east of the plaza, still functions as such, and boasts crenelated towers at each corner. The *comandancia* (police station), on the northwest side of the plaza, displays a large archaeological collection. Calle Central, east of the plaza, has been renamed **Calle Real** and boasts many fine colonial structures.

A lively setting for relaxing is the **Hacienda La Chácara** (see p. 261), a sugarcane farm and cattle ranch where *sabaneros* and hostesses in traditional dress serve up a cocktail of typically Guanacastecan music, dance, and food, with bull-riding thrown in to boot. Visits to this Fiesta Brava can be arranged through the Casa de la Cultura.

Liberia has taken on an increasingly important role in recent years, following the 2002 opening of the Daniel Oduber International Airport, 7 miles (11 km) west of town. It is mostly used by charter flights delivering package vacationers to the beaches about an hour away. ■

Parque Nacional Rincón de la Vieja

The velveteen cone of Rincón de la Vieja (meaning "old woman's corner") makes a theatrical backdrop that dominates the landscape of northern Guanacaste and offers active travelers a variety of invigorating attractions within the 34,800-acre (14,080 ha) park.

This volcano is the grandest of the fiery giants that make up the Cordillera de Guanacaste. The park spans an elevation range of 5,000 feet (1,525 m) and protects markedly different vegetation on its rain-soaked Caribbean and

The active volcano Rincón de la Vieja on a quiet day

INSIDER TIP:

The Rincón Corobici restaurant, 10 minutes past Cañas on the Inter-American Highway to Liberia, offers excellent ambience, particularly in the evening when flocks of egrets come to roost outside.

—SUSAN PERRY
National Geographic field researcher

seasonally parched Pacific sides—from savanna to montane rain forest to upper-level dwarf cloud forest. Rain clouds cloak its summit, spawning swift rivers that radiate in every direction, gouging deep ravines into its concave sides. The volcano has two peaks—**Rincón de la Vieja** (5,925 feet/1,806 m) and **Santa María** (6,256 feet/1,916 m). The nine craters include the Rincón peak's bowl-shaped, gently steaming **Von**

Seebach Crater—a reminder that this is an active volcano.

Casona Santa María is an adobe farmstead housing the park headquarters and an exhibition. The hacienda was purchased by Costa Rica's national park service from former U.S. President Lyndon Johnson. The headquarters and the **Las Espuelas Ranger Station** (Las Pailas), farther north, can be reached from Highway 1 via dirt roads.

The volcano's lower western slopes are mostly occupied by working cattle haciendas, which provide lodging and horseback riding. Key among them are **Hotel Hacienda Guachipelín** (see p. 262) and the **Rincón de la Vieja Lodge** (see p. 248), where you can traverse the forest canopy in a harness. The many mammal species here include tapirs, seen at higher elevations. ∎

**Parque Nacional
Rincón de la
Vieja**

🅰 Map p. 101
✉ 16 miles (26 km)
  NE of Liberia
☎ 2661-8139
💲 $$
www.sinaccr.net

A Walk to the Top of Rincón

The soaring mass of Rincón de la Vieja draws hardy hikers up its jungle green sides in search of rare wildlife and the satisfaction of ascending the summit. Hot springs, mud pools and "ovens"—evidence of vibrant geothermal activity—make diverting landmarks along this rewarding two-day walk. Take a tent and sleeping bag for the night on the mountain.

It is a straightforward hike, beginning at the **Casona Santa María ❶** Ranger Station on the southwestern side of the volcano. There is a basic campsite 400 yards (365 m) from the hacienda, or you can sleep in dormitory-style accommodations in the ranger's *cabina* by prior arrangement *(tel 2661-8139 or 2233-4160)*. You will need to bring your own sleeping bag and blanket. The hike to the summit covers 8.3 miles (13.3 km), with an elevation gain along the way of 3,614 feet (1,100 m).

Head out along the old roadway that leads west from the ranger station. After half a mile (0.8 km) you pass the **Sendero Bosque Encantado ❷** ("enchanted forest trail") on your left, making an interesting side excursion into old growth forest that abounds with orchids, including *guaría morada,* the national flower. The main trail continues 0.6 mile (1 km) to another side trail marked **Aguas Termales ❸** ("hot springs"); you should save your visit for the return journey (when you will be better able to appreciate a soothing celebratory soak). About 2.5 miles (4 km) farther along take the right-hand trail, uphill, at the Y-junction. The landscape opens up at the top and you can make a short detour—marked as **Pilas de Barro ❹** ("mud pots")—to where boiling mud explodes in great belching bubbles and the superheated mineral-rich pools are tinged with a rainbow of colors. Stay away from the overhanging edges of the pools; they are often insecure underfoot.

Continuing along the main path, you will pass through former cattle pasture that is being slowly regenerated with native forest. Steam rises mystically over the treetops, luring you along another short trail to your right that de-

posits you at **Las Hornillas ❺** (ovens), where fumaroles (vapor geysers) hiss like teakettles, spitting up odoriferous steam and gases—hydrogen sulfide and sulfur dioxide. Again, use caution when walking around the "stove pipes." Continue half a mile (0.8 km) on the steep main trail to the **Río Colorado ❻**, where there is a basic campsite on the riverbank. Just beyond that is the **Las Espuelas Ranger Station ❼**, sometimes called Las Pailas, 4 miles (6.4 km) from Santa María. You can pitch a tent here. Plan on getting up around sunrise and ascending to the summit in time to beat the clouds, which generally tend to form in mid-morning.

It is a 6-mile (10 km) ascent through pre-montane and montane rain forest festooned with bromeliads and epiphytes, including hundreds of the park's renowned orchid species. The forests vibrate with birdsong; look for the turkey-like black guan, a raucous bird that hops about in the branches. The trail snakes upward through bamboo, then through stunted dwarf forest near the edge of the tree line. About 3 miles (5 km) above Las Pailas, you will pass a meager campsite—set amid the gnarly copey clusia, a cloud forest species with waxy leaves that perfume the air. You are now only a few hundred yards below the ridge, attained by a scramble up loose lava scree. **Von Seebach Crater ❽** is half a mile (0.8 km) away. The way is marked by cairns, but it is easy to lose the trail when the clouds set in, whipped up by a cold wet wind swirling about the summit like a mad maypole. Volcanic eruptions occasionally obliterate the summit trails.

With luck, the sky will be scintillating blue overhead and the last 1.5 miles (2.5 km) across the lava-strewn saddle to the smoking summit of **Volcán Rincón de la Vieja** will be clear. You can revel in the vast views, which are phantasmagoric in their infinity, with the Pacific and Caribbean shimmering on hazy horizons. With proper planning, you might camp on the beach at **Laguna los Jilgueros** ❾, which is southeast of the Von Seebach Crater and surrounded by a ravaged moonscape like a scene from Dante's *Inferno*—there is a chance at both dawn and dusk to watch super-shy tapirs drink at the pea green lake that sits in the saddle between the Von Seebach and Rincón Craters.

This hike is best tackled in the dry season (*Nov.–April),* with January to April being the best months. Ticks and other biting insects inhabit the thick elephant grass that can grow as tall as your shoulder. It is recommended that you wear long pants tucked into socks, especially around campsites. Take insect repellent, sleeping bags, good camping gear, and warm, water-repellent clothing—as much as 200 inches (500 cm) of rainfall douses upper elevations each year.

NOT TO BE MISSED:

Aguas Termales • Pilas de Barro • Von Seebach Crater

- Also see area map p. 101
- ► Casona Santa María
- ⬌ 8.3 miles (13.3 km)
- ⏲ 2 days (1 night on mountain)
- ► Laguna las Jilgueros

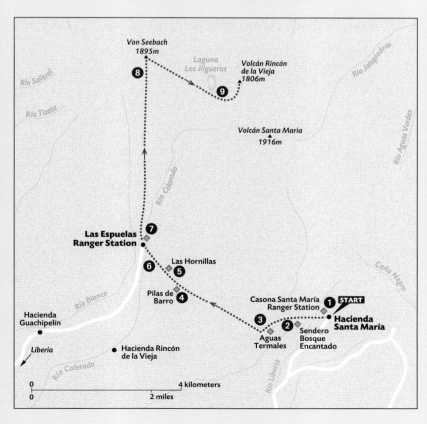

Parque Nacional Guanacaste

Wellspring of the Río Tempisque, the watershed of the Orosí and Cacao Volcanoes was protected in 1989 and enshrined in this national park, a rugged, rarely visited world devoid of tourist services and appealing to those with a spirit of adventure.

Armadillos are at home in the dry forests of Guanacaste.

Parque Nacional Guanacaste

🏛 Map p. 100
☎ 2666-5051
💲 $$

The 207,560-acre (84,000 ha) Parque Nacional Guanacaste is the keystone in the 2,742,810-acre (1,110,000 ha) **Guanacaste Conservation Area**—an amalgam of contiguous parks and reserves. The park is a mosaic extending from lowland savanna to cloud forest atop its two volcanoes: **Orosí** (4,879 feet/1,487 m) and **Cacao** (5,443 feet/1,659 m). Much of the former cattle range at their western bases is being returned to dry deciduous forest in an effort to fuse the disparate native habitats and create migratory corridors for the profusion of wildlife found here.

The main entrance to the park is via **Quebrada Grande,** accessed from Highway 1 at Potrerillos via a 6-mile (10 km) dirt track. Beyond **Gangora,** hike 3 miles (5 km) to the **Cacao Field Station** on the south side of Cacao at 3,350 feet (1,021 m). From here, you can hike through cloud forest, watching for wildlife as you head for the summit, 1.5 miles (2.5 km) beyond Cacao. Another trail slopes down through montane moist forest and seasonally dry moist forest to the spot where **Maritza Field Station** is linked to Highway 1 by a trail from the Cuajiniquil turnoff. Maritza, the main ranger station, has basic dormitories. You can hike to the summit of Orosí via **El Pedregal,** an archaeological site where pre-Columbian petroglyphs peer through mosses on the **Llanos de los Indios** (the plain of the Indians).

On the Caribbean side, the **Pitilla Field Station**, set in premontane rain forest (good for birding) is reached via a dirt track from **Santa Cecilia,** 18 miles (29 km) east of Highway 1. ■

Parque Nacional Santa Rosa

This national park, the first to be established in Costa Rica, boasts an abundance of human and natural history. Sea-girt on two sides, Santa Rosa has fine beaches washed by rugged surf. Good camping facilities help make this one of the country's most appealing wildland attractions.

Its 122,350 acres (49,512 ha) enfold ten distinct habitats, home to about 115 mammal species and more than 250 species of birds—all easily seen amid the predominant landscape of dry deciduous forest, where anteaters, deer, iguanas, and howler, spider and white-faced monkeys are preyed upon by five species of cats, including rarely seen jaguars. In the scorching heat of the dry season, the forests explode in vibrant color, birds and beasts gather at precious water holes, and wildlife viewing is easy for patient and silent visitors.

The park is divided into two sections. To the south is the larger **Santa Rosa sector,** where armored vehicles rust amid tall grass west of the entrance gate, marking an ill-fated invasion by Nicaraguan troops in 1955. The park headquarters, which houses a museum, is a replica of **La Casona,** where in 1856 Costa Rica's ragtag army of peasant soldiers routed William Walker and his mercenaries (see p. 29). The original hacienda was destroyed by arsonists in 2001.

Numerous trails branch out from La Casona through the dry forest. The **Naked Indian Trail,** named for the gumbo-limbo trees whose peeling bark exposes a red trunk, makes an easy loop; the **Los Patos Trail** is good for spotting rare mammals. Visitors with rugged four-wheel-drive vehicles can descend the 8-mile (13 km) track to

Playa Naranjo, which is flanked by headlands and beloved by surfers for its tubular waves. Nearby **Playa Nancite** is off-limits to visitors, for here one of nature's miracles plays out each summer as Ridley turtles—as many as 10,000 at a time—swarm ashore to lay eggs. Crocodiles lurk in the mangrove swamps that back the shore.

To the north is the **Murciélago sector,** which extends along the

INSIDER TIP:

Swimmers and even waders should avoid estuaries and the mouths of rivers, particularly at Playa Naranjo and Playa Potrero Grande, where crocodiles are a real and present danger.

—MICHAEL H. GRAYUM
National Geographic field researcher

Santa Elena peninsula. Rarely visited white-sand beaches sparkle like diamonds. Bring camping gear. Pelicans and frigatebirds wheel overhead. **Hacienda Murciélago,** once owned by the Nicaraguan Somoza family, was the site for Oliver North's secret airstrip during the Contra era. Fishermen will take you to the **Islas Murciélagos** (Bat Islands), renowned for their superb diving potential. ∎

Parque Nacional Santa Rosa

- Map p. 100
- 4 miles (6.4 km) W of Hwy. 1, 20 miles N of Liberia
- 2666-5051
- $$

More Places to Visit in Guanacaste

Africa Mía

One senses that this wildlife park's giraffes, ostrich, and zebras feel at home in the grasslands of Guanacaste, which closely replicate the African savannas. Opened in 2005, Africa Mía hosts a panoply of creatures. Giraffes stretch their necks to nibble thorny acacias as antelope, eland, gemsbok, and warthog trot past. The park also has camels, watusi cattle, and peacocks, as well as monkeys and other animals endemic to Costa Rica. Guided tours are offered aboard open safari vehicles.
www.africamia.net   ⚠ Map p. 101
✉ 5 miles (8 km) S of Liberia ☎ 2661-8161 🕐 Guided tours 💲 $$$

Bahía Salinas

Several fine beaches line this flask-shaped bay, including the sugar white Playa Pochotes, which is backed by glistening salt pans picked upon by wading birds and mangroves where crocodiles lurk. The bay is enfolded to the south by Punta Descartes, which opens to the northwest and garners winds off the

INSIDER TIP:

In season (mainly June to September), restaurants in La Cruz offer a delicious *refresco* (drink) made from the fruits of *pitahaya*, a cactus native to the region.

—MICHAEL H. GRAYUM
National Geographic field researcher

open sea making it a nirvana for windsurfers, who are served by the Eco-Wind Surf Center *(tel 2228-7146, www.ecoplaya.com)* and Kite Surf Center *(tel 8826-5221, www.suntoursand fun.com)*. A few rustic fishing hamlets remain, tethered to a hard life at sea. A craggy isle covered with drought-resistant shrubs—
Refugio Nacional de Vida Silvestre Isla

Bolaños—studs the bay. This island is a protected nesting site for frigatebirds, American oystercatchers, brown pelicans, and boobies. The island is off-limits to visitors.
⚠ Map p. 100 ✉ 4 miles (6.4 km) W of La Cruz

Ecolodge San Luís & Research Station

This private research center of the University of Georgia welcomes tourists to its 165-acre (67 ha) reserve and working farm in the small hamlet of San Luís, whose residents are being integrated into a project to develop a model for sustainable development. Montane wet forest and cloud forest provide opportunities for birding and viewing wildlife on foot or horseback, and visitors are welcome at the research facilities for lectures and classes on local ecology, or to help out in the fields. Participatory educational workshops and cultural activities are offered for both resident students and ecotourists. Accommodation is available in comfortable *cabinas*.
www.uga.edu/costarica   ⚠ Map p. 101
✉ 5.5 miles (9 km) SE of Santa Elena
☎ 2645-8049

Parque Megafauna Monteverde

Children will love this educational facility situated beside the Inter-American Highway. The main draw is a mile-long (1.6 km) loop trail featuring life-size sculptures of dinosaurs and other prehistoric creatures, as well as eight extant Costa Rican animals threatened with extinction. You can walk through an enclosed butterfly garden, and a gallery featuring a portion of the Jewels of the Rain Forest Bio-Art Exhibition (much of the exhibition is at Selvatura; see p. 111), with fascinating insects from around the world. The park is designed to educate about ecological fragility.
www.monteverde.net   ⚠ Map p. 101
✉ Chomes de Puntarenas, on Inter-American Hwy. ☎ 2638-8229 💲 $$

Diamond-dust beaches, emerald golf courses, superb sportfishing, scuba diving, and surfing in an otherwise sleepy region

Nicoya

The hawksbill turtle has a beaklike mouth.

Nicoya

Sand and sea are the names of the game in Nicoya, a mountainous crab-claw peninsula that hooks around the Golfo de Nicoya. Visitors love its white-sand beaches, unique in the nation, and enjoy a six-month dry season, when the sun dances incandescently on the sea beneath a virtually ever blue sky.

Northeastern Nicoya is an undulating plain fringed by wetlands fed by the Río Tempisque—fabulous for birding—that open into the Golfo de Nicoya. The region's few towns speckle well-paved Highway 21, which runs north to south down the plain, east of the low-slung mountain range. Much of the land has been denuded for cattle ranching, the predominant industry since colonial days. Prior to the depredations of the Spanish, the peninsula was the home of the Chorotega, whose legacy can be seen in distinctive pottery. Tiny Guaitíl is at the center of a Chorotega cultural rebirth.

Local life still revolves around fishing and ranching, and Nicoya moves at a sleepy bucolic

NOT TO BE MISSED:

pace. A half dozen burgeoning resorts dot the rugged shoreline, though Tamarindo is the only coastal town of significant size or sophistication. While all of San José seems to descend on weekends and holidays, Josefinos tend to flock to a fistful of beaches, and visitors find it relatively easy to escape the madding crowd despite the fact that three-quarters of the nation's hotel rooms are along Nicoya's sugar white northern beaches. Two experiences stand out: watching leatherback turtles nesting at Playa Grande, and witnessing the awesome spectacle of the *arribadas*—synchronized nesting of Ridley turtles at Playa Ostional that occurs at predictable times every year. Parque Nacional Marino Las Baulas and Refugio Nacional de Vida Silvestre Ostional protect these precious havens.

In southern Nicoya, the lush tropical moist forests of Reserva Natural Absoluta Cabo Blanco and Refugio Nacional de Vida Silvestre Curú protect their own wildlife wonders.

Recent years have brought an explosion of construction. Due to a contentious decision during the Rafael Calderón administration (1990–1994) to target the untapped deluxe vacation market, Bahía Culebra is shaping up to become a mini-Cancún. The Gulf of Papagayo Project stalled in the mid-1990s under charges of corruption and environmental abuse; it is now moving ahead under more careful surveillance. The nation's second airport—the Daniel Oduber International Airport—opened in 1995, fostering a huge boost to the region.

New golf courses offer relaxed pleasures, though they are draining the drought-stricken region's aquifers. Waves pump ashore, providing thrills for surfers. Despite low visibility, scuba divers rave about eye-to-eye encounters with giant groupers and other fish. And sportfishing is world-class, centered on the Golfo de Papagayo, where marlin run thick and fast. Ashore, cavers can escape the searing summer heat in the cool caverns at Parque Nacional Barra Honda.

Most roads linking coastal hamlets are unpaved and covered with fine dust in the dry season and are hard to access in the rainy season except in a four-wheel-drive vehicle. Some rivers still need to be forded—adding to the adventure of exploring—and due care should be taken. ∎

Golfo de Nicoya

The isle-studded, mangrove-fringed Golfo de Nicoya is a slender sleeve of shallow water separating the Península de Nicoya from mainland Guanacaste, exposing mudbanks during low tide and forming an aquatic haven for crocodiles and profuse birdlife.

Roseate spoonbills feed in the mudflats of the Golfo de Nicoya.

Golfo de Nicoya
Map p. 131
Visitor Information
☎ 2685-5417
🚢 Coonatramar R.L. (Naranjo): 2661-1069; Ferry Peninsular (Paquera): 2641-0515
💲 $ For ferry (passenger), $$ For ferry (car)
www.coonatramar .com

Settlements are few along the banks of the gulf, where mangroves envelop vast acres fed by the Río Tempisque's sediment-laden waters. **Tempisque Safari Ecological Adventure** *(2 miles/ 3.2 km N of Puerto Humo, tel 2698-1069, $$$$)* is a wildlife center exhibiting scores of exotic creatures; a guided tour includes a boat trip.

The largest of the gulf isles is **Isla Chira,** a favored nesting site for frigate birds, which hang in the sky like kites. Roseate spoonbills grub about in the mudflats and salt pans—*salinas*—from which a few hardy inhabitants eke a living extracting salt. Precious nesting sites of brown boobies, frigatebirds, and other seabirds are also protected on scrub-covered **Isla Guayabo** and **Isla Negritos,** two tiny isles at the mouth of the gulf. Guayabo,

uniquely, is a winter nesting site for peregrine falcons. Both isles are off-limits to visitors. Dolphins and whales cavort in the open waters.

Isla San Lucas, off the southeast tip of Nicoya, was a sacred burial place for pre-Columbian Indians. In the 19th century its barren wastes were turned into a hellish prison. Ghosts seem to haunt the forlorn isle, a national wildlife refuge being developed for tourism; the prison is to be restored as a museum, and nature trails are being laid out. Visits can be arranged with tour companies in Puntarenas.

Tempisque bridge spans the wide mouth of the river, linking Highway 1 with the Península de Nicoya. Ferries operate between Puntarenas and **Playa Naranjo** and **Paquera,** providing access to southern Nicoya. ■

Parque Nacional Barra Honda

Riddled with stygian chambers like holes in Swiss cheese, Barra Honda— unique in the nation— offers cavers an exciting challenge. Not all of its appeals are subterranean, however; above ground, its hiking trails thread a wonderful, wildlife-rich world of dry forests.

Barra Honda comprises a 5,670-acre (2,295 ha) wilderness of pitted limestone uplands that rise west of the Río Tempisque floodplain, from which eons of weathering have carved out caverns. Of the 42 known caverns, only 19 have been explored. The deepest, **Caverna Santa Ana**, extends to almost 800 feet (240 m) underground.

The only cavern open to the public in Parque Nacional Barra Honda is the **Caverna Terciopelo,** accessed by a ladder that descends 100 feet (30 m). The cavern boasts

Stalactites drip from the ceiling of the Terciopelo Cave in Barra Honda park.

INSIDER TIP:

Drink the water in Nicoya—it has off-the-charts levels of calcium, and if you drink enough, it amounts to taking a supplement.

—DAN BUETTNER
National Geographic author

spectacular dripstone formations, including one known as "The Organ" that fills the cave with haunting chimes when struck. Terciopelo's three distinct chambers are named for the formations within, with the most obvious being **Mushroom Hall.** In the **Hall of the Caves,** it's fun to project your imagination onto the crystal

structures—a lion's head? entwined lovers? And **Caverna Nicoya** contains pre-Columbian remains dating back two millennia.

Barra Honda also is ideal for terrestrial exploration—convoluted trails stipple the hilly, scrub-covered landscape. Pick up trail maps and hire a guide at the ranger station. **Cerro Barra Honda** (1,459 feet/ 445 m) offers a tremendous vantage over the country below. Take plenty of water, plus a camera to capture anteaters, monkeys, scarlet macaws, or other exotic denizens of the relatively open dry forest.

The caves have "homegrown" species; among them are endemic blind fish and salamanders that have adapted to absolute darkness. The bats here have deposited so much guano that one cave is called **Pozo Hediondo**—"fetid pit". ■

Parque Nacional Barra Honda

🔺 Map p. 131

✉ Hwy. 18, 10 miles (16 km) E of Nicoya

☎ 2659-1551; or guided tours c/o Asociación de Guías Ecologistas de Barra Honda: 2659-1716

🕐 Closed Easter week

💲 $$$

Mangroves

Mangroves are a distinctive tropical habitat with halophytes—plants that exist in salty conditions—although they also thrive in fresh water. Five species—black mangrove, buttonwood mangrove, red mangrove, tea mangrove, and white mangrove—are found in Costa Rica, and each has evolved its own unique method for ridding itself of salt—from secreting it through leaf glands to preventing it from being taken up by the roots.

The glutinous mud that mangroves call home is so dense that it contains almost no oxygen. The mud is also acidic, and the nutrients upon which mangroves feed lie not deep down but near the surface, where decomposing organic debris drops from above or is deposited by the receding tides. Thus, most mangroves form aerial roots, drawing oxygen in through spongy bark and giving the appearance that the mangroves are walking on water. Black mangroves differ, preferring to send forth underground roots that sprout long lines of offshoots, called pneumatophores, that stick up from the ground like upturned nails.

The tangled spiderweb of interlocking roots helps stabilize land, protecting it against erosion by waves while acting as a pioneer land builder by filtering out the silt brought down to the sea by Costa Rica's turbulent rivers. The nutrient-rich muds foster the growth of microorganisms that form a food source for larger species, such as shrimps and snails. Many creatures live on the buffet, including stilt-legged wading birds that pick tiny, shrimp-like amphipods from the glistening mud. The redolent mangroves are also important nesting sites for cormorants, pelicans, kingfishers, and frigatebirds, which deposit their guano atop

Crab

Kingfisher

Red mangrove

Frigatebirds

the mud, fertilizing the mangroves and speeding their growth.

Mangroves also serve as aquatic nurseries for creatures such as crustaceans, fish, oysters, sponges, and even stingrays and baby sharks. These habitats are so important to marine species that the destruction of mangroves has an inordinately harmful effect on the entire marine ecosystem.

Raccoons, lizards, and snakes abound, too, as do insects, including a species of mangrove ant that is only found here. Many animal species are unique to mangroves, such as the yellow mangrove warbler (*Dendroica petechia*), an insectivorous migrant that's present from August to May; and the arboreal mangrove tree crab (*Aratus pisonii*), a leaf-eater that is stalked by another arboreal crab species, *Goniopsis pulchra*, and is thereby forced to spend a life away from water in the crowns of the mangroves.

Mangrove Proliferation

Mangroves propagate swiftly, and often establish new colonies far removed from the parent plants—this is thanks to a splendid reproductive system. The mangrove blooms briefly in spring, then produces a fruit from which sprouts a fleshy seedling shaped like a plumb bob. This pendulous seed, which can grow to a foot (30 cm) in length, germinates on the branch then drops like a dart. At low tide, they stick upright in the mud and instantly send out roots. Seeds that hit water float on the tides like half-filled bottles. They are astoundingly hardy and can survive sea journeys of several hundred miles, often traveling for a year or more before touching a muddy shore, where they anchor themselves and begin a new colony.

A seedling can grow 2 feet (60 cm) or more within its first year. By its third year it has become a mature bush and begins sprouting seeds that establish themselves around the parent's prop roots. Within a decade a mangrove colony has been formed and the process of silting is well under way as the colony creeps farther and farther out to sea. As the land builds up in their lee, they may eventually strand themselves high and dry and die on land of their own making.

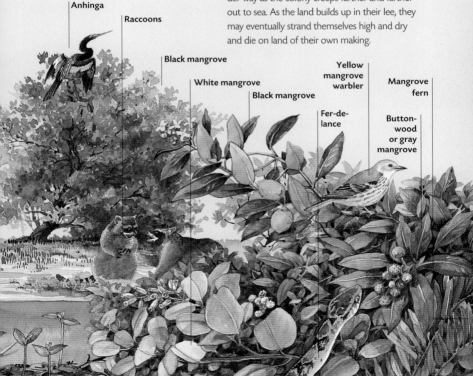

Anhinga

Raccoons

Black mangrove

White mangrove

Black mangrove

Yellow mangrove warbler

Mangrove fern

Fer-de-lance

Button-wood or gray mangrove

Heartland of the Chorotega

Nicoya's heartland maintains a regional pride as the wellspring of a newly resurgent Chorotega heritage. The countryside is still worked in the traditional manner: Ox-drawn plows and carts are familiar icons tended by *campesinos* in soiled cotton linens and straw hats, each with a machete and a gourd canteen by his side.

The solemnity of Catholic processions finds form in Nicoya's Easter festivities.

Nicoya

 Map p. 131

By some accounts the oldest town in the country, **Nicoya,** administrative capital of the region, serves agricultural communities for miles around. A settlement existed here and served the same purpose prior to arrival of Spanish conquistador Gil González Dávila (?–1526), who named his colony for the local Chorotega Indian chief. Nicoya was the center of the Chorotega culture, and well-defined trade routes radiated as

far as Nicaragua. The nation's oldest extant church—**Iglesia de San Blas**—is here, a squat 16th-century adobe affair on the tree-shaded main plaza. The town comes alive each December 12 for the **Festival of La Virgén de Guadalupe,** a celebration that combines Catholic beliefs with the Chorotega legend of La Yeguita, which tells of two brothers spared by a mare from killing one another over a Native American princess. There are no other attractions, but the town has several banks, a hospital, and other key services.

Santa Cruz, situated 12 miles (19 km) north of Nicoya astride Highway 21, is renowned as the "folkloric city" for its civic fiestas. Each January 15 and June 25, beer and *chicha* (corn liquor) flow freely, citizens kick up their heels by dancing the Punto Guanacasteco, and the bullring resounds with the cheers of spectators. **Plaza Bernabela Ramos** has some notable statues plus a ruined colonial church and the modern building that has replaced it.

Guaitíl

There is a splendid charm and vitality to this hamlet, 7 miles (11 km) east of Santa Cruz. Guaitíl

marks the heart of the renaissance of Chorotega cultural pride, and local residents carry proudly the dark, robust facial features of their Indian forebears.

INSIDER TIP:

In Nicoya, many people reach a healthy age of ninety. In fact, this piece of real estate has one of the highest rates of centenarians in the world. So if someone you meet looks like they are a hundred, they probably are.

—DAN BUETTNER
National Geographic author

Santa Cruz
 Map p. 131
Visitor information
✉ One block S of Plaza de los Mangoes
☎ 2654-4123

Jade

The pre-Columbian Chorotega were masters at crafting jade. They used the string-saw carving technique, in which a hole is drilled and a string is inserted through it, then repeatedly drawn back and forth like a saw. This enabled them to create detailed figures of frogs, crocodiles, eagles, jaguars, and humans; the latter were often shown engaging in the most worldly of pleasures. Archaeologists have found no local source for the semiprecious stones, which more advanced northern cultures introduced to the Chorotega around 400 B.C.

The village, which squats amid parched cattle country, is lined with stalls of pottery made in the traditional manner: turned by hand on wheels and fired in wood-fueled, open-hearth kilns, finished with jade grinding stones that local matriarchs believe have magical powers and then painted with animal motifs.

The artists are organized in cooperatives. Visitors are welcome to stop at family workshops where the homespun craft is performed in front yards beneath spreading shade trees. The **Eco-Museo de la Cerámica Chorotega** *(tel 2681-1563, www.ecomuseosanvicente .org),* in the adjoining village of San Vicente, honors the cultural traditions and is a center for several annual fiestas. ∎

The Northern Beaches

Cupped by bays and coves gilded with a dusting of sugary beaches, northern Nicoya's rugged shoreline—the nation's laid-back "riviera"—provides a variety of choices for vacationers seeking sun, sand, and sea. All of Costa Rica's ubiquitous nature highlights are on hand.

White sand lines the protected cove at Playa Flamingo.

The Northern Beaches

 Map p. 130

Easily accessed from Liberia along well-paved Highway 21, Nicoya's northern beaches extend southward from the Bahía Culebra to Bahía Tamarindo in scalloped relief, set in deep basins which are separated by scrub-covered headlands. The nation's major resort developments are concentrated here. Playa Flamingo, Playa Hermosa, Playa Tamarindo, and the all-important Bahía Culebra are nodes for the burgeoning flock of self-contained upscale resort complexes that are reshaping the face of the region. Between them are lesser resorts where local fishing communities cling to a simple life by the sea. Sportfishing, scuba diving, and surfing are favorite pastimes. And golfing is new to the region—a contentious use of precious water and a source of growing conflict between government and local communities concerned about the effects of tourism on their lives.

Weekends and holidays get crowded, when Josefinos flood lemming-like from the capital to sun themselves and swim in the surf conjured by the breeze from the warm Prussian blue sea. Be warned, because the most popular beaches get terribly littered in the wake of these weekend invasions.

Bahía Culebra

This massive horseshoe-shaped, cliff-rimmed amphitheater is held in the pincers of **Punta Ballena** to the south and **Península de Nacascolo**—an archaeologically precious region of pre-Columbian sites—hooking around to the north. Its setting is dramatic and the sublime vistas across its aquamarine waters are made more so by the dramatic backdrop of Rincón de la Vieja volcano looming to the east.

The previously uninhabited Bahía Culebra is at the center of the largest development project attempted in this part of the Central American isthmus. The Gulf of Papagayo Project, named for the vast gulf into which the bay opens, was initiated in 1993 by the Rafael Calderón administration with ambitions to push Costa Rica into the big league of resort tourism—with 15,000 hotel rooms, two golf courses, self-contained residential communities, a massive marina, and other resort facilities. Most of the score of beaches that nestle in coves that rim the bay between rocky headlands have been earmarked for development.

Take your pick from several completed resort hotels at **Playa Arenilla** and **Playa Buena** to the south, and **Playa Manzanillo** and **Playa Nacascolo** to the north. The 2003 opening of the **Four Seasons Resort at Papagayo Peninsula** (see p. 248) brought a new panache to the project, along with a championship golf course

that was created by visionary designer Robert Trent Jones, Jr. A Ritz-Carlton is due to open here. And the **Ellerstina Costa Rica Polo & Equestrian Beach Club** (*www.ellerstinacr.com*), overlooking Playa Cabuyal, serves its upper-crust members. Nearby, the **Witch's Rock Canopy Tour** offers a zipline jaunt through the forest.

Around Playas del Coco

Playas del Coco is a small fishing village popular with Tico youth who pack in as tightly as sardines on weekends and holidays to tan

Many of the beaches that are frequented by tourists are also frequented by thieves. Leave all of your valuables at home or bring them with you to the beach, keeping the car empty.

—BEN HORTON
National Geographic field researcher

their bodies, play volleyball, and flirt beneath the palms. Their informal hangout is the small central plaza, ringed by bars. Pelicans perch on the fishing boats anchored in the mile-wide (1.6 km) horseshoe-shaped bay. The noisy partying climaxes in January with the civic fiesta's beauty contests, rodeos, and over-the-top revelry.

To the north lies **Playa Hermosa**, a gray-sand beach with tide pools at the northern

Witch's Rock Canopy Tour

✉ 22 miles (35.4 km) W of Liberia

☎ 2667-0661

💲 $$$$

end. The beach is in the throes of development yet manages to retain its laid-back appeal. This is enhanced toward its southern end by nets that drape old fishing shacks drawn up on the sands. Farther north, on the southern cusp of Bahía Culebra, lies **Playa Panamá,** offering grand views and a choice of moderately priced to deluxe accommodations. You can hike inland 600 yards (550 m) to the community of **Panamá** along a dirt road good for spotting wildlife.

A dusty dirt road leads 2 miles (3.2 km) south from Playa del Coco to **Playa Ocotal,** a secluded beach with tide pools that is known as a base for sportfishing and scuba diving excursions in the Golfo de Papagayo. The snorkeling is good, particularly at Las Corridas, where sea horses float among soft corals.

Around Playa Flamingo

No, there are no flamingoes in Costa Rica, and this beach resort is also called **Playa Blanca**—White Beach—particularly by promoters. In combination, its sparkling sands and setting are as alluring as any other beach in the nation. The stunning mile-long (1.6 km) scimitar of silver lamé unspools within the cusp of rocky headlands speckled with luxurious villas of wealthy Ticos and gringos.

Despite the presence of a few modest resort hotels, the colloquial title of Acapulco of Costa Rica belies the paucity of nightlife and other tourist facilities. Flamingo was once Nicoya's major sportfishing center; the marina closed in 2005.

The commercial development extends along Bahía Potrero, whose gray sands sweep north to the rustic fishing hamlet of **Potrero**

and, beyond a rocky headland, to the white sands of **Playa la Penca,** backed by a vital mangrove estuary good for spotting coatis, iguanas, monkeys, parrots, and roseate spoonbills amid the rare saltwater forest. The dirt road dips and rises, eventually depositing you at **Playa Pan de Azúcar,** a splendid cove. **Isla Santa Catalina,** a precious nesting site for seabirds such as bridled terns, is just offshore. Northeast of Portrero, the **Congo Trail Canopy Tour** *(tel 2666-4422)* offers zipline thrills, plus snake and butterfly exhibits.

The explosion that has come to Nicoya's beaches has hit the funky fishing hamlet of **Brasilito,** a mile (1.6 km) south of Flamingo, with megaton force. This community has been forced into the modern era by the construction of the **Paradisus Playa Conchal Beach & Golf Resort** (see p. 249), set immediately south of the village at **Playa Conchal.** The half-mile-long (0.8 km) beach of powdered sugar—actually pulverized seashells—shelving into warm turquoise waters is ideal for snorkeling. Water sports are available. The spectacular 18-hole golf course, studded with lagoons, is another creation of Robert Trent Jones, Jr. Alas, much of the wildlife that once inhabited the dry forests hereabouts has been chased away.

From **Huacas,** 4 miles (6.4 km) south of Brasilito, a dirt road leads west via **Matapalo** to **Playa Real,** a secluded gem of a beach hidden within the cusp of headlands. You can wade in tidal pools, and a rugged islet attached to the shore by a short isthmus provides a nesting site for pelicans that perch on rustic fishing boats that bob in the bay. ∎

Parque Nacional Marino Las Baulas

This marine national park encompasses a stunning long beach white as flaming magnesium and known as the nation's preeminent nesting site for leatherback turtles. Waves pound ashore all year, drawing the surfing cognoscenti.

Parque Nacional Marino Las Baulas protects 1,100 acres (445 ha) of Pacific shoreline and an additional 54,000 acres (21,850 ha) out to sea, safeguarding environments vital to the endangered leatherback turtle, whose females lay their eggs on **Playa Grande.** The females come ashore to lay during the cool nights, October through April. They prefer a full moon—a boon to tourists who can watch the awe-inspiring spectacle under the scrutiny of local guides. This magnificent white beach unfurls along the north shore of **Bahía Tamarindo** and suits the leatherback's need for a deep-water approach that minimizes the distance it has to crawl to nest.

The park's creation in 1990 is seen as a victory over commercial egg poachers, including members of the local community who today derive their livelihood protecting the turtles for ecotourism income.

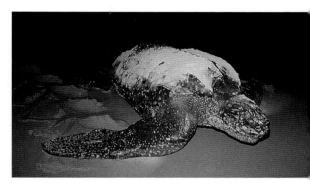

Heeding instincts, a female leatherback drags herself ashore.

Although visitation is regulated., developers have nonetheless been permitted to erect hotels abutting the beach, boosting the numbers of trampling feet. To learn about turtle ecology, visit **El Mundo de la Tortuga,** a superb museum with audiovisual displays.

Dry forest and mangroves behind the beach are laced by trails good for spotting birds, crocodiles, and monkeys. ∎

Parque Nacional Marino Las Baulas
- 🅰 Map p. 130
- ✉ 5 miles (8 km) W of Huacas & 35 miles (56.3 km) W of Liberia
- ☎ 2686-4967
- 🕐 Turtle watching Oct.–April
- 💲 $

El Mundo de la Tortuga
- ✉ 200 yards (183 m) inland from the beach
- ☎ 2653-0471
- 🕐 Call for details
- 💲 $$

Leatherback Turtles

The world's largest reptile traces its lineage back to the antediluvian dawn. Males can grow to 10 feet (3 m) in length and weigh 2,000 pounds (900 kg)—and yet their brains weigh less than an ounce (28 g)! The leatherback has an internal skeleton and a leathery exterior of thick, cartilaginous skin, and is insulated from extreme cold by a thick layer of fat. This turtle is powered by huge flippers and tapered for streamlined motion. It can dive to 4,000 feet (1,220 m) in pursuit of jellyfish—its favorite food.

Marine Turtles

Seven species of fast, graceful marine turtles (Chelonidae) roam the world's oceans, from the diminutive Ridley, which rarely grows to more than 30 inches (75 cm) long, to the Cadillac-size leatherback. The turtle, which boasts a remarkable physiology that includes an external skeleton and a toothless jaw that acts like a paper cutter, dates back 200 million years, proving an incredible ability to adapt and endure.

A biologist releases olive Ridley hatchlings from a study nest at Playa Nancite.

Turtle populations are endangered worldwide and several species are nearly extinct. After the discovery of the New World, turtle meat became a staple of seamen cruising these waters. Turtles also were harvested to indulge Europe's taste for turtle soup. In Costa Rica, the green turtle population has been reduced to only three remaining major nesting sites.

Turtle populations continue to face domestic pressures, although all of the nation's major nesting sites are now protected. Raw eggs, valued for their reputed aphrodisiac properties, are imbibed in local cantinas, and nest poaching still goes on despite laws against it. Natural predators also snatch up hatchlings as they flail their way to the sea. Adult turtles face capture in shrimpers' nets or by commercial pirates. And turtles nest on the same beaches beloved by developers.

Nature's Miracle

Adults navigate vast distances, often crossing oceans, on foraging forays. Males spend their entire lives—up to half a century—at sea; only females return to land. Each female returns to shore every two or three years during high tide, usually by night, and often under the full moon to ease her climb up the beach.

After finding a spot above the high tide mark, she uses her front flippers to scoop a hollow and digs a pit with her back flippers. In this she lays an average of 107 spherical, golf-ball-size eggs. "There is a great deal of biology packed into that figure," said turtle expert Dr. Archie Carr (1909–1987). "The whole race and destiny of the creature are probably balanced at the edge of limbo by the delicate weight of that magic number." Any fewer and predators prevail and the species wanes.

Once the first egg drops, the turtle will proceed with egg laying oblivious to any intrusion. After shoveling the sand back into place and thumping it down with her body, she flings sand about to hide her nest, then heads back to sea. If no longer producing eggs, she swims off. If the turtle is still receptive, she will remain near shore where the males take turns mounting her. Females often nest several times in one season.

Whither the Youth?

After incubating in the warm sand for around seven weeks, the eggs hatch. Hatchlings are usually the same gender in each nest, due to the temperature of the sand (cooler for males), with 2 to 3°F (1°C) making the difference. They emerge from their eggs together, dig their way up to the surface, and wait until night to make their mad dash to the sea.

Baby turtles are programmed to head for the ocean horizon and are easily disoriented by other lights. Hotel guests who leave their lights on often find baby turtles at their door. Once at sea, hatchlings paddle maniacally for several days. Then they are rarely seen until some come back as big as a chest of drawers. Recent genetic evidence bears out the long-held belief that turtles return to their natal beaches. How they accomplish this navigational feat is unclear.

Turtle Viewing

Five species of turtle lay their eggs on Costa Rica's beaches, and can be seen nesting at any time of year. Leatherback turtles (see p. 141) come ashore from October through April at Playa Grande in Nicoya and at Refugio Nacional de Vida Silvestre Gandoca-Manzanillo on the southern Caribbean shores. Green turtles can be seen at Gandoca-Manzanillo and Parque Nacional Tortuguero, where as many as 35,000 turtles come ashore between June and November. The most awe-inspiring site is the *arribada* (see p. 144), or mass nesting, of olive Ridley turtles occurring at Playa Ostional and Playa Nancite *(off-limits)* in Nicoya, where tens of thousands of turtles swarm ashore during full moons between July and December. Hawksbill turtles nest singly and in far smaller numbers at select beaches throughout the nation, and loggerhead are found on the Caribbean shore.

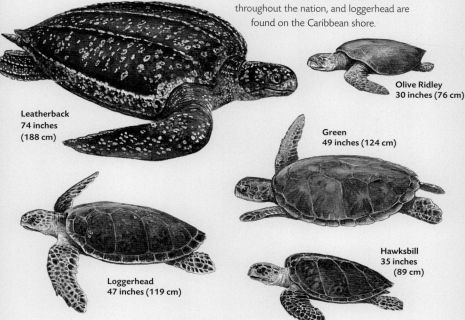

Leatherback
74 inches
(188 cm)

Olive Ridley
30 inches (76 cm)

Green
49 inches (124 cm)

Loggerhead
47 inches (119 cm)

Hawksbill
35 inches
(89 cm)

EXPERIENCE: Saving the Turtles

Marine turtles have lived in the oceans for more than 100 million years. Today, the world's six marine turtle species are endangered. Tens of thousands of turtles are killed every year by fishing gear and ocean pollution. Others are illegally killed for food or commercial reasons, while poaching of eggs and destruction of nesting sites are among a panoply of other threats that threaten to reduce the populations beyond the point of no return (see pp. 142–144). The turtles' future existence could depend on human efforts to safeguard their precious nest sites.

Guided by an internal compass, a green turtle follows its destiny.

Costa Rica is a world-leader in efforts to protect marine turtles. As part of a plan designed to help save the Ridley, for example, the residents of Ostional hold a unique license to harvest the turtles' eggs and sell them. Because so many turtles pack the beach during the *arribada* (or egg-laying) season, eggs laid on the first few nights are often destroyed by turtles on subsequent nights. At the same time, incubating eggs are often dug up and destroyed when another arribada occurs before the first batch has hatched. By allowing local residents to legally harvest a quota of eggs—those that would likely be destroyed anyway—during the first 36 hours of each arribada, bacterial infections have been reduced and significantly more eggs are hatching.

Similarly striving to help save marine turtles, several conservation organizations run programs in Costa Rica that are always seeking volunteers.

Caribbean Conservation Corporation: The largest and oldest of the entities active in Costa Rica, CCC focuses its efforts at Tortuguero, one of the world's oldest and largest green turtle nesting sites. Volunteers are needed to assist with turtle tagging and monitoring. *(4424 NW 13th St., Ste. A1 Gainesville, FL 32609, tel 2224-9215 or 352/373-6441, www.ccc turtle.org)*

Earthwatch: Working at Playa Grande (see p. 141), Costa Rica's principal leatherback nesting site, volunteers count eggs; protect hatchlings; monitor, measure, and tag nesting turtles; and perhaps even help attach transmitters to adults to monitor their migration. *(3 Clock Tower Pl., Ste. 100, Maynard, MA 01754, tel 978/461-0081 or 800/776-0188, www.earthwatch.org)*

Sea Turtle Conservation Network: This organization focuses its marine conservation efforts at Cahuita, Gandoca-Manzanillo, Ostional, and the Osa Peninsula's Playas Carate and Pejeperro. You'll patrol beaches to keep poachers away, collect research data, and give a helping nudge to newborn hatchlings flailing to reach the sea. *(P.O. Box 2164 3000, Heredia, Costa Rica, tel 2261-3814, fax 2260-5789, www.latin americanseaturtles.org)*

Tamarindo

This once sleepy fishing village has been catapulted from obscurity to become Costa Rica's most sophisticated and popular beach resort, offering a base for exploring Parque Nacional Marino Las Baulas and the wildlife-rich ecosystems adjoining it.

Tamarindo looks west over a deep bay and the long silver sweep of Playa Grande, which is separated from the village by the Río Matapalo unfurling majestically to the northeast. The beach is lackluster, though tide pools offer interest at low tide. **Isla Capitán** beckons a short distance offshore, and pelicans perch on fishing boats at anchor.

Surfers come here for the waves. Several local tour operators run surf trips to more remote spots, though, including the unspoiled **Playa Langosta.** Sportfishing and scuba diving trips are also available. And **Blue Trax Tours** (tel 2653-

Sunset is the only real reason to stash the surfboard at Tamarindo.

1705) offers ATV adventures.

Tamarindo's greatest natural appeal is the **Refugio Nacional de Vida Silvestre Tamarindo,** protecting 1,000 acres (400 ha) of mangrove-riddled wetlands and dry forests at the estuary of the Río Matapalo, which extends inland from Parque Nacional Marino Las Baulas. Monkeys can sometimes be seen cavorting on at the tip of Playa Grande. Crocodiles lurk in the brackish waters. Waterfowl abound. And ocelots, deer, and several other endangered species have reappeared in recent years. You can hire canoes or take organized boat excursions.

Tamarindo's growing popularity has spawned chic cafés and upscale hotels under the aegis of European and North American proprietors. Be warned, however, that crime is now rife, and drugs and prostitution have tarnished its reputation. ∎

Watch Out!

Try to avoid becoming one of the many victims of scams and petty crimes:

- Keep your credit card in sight during transactions, and make sure the imprints are destroyed.
- If you get a flat tire, be wary of "good Samaritans" offering to help but who may try to rob you.
- Never accept unsolicited help with your luggage, as you may never see it again.
- Watch merchants when you pay with a large bill. They may switch it with a counterfeit and try to unload the bogus bill back on you, claiming it's a fake.

Refugio Nacional de Vida Silvestre Tamarindo

- 🅰 Map p. 130
- ✉ Tamarindo
- ☎ 2296-7074
- 🕐 Call for details
- 💲 $$

Refugio Nacional de Vida Silvestre Ostional

Around Ostional there are almost always turtles in the water, particularly during the July to December nesting season, when battalions of helmeted turtles storm ashore in an astonishing example of synchronized reproduction.

The Nosara beaches, with Playa Ostional in the background

Refugio Nacional de Vida Silvestre Ostional

✉ 3 miles (5 km) W of Nosara

☎ 2682-0470

💲 $$

This 613-acre (248 ha) reserve protects three critical nesting sites for olive Ridley turtles—Playa Ostional, Playa Nosara, and Playa Guiones—extending along 9 miles (15 km) of shoreline between **Punta India** and **Punta Guiones.** The refuge centers on

the coastal hamlet of **Ostional** midway down a gray-sand beach that is one of the world's most important turtle hatcheries. The Ridley, known as the *lora,* has hit on a clever idea to ensure its survival: an occurrence known locally as an *arribada.* Playa Ostional is one of two arribada sites in Costa Rica and nine worldwide.

During full moon periods, tens of thousands of turtles congregate offshore, then surge ashore like armored battalions. Each arribada can occupy an entire week as wave after wave of turtles come ashore: often as many as 150,000! Stragglers come ashore at other times of year, as do leatherbacks between October and January.

All beach-going visitors must report to the **ranger station** or the **turtle cooperative** *(tel 2682-0470, http://ostionalcr.tripod.com)* in the village center. Guides *($$)* are compulsory for visits, and a video is shown prior to stepping onto the beach.

Southward Playa Ostional melds into **Playa Nosara,** which had its first arribada in 1997. The recovery of the turtle population at Playa Ostional has been such a success that overpopulation has resulted in spillover onto adjacent beaches. Both these beaches are backed by steep forest-clad hills that are good for hiking. The **Río Montaña** and **Río Nosara** tumble down from the hills and snake across the coastal plain, forming a tangled estuary of mangroves and forests full of play-acting monkeys, coatis, iguanas, and more than 190 species of birds, including parrots. You can take several boat trips locally.

Nosara

The Río Nosara is hemmed by a craggy headland, **Punta Nosara,** in whose lee a cove with a blow-hole and cave full of bats lies cupped by **Punta Pelada.** Punta Pelada offers stupendous views over **Playa Guiones,** a wide coral-colored beach arcing 2 miles (3.2 km) south. Tidal pools tempt you to wade the knee-deep shallows, and rollers crash ashore, luring the many surfers.

Behind Playa Guiones is Beaches of Nosara, a residential area for North Americans and Europeans, which extends up into the Fila Hor-migosa Mountains. A few cafés and small hotels, plus the **Nosara Yoga Institute** *(tel 2682-0072; see side-bar below),* nestle amid the foliage, connected by a maze of dirt roads. Howler monkeys are often seen by the beach. Crocodiles, monkeys, and a wealth of other creatures are easily seen in **Reserva Biológica Nosara** *(tel 2682-0035, www.lagarta. com),* at the river estuary.

An airstrip is located in the middle of the main village, **Bocas de Nosara,** an attractive rustic hamlet redolent of *campesino* life. It is on the south bank of the Río Nosara, 3 miles (5 km) inland of Playa Guiones. ∎

EXPERIENCE: Learn Yoga in Costa Rica

Seeking to balance mind, body, and spirit in an environment of natural beauty and tranquility? Costa Rica has evolved as one of the world's premier destinations for yoga vacations. Barely a year goes by without half a dozen new venues being added to the roster. A handful are dedicated yoga facilities. Others range from wilderness lodges or deluxe beachfront hotels with yoga dojos where you can harmonize the rhythms of your inner self to those of Mother Nature. Here are a few key venues

Luna Lodge *(tel 8380-5036, www.lunalodge.com),* within minutes of Parque Nacional Corcovado on the Osa Pen-insula, has an open-air dojo overhanging the rain forest hillside with a view of the Pacific Ocean. Week-long yoga retreats are offered by nonresident masters. Programs in tai chi and tantric intimacy are also given. Wildlife abounds on the property. Sleep in a bungalow or the lodge.

Nosara Yoga Institute *(tel 2682-0071, www.nosara yoga.com)* in Nicoya, run by renowned yoga masters Amba and Don Stapleton, is the largest and most respected of Costa Rica's dedicated yoga facilities. Surrounded by rain forest in the hills above the Nosara beaches, it's a mag-nificent venue that special-izes in advanced techniques geared to training for yoga professionals.

Samasati Nature Retreat *(tel 2756-8015, www .samasati.com),* on the Caribbean coast, is a rustic mountainside eco-resort specializing in yoga. It offers twice-daily classes, plus ongoing week-long retreats, and training for yoga professionals. Special programs have included yoga and humanitarian ser-vice retreats that include volunteering at a local orphanage and school.

Sámara to Malpaís by 4WD

There is no shortage of adventure in Costa Rica, where one of the best to be had is this 57-mile (91 km) drive along the rugged southwestern shore of Nicoya. You will need a sturdy four-wheel-drive vehicle and an Indiana Jones spirit to tackle the rough dirt track that turns travel into a minor expedition, especially in the wet season when fording swollen rivers (see sidebar p. 151) can add to the adrenaline rush.

This rutted dirt road clambers over mountainous headlands and down to hidden beaches passing forlorn fishing villages and farming communities separated by long stretches of jungle-green shoreline. There are no road signs, and the roads have many deceptive forks in them. Fill up before setting off: There are no gas stations. Don't attempt this drive late in the day.

Begin your journey in **Sámara ❶**, reached from Nicoya township via Highway 150, a well-paved road. This offbeat funky fishing hamlet and resort is popular with budget-conscious European travelers and young Ticos. It has gained a few upscale touches of late but nonetheless retains its slightly raffish, impecunious charm, assisted by vultures hopping about the sand-blown unpaved streets. Sámara is set in a deep basin and faces onto a handsome horseshoe bay where pelicans dive for fish and surf rolls in, bringing the surf crowd to town.

Immediately south of town, the dirt road narrows and begins to dip and rise before spilling you onto **Playa Carrillo ❷**, a sliver of white sand with an eponymous fishing hamlet—a base for sportfishing sorties—tucked into the cove at the southern end of the beach. Farther beaches lie hidden along the shore as the road runs inland, parallel to the coast, deteriorating all the while. Leatherback and Ridley turtles nest all along the jungle shore, including at **Playa Islita ❸**, beyond which the track begins a stiff climb that would challenge a goat. The hilltop **Hotel Punta Islita** (see p. 250) makes a perfect break-point thanks to the magnificent vistas to be enjoyed from the bar and excellent restaurant.

You then spiral down to the hamlet of **Islita ❹**—with trees and public structures which are

adorned as the **Open-Air Contemporary Art Museum**—and ascend again over **Punta Barranquilla,** with the narrow dirt road clinging magically to the mountainside. Though the road seems to descend into oblivion from above, it disgorges you at **Playa Corazalito ❺**. Farther south come **Playa Bejuco ❻** and **Playa Coyote ❼**, both good for turtle spotting, with the road running inland parallel to a shore backed by thick wetland swamp teeming with wildlife. You will also pass inland of **Playa San Miguel** and through the hamlet of **Pueblo Nuevo** en route to the crossroads of **San Francisco de Coyote ❽**, where the going begins to get tricky. Unpaved Highway 162 links San Francisco to Highway 21, and continues southwest along the **Río Jabillo,** which you must ford. The road is subject to flooding, but as long as you can resist being carried off into the mangroves, you will get through. The river winds through mangroves that form a haven for egrets, snakes, turtles, and other wildlife. Don't be surprised to see a crocodile padding across the road.

After twisting for 4 miles (6.4 km), turn right at the Y-fork beside the sugarcane field.

This will bring you to the **Río Bongo,** a seemingly shallow crossing that can make your pulse quicken. A short distance beyond the river, you will pass **Salon La Perla India 9**, at a road junction. Here you have a choice: by going straight, you will emerge near **Playa Bongo,** where at low tide (and *only* at low tide!) you

Santa Teresa. In the wet season, or after a downpour, the mud can be deep. Surf pounds the beaches that line the jungle green shore, drawing surfers. Rustic hotels and surf camps announce your arrival in the offbeat surfers' resort of **Malpaís 11**, where you can pick up the paved road that links to Highway 160.

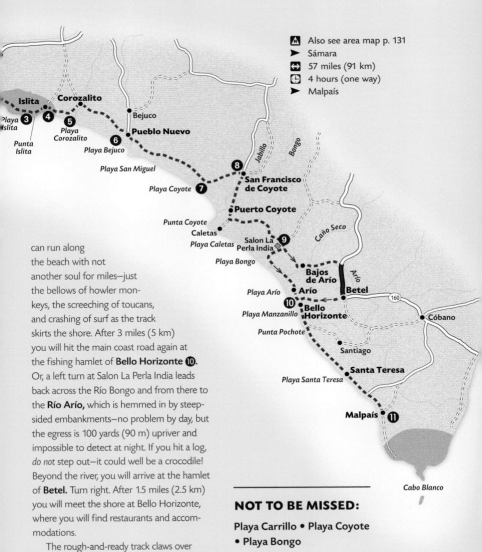

Also see area map p. 131
Sámara
57 miles (91 km)
4 hours (one way)
Malpaís

can run along the beach with not another soul for miles—just the bellows of howler monkeys, the screeching of toucans, and crashing of surf as the track skirts the shore. After 3 miles (5 km) you will hit the main coast road again at the fishing hamlet of **Bello Horizonte 10.** Or, a left turn at Salon La Perla India leads back across the Río Bongo and from there to the **Río Arío,** which is hemmed in by steepsided embankments—no problem by day, but the egress is 100 yards (90 m) upriver and impossible to detect at night. If you hit a log, *do not* step out—it could well be a crocodile! Beyond the river, you will arrive at the hamlet of **Betel.** Turn right. After 1.5 miles (2.5 km) you will meet the shore at Bello Horizonte, where you will find restaurants and accommodations.

The rough-and-ready track claws over **Punta Pochote** and follows surf-washed **Playa**

NOT TO BE MISSED:

Playa Carrillo • Playa Coyote
• Playa Bongo

The Eastern Shore

Nicoya's serrated eastern shore runs southwest like a great saw, deeply indented with swampy coves and beach-lined bays in the lee of sheer cliffs. Tropical dry deciduous forest merges into moister jungle replete with wildlife, protected in several prime retreats including Costa Rica's most exquisite island.

White sands and jade waters draw day-cruise boats to anchor at Isla Tortuga.

Profelis Wildcat Center

✉ San Rafael de Paquera, 5 miles (8 km) NW of Paquera

☎ 2641-0644

🕐 Open Mon.–Fri. by appt.

💲 $$

www.grafischer.com/profelis

Refugio Nacional de Vida Silvestre Curú

🗺 Map p. 131

✉ Hwy. 160, 2 miles (3.2 km) S of Paquera

☎ 2641-0590

💲 $$

www.curu.org

From **Paquera,** Highway 160 writhes over rugged headlands. The road is mostly unpaved and badly deteriorated, but grand coastal vistas make amends for this. The largest indentation is **Bahía Ballena,** named for the whales that sometimes visit the bay. Travelers can choose from several resort hotels around **Tambor,** a small fishing village. Caimans and waterfowl are among the wildlife to be seen in the mangrove swamps to the northeast at the estuary of the **Río Pánica.** The **Tango Mar Hotel,** 3 miles (4.8 km) south of Tambor (see p. 250), offers a nine-hole golf course and sits over its own splendid beach. Inland, the **Profelis Wildcat Center** breeds and rehabilitates wild cats for reintroduction into their natural habitats. Visitors are welcome; call for times.

Highway 160 runs to **Cóbano,** a crossroads gateway to Malpaís (see p. 149) and to Reserva Natural Absoluta Cabo Blanco (see p. 152). The latter is reached via **Montezuma,** a quintessential laid-back retreat with coral-colored beaches featuring rocky outcrops and tidal pools. The village has a reputation for attracting New Age types with its inexpensive accommodations and health-food cafés; a local citizens' association tends it conscientiously. You can cool off in the waterfalls that cascade down from the forest-clad hills where monkeys cavort in open view.

The dusty coast road continues west to the hamlet of **Cabuya,** which provides access to Cabo Blanco. At low tide you can cross the causeway to **Isla Muertos** ("isle of the dead"), which served as a cemetery since pre-Columbian times.

Between Cóbano and Montezuma, the **Montezuma Canopy Tour** *(tel 2642-0808)* lets you whiz through treetops full of wildlife.

Refugio Nacional de Vida Silvestre Curú

Tucked within the shore of Golfo Curú, this 208-acre (84 ha) jewel forms the nucleus of a 3,000-acre (1,214 ha) private cattle hacienda. Two-thirds of the ranch is smothered in primary forest that extends along 3 miles (5 km) of shore and into the hills behind. Its Lilliputian scale notwithstanding, Curú's habitats range from mangrove swamps along the banks of the Río Curú to deciduous forest atop the hills. You can expect to see caimans and howler and capuchin monkeys. Agoutis, ocelots, pumas, sloths, endangered spider monkeys, and white-tailed deer are also present, along with more than 150 species of birds. Both hawksbill and olive Ridley turtles lay eggs at **Playa Curú, Playa Colorado,** and **Playa Quesara.** A boggy trail leads to a spider monkey enclosure.

Isla Tortuga

This emerald jewel in sea of aquamarine 2 miles (3.2 km) offshore of Curú is everything you hope a tropical isle will be—white-rimmed, shaded by palms, lapped by waves washing lazily onto the beach. Tortuga's 770 acres (312 ha) of forested hills rise steeply from the shore.

This idyll draws day-trippers on cruise tours from Puntarenas, who come to snorkel, tour in glass-bottom boats, and paddle kayaks and water bicycles. Others flock

EXPERIENCE: Fording Rivers the Right Way

Fording unbridged rivers is part of the fun of off-road driving in Costa Rica. The dry season normally poses few problems; the wet season, however, requires more caution, as rivers swell and may be impassable.

Before attempting to cross, assess the current and riverbed. Scout on foot for deep channels that may be hidden in murky water. If it's too deep to wade, it's too deep to drive. And don't forget to calculate the height of your doorsills to avoid a flooded compartment. Open your windows and door locks beforehand (in case the engine stalls). Enter the river slowly. Rushing in will create a wave that washes over the hood. You don't want to swamp the engine and stall and risk getting washed downriver. Stay in low gear and keep a heavy foot on the accelerator. Sometimes the best route isn't always a straight line across. If the river looks dangerous to cross, it probably is.

here simply to laze in a hammock and soak up the sun with a *coco loco* (rum, coconut milk, and coconut liqueur served in a husk) in hand. **Calypso Cruises** (see p. 263) was the company that pioneered the cruises and they still lead the way, whisking guests from Puntarenas aboard a state-of-the-art catamaran, *Manta Ray*. Weekend crowds are best avoided. ∎

Reserva Natural Absoluta Cabo Blanco

Dangling off the tip of Nicoya, this 2,896-acre (1,172 ha) reserve lies at the boundary between tropical dry and tropical wet ecosystems and is known for its rich biodiversity, including Pacific tropical lowland forest unique to southwest Nicoya. For hardy hikers (with a trail guide and plenty of water) the rewards are enriching.

A pelican wings homeward at Cabo Blanco.

**Reserva Natural
Absoluta Cabo
Blanco**

🅰 Map p. 131

✉ 10 miles (16 km)
SW of Cobano

☎ 2642-0093

🕐 Closed
Mon.–Tues.

💲 $$

The reserve wraps around the southwestern shores of Nicoya, protecting precious mountain forests. In 1963, Costa Rica's national park system was born here—the culmination of the remarkable dedication shown by Olof Wessberg, a Swedish immigrant who arrived to find the lush wilderness under siege. Ultimately, this ceaseless campaigner paid with his life—he was murdered in 1975—for the wilderness he managed to save. A plaque at the **ranger station** at the end of the road 5 miles (8 km) west of Montezuma commemorates his work. From here a trail leads into the park.

Sendero Sueco is a stiff climb over steep ridges before dropping down to lonesome **Playa Balsita** and **Playa Cabo Blanco,** separated by a great headland. The crushed-diamond beaches have tidal pools

good for spotting sea urchins and starfish. From Balsita, **Sendero El Barco** follows the coast west before climbing inland and looping north. Don't try walking the shoreline trail except at low tide—you might get cut off! Rising out of the ocean about a mile (1.6 km) offshore is **Isla Cabo Blanco,** strung like a pearl off the southern tip. It gains its white hue from guano deposited by a large colony of brown boobies and other seabirds.

The park was initially off-limits, but visitors have been permitted entry since 1989; the trail system remains limited, however, making most of the park inaccessible. Species you might spot include anteaters, coatis, sloths, and boa constrictors and other snakes, plus howler, capuchin, and spider monkeys. With great fortune, tepezcuintles or agoutis might run across your path, chased by an ocelot or puma. Peccaries are also abundant and not to be trifled with. Sulfur-winged parakeets chatter in treetops that soar to 150 feet (45 m), and crested caracaras, elegant trogons, and herons are among the scores of other rainbow-hued birds.

Be aware that the park is now under threat from too many visitors, and wildlife species have increasingly retreated to the park interior, bringing calls for renewed restrictions. ■

A coastal strip of surf-pounded shore walled by jungle-clad mountains, offering adventure, fantastic wildlife, and splendid accommodations

Central Pacific

Breakers wash up to the rain forest in Parque Nacional Manuel Antonio.

Central Pacific

It is not hard to see why the Central Pacific region has become one of the country's most visited areas, attracting visitors seeking a medley of treats from easygoing immersions in nature to wild white-water rides on mountain rivers.

A large percentage of visitors come here specifically to visit Parque Nacional Manuel Antonio, a shining star in the park system, within walking distance of more than 60 fine hotels. Backed by kelly green mountains, the surf-washed beaches offer something for everyone, whether they are surfers in search of the ultimate wave or sybarites seeking a poolside retreat at Playa Jacó, Costa Rica's party-hearty resort town that is the yang to Manuel Antonio's yin.

Everything happens down on the coastal plain. To the north, rugged spurs of the Talamancas curl around the plain and crash to the coast, dramatically marking the transition from dry to wet life zones. South of Jacó the mountains recede and the plains open out,

dominated by cattle farms and, farther south, row upon row of sturdy palms grown for palm oil and centered on the town of Parrita. Still farther south, the plain is crimped by a range of coastal mountains—the Fila Costeña—that seem to rise straight up from the sea.

A single highway—Highway 34—runs parallel to the coast, with peekaboo views of the blue Pacific. It's in good shape as far as Quepos—though follow the posted speed limits; police prey on visitors. A maddeningly pot-holed and unpaved section between Quepos and Dominical forges a dusty path through a string of tidy little plantation villages. It was as late as 1996 before the highway pushed beyond Punta Uvita, providing a link with Golfo Dulce and the Inter-American Highway via the rugged rain forest of the Brunca Coast. Highway 34 is currently being widened and paved to become the new Inter-American Highway.

Lonesome gray-sand beaches stretch for miles in a long daisy chain, one after the other, separated by rugged headlands. Many beaches are hidden from the main highway by thick stands of forest. The wide-open coastline receives waves head-on and offers fantastic surfing, though swimming is dangerous everywhere due to strong riptides.

Several beaches, including Playa Herradura, have long been popular weekend destinations for Josefinos. Today this once languid hamlet is the setting of a golf course and the nation's largest marina. Nearby Jacó has traditionally served a budget-minded Canadian market, plus surfers drawn to the endless swells. The resort has gained a modicum of sophistication in recent years, as has Quepos, a sportfishing center that now boasts a lively restaurant and night scene. A mega-marina will soon open here.

The forested mountains are popular for both hiking and horseback riding—activities offered in mountain retreats such as Escaleras and the Rainmaker Conservation Project. The rivers that tumble out of the mountains provide enthralling white-water rafting. Below, the rivers meander lugubriously through swathes of mangroves and riparian forest that provide vital habitats for a Noah's Ark full of wildlife. Crocodiles are numerous, notably in the estuary of the Río Tárcoles. And Parque Nacional Carara and Parque Nacional Manuel Antonio offer even the least intrepid souls the opportunity of coming face to face with wildlife. Manuel Antonio has a coral reef and picturesque beaches. ■

NOT TO BE MISSED:

A crocodile safari on the Río Tárcoles   157

The cliff-top ocean views from the restaurants at Villa Caletas   158

Sportfishing from Quepos   161

Snorkeling at Parque Nacional Manuel Antonio   162–163

Surfing at Dominical   166

Canopy tours at Refugio Nacional de Vida Silvestre Barú   167

Parque Nacional Carara & Río Tárcoles

Though small, Carara—a Huetar Native American name meaning "crocodile"—is astoundingly rich. This seminally important national park lies at the meeting point of the dry and wet climatic zones, marking the shift from predominantly Mesoamerican to Amazonian influences.

Groom with a view: White-faced capuchin monkeys are easy to spot in Parque Nacional Carara.

Parque Nacional Carara

- Map p. 154
- Hwy. 34, 14 miles (22.5 km) S of Orotina
- 2200-5023
- $

Carara protects the last major stand of transitional forest on the isthmus; representative species from both ecosystems abound within its 11,613 acres (4,700 ha). A broad river flows to a sweeping mangrove and wetland system teeming with birdlife.

Carara

A one-hour drive from San José, Carara shrouds the westernmost foothills of the Talamancas. It owes its existence in part to the stewardship of the Cervantes family, who protected the lush mountain watershed on their huge cattle ranch, Finca La Coyola, before handing it to the National Parks Service in 1977.

The profusion of tree species belies Carara's scale. Hardwoods soar over the evergreen forests that cloak **Cerro Bijagualito** (2,188 feet/667 m). Access is via a mile-long (1.6 km) loop trail— **Sendero Las Araceas**—from the **Quebrada Bonita Ranger Station** beside Highway 34, 2 miles (3.2 km) south of the **Río Tárcoles,** which forms the reserve's northern boundary. Just south of the bridge over the Río Tárcoles, a second trail—**Sendero Sura**—follows the river inland for 3 miles (5 km). The terrain is fairly flat, making access easy for everyone.

You are almost assured of seeing capuchin monkeys. Endangered spider monkeys are also present, plus howler monkeys, coatis, great anteaters, ocelots, peccaries, and, in moister sections, poison dart frogs hopping on the forest floor.

Birding is especially rewarding. The riverbanks are good places to spot kingfishers. Parrots abound. And toucans are everywhere. So are their cousins the fiery-billed aracari. The most colorful denizen, and reason enough to visit, is the endangered scarlet macaw. At least 100 pairs breed in Carara, where their nests are guarded against poachers. Time your arrival for dawn or dusk and you can see the flock migrating between Carara's tropical wet forest interior and the mangrove forest at the mouth of the Río Tárcoles, where they roost.

What a Croc

Despite their rather fearsome reputation, crocodiles are good parents. Female crocs build nests of compost above the high-water mark, in which they lay 30 to 70 eggs. They tend their nests assiduously; then, when they hear the first squeaks of hatchlings, they carefully dig open the nests and take the little ones into their mouths to carry them to the water. The male croc helps guard the nursery.

INSIDER TIP:

If you encounter a band of monkeys moving through the treetops, stay still and silent for a while after they've passed. All manner of exotic mammals may emerge to forage on fruits the monkeys drop.

—CHRISTOPHER P. BAKER
National Geographic author

Numerous archaeological sites have been excavated, though none are open to visitors. To minimize human impact, visits are limited to 60 people at one time, and to a small lowland section of the park. Insects abound, so bring repellent. Carara's weather is seasonal: March and April are the driest months. Guides can be hired through the **Asociación de Guías del Pacífico Central** (tel 8826-7438).

Río Tárcoles

Highway 34 crosses the **Río Tárcoles,** where crocodiles are almost always present, basking motionless as logs on the banks. You have a grandstand view from the bridge on the main highway. Close-up views of these monsters can be arranged through **Jungle Crocodile Safari** (tel 2637-0338, *www.junglecrocodilesafari.com*), at the funky village of Tárcoles. Dozens of the reptiles gather near the mangrove-lined river mouth, and you may even get to see one or more of these awesome beasts being hand-fed by your guide.

The estuarine mangroves also form one of the richest repositories of avian fauna in Central America. More than 400 species have been recorded—an astonishing number that includes roseate spoonbills, a significant breeding population of scarlet macaws, and boat-billed herons, named for their broad keel-shaped beaks. ■

Jacó

The nation's most popular resort has been drawing visitors for more than two decades. Though its own appeal seems limited, its proximity to San José assures a regular local clientele. Jacó also remains steadfastly popular with Canadian charter tourists—so much so, in fact, that the maple-leaf flag flutters above the town.

Fishing boats on the shores of the beach at Jacó, Costa Rica's most developed resort area

Pura Vida Botanical Garden

🅰 Map p. 154

✉ 3 miles (5 km) E of Táracoles

☎ 2200-5040

💲 $$$

www.puravida garden.com

Pacific Rain Forest Aerial Tram

✉ 2.5 miles (4 km) E of Jacó

☎ 2257-5961

💲 $$$$

www.rainforest tram.com

Jacó, 9 miles (15 km) south of Parque Nacional Carara, remains Costa Rica's most developed retreat. Hotels, restaurants, surf shops, and travel services line the sole drag, which runs parallel to Highway 34. Jacó's unpretentious character appeals to party-loving Josefinos and to the young, carefree surf crowd who lend the town an irrepressibly offbeat edge. It is slowly gaining sophistication, however, helped along by the deluxe **Los Sueños Marriott Ocean & Golf Resort** (see p. 252) north of town at Playa Herradura and by **Villa Caletas** (see p. 170), a stunning cliff-top resort hotel featuring fine dining and classical concerts.

Flanked by headlands, the palm-fringed beach of gray sand extends for 2 miles (3.2 km). Tidal pools beneath the headlands can be tempting, but beware of the strong riptides. Try horseback riding on the beach, or arrange an excursion with a tour company. Offshore, **Isla Herradura** is an important nesting site for seabirds.

Pura Vida Botanical Garden, in the mountains outside town, has manicured self-guided trails; its riotous colors and scents draw birds in profusion. To view wildlife amid native forest, ride the **Pacific Rain Forest Aerial Tram,** which ascends leisurely into the coastal mountains, offering eye-level encounters with monkeys and other canopy dwellers. ■

Lonesome Beaches

The long, linear coast south of Jacó is a necklace of surf-pounded beaches that are divided by estuaries where silt-laden rivers snake through swamps and mangrove. These beaches offer a rare chance to play Robinson Crusoe, although the tourist industry has begun to stir.

South of Jacó, Highway 34 crests a steep headland—**Punta Guapinol**—where you have your first magnificent view of the beaches, beginning with **Playa Hermosa** rolling southward for 6 miles (9.6 km) like a ribbon of silver lamé, with tiny surfers like ants rolling in on the waves. Don't get too close to

Walking the beaches at night with a flashlight can sometimes afford a glimpse of sea turtles that have come ashore to lay eggs.

—BEN HORTON
National Geographic field researcher

the cliff edge, as it is unstable in places. An international surfing championship is held here annually. The beach has its share of budget accommodations catering to the laid-back surf crowd, as well as more upscale accommodations.

The central and southern parts of the beach are backed by a wetland area offering birders the splendid delight of viewing stilt-legged waders, kingfishers, parrots, and other exotic species. **Punta Judas** separates Playa Hermosa from **Playa Esterillos Oeste, Playa Esterillos Central,**

and **Playa Esterillos Este,** three ruler-straight beaches backed by palms and thick tropical forest, and kept clean by pounding surf. Playa Esterillos Oeste is intriguing for the fossils that can be seen in the rocks at the northern end of the beach. Horseback rides are offered at **Rancho Monterey** *(tel 2778-8001, www.montereycr.com).* Farther south

At low tide, when the sea recedes up to 200 yards (180 m), the sparkling sands are ideal for long, solitary walks.

are the **Río Palma** and **Río Parrita,** which feed the vast wetland systems that back **Playa Palma** and **Playa Palo Seco.**

Deep in the mountains inland, **Sky Mountain** *(tel 2770-8325, www.canopycostarica.com)* offers zipline thrills across a mountain gorge, with spectacular coastal vistas. It also has horseback rides. ∎

Quepos

Quepos is known as a sportfishing center whose fortunes were boosted by Parque Nacional Manuel Antonio (see pp. 162–163), 4 miles (6.4 km) away. It is a service-and-entertainment center for the hotels that line the hilly road between the town and the park.

The nighttime scene in Quepos ranges from a Texas saloon to a small casino.

Quepos
🅰 Map p. 154

Visitor Information
✉ Calle Central, Ave. 3, Lynch Travel
☎ 2777-1170
www.lynch travel.com

Quepos nestles at the foot of a bay 2 miles (3.2 km) southwest of Highway 34. In the 1930s, banana plantations were established here and Quepos became a key shipping port. Alas, banana blight swept through the hills in the 1950s, and the Standard Fruit Company switched its interest to African palms.

Today, Quepos's fortunes rest squarely on tourism. Small hotels, hip restaurants, and nightclubs have proliferated. The town hosts a Carnival each February that attracts visitors. The 196-slip **Pez Vela Marina** (www.marinapezvela.com), set to open in 2009, promises an electrifying boost for the town.

The compact town center melds northward into the fishing village of **Boca Vieja;** its ramshackle wooden houses perch rather precariously on stilts over the dun-colored waters of the mangrove-lined **Estero Boca Vieja.** More handsome clapboard homes hide in the hills south of town, where the Standard Fruit Company once had its residential compound. Do not swim off the gray-sand beach that fronts the town; as a result of a local sewage problem, the bay is polluted.

Nearby is the **Río Naranjo,** which spills down the flanks of the **Fila San Bosco** mountains and is popular for white-water rafting excursions. Horseback rides are available at several nearby estates. But by far the biggest activity is sportfishing—with marlin the main lure in the December to April peak season. Several outfitters berth their sportfishing vessels here, and usually are available to take you out at short notice.

The **Finca Naturales Wildlife Refuge & Butterfly Garden,** south of Quepos on the road to Manuel Antonio, provides an immersion in lepitodera lore. This 30-acre (12 ha) "living laboratory of nature conservancy" features trails, plus netted flyways and butterfly exhibits. It also includes reproduction facilities for such endangered animals as the tepezcuintle. Take the guided nocturnal tour; trails with ultraviolet lights show off the insects' markings, visible only to potential mates with ultraviolet vision.

Damas Estuary

This vast wetland system extends northwest of Quepos for 12 miles (19 km). The **Río Palo Seco** and **Río Damas** wash large volumes of silt down from the mountains to make the estuary a Minotaur's maze of interconnected channels, some of which open into broad lagoons while others peter out in narrow cul-de-sacs.

Boat and sea-kayaking trips depart from **Damas wharf** for "mangrove safaris" (see p. 264). You are sure to see crocodiles, monkeys, and countless wading birds. With luck you might spot raccoons and their native cousins, coatis. Mosquitoes whine in your ears: Bring repellent. And watch for snakes.

Isla Damas pins the main estuary and is good for walks. Its attractions consist of a small zoo and a floating restaurant. ∎

Finca Naturales Wildlife Refuge & Butterfly Garden
- ▲ Map p. 154
- ✉ 2.5 miles (4 km) S of Quepos
- ☎ 2777-0850
- 💲 $$$
- www.butterfly gardens.co.cr

EXPERIENCE: Dining & Cooking Like a Local

There's no shortage of impressive restaurants in Costa Rica serving international cuisines. The tourism industry has brought professionally trained chefs whose menus have little in common with native traditions, nor a particular attachment to Costa Rica. But you'll come to appreciate the country more, and save money, if you adopt local habits when dining.

Look for *bocas,* savory snacks served at most self-respecting bars. *Sodas* are small family-run roadside eateries. Distinctly no-frills, they serve simple local fare, including *casados:* inexpensive set meals served on one plate, consisting of a salad, a starch, and a main course. Casados have either beef, chicken, or fish with beans and rice or potatoes, plus vegetables, fried yucca, and salad.

Or, learn to cook local fare: **Creole Cooking School** Three-day culinary retreats teach Creole cookery in Alajuela in the Central Highlands. You'll learn about using local ingredients such as coffee and cocoa to make such traditional dishes as mole, tamales, and empanadas. *(Inn at Coyote Mountain, San Francisco de Piedades Sur, tel 8383-0544, www .cerrocoyote.com)*

Hacienda Tayutic Owner Doña Eileen Victory teaches how to prepare Costa Rican meals infused with traditions passed down from pre-Hispanic cultures, yet with a gourmet touch. You'll be begging for her recipes! Your venue is a coffee, sugar, and macadamia plantation with an upscale lodge, near Turrialba. *(Santa Cruz de Turrialba, tel 2280-8686, www .haciendatayutic.com)*

Parque Nacional Manuel Antonio

Tucked into a rugged cranny midway down the Pacific coast, pocket-size Parque Nacional Manuel Antonio embodies many of the diverse attributes that visitors hope to see in Costa Rica. The popular park offers white-sand beaches, a coral reef, and rain forest teeming with wildlife that loves to put on a song and dance.

Many beaches in the Central Pacific, such as this one at Manuel Antonio, are deserted.

Parque Nacional Manuel Antonio

- 🅰 Map p. 154
- ✉ 4 miles (6.4 km) S of Quepos
- ☎ 2777-0654 or 2777-5155
- 🕒 Closed Mon.
- 💲 $$

The 1,685-acre (682 ha) park is set on a blunt-nosed peninsula backed by forested hills; it also includes the waters of the Pacific on three sides. The peninsula is in fact a tombolo: a slender, low-slung sand spit connecting two larger sections of land—in this case, a former island called **Punta Catedral,** which seems to hang on the map like a pearl. You can hike to its summit via a steep trail at the end of **Playa Espadilla Sur,** a quarter-mile (400 m) scimitar that forms the tombolo's west side, one of four white beaches in the park.

On the east side, the smaller **Playa Manuel Antonio** is the prettiest of the bunch, curling around its deep flask-shaped bay like a shepherd's crook. A small coral reef a short distance offshore is perfect for snorkeling; the water clarity is best during the dry season (Nov.–April). There are plenty of tidal pools, too, good for wading out into the crystal clear shallows to spot sea stars and crayfish. And Pacific green and olive Ridley turtles come ashore to lay eggs. Pre-Columbian Native Americans captured them; you can still see traps hollowed into the rocks and exposed at low tide. The turtles swam in at high tide and got caught in the scalloped basins when, exhausted after their exertions ashore, they tried to struggle back to sea with the receding tide.

The park entrance is 600 yards (550 m) east of Manuel Antonio hamlet, at the east end of Playa Espadilla. You can wade across the mouth of the **Río Camaronera;** a boatman will ferry you across at high tide. Wide, well-maintained trails perfect for wildlife viewing lead into tropical forest. Sightings of certain species are virtually guaranteed by following the easy **Sendero Perezoso** (Sloth Trail). Cheeky capuchin monkeys chatter within arm's length in the trees that shade the beaches (it is best not to get too close; they can be aggressive). Away from the shore you can see howler monkeys, iguanas, and sloths high up in the trees, while many a hiker reports seeing a coati scamper across the path. Toucans and parrots are commonly seen, and threre's always the hope of spotting a scarlet macaw.

A more adventurous hike along the **Sendero Mirador** (Mirador Trail) leads into the farther reaches of the forest, where with luck you might encounter spider monkeys; Manuel Antonio is home to a population of more than 350 of this endangered species. The steep trail, which is muddy in the wet season, leads to a *mirador* offering fabulous views over the park and out to sea.

The park has proved so popular in recent years that it has begun to feel the adverse effects of all those trampling feet. In 1997, a daily quota of visitors was introduced: No more than 600 are permitted to enter.

The Road to Manuel Antonio

Manuel Antonio's umbilical cord is a narrow serpentine highway that connects it to Quepos, some 4 miles (6.4 km) to the north. The forest-fringed road clambers over a steep headland and wriggles along the ridgetop, offering teasing views best enjoyed from one of the scores of hotels and restaurants that command grandstand seats.

Zapped by Sap

Poisonous manchineel trees *(Hippomane manicinella)*, colloquially called "beach apple" or *manzanillo*, shade the beaches of Manuel Antonio. Make sure to avoid sitting underneath them; the sap is caustic. The fruits are poisonous, and simply touching the bark causes severe skin irritation. If you are camping, do not burn the wood, which gives off a poisonous smoke.

A **Fairchild C-123 airplane,** formerly used by the CIA—now converted to a bar and restaurant—stands by the road on top of a hill that is midway between Quepos and Manuel Antonio.

Dirt trails lead down through the forests that cascade into carefully secreted coves. The road drops down to the bustling hamlet of Manuel Antonio, which clings to the edge of the popular **Playa Espadilla** and then dead-ends at the national park entrance. ■

Sportfishing

The waters off Costa Rica have far more fish than fishhooks, making the country one place from which you can return home with tales of the one that didn't get away. The angling on the Pacific coast differs markedly from that on the Caribbean; in each case, however, feisty game fish are guaranteed to give anglers a rod-bending fight to remember.

Sportfishing is popular and fruitful in Costa Rica for serious anglers and novices alike.

Every season you can be sure that at least one International Game Fishing Association (IGFA) record will be broken in Costa Rica. The nation holds the world record for sailfish and marlin catches in international tournament history. It has also posted more "grand slam" records—all three species of marlin and one or more sailfish caught the same day—than anywhere else in the world.

More than a dozen dedicated sportfishing lodges cater to serious anglers with package programs. Most are operated by North Americans and follow a similar regimen, using top-rated boats and equipment plus skilled guides. Scores of smaller outfitters also offer half- and full-day sportfishing trips from beach resorts up and down the Pacific coast. Most operate a catch-and-release policy to

ensure the continued health of the game fish population. Four people can expect to pay $350 to $500 for half a day fishing and $450 to $700 for a full day.

The Pacific

On the Pacific side, game fish run offshore year-round and snagging the big one comes really easy. In good years the big fish seem to be jostling for space and the Pacific Ocean seems to boil with marlin, tuna, and wahoo fighting to get a bite on your hook. Seasons vary, however. Sportfishing often slumps as a response to the climatic changes caused in El Niño years, when fish seem to disappear. Then they come back with a vengeance, with big marlin streaming through the Pacific waters like salmon following the urge to spawn.

INSIDER TIP:

Even if you aren't a sport fisherman, it's well worth getting your snorkeling gear and having a boat take you off the coast to see spinner dolphins. They can school by the hundreds and give a great show with their aquatic acrobatics.

—BEN HORTON
National Geographic field researcher

The big draw is the blue marlin—the "bull of the ocean." They are present year-round, though the big run begins each year in May, with June and July being the prime months. Then, too, tuna school close to shore and the dorado begins to peak. In general, the fish move seasonally, with summer months offering the best catches in the **Golfo de Papagayo,** while winter months are best in southern waters centered on the **Golfo Dulce. Playa Flamingo** and **Tamarindo,** and **Quepos** and **Golfito,** respectively, are the main sportfishing centers. High winds during the winter in the Golfo de Papagayo make fishing dangerous, and many operators move their fleets south for the season.

The Caribbean & Lowlands

The Caribbean side is different, with off-shore fishing limited. Here anglers cast their light-tackle lures in river estuaries, backwater lagoons, and wide rivers that extend inland from **Tortuguero** and **Barra del Colorado,** the two sportfishing centers. The fish of choice is tarpon, a tempestuous "silver bullet" that can weigh up to 150 pounds (68 kg). Unsurprisingly, Costa Rica is the world's premier site for tarpon, which puts up a fight like no other.

Large trophy-winning snook, a smaller yet aggressive adversary weighing up to 30 pounds

(14 kg), can also wear you out. Costa Rica holds the all-tackle IGFA world record for this fish. They return from the Caribbean Sea to spawn in the calm river mouths from August to January, when anglers stand knee-deep in the estuaries, or in the surf where the best catches are reeled in. *Calba*, or smaller snook, also run in midwinter, providing good sport on lighter tackle. And in the ocean, large jacks and barracudas can be caught year-round. Both are voracious; barracuda is so rapacious that it will even go for a shoestring.

Huge tarpon are among the game fish in Costa Rica's waters.

The granddaddy of the Caribbean rivers is the **Río Colorado,** fed by the Río San Juan, which can both be fished far inland from Tortuga Lodge (see p. 256) in Tortuguero, a fistful of lodges at Barra del Colorado, or aboard dedicated sportfishing houseboats that offer three- to seven-day packages (see p. 264). Inland, the waters of Lago Caño Negro also offer superb opportunities for tarpon and snook, while **Laguna de Arenal** is renowned for its *guapote* (rainbow bass).

Dominical

Well on its way to becoming the Pacific coast capital of cool, Dominical is synonymous with surfers and a laid-back lifestyle. This former fishing village situated beside the estuary of the Río Barú also makes an excellent jumping-off point for hiking and horseback riding in the surrounding mountains.

Surfers flock to Dominical to test themselves on its Pacific breakers.

Dominical

🗺 Map p. 155

Dominical's barefoot, casual dress code appeals to vacationers seeking a refuge that shuns pretension. The college crowd joins middle-aged misfits with sun-bleached hair and ankle beads to make waves by day and party by night at colorful bars and cafés run by transplanted gringos.

The hamlet backs a 2-mile-long (3.2 km) gray-sand beach that runs south from the mouth of the **Río Barú,** along whose banks hundreds of roosting egrets gather at dusk. You can walk along the beach to the hamlet of **Dominicalito** beneath the rugged headland of

Punta Dominical. Surfers rave about Dominical's beach breaks, but the riptides are a danger to swimmers. Both whales and dolphins can sometimes be seen from the shore.

Between Quepos and the village of Dominical, a distance of some 30 miles (48 km), rugged ranges push up hard against the coast and the narrow Highway 34—the Costera Sur—is pinned between forested mountain and mangrove-lined shore. Though Highway 34 passes through long stretches of almost uninhabited forest, it still offers attractions for the adventurous: horseback riding at **Rancho**

Savegre *(tel 8834-8687, www.costa ricahorsevacation.com);* surfing at **Playa Guapil** and **Playa Matapalo.**

Inland, the mountains are renowned for waterfalls, notably **Cataratas Nauyaca** *(tel 2787-8013, www.cataratasnauyaca.com),* tumbling more than 200 feet (60 m). Nearby, at **Platanillo,** high above Dominical in the valley of the Río Barú, **Parque Reptilandia** has one of the country's largest snake exhibits, with dozens of species, plus poison dart frogs, crocodiles, and other reptiles.

Refugio Nacional de Vida Silvestre Barú

This private reserve, on former farmland at Hacienda Barú, offers an array of natural treats on trails through cocoa plantation and pasture and into the thick of forest and mangrove backing a beautiful beach—**Playa Barú**—cleansed by surf that brings ashore hawksbill and olive Ridley turtles. Anteaters, iguanas, monkeys, ocelots, and even rare tayras and jaguarundis are among the mammal species here. And the birding is fabulous, with more than 300 species from roseate spoonbills to anhingas. The local ecology is explained in exhibits at an **interpretive center.**

The property also features pre-Columbian archaeological sites, as well as a canopy tour and jungle tent camp. Kayaking and horseback rides are offered.

Escaleras

Escaleras ("staircase") refers to the mountain range that steps steeply inland of Dominicalito, accessed by dirt roads that clamber up from the main coast highway. The exuberantly forested mountains

Riptide Dangers

By far the greatest danger facing visitors to Costa Rica is that of being caught in a riptide. These ferocious ocean currents occur when the volume of incoming water is so great that the waves form a dam preventing the water's retreat. Swimmers caught in the current will be dragged out to sea. The natural instinct is to strike for shore—a big mistake. Riptides are so powerful that even the strongest swimmer can quickly tire and drown. The key to escaping is to swim parallel to shore (i.e., perpendicular to the current). Riptides migrate along the beach, and can form and dissipate quickly. Their presence is often betrayed by a still, glassy surface in the midst of waves.

provide rewarding hiking and horseback riding along sometimes daunting trails. One leads to the **Pozo Azul** ("blue hole"), where you can take a shower in the chill waters of a thunderous cascade.

Escaleras is blessed with a variety of accommodations, each as distinct as a thumbprint—from the cozy rusticity of **Reserva Biológica La Danta** *(cell tel 8396-6206, by appt.),* which offers an immersion in a true *campesino* lifestyle, and **Bella Vista Lodge** (see p. 263), which resembles a rustic Western-style dude ranch, to luxurious villas with their own swimming pools inset like sparkling jewels in the green hillside. ∎

Parque Reptilandia

🗺 Map p. 155

✉ Hwy. 243, 7 miles (11 km) E of Dominical

☎ 2787-8007

💲 $$$

www.crreptiles.com

Refugio Nacional de Vida Silvestre Barú

🗺 Map p. 155

✉ Hwy. 34, 1 mile (1.6 km) N of Dominical

☎ 2787-0003

💲 $$ (guided tours)

www.hacienda baru.com

The Brunca Coast

Development is still relatively nascent on the Brunca Coast, one of the last ocean stretches to be placed within easy reach of tourists following the completion of the Costera Sur Highway. Nonetheless, a prime wildlife refuge and a marine refuge grant potentially thrilling encounters, while mountain farms offer forays far from the madding crowd.

Wild and undeveloped—so far—the Brunca Coast is a virgin beauty.

Reserva Biológica Oro Verde

- 🏔 Map p. 155
- ✉ 9 miles (14.5 km) SE of Dominical
- ☎ 2743-8072
- 💲 $$$ (horseback & birding tours)

www.costarica
birding-oroverde.com

The Brunca Coast, named for a local Indian group, extends south from **Punta Uvita,** 9 miles (15 km) south of Dominical, to the mouth of the **Río Terraba** and the **Bahía de Coronado.** A range of mountains—the **Fila Costeña**—runs parallel to the thread-thin coastal plain. Pleated in folds of velveteen foliage, the mountains are good for hiking and horseback rides at **Reserva Biológica Oro Verde,** where the Duarte family specializes in birding tours of their farmstead.

Down by the shore, **Refugio Nacional de Vida Silverstre Rancho Merced,** situated on the north side of Punta Uvita, protects a vital mangrove ecosystem and patches of primary forest on a 3,130-acre (1,267 ha) privately owned cattle farm that offers horseback rides.

Highway 34—wide, fast, and unpaved—hugs the shore south of Punta Uvita, tracing a series of lonesome, miles-long, palm-shaded beaches. Sea kayaking is a popular activity; the caves on the south side of **Punta Piñuela** are a favorite destination. Note, however, that the seas are rough and the journey is not for the faint of heart.

The plain fans out to the south, where the Río Terraba spills into the ocean through a vast swampland—the **Delta del Terraba.** This labyrinthine delta makes up Costa Rica's most extensive mangrove system, providing an invaluable home for crocodiles, caimans, and innumerable waders and waterfowl. You can explore this rich and redolent world by boat or kayak, easily arranged from any of the fistful of ecologically focused hotels, centered on the inland community of **Ojochal**. This sleepy village boasts a large French-Canadian community, plus a selection of restaurants offering gourmet cuisine.

Parque Nacional Marino Ballena

The 9 miles (15 km) of shoreline from Punta Uvita to Punta Piñuela is protected within Parque Nacional Marino Ballena. The park forms a quadrant that extends 10 miles (16 km) out to sea, encompassing 11,120 acres (4,500 ha) of inshore ocean. It is named after the Pacific humpback whales that gather here at predictable times each year to mate and give birth. Bottlenose and common dolphins can be seen frolicking offshore year-round; they weave their way through the bow waves of boats like ribbons of silver.

The nation's largest coral reef is found within the park, surrounding a small island that is connected to Punta Uvita by a tapering tombolo. The reef also extends in patches southward toward **Isla Ballena**. Between, rising from the sea like witches' fingers, are **Las Tres Hermanas** (The Three Sisters), rock formations atop which boobies, frigatebirds, and pelicans all maintain nesting sites.

The undersea world here is enthralling. Plentiful hard corals, sponges, and sea anemones sway to the rhythm of the ocean currents. Snorkeling and scuba diving are available from Piñuela, but snorkelers should beware

the rough seas. At low tide, try wading in the tidal pools at the tip of Punta Uvita. With good timing, you may even be blessed with the exhilarating sight of female marine turtles coming ashore to lay their eggs, notably at the namesake **Playa Tortuga** *(Sept. and Oct. are the best months to visit)*. Both olive Ridley and hawksbill turtles are a frequent sight.

For the Love of Pod

You can depend on seeing humpback whales close to Costa Rica's shores. Two populations migrate from colder Californian (July–Oct.) and Antarctic (Dec.–March) waters to court and calve. These gentle giants reach lengths of 50 feet (15 m), weigh up to 40 tons (36.3 tonnes), and wear their fingerprints on their tails; each animal has its own distinctive markings. Individuals sighted in Costa Rica have been seen as far north as Alaska. Watch for their explosive exhalations of breath. With luck, you may witness a Herculean leap called breaching.

Though this is a national park, camping is allowed. A small donation is suggested for both daily and overnight use. There is no centralized park entrance, but ranger stations are located in the tiny community of Bahía, at Piñuela, and at the park headquarters at Playa Ballena. ∎

Refugio Nacional de Vida Silvestre Rancho Merced

- Map p. 155
- 9 miles (14.5 km) SE of Dominical
- 2771-4582
- $$ (guided horseback tour)

www.ranchola merced.com

Parque Nacional Marino Ballena

- Map p. 155
- 12 miles (19 km) S of Dominical
- Palmar Norte: 2786-7161
- Donation

More Places to Visit in the Central Pacific

Rafiki Safari Lodge

Inspired by the classic lodges of Africa, this thatched mountainside nature lodge overlooks the raging Río Savegre in the thickly forested upper Savegre Valley. White-water rafting and kayaking are offered. In the dry season, visitors can cast for mojarra, snook, and other fish. A 328-foot-long (100 m) waterslide whisks you into a freshwater pool. Using techniques successfully developed in their homeland, the South African owners have initiated a tapir breeding and reintroduction program in the 700-acre (28,111 ha) rain forest reserve, accessed by trails. www.rafikisafari.com ▲ Map p. 154 ✉ 6 miles (10 km) E of El Silencio, 12 miles (19 km) E of Hwy. 34 ☎ 2777-2250 💲 $

Rainmaker Conservation Project

This private 1,500-acre (600 ha) reserve in the **Fila Chonta** range is a realm of lush forests. It's part of the **Quepos Biological Corridor,** contiguous forest reserves that create a migratory path for wildlife that ranges as far afield as the Talamancas. Rainmaker covers four separate habitats, from lowland tropical moist forest to cloud forest at 5,600 feet (1,700 m). Trails lead to waterfalls and natural pools, and to the **Damas Caves**, with fanciful dripstone formations. Treetop suspension bridges make up an aerial boardwalk, fantastic for eye-to-eye encounters with wildlife. Horseback rides are available; a visitor center provides a good background to the reserve and its history. www.rainmakercostarica.com ▲ Map p. 154 ✉ E of Hwy. 34 ☎ 2777-3565 💲 $$$$

Villa Caletas

Built in the style of a Roman villa, opulent Villa Caletas stands out, even in a country with many unique hotels. This stunning place boasts a spa and two restaurants overlooking the ocean. Guests can swim in the infinity pool or at a private beach nearby. A Greek amphitheater carved into a cliff seats 150. www.hotelvillacaletas.com ▲ Map p. 154 ✉ Hwy. 34, 4 miles (6.4 km) N of Jacó ☎ 2637-0505

EXPERIENCE: Contributing to Community Development

Nothing is as satisfying as knowing that you have contributed to local welfare at a grassroots level. You can give your time by acting as a role model for children, learning about traditional customs, and contributing to the care, education, and development of vulnerable local communities and their environments. Here are some key organizations.

ATEC (tel 2750-0191, www.greencoast.com/atec) promotes culturally and ecologically sound tourism by helping local associations and families derive economic benefits from their natural resources. It specializes in excursions into indigenous reserves. **Costa Rican Association of Community-Based Rural Tourism** (tel 2248-9470, www.actuarcos tarica.com) is a network of rural community cooperatives that foster local tourism, educating visitors on the way of life of fishermen, peasants, and indigenous families. **Tiskita Foundation** (tel 2296-8125, www .tiskita-lodge.co.cr) fosters community development around Pavones and Punta Banco, offering opportunities to work in education, health, environmental, and engineering projects. **uVolunteer** (tel 971/ 252-1334 or 2407-6856, www.uvolunteer.org) places volunteers on a two-week to six-month basis in a wide range of projects throughout Costa Rica, from reforestation to working in an orphanage.

A vast swath of wet and wild rain forest abutting Panama at Costa Rica's remote southwest corner

Zona Sur

One of Zona Sur's elusive jaguars

Zona Sur

Known for lush forests and abundant wildlife, this rainy southwestern quarter of the country's nether-reaches' appeal is epitomized by a remote national park protecting the largest extant primeval rain forest along the Pacific coast of Central America.

The region is hemmed inland by the soaring Fila Costeña mountains, along whose base the Inter-American Highway (Highway 2) runs ruler straight to the Panamanian border. To the northwest lies a broad plain—the Valle de Diquis—drained by rivers that flow north and braid the mangrove estuaries of the Delta del Terraba. To the southeast is the Valle de Coto Colorado, drained by an eponymous river and its tributaries, which flow westward into the shallow Golfo Dulce.

The banana plantations blanketing the two major valleys are the economic mainstay of the sleepy towns of Palmar Norte and Ciudad Neily. Golfito, the colorful and somewhat forlorn capital of the region, has a lassitude typical of tropical ports and derives much of its income from a duty-free zone and sportfishing. Paso Canoas, at the Panama border, is also a duty-free zone.

Costa Rica and Panama share the Península de Burica, which tapers at the country's southernmost tip, with nothing but the blue expanse of the Pacific beyond. Most of the peninsula is

protected as tribal land of the Burica Indians. Many of the beaches are prized nesting sites for marine turtles. Whales frequent the warm waters, and the open ocean and Golfo Dulce draw anglers seeking to snag blue marlin, dorado, tuna, wahoo, or other big-game species.

Hooking around the gulf

CENTRA[L]

Delta del Térraba

Bahía de Coronado   Isla Zacate

RESERVA FORESTA[L] DEL HUMEDAD INTERNACIONAL TERRABA-SIERPE

Isla Violín

Punta Violín

Punta Sierpe

Bahía Drake

RESERVA BIOLÓGICA ISLA DEL CAÑO

Agujitas

Isla del Caño

Refugio Nacional de Vida Silvestre **Punta Río Claro**

Playa San Josecito

Reserva Biológica Campanario

San Pedrillo

PARQUE NACIONAL CORCOVADO

Punta Llorona

Laguna Corcovado

Playa Llorona

Sirena

0   20 kilometers
0   10 miles

Isla del Coco

Isla Manuelita

Punta Agujas

Bahía Weston   Bahía Chatham

Bahía Wafer   Punta Ulloa

Cabo Barreto

634m Cerro Iglesias

PARQUE NACIONAL ISLA DEL COCO

Cabo Atrevida

Cabo Lionel

Cabo Dampier

0   2 kilometers
0   1 mile

to the north is the Península de Osa, a rugged region still mostly covered in sweet-smelling primary rain forest. Wildlife viewing is stellar, reaching its zenith in Parque Nacional Corcovado. Scarlet macaws are particularly numerous here, and many of the rarest animals—such as tapirs and jaguars—still thrive, albeit rarely seen.

The Osa is ravaged by loggers (often illicit), and oreros (gold hunters) still sluice the rivers seeking nuggets from the veins that once provided the Diquis Indians with raw material for their ancient finery.

The legacy of pre-Columbian culture can be seen in the many bolas (see p. 178), perfect spheres of granite found in the ground only here. A major source is uninhabited Isla del Caño. Scuba diving is highly rated, notably at Isla del Coco, 300 miles (480 km) due south, and out of Bahía Drake, a rustic hamlet on the Osa's hard-to-reach western shore.

Corcovado Conservation Area links reserves and protected areas, such as wetlands supporting crocodiles and waterfowl, which you can see in the deltas of the Río Coto and Río Terrabas. Several reserves occupy a small mountain range separated from the Fila Costeña by the valley of the Río Esquinas, which links the Valle de Diquis and Valle de Coto Colorado. ■

Península de Osa & Isla del Caño

Acclaimed for its astonishing biodiversity, the Península de Osa is swaddled in the largest expanse of tropical rain forest along the Pacific coast of the isthmus. Beach lovers can choose from a panoply of endearing beaches, where the surfing is fabulous and a bevy of top-ranked eco-lodges belie the "final frontier" feel.

The rugged Península de Osa demands much of hikers.

Península de Osa & Isla del Caño

🗺 Map pp. 172–173

The Península de Osa receives more than 200 inches (500 cm) of rain annually, mostly from April to December. Much of its jungle-cloaked interior is banked within **Parque Nacional Corcovado** (see pp. 182–183), created in the 1970s to guard against human encroachment. However, much of the Osa is owned by logging companies which still fell hardwoods. *Precaristas* (squatters) continue homesteading by clearing forest, and the rivers here bear gold that in past decades has brought would-be millionaires with chain saws and shovels in hand.

The former gold-mining villages of **Los Patos** and **Dos Brazos de Río Tigre** now cater to ecotourism, offering horseback riding and guided hikes into Corcovado.

Puerto Jiménez

Tiny Puerto Jiménez, on the peninsula's east side and reached from the Inter-American Highway via Carretera 245, is the Osa's sole town. It attracts the college and counterculture crowd, and travelers seeking sea kayaking, surfing, and other adventures. The town clings proudly to a colorful past based on the antics of prospectors (not to mention of prostitutes who charged by the ounce). Beside the airstrip is the administrative office for Parque Nacional Corcovado.

A dun-colored beach offers views across the gulf. Eastward, in the mangrove estuary of the **Río Platanares,** crocodiles and caimans cool off in brackish waters, white-faced monkeys cavort in the branches, and scarlet macaws fly overhead. Beyond is **Playa Platanares,** a major turtle nesting site.

Northwest Shore

On Osa's remote northwest side, and popular with yachters, is palm-fringed **Bahía Drake** (Drake Bay). At **Agujitas,** the **Original Canopy Tour** *(tel 2291-4465, www.canopytour*

INSIDER TIP:

Kayak up the small river (Río Agujitas) at Drake Bay Lodge at high tide. It is a short trip through a pleasant forest with some nice swimming holes.

—JOHN CALAMBOKIDIS
National Geographic field researcher

.com, $$$) offers treetop adventure by suspended walkway and zipline; and **Costa Rica Adventure Divers** (tel 2231-5806, www.costaricadiving .com) organizes scuba trips.

Getting to Bahía Drake is half the fun—it is a two-hour boat trip down the Río Sierpe. Although a dirt road now links Agujitas with Rincón, Bahía Drake may strike you as having changed little from the day in March 1579 when Sir Francis Drake deliberately beached his *Golden Hind* here. Running water, for example, still means a boy with a bucket. Telephones and electricity, however, arrived for the millennium.

To the south is **Río Agujitas,** flowing down a canyon good for kayaking. Whale-watching trips take visitors to see the humpback whales. Hikers can reach Parque Nacional Corcovado, with pearly beaches washed by warm waters (beware of riptides; see sidebar p. 167) via 8 miles (13 km) of coastal trail.

On the hillsides above **Playa Caletas** is the 1,235-acre (500 ha) **Refugio Nacional de Vida Silvestre Punta Río Claro,** which abuts Corcovado and protects an array of wildlife. Scarlet macaws squawk noisily, as do toucans, parrots, and monkeys. Self-guided trails provide access to this pristine world. Nearby, **Reserva Biológica Campanario** offers simple accommodations and a field station where ex–Peace Corps volunteers now lead treks.

Reserva Biológica Isla del Caño

On the horizon 10 miles (16 km) west of Osa, Isla del Caño hovers tantalizingly. Local lodges offer day excursions *(overnight stays not permitted).* The 740-acre (300 ha) island was a sacred burial site for pre-Columbian Indians; many *bolas* and archaeological sites have been excavated and can be seen beside forest trails. Olive Ridley turtles skim reefs to nest on coral-sand beaches. Snorkeling is enthralling and whales and dolphins gather in the warm waters farther out. ∎

Refugio Nacional de Vida Silvestre Punta Río Claro

- 🅰 Map p. 172
- ✉ 5 miles (8 km) S of Bahía Drake
- ☏ 2877-3535
- 💲 $$

www.puntamar enco.com

Reserva Biológica Campanario

- 🅰 Map p. 172
- ✉ 8 miles (13 km) S of Bahía Drake
- ☏ 2258-5778
- 💲 $$

www.campanario.org

Gold

In the streams of the Osa, the Diquís Indians found gold flecks, which they melted down to create their fine pre-Columbian jewelry. Later, Spanish conquistadors searched in vain for the fabled gold mines of Veragua. In the 1980s, when the United Fruit Company pulled out of Zona Sur, unemployed workers poured into Corcovado, destroying countless acres in a fit of gold fever that ended with their violent ouster in 1986. A few *oreros* (prospectors) still work the streams seeking the eternally elusive nugget that will land them on Easy Street.

A Drive Along the Osa

A single road—Highway 245—probes the peninsula and snakes along the western shore of the Golfo Dulce, curls around Cabo Matapalo, and peters out at Carate, midway along the southern coast.

It's only 73 miles (117 km) from the Inter-American Highway to Carate, but don't let that distance mislead you. Although the road is paved and in relatively good condition for the first third of the trip, conditions deteriorate thereafter; beyond Puerto Jiménez, the journey becomes an adventure. You will need a four-wheel-drive vehicle to make a fun trip of what could otherwise be an ordeal.

Highway 245 begins at **Chacarita ❶**, a trucker's stop at the junction with the Inter-American Highway. From here the well-paved road sweeps southwest, undulating like a roller coaster, with giant hardwoods—mahogany, kapok, and strangler figs—framing your passage in shades of lustrous green. After 10 miles (16 km) you get your first dramatic view of the sea. You will pass cattle ranches freshly hewn from the lush green forest, and huge logging trucks may thunder past in the other direction, hauling loads of precious hardwoods. After 25 miles (40 km) you arrive at the hamlet of **Rincón ❷**, where the paved road gives out. Here the views open up like fanciful Hollywood creations, with an endless vista sweeping eastward across the length of the Golfo Dulce all the way down to Panama and southward across the immensity of the Península de Osa, swollen with billowing greenery like a violent sea.

The road, now dusty, bumpy, and badly potholed, drops down to **La Palma ❸**, 7 miles (11 km) south of Rincón. Turn left at the T-junction for Puerto Jiménez, 18 miles (29 km) southeast. The road parallels the shore inland, offering occasional tantalizing glimpses north toward the Fila Golfito mountains. Just before Puerto Jiménez, you might detour through the valley of the Río Tigre to the community of **Dos Brazos,** where the former gold-mining community operates a

cooperative that leads gold-panning tours.

If you are low on gas, you should fill your tank up at **Puerto Jiménez ❹**, as there is none to be had farther along. The road is mostly level for the 10 miles (16 km) to **Cabo Matapalo,** the snub-nosed southeasterly tip of Osa. Your route is lined with ranches on one side and numerous handsome beaches on the other, notably **Playa Tamales** and **Playa Sombrero,** beloved of surfers for the terrific swells that peak in midsummer. For the best view around, stop at **Lapa Ríos ❺** (see p. 253), a cliff-top eco-lodge surrounded by greenery, with a soaring *mirador*—lookout tower—offering spectacular views over the coastline and, inland, a 1,000-acre (400 ha) private rain forest reserve accessed by trails.

From here, the going begins to get fun. You will ford a few streams (the mightier flows that used to set your heart racing—particularly after torrential rains—are now bridged), and in places the gradient grows acute enough to challenge a goat. In really wet weather you will need a low gear to call on as you walk your vehicle up and over hills that can have you slithering back 2 feet for every 3 that you gain. In some places the foliage closes in on the road, brushing against you. Signs of human habitation gradually peter out and you begin to feel that you are all alone in the world. But no: 27 miles (44 km) from Puerto Jiménez, you arrive at **Carate ❻**, where the road comes to a stop beside an airstrip by a brown-sand beach that stretches endlessly westward, and is backed by the teeming jungle of Parque Nacional Corcovado (see pp. 182–183).

NOT TO BE MISSED:

Dos Brazos • Cabo Matapalo • Lapa Ríos

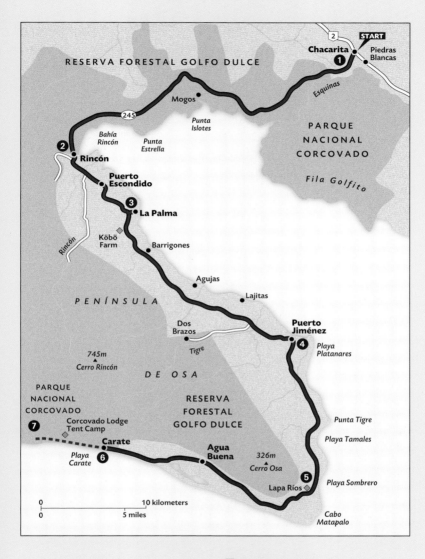

Plan in advance and book a canopy tour at **Corcovado Lodge Tent Camp** (see p. 253) on the edge of **Parque Nacional Corcovado ❼**, 1 mile (1.6 km) west of Carate. You can drive along the beach at low tide, but don't get stuck on the way back! A tree house situated 90 feet (27 m) up offers a monkey's-eye view of the rain forest

Also see area map p. 173
► Chacarita
↔ 73 miles (117 km)
🕒 3 hours (one way)
► Parque Nacional Corcovado

canopy. Scarlet macaws fly past as guests move among the treetops in a boatswain's chair—a fitting finale to an adventure drive.

Río Sierpe & the Valle de Diquis

Emerald points of land and the sea green of mangroves paint the view across the slate-smooth Valle de Diquis. The birding is fabulous along the banks of the Río Sierpe and Delta del Terraba.

Río Sierpe & the Valle de Diquis

△ Map
pp. 172–173

At the north end of the Valle de Diquis is the broad **Río Terraba,** which flows down from the Valle de El General and pours out of a canyon to begin its meandering route to the sea through a vast mangrove system. **Palmar,** the only town of significance, spans the banks of the silt-laden river. The sleepy settlement has a significant population of Chinese who dominate the restaurant trade. In a grassy plaza on the south side of town is a sight worth seeing: an old steam locomotive and, next to it, a pre-Columbian bola.

The town's fortunes rise and fall with those of the banana crop. Land south of the river is swathed

in banana plantations penetrated by a grid of dirt service roads that after 9 miles (15 km) will deposit you in the funky riverside hamlet of **Sierpe.** The village, which sits on a great loop of the **Río Sierpe,** is surrounded by swamps and *manglares*

INSIDER TIP:

Mosquito nets pack easily and only cost about 15 dollars at a sporting goods store. Buy the biggest one you can; it's best to have a net that drapes all the way to the floor.

—BEN HORTON
National Geographic field researcher

(mangroves) that form the **Reserva Forestal del Humedad Internacional Terraba-Sierpe,** which runs along the 25-mile (40 km) shoreline between the mouths of the Sierpe and Terraba Rivers. The waterways form a convoluted lacework that opens into a series of wide tidal *esteros* (estuaries) and isles. Most of the nature lodges here offer guided wilderness excursions. Dugout canoes and motorboats also depart Sierpe's small dock on forays sure to provide close-up encounters with crocodiles, caimans, and scores of exotic bird species. **Tours Gaviota de Osa** *(tel 2788-1212, www.tgaviotas .com)* is recommended. ∎

Bolas

Pre-Columbian *bolas*— man-made granite balls with the perfect sphericity of glass beads—litter the Zona Sur, where they lie deep in luxuriant undergrowth. They measure from a few inches to 10 feet (3 m) wide and weigh up to 15 tons (14 tonnes). Some are found singly; others occur in groups of 20 or more. Were they religious totems? No one knows. How were they made? No one seems to know that either—though one plausible theory suggests that boulders were tumbled like ball bearings at the base of mighty waterfalls.

Life in the Lowland Rain Forest

The lushest environments on Earth, lowland rain forests teem with animal life. Of the world's estimated five million plant and animal species, as many as two-thirds inhabit this sodden world of throttling green, each species interdependent on other species in a complex web of unseen creatures on the move.

Within the dense lowland rain forest the air is cool and dank and underwater green, heavy with a silence that seems to ignore the crushing intensity of the sun dancing on the vast green ocean of the forest canopy above. What first appears to be silence and stillness is actually alive with liquid, musical calls and the whistles, squawks, and raucous screeches of parrots squabbling among the high branches. Peccaries and jaguars roam unseen in the cobalt shadows, while bats roost in the towering grottos of hollow trees. A brilliant blue tanager flashes by, its short stubby wings especially adapted to maneuver between densely packed branches, followed by an enormous turquoise morpho butterfly that floats by like a flashing neon sign. High in the canopy, silhouettes move slowly in the shadows. Perhaps a band of spider monkeys swinging hand over hand, foraging for fruiting trees, while eagles soar high above the canopy, hoping to snatch up an iguana innocently crawling along a branch.

This baby spider monkey has a good chance of survival in the rain forest.

A Complex Ecosystem

At first glance, the overwhelming riot of greenery might suggest that the rain forest is a place of disorganized chaos. In fact, it has a well-evolved structure. Although difficult to appreciate from the ground, the rain forest is actually built up of layer upon layer of overlapping habitats, like a Russian doll, each with its own characteristic amalgam of flora and fauna interrelated in a unique dynamic. As biologist Paul W. Richards, the father of modern rain forest science, has noted: "Tall trees, short trees, vines and epiphytes each have a specific role in the general scheme of things. And animal life in turn is well fitted into the overall architecture of the rain forest. In the jungle, in short, there is a place for everything—and everything remains pretty much in its place."

An "Undiscovered Continent"

The abundance is truly prodigious, and the overwhelming majority of species are far smaller and far less noticeable than the species most of us recognize easily. Insects—in particular beetles and ants—predominate. A single tree can harbor more than 10,000 beetle species. The relative paucity of undergrowth in lowland rain forests is such that by far the greatest diversity and concentration—some 90 percent fauna—exists unseen in the treetops. The forest floor is a relatively stagnant world by comparison. The sunlit canopy is a factory of fecundity teeming with animals, birds, and insects—most species being unique to their lofty realm. This universe of the canopy is a final frontier of scientific research, one of the last outposts of relative obscurity, what the 19th-century naturalist William Beebe described as an "undiscovered continent." Only in recent years have scientists begun to study life in these cathedral-like vaults—an experience now made easy for lay visitors with canopy tours by suspended walkways or in harnesses.

Countless animal species spend their entire lives in the canopy and have evolved to avoid the need to come down to the ground. Humus accumulates so thickly on high branches that subspecies of arboreal earthworms have evolved, while arboreal snakes have developed which can stiffen their elongated bodies to bridge gaps between trees. Many mammal species have also adapted for climbing and leaping: The spider monkey's muscular tail, which can support the animal's whole weight, has a sensitive fingertip-like pad that makes it good for grasping. And tailless sloths move lethargically from branch to branch using hooked claws perfectly adapted for a life in the trees. Frogs, mice, scorpions, and even a species of crab are among the many terrestrial creatures that have adapted to a life high above the ground.

Although it may not be obvious, animals tend to move on known, well-worn routes through the canopy, rather like traffic streaming along major highways. Where howler monkeys and anteaters might pass by day, a kinkajou makes nightly forays, followed perhaps by a chocolate brown tayra prowling silently, with its teeth bared in a toothy grimace. Well-camouflaged snakes such as the green tree viper lie patiently in wait for prey such as opossums or mice.

Ironically, the voluptuousness of this fecund realm is not derived from the soil, which is nutritionally barren. Whereas in deciduous forests, leaves drop simultaneously, accumulate, and build up a rich layer of humus, leaf fall in tropical forests occurs throughout the year. The leaves that drop decompose quickly as a result of the constant heat and daily rains, so that their nutrients are swiftly reabsorbed into the canopy without allowing any buildup in the soil. Over millions of years, tropical soils have been leached so efficiently that only aluminum and iron oxides remain in quantity. This rust red earth is acidic, further adding to the destruction of nutrients. Homesteaders convinced of the richness of tropical soils are swiftly brought down to Earth. Within two or three years, the land they clear and plant for farming is usually left sterile.

Lowland Rain Forest

A harpy eagle perches in the treetops, its sharp eyes searching for prey below.

Spider monkeys live among canopy plants that enfold the boughs of the forest ceiling.

Relatively sparse foliage at lower levels lets the tanager and the tayra move freely.

Tapirs roam the light-starved forest floor.

A macaw soars over the emergent layer, where scattered giants top the canopy.

Toucans and howler monkeys live high in the canopy.

Branching out at low level, understory trees form a sub-canopy.

A katydid and a mantis rest in the thin leaf litter.

Parque Nacional Corcovado

This crown jewel of rain forest biology forms a mini-Amazon whose appeals are worth the discomforts of sodden humidity and rains—up to 25 feet (8 m) per year at higher elevations. In the tropics, water (and lots of it) spells life. From crocodiles in the marshy wetlands to sleek jaguars on the prowl, Corcovado has earned a reputation for some of the nation's best wildlife viewing.

Raucous keel-billed toucans are common in Corcovado.

Parque Nacional Corcovado

🅰 Map pp. 172–173

✉ 30 miles (48 km) SW of Puerto Jiménez

☎ 2735-5580

💲 $$

Corcovado was established in 1975 to protect 103,259 acres (41,787 ha) of tropical rain forest in addition to seven other distinct habitats, which include rare jolillo palm forest, freshwater swamp, mangrove swamp, alluvial plains forest, prairie forest, cloud forest, and even areas of montane forest on the upper slopes of **Cerro Rincón** (2,444 feet/745 m).

You can enter the park either from the northwest via the **San Pedrillo Ranger Station;** from the northeast via the **Los Patos Ranger Station;** or from the southeast via the **La Leona Ranger Station.** The park headquarters is at **Sirena,** in the heart of the park. Basic dorm rooms are available at Sirena; you can camp at any of the ranger stations. You also can easily visit the park from any of a half dozen or so eco-lodges that fringe the shore just outside the park boundaries.

Abundant Wildlife

This lush ecological Eden boasts wildlife in astonishing abundance.

Around one-tenth of all mammal species in the Americas live in the park. You are certain to see howler and capuchin monkeys, and possibly even endangered squirrel monkeys. Anteaters are common, as are peccaries and tapirs. One of

Hiking

Though Corcovado can only be seen on foot, no place in Costa Rica will more richly reward your effort with magnificent wildlife. Arm yourself with the Instituto Geográfica Nacional (see p. 257) 1:50,000 map, as trails are poorly marked. You can go it alone, or hire guides in Puerto Jiménez. You will need good walking shoes, bug spray, and water. Watch out for venomous snakes, especially fer-de-lances, pit vipers with yellow-brown backs and pink bellies; their bite can be fatal in minutes.

The 24-mile-long (39 km) main trail from La Leona to San Pedrillo mostly follows the beaches. Allow two days, including a side trip to Laguna Corcovado from Sirena, 9 miles (15 km) northwest of La Leona. Midway between Sirena and San Pedrillo, cool off beneath Catarata La Llorona, which plunges 100 feet (30 m) onto the beach. You can also hike from Los Patos to Sirena (13 miles/21 km). Rivers must be forded on all trails; tackle these at low tide, not the least to avoid tangling with crocodiles.

the best places for viewing tapirs is **Laguna Corcovado,** where the timid, strange-looking creatures commonly come to drink at dawn and dusk. After dark you can watch bats swoop down to pluck fish from the water. And Corcovado is one of the few places in the country where sightings of jaguars and other big cats are common. These cats also hang out around the lagoon, as do large, fast, toothy crocodiles.

Corcovado's forests vibrate with the squawking and chirrups of countless birds. Of the nearly 400 bird species, 1 species and 17 subspecies are endemic—found only here. Egrets, herons, and ibises pick among the sedge wetlands, where jacanas can be seen walking across water, tiptoeing across the lily pads by using the ultrawide span of their toes to disperse their weight. Even the harpy eagle, recently considered locally extinct, has been seen with increasing frequency. And nowhere else in Central America has such a large population of scarlet macaws—about 1,200 birds. You are sure to see them feeding on almond trees as you walk along the beach, or flying overhead in pairs.

There are in excess of 115 reptile species, including poison dart frogs that hop about the jungle floor like enameled porcelain figurines. You may even spot the diminutive red-eyed tree frog or a species with transparent skin, appropriately called the glass frog. Do not be surprised to come across female marine turtles as you walk along the miles of beaches: Hawksbills, leatherbacks, olive Ridleys, and Pacific greens all lay their eggs above the high-water mark. ■

Golfito & the Golfo Dulce

The erstwhile "banana capital" Golfito, capital of Zona Sur, is long on authentic character. It makes a perfect base for sportfishing in the gulf, hiking in nearby rain forests, boating along the mangrove-lined shores, and snorkeling at remote beaches where both surfers and marine turtles come ashore.

Golfito's ramshackle harbor once presided over a huge banana-exporting operation.

Golfito

📍 Map p. 173

Visitor Information

☎ 2775-1614

Refugio Nacional de Vida Silvestre Golfito

📍 Map p. 173

✉ 0.5 mile (0.8 km) E of Golfito

☎ 2789-9092

💲 $$

Golfito

Highway 14 dead-ends in Golfito, connecting it to the Inter-American Highway, 16 miles (26 km) away. The town itself sprawls along 5 miles (8 km) of shoreline paralleled inland by steep jungle-clad mountains. Its sultry setting midway down the eastern shore of Golfo Dulce is not ideal, as the hills enclosing the gulf preclude breezes from reaching Golfito, which stews.

The town was born in 1938, when the United Fruit Company established its plantations nearby and built the town from scratch in a unique plantation style. Golfito swiftly became the main banana shipping port in Costa Rica. World War II injected new vigor when the U.S. military arrived. The good times ended abruptly in 1985 when "Big Fruit" pulled out. To offset the decline, the government created a duty-free zone where Costa Ricans can purchase $500 worth of goods every six months. The many basic hotels here cater to this itinerant trade. A considerable expatriate population includes a good number of yachters who arrived and succumbed to a spell from which they have never escaped. Others have washed up in more ways than one.

The **Pueblo Civil,** to the east, is a bedraggled section where the main bars and services are located.

INSIDER TIP:

The word "ecotourism" can be used to attract business, but some places build roads through the rain forest and cut down trees to build lodges. Do a little research beforehand.

—BEN HORTON
National Geographic field researcher

Highway 14 meanders north past the Muelle de Golfito banana-loading dock and into the tranquil **Zona Americana,** once the administrative center of the United Fruit Company, with colorful, two-story clapboard houses atop stilts. The airstrip and duty-free shopping compound—*depósito libre*—are here.

A stiff hike uphill leads to the **Refugio Nacional de Vida Silvestre Golfito,** which protects 3,235 acres (1,310 ha) of forested hills boasting all four species of monkeys plus scarlet macaws, among other impressive creatures. Water taxis depart from Muelle de Golfito for **Playa Cacao,** a ten-minute trip to a small beach with idyllic views across the bay.

Around the Gulf

North of Golfito, steep mountains flank the gulf shores and emerald forests spill down to lonesome brown-sand beaches—**Playa Cativo, Punta Encantado,** and **Playa San Josecito**—where eco-lodges offer hiking, horseback riding, snorkeling, and kayaking just a quick water-taxi ride from Golfito. Visit the **Casa de Orquídeas,** at Playa San Josecito, where guided tours lead through a botanical fantasia of orchids and ornamentals two decades in the making.

Mountains compose the **Esquinas** part of Parque Nacional Corcovado, a park that embraces **Parque Nacional Piedras Blancas;** funded by the Austrian government, it's also called "rain forest of the Austrians." The **Esquinas Rain Forest Lodge** (see p. 253), which is run as a local cooperative, offers guided nature hikes.

A 10-mile (16 km) water-taxi trip southeast from Golfito, (44 miles/71 km by road) lands at **Zancudo,** a charmingly funky hamlet—popular as a sportfishing center—sprawling along a sand spit that separates the **Coto Swamps** from the sea. You can explore mangrove and wetland ecosystems by kayak or on guided boat excursions (see p. 264)—a chance to photograph river otters and crocodiles.

A dusty track leads south from Zancudo to the fishing community of **Pavones,** legendary for what is ostensibly the longest surf ride in the world. Rocky outcrops puncture the dramatic shore, where marine turtles also pop up out of the surf, mainly from August to December. The road dead-ends at **Punta Banco,** 5 miles (8 km) south of Pavones, at the gateway to the **Reserva Indígena Guaymí de Conte-Burica** *(closed to the public)* and the **Península de Burica.**

Stop at **Tiskita Lodge** (see p. 253), a fruit farm with a rustic lodge set on a mountain ridge. It is backed by a private 370-acre (150 ha) rain forest that awaits exploration. Well-maintained trails lead to waterfalls and plunge pools. The birding is stupendous, assisted by a booklet for self-guided tours. ∎

Casa de Orquídeas
- Map p. 173
- Playa San Josecito
- 8829-1247
- Guided tours Sun.–Thurs.
- $$ (guided tour)

Parque Nacional Piedras Blancas
- Map p. 173
- Within Esquinas sector of Parque Nacional Corcovado
- 2775-0901
- $$$ (guided tour)

Isla del Coco

For anyone with the time and resources, Isla del Coco will make a memorable high point of a Costa Rica visit. This island, a geographic oddity 300 miles (480 km) southwest of Costa Rica, receives only a fistful of visitors. Yet it is the nation's prime dive spot—not to mention one of its most important seabird rookeries and a repository for endemic bird species.

A male frigatebird inflates his credentials as a mate, hoping to lure a female flying overhead.

Isla del Coco
🗺 Map p. 172

Visitor Information
☎ MINAE, National Parks Service: 2282-0022

www.sinac.go.cr

Geographically part of the Cocos volcanic chain that extends south to the Galápagos Islands, this island is wed to Costa Rica by a purely political link. The youthful 20-square-mile (52 sq km) island pierces the Pacific and reaches 2,080 feet (634 m) atop **Cerro Iglesias.** Relatively young, it owes its genesis to a hot spot—a point in the seabed where molten magma has welled up from deep within the Earth's bowels, giving birth to a chain of submarine volcanoes as the Pacific plate has slowly moved over it (see pp. 118–119).

Feral pigs are the only mammal species, but Isla del Coco shares several bird species with its southerly cousins: a subspecies of Galápagos finch plus blue- and red-footed boobies. Endemic

species include the Cocos flycatcher and Cocos Island cuckoo. Frigate-birds use the steep bushy cliffs for launch pads, and the snowy white tern, locally called the Holy Spirit bird *(espiritú santu),* soars overhead.

Isla del Coco is a UNESCO World Heritage site. Traipsing the island is by permit only, although yachters dock here, as do scuba divers operating from live-aboard dive vessels (see p. 264), which provide the only transport to the island. The diving here is daunting—and exhilarating. Swirling currents stir up nutrients upon which fishes thrive, drawing hammerhead and white-tipped sharks in abundance. The thrill of diving amid schooling hammerheads is one of the island's greatest draws. Encounters with harmless whale sharks and giant manta rays are also common. And inshore snorkeling amid the coral reefs reveals a world more beautiful than a casket of gems.

Following its discovery in 1526, the island became a popular stop-over for pirates and other mariners. Many a pirate supposedly buried his treasure here, though scores of expeditions have scoured the island to no avail. Today, the Ministry of Natural Resources leases the island to treasure hunters, charging hefty fees. At **Bahía Chatham,** the main anchorage, you can see the etchings carved into the face of the cliff by sailors from centuries past. This is the only secure anchorage. ∎

Extreme contrasts of valley and mountain, superb
botanical gardens, premier white-water rafting, and
the country's highest peak

South Central

Guaria morada, Costa Rica's
national flower

South Central

This region encompasses the nation's most rugged terrain. Much of it is part of the Talamanca Massif, whose igneous and sedimentary rocks (many lifted from the ocean bed) underlie rugged forest and, higher up, wind-scoured alpine grass-lands. Few people live in these gargantuan ranges; much of the area remains unexplored, tempting intrepid adventurers.

Most of the vast massif is enshrined as Parque Internacional La Amistad; shared with neighboring Panama, the park covers a whopping 479,000 acres (193,929 ha). It encompasses many indigenous and biological reserves, plus Parque Nacional Chirripó, and is crisscrossed by a network of rarely used trails.

Two fertile valleys are sandwiched between the Talamancas and the Fila Costeña coastal range to the west. The Valle de El General, 60 miles (96 km) long by 20 miles (32 km) wide, is drained by the Río General, which is fed by rivers that thunder down from the massif and provides some of the country's best white-water rafting. To the south, the Río Coto Brus and its tributaries drain a short, eponymous valley. The two rivers merge to form the Río Térraba, which funnels west through a steep gorge in the Fila Costeña and links the region with Golfo Dulce.

The steepled Talamancas reach 12,530 feet (3,819 m) atop Cerro Chirripó, whose summit is usually hidden from view by clouds whipped up by a wind that brings torrential rains from the Caribbean. Yet the valleys are so sheltered that they bask in a balmy Mediterranean climate. This, combined with the richness of alluvial soils washed down from the mountains, lends the Valle de El General great importance as the nation's breadbasket. The sun shines benevolently upon pineapple plantations and other fruit fields here, while the flanks of the Valle de Coto Brus are adorned with dark green coffee bushes.

Despite its agricultural vitality, the region developed late in colonial history and remained sparsely settled until the Inter-American Highway reached it in the late 1950s. Before this, poor farmers hauled their produce to market in Car-

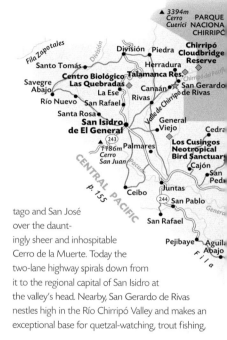

tago and San José over the daunt-ingly sheer and inhospitable Cerro de la Muerte. Today the two-lane highway spirals down from it to the regional capital of San Isidro at the valley's head. Nearby, San Gerardo de Rivas nestles high in the Río Chirripó Valley and makes an exceptional base for quetzal-watching, trout fishing,

NOT TO BE MISSED:

Costa Rica
color-coded by region

San José

2251m
Cerro
Matama

CENTRAL HIGHLANDS
p. 68

THE CARIBBEAN
p. 219

Fila de Matama

Estrella

Teliré

Valle de
Talamanca

Teliré

SanJosé
Cabécar

Coén

Lari

Cordillera

819m
Cerro
hirripó

PARQUE

2435m
Cerro
Punlbeta

Fila Dúrika

INTERNACIONAL

San Pedro

3280m
Cerro Dúrika

LA AMISTAD

Uren

Esperanza

RESERVA
INDÍGENA
UJARRÁS/
DÚRIKA

Estación
Altamira

Angel
Arriba

Talamanca

3078m
Cerro
Utyum

3554m
Cerro
Kámuk

Ujarrás

Volcán

Cacao

Cañas

Buenos
Aires

Cabagra

RESERVA
INDÍGENA
CABAGRA

3122m
Cerro Nai

2558m
Cerro Aká

PANAMA

Peje

CARRETERA
INTERAMERICANA

2

Cabagra

Valle de
l General

Brujo

Mosca

Costeña

Pilas
Colinas

Térraba

General

Helechales

3162m
Cerro
Echandi

Boruca
RESERVA INDÍGENA
BORUCA

Paso
Real

Currê

Potrero
Grande

ZONA PROTECTORA
LAS TABLAS

La Amistad
Lodge

2486m
Cerro
Pando

Cajón

Vueltas

237

Valle de Coto Brus

Cotón

Chánguena

Jabillo

Coto Brus

Coto Brus

Santa Elena

Alturas

Progreso

Fila

Limón

Sabanilla

Costeña

Gutiérrez Braun

La Mellizas

Brisas

ZONA SUR
p. 173

1707m
Cerro
Anguciana

Limóncito

San
Vito

Copal

Las Cruces
Biological Station

Sabalito

Finca
Cántaros

Agua
Buena

and soaking in hot
springs. The only
other town of conse-
quence—San Vito, unusual for
its pervasive Italian heritage—sits
on the Fila Costeña's northern flanks, at
the head of the Valle de Coto Brus.

The South Central region is also the heartland of indigenous culture. In secluded mountain
valleys, members of the Boruca and Guaymis
tribes live on indigenous land held in trust.
Several reserves are opening to tourism. ∎

0   20 kilometers
0   10 miles

The Route to San Isidro

Tourism has bypassed this peaceful valley, despite the fact that the all-important town of San Isidro is a gateway to Parque Nacional Chirripó—set in a vale popular with rafters, hikers, and birders. The Valle de El General is devoted to agriculture, mainly fruit plantations and flower farms raising tropical plants for export.

A blue-crowned motmot pauses for lunch at Los Cusingos Neotropical Bird Sanctuary.

The descent into the valley from San José via the Cerro de la Muerte is a head-spinner, as the narrow Inter-American Highway (Highway 2) spirals down more than 9,000 feet (2,745 m) in just 20 miles (32 km). On clear days views are sublime, with the valley spilling away below, green and flat as a billiard table.

The **Centro Biológico Las Quebradas,** at the base of Cerro de la Muerte, is a good place to spot quetzals. Accessed by a turnoff north of San Isidro, east of the Inter-American Highway, it has 5,930 acres (2,400 ha) of primary forest, including cloud forest at higher reaches. Trails are difficult.

A cliff-top statue of Christ floats over the highway 1 mile (1.6 km) north of the roadside community of **San Rafael,** at Km 104.

San Isidro de El General

The main market and center for the region is this unprepossessing town, known by its municipal name of Pérez Zeledón. The town comes alive during its **Fiesta Cívica** in late January when farmers and their families thrill to the rodeos and mariachis; and on May 15, when *boyeros* (oxcart drivers) celebrate with a colorful parade highlighting an entire month given to honoring San Isidro, patron saint of farmers.

The town offers few attractions; its primary role is as a service center for fuel and as the gateway to Dominical and the Central Pacific, and to Parque Nacional Chirripó. Nonetheless, the concrete cathedral in modernist style, one block east of the modest **plaza** at Calle Central and Avenida 0, is worth a peek for the stained-glass windows, and the meager **Regional Museum and Cultural Center Pérez Zeledón** *(tel 2771-5273),* on Calle 2 between Avenida 0 and 1, offers a glimpse into the culture of *campesinos* and that of the indigenous peoples.

The Valley

South of San Isidro, the warm air is filled with the aroma of *piñas* (pineapples). Soon you are surrounded by fields of pineapples in tidy rows rolling to meet the horizon. The vast commercial enterprise is centered on **Buenos Aires,** 40 miles (64 km) southeast of San Isidro. You can

visit Parque Internacional La Amistad (see pp. 198–199) from here, by way of Ujarrás, to see the nation's largest park and adjacent biological and indigenous reserves.

Between Buenos Aires and San Isidro on the western bank of the Río Peñas Blancas is **Los Cusingos Neotropical Bird Sanctuary.** Situated near Santa Elena on the lower slopes of the Talamancas, this 350-acre (142 ha) reserve was the longtime home and research site of Alexander Skutch (1904–2004), who co-wrote *Birds of Costa Rica* with Gary Stiles. The Tropical Science Center now manages Los Cusingos, which was named after a small, orange-billed toucan *(Pteroglossus frantzii),* for ecological tourism and bird observation. Trails also go past Indian petroglyphs. ■

Centro Biológico Las Quebradas
- Map p. 188
- 1.5 miles (2.5 km) N of Quebradas
- 2771-4131
- Closed Mon.
- $$

San Isidro de El General
- Map p. 188
Visitor Information
- 2770-9393

Los Cusingos Neotropical Bird Sanctuary
- Map p. 188
- Quizarrá de Pérez Zeledón
- 2200-5472
- Reservations required
- $$$
www.cct.or.cr

Considering a Move to Costa Rica?

According to the Departamento de Migración y Extranjería, some 300,000 foreigners live permanently in Costa Rica. Many are Europeans and North Americans who came to vacation and discovered a "calling." They followed their heart or gut, inspired by the country's physical beauty, easy pace, and salubrious climate. Others are drawn by its benefits as a retirement destination: Costa Rica has a stable democratic government, a well-educated workforce, excellent telecommunications, and a relatively high standard of living. It's also remarkably inexpensive.

Foreigners can even start a business while here on a tourist visa. Three principal options for residency allow foreigners to own a business but not to work for wages. *Pensionado* (pensioner) status requires

you to prove that you have at least $600 a month in pension income, and to spend at least four months in Costa Rica. *Rentista* (small investor) status, for non-retirees, also requires a four-month residency, plus proof of a guaranteed monthly income of $1,000. An *Inversionista* (large investor) must invest a minimum of $50,000 in tourism or another "priority sector," and a six-month residency is required.

Though non-resident foreigners enjoy most of the same property rights as Costa Ricans, they can only own up to 49 percent of beach property. Be aware that anyone can be a realtor: No license or exam is required, and the the field is full of scam artists. The **Association of Residents of Costa Rica** *(tel 2233-8068, www.arcr.net)* is a good starting point for information.

A Walk in the Clouds

Cerro Chirripó (12,530 feet/3,819 m) lures intrepid hikers seeking the satisfaction of hiking to the top of Central America's highest peak. This nontechnical ascent demands no more of you than stamina, determination, good hiking shoes, and a sleeping bag to guard against the cold during an overnight stop at cloud-hung heights.

Clouds swirl hauntingly among the mid-elevation forests.

The peak crowns a 123,920-acre (50,150 ha) national park that is a high-mountain refuge of pristine, rugged splendor. When hiking this forbidding terrain, it's easy to appreciate why pre-Columbian Indians believed the mountain was sacred. The park remains a sanctum of a different sort: Endangered wildlife—including tapirs and jaguars—are numerous. A side trek to the Savannah of the Lions gives you a good chance of spotting pumas. And because you ascend through three distinct life zones, the birding is excellent.

Before setting off, visit park headquarters in the hamlet of **San Gerardo de Rivas ❶**, 1 mile (1.6 km) south of San Gerardo, to pick up a visitors' guide and a trail map; inquire here about hiring an *arriero* (guide/porter, $$$ per day). No camping is permitted, but you can cook at a refuge hut. The 9-mile (15 km) ascent covers 7,500 feet (3,035 m), so dress to foil the rain and the wind. The National Parks Service

(tel 2283-8004) allows no more than 60 people on the trail at one time. Hikers must register for three-day stints in the park, so book ahead *(reservations accepted Mon.–Fri.);* payment should be made at the San Gerardo ranger station *(tel 2742-5083, $$$ two days, $$ per extra day).*

The Trek

Begin your two- or three-day round-trip trek at San Gerardo de Rivas, where the **Sendero Termometro trailhead ❷** is well marked. Begin at dawn, as the first day's haul takes six to twelve hours, depending on the weather and personal fitness. Rains frequently deluge the mountain in the afternoons.

From here, follow the dirt road east. Go right at each of two Y-forks, until you see a fence marked Sendero al Cerro Chirripó. The 1-mile (1.6 km) track crosses mostly open pasture, good for birding, then another sign points to the official trail. The route becomes steeper (notably so beyond the **Llano Bonito ③** marker) and you begin a tough uphill climb along **La Cuesta del Agua.** Fill up on water (which you should boil or treat with chlorine tablets) from the trailside stream. After about two hours on this "staircase" you will crest at **Monte Sin Fé ④** (Mountain Without Faith), where you can rest and listen to the sounds of the forest: birds, howler monkeys, and the wind in the trees. A *refugio natural*—wooden shelter—marks the halfway point.

Mists swirl overhead as you enter the cloud forest at 7,500 feet (2,300 m)—a haunting world of gnarled trees festooned with epiphytes and old man's beard. The 2-mile (3.2 km) ascent is known as **La Cuesta de los Arrepentidos** (Repentants' Hill), ending in the salvation of the **Centro Ambientalista El Paramó ⑤** *(tel 2777-8040)*, a simple *albergue* (hostel) beside the **Río Talari** in the saddle between **Cerro Crestones** and **Cerro Paramó.** The hostel has a self-serve kitchen, but cooks will prepare meals by advance request. The hut sits beneath unusual rock formations called **Los Crestones ⑥**.

After a chilly night at Centro Ambientalista El Páramo (bring a warm sleeping bag), you should

be back on the trail at dawn to beat the fogs that shroud the peak by mid-morning. The 3-mile (5 km) hike leads past waterfalls and through the **Valle de los Conejos ⑦** (Valley of the Rabbits), amid alpine grasslands. After about 90 minutes you will reach the summit. With luck, the sun will shine and you can enjoy the views. The peak is surrounded by lakes good for a dip.

Expect the clouds to appear soon, and the wind to whip around the summit—time to head back to San Gerardo, to make it by late afternoon. Or you can explore summit trails, and extend your stay on the mountain.

NOT TO BE MISSED:

San Gerardo de Rivas
• Monte Sin Fé • Los Crestones
• Valle de los Conejos

🅼 Also see area map p. 188
▶ San Gerardo de Rivas
↔ 11.5 miles (18.4 km)
🕐 2–3 days (1 night on mountain)
▶ The summit

Valle de Chirripó

Due east of San Isidro, a deep valley cleaves the Talamancas; the rock-strewn Río Chirripó tumbles between its steep flanks. The secluded valley is popular with fly fishermen, white-water enthusiasts, and birders on the trail of quetzals.

A tamandua anteater

Valle de Chirripó
 Map p. 188

Chirripó Cloudbridge Reserve
 Map p. 188
✉ 1 mile (1.6 km) NE of San Gerardo de Rivas
☎ 2771-1866
💲 Donation

www.cloudbridge.org

Talamanca Reserve
 Map p. 188
✉ 2.5 miles (4 km) NE of San Gerardo de Rivas

Several interesting sites lie on the road leading through the valley, whose balmy microclimate is perfect for growing fruits. You can buy apples, citrus, peaches, and other treats from roadside stalls.

Four miles (6.5 km) into the valley is **Rivas,** a rustic hamlet and the setting for **Rancho La Botija** *(tel 2770-2146, closed Mon., $),* a farm famous for its traditional hand-operated *trapiche* (sugarcane press) and a boulder etched with pre-Columbian petroglyphs. Its restaurant is charming and visitors can enjoy horseback rides and dips in the swimming pool.

Beyond Rivas, the paving gives way and the dirt road narrows and scrambles tenuously into the upper reaches of the valley.

Around San Gerardo de Rivas

About 14 miles (22 km) east of San Isidro, **San Gerardo de**

Rivas—headquarters for Parque Nacional Chirripó—is an alpine village poised above the Río Chirripó, which runs wild and effervescent as champagne in the lee of the Talamancas. The aroma of pine trees and log fires scents the crystal-clear air. The nearby hamlet of **Canaán,** immediately south, is a center for coffee production. Together these villages offer a selection of rustic *albergues,* including the **Albergue Montaña El Pelícano** *(tel 2390-4194),* a small hostel that includes the **Museo El Pelicano,** whose owner—Rafael Elizondo Basulto—crafts sculptures from wood and stone. A race of near-marathon length from San Gerardo to the top of Cerro Chirripó is held each February for local runners; the winner completes the contest in a matter of hours.

A dirt road leads northwest from San Gerardo de Rivas and follows the **Río Blanco** to the trail for **Aguas Termales** (Hot Springs), which you can reach via a 20-minute uphill trail.

Chirripó Cloudbridge Reserve, at the end of the dirt road east of San Gerardo, offers forest hikes on the mid-level slopes of Chirripó. This 430-acre (174 ha) private cloud forest has trails and guides. Don't be surprised to see spider monkeys and tayra here. Nearby, **Talamanca Reserve** *(tel 2777-1215, www .talamancareserve.com)* also has trails, including for ATVs. ∎

EXPERIENCE: Learn Spanish in Costa Rica

Costa Rica is renowned as a center for Spanish language instruction. There are dozens of schools to choose from in San José. Heredia and Alajuela have also evolved as centers for learning Spanish. And there's no shortage of dedicated language schools in the beach resorts of Nicoya and in other key tourist resorts, such as La Fortuna and Monteverde. You can choose from a one-week quick immersion class to month-long (or longer) intensives.

It helps that Ticos enunciate with very clear diction, and that the country offers so much to see and do when class is out. Spanish language courses are also a tremendous way to immerse yourself in local culture, not least because most schools have their students room with local families. And many combine language instruction with classes in local dance and cultural mores. Some combine excursions.

Rarely do classes take up more than 20 hours per week; the norm is 4 hours daily, Monday to Friday. Check to ensure that classes are small—the more personal attention you can get, the better. If you seek one-on-one tutoring, make sure it's available before signing up. Costa Ricans are very patient, so don't be afraid to practice what you are learning outside of the classroom.

Here are a few reputable schools:

The **Costa Rican Language Academy** *(tel 2280-1685, www.spanishandmore.com),* in San José's university district, is completely owned and operated by Costa Ricans, and all of the teaching staff are native Spanish speakers. It also has Latin dance classes, and cooking classes, and contributes 3 percent of tuition funds to conservation.

The **Forester Instituto Internacional** *(tel 2225-3155,www.fores.com),* in San José, was founded in 1979 and offers beginner to advanced classes, including short-term immersion classes of one- to four-weeks and longer term sessions. This school is used by several foreign universities for their study abroad Spanish programs.

The **Institute for Central American Development Studies** *(tel 2225-0508, www.icads.org),* in the San Pedro suburb of San José, provides Spanish instruction while emphasizing knowledge about political, social, and environmental issues. ICADS supplements intensive conversation, grammar, and practice with guest lectures and discussions on culture, the environment, political processes, women's issues, and development, as well as site visits that create opportunities for additional total immersion learning.

Intensa *(tel 2281-1818, www.intensa.com)* has campuses in San José, Alajuela, and Escazú. Founded in 1980 by North American linguist Robert Patterson, it was a pioneer in Spanish language instruction in Costa Rica. The approach combines classroom learning with interactive excursions.

Sámara Language School *(tel 2260-8480, www.samaralanguageschool.com)* offers instruction in Sámara by the beach and provides options for homestays or hotel accommodation. It has activities from cooking to yoga, and you can volunteer to teach local children.

Spanish Abroad *(tel 888/722-7623, www.spanishabroad.com)* is the largest language school in Costa Rica, with nine locations that include La Fortuna (Arenal), Manuel Antonio, Monteverde, and Tamarindo. You can mix and match locations, with classes starting every Monday of the year.

Spanish for Success *(tel 866/310-7600, www.spanishforsuccess.com)* has outlets in Heredia, Manuel Antonio, and Sámara, as well as San José. In addition to regular Spanish classes, it offers special-interest language instruction, such as for teens, families, and medical staff.

White-water Rafting

Costa Rica is a white-water paradise, and rafting is a popular outdoor activity. As you plunge like a log down a flume through a no-man's land of dark, brooding rain forest, rafting provides the ultimate combination of thrills and natural beauty. Below the mountains, the rivers settle down, flowing for mile after mile in solitude and peace. The country's combination of high mountains and plentiful rain produces scores of runnable rivers—enough to keep even experienced rafters occupied for weeks.

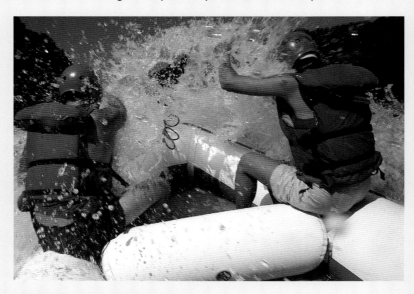

A wet and wild moment on the Río Pacuare

The country boasts some of the most diverse and spectacular river runs on the continent. Depending on the river chosen, you'll pass through several life zones as you tumble through canyons overhung with tropical foliage. You are sure to find something that appeals to you. Travelers have gotten more adventurous in their demands, taking up paddles with gusto; river trips are now also available for the physically challenged.

Whatever the time of year, you'll find a river trip being offered. Major rivers such as the Pacuare, the Reventazón, and the Corobicí are run year-round. Others are seasonal, depending on water levels. In general, the best times are May to June and September to October, when water levels are high and the rainy season serves up more potent excitement. The Río General and the Río Chirripó—two mammoth rivers in South Central that tumble out of the Talamancas and cascade through great gorges—are often compared with California's Tuolomne and Idaho's Middle Fork of the Salmon.

Choose Your Adventure

The Río Reventazón in the Central Highlands is the intoxicating Dom Perignon of white water, a river that will have you laughing with sheer delight. It and the adjacent Río Pacuare are considered the quintessential rivers on which to experience an immersion in the rain forest environment. Both rivers pour down through mountain gorges and spill onto the Caribbean plains. Monkeys and toucans screech in the canopies en route, and there are waterfalls and tranquil stretches that allow quiet contemplation of nature.

In Guanacaste, the lazy Río Corobicí offers an entirely different experience, perfect for children. This short, relatively calm river flows through a dry forest environment. Its waters—controlled by dam and released year-round—draw to its banks all manner of wildlife, from howler monkeys and giant iguanas to herons and snakes.

Prepare to Get Wet

Rivers are rated from Class I (flat water, considered a "float" trip) to Class V (high waves, deemed suitable for experts only). No prior experience is necessary for Class I to III runs; some companies accept beginners on Class IV runs as well. Life vests and helmets are mandatory, but the tour operator will supply all equipment (plus expert guidance). The industry

was established by North American experts and is operated to strict professional standards. More than 20 established companies operate rafting trips under the watchful eye of government regulators. Most companies offer paddle trips, where you and your raftmates do the work of powering through a rock-pocked slalom course while your guide controls things from the rear.

On some rivers, all you need to wear is a swimsuit, a T-shirt, and river sandals or sneakers that you don't mind getting wet. Expect to get drenched on Class III to V rivers—that's half the fun! A wet suit is recommended for the upper reaches of such high-mountain rivers as the Río General and Río Chirripó. Remember to take plenty of sunscreen—you'll be out in the sun all day—as well as a set of dry clothes and shoes to change into at float's end. On overnight trips you will sleep in tents or jungle lodges, where the day's rafting guides often rematerialize as the evening's chefs.

EXPERIENCE: Down the River

Outfitters offer river rafting throughout Costa Rica. The best seasons are May to June and September to October. Trips vary from half-day to four- and five-day excursions. Here are what the different regions offer and some of the the best outfitters:

In the Central Highlands, Ríos Reventazón and Pacuare offer one- or three-day runs with Class III or IV rapids year-round. In Guanacaste, the Río Corobicí is a calm float, with short rapids year-round. In the Central Pacific, Ríos Naranjo and Savegre offer Class III and IV rapids. In South Central, Ríos General and Chirripó are Class III or IV experiences. In the Northern Lowlands, Ríos Peñas Blancas and Sarapiquí offer Class II and III rapids.

Adventures Manuel Antonio *(Manuel Antonio, tel 2777-1084, www.adventure manuelantonio.com)* offers rafting in the Central Pacific. **Aguas Bravas** *(Puerto Viejo tel 2292-2072, www.aguas-bravas.co.cr)* runs trips in the Northern Lowlands. **Costa Rica Expeditions** *(San José, tel 2257-0766, www.costaricaexpeditions. com)* leads groups in the Central Highlands and South Central. **Costa Sol Rafting** *(tel 2431-1183, www.costasol*

rafting.com) offers trips in the Central Highlands and the Northern Lowlands. **Desafío Adventure Company** *(tel 2479-9464, www. desafiocostarica.com)* rafts the Northern Lowlands. **Ríos Tropicales** *(San José: tel 2233-6455, Quepos: tel 2777-0082, www.rios tropicales.com)* runs trips in Central Highlands, Central Pacific, and Northern Lowlands. **Safaris Corobicí** *(Cañas, tel 2669-6191, www.nicoya.com)* leads groups in Guanacaste.

Parque Internacional La Amistad

Beyond the pale of human incursion, the vast Talamanca Massif is a last frontier for tourism. Here Costa Rica's wildest terrain has been enshrined for posterity in a mammoth park—the nation's largest—that the country shares with its southern neighbor, Panama.

The 479,200-acre (193,920 ha) Parque Internacional La Amistad girdles the Talamancas, a great tectonic massif thrust from the ocean over several

Fed by torrential rains, a stream rushes to join one of the mighty rivers of La Amistad.

million years and twisted into a number of ranges. Unlike the mountains in the northern part of Costa Rica, the Talamancas are not volcanic, but instead are composed of sedimentary rock and igneous intrusions. Rising with a heartrending loveliness, these mountains span a width of 50 miles (80 km) and make up a fifth of the national territory.

La Amistad

La Amistad, which extends south into Panama, begins at barely 450 feet (137 m) above sea level along the southern Caribbean shore and rises to the dizzying heights of Cerro Chirripó. The park spans eight of Costa Rica's twelve life zones, encompasses other national parks, and shelters the largest repository of animals, birds, and tropical forest in the nation. On the Caribbean slopes, La Amistad protects the largest area of montane rain forest in Central America, rising above 3,500 feet (1,060 m) to a prodigious expanse of cloud forest—home to the largest concentrations of quetzals in the country. The mountain fastness is a last refuge for several endangered species. Tapirs thrive in the isolation, as do pumas and jaguars. And harpy eagles still soar above the southern Talamancas.

Hiking is a true adventure but should only be undertaken with adequate preparation. The park has scant facilities but the head-quarters in San Isidro provides information, as does the CONAI (Comisión Nacional de Asuntos Indígenas, or National Commis-sion for Indigenous Affairs) office at **Ujarrás**. An arduous trail across the mountains begins at Ujarrás and ends in the **Reserva Biológica Hitoy Cerere** (see p. 228).

INSIDER TIP:

Hire nature guides, even if you are an experienced naturalist. Their eyes are better than yours, and they know the habits of the local fauna.

—JOHN LONGINO
National Geographic field researcher

A local guide is a prerequisite for a trans-Talamanca journey; travelers planning to make the crossing must register in advance with CONAI. The park head-quarters provides a list of ranger stations from which you can hike into the park. Above the village of El Carmén, the **Estación Altamira** *(tel 2730-0846)* has a small mu-seum and camping facilities.

Reserva Indígena Ujarrás (7.5 miles / 12 km NE of Buenos Aires) protects lands of the Cabécares indigenous people, who are open-ing up to ecotourism.

EXPERIENCE:
Kibbutz-like Living in Costa Rica

In search of a communal living experience? Costa Rica has a couple of options: **Durika Biological Reserve** *(tel 2730-0657, www.durika.org)*, high in South Central's Talamanca mountains and accessed by a daunting 4WD track, is a 21,000-acre (8,500 ha) reserve centered on a self-sufficient, ecologically focused commune with about 30 permanent members. It offers accomo-dations to visitors who can help milk the goats, or with reforestation and conserva-tion projects. Guided excursions are offered. **PachaMama** *(tel 2289-7081, www .pachamama.org)* may be perfect for those on a spiritual quest. Led by a quasi-guri named Tyohar, this Nicoya eco-sensitive commune for transient free spirits is inspired by East-ern mysticism. It offers art and movement classes, meditation, and has a kindergarten for families with children. Relations with nearby communities are somewhat strained.

Nearby, at **Durika Biological Reserve,** a farm and reforestation area on a 21,000-acre (8,500 ha) private reserve, you can assist the local community in their efforts to conserve the land. The daunting mountain road is a true challenge; consider taking a jeep-taxi from Buenos Aires.

You do not have to be Indiana Jones to probe the park. A good base for exploring is the homey **La Amistad Lodge** (see p. 254), within the Las Tablas Protective Zone abutting the southeastern border of the park and accessed by four-wheel drive. Its 40 miles (64 km) of trails lead to two basic high-mountain camps at a 6,000-foot (1,830 m) elevation. ∎

Parque Internacional La Amistad
🅐 Map pp. 188–189
☎ 2730-0846 or 8200-5355
💲 $$
www.sinac.go.cr

Reserva Indígena Ujarrás
🅐 Map p. 189

Durika Biological Reserve
🅐 Map p. 189
✉ 13 miles (21 km) NE of Buenos Aires
☎ 2730-0657
www.durika.org

A Drive Around Valle de Coto Brus

Superbly scenic yet forsaken by tourists, the Valle de Coto Brus carves a deep gorge between the Talamancas and Fila Costeña. Highway 237 runs the length of the valley along the flank of coastal mountains, offering elevated vistas over the vale; in the distance, the southern peaks of the Talamancas rise grandly to mauve-colored, cloud-shrouded heights.

Your journey begins at the community of **Paso Real ❶**, at the eastern end of the Valle de El General, where the Río General and Río Coto Brus merge to form the **Río Terraba,** which flows south and carves a deep gorge in the Fila Costeña. About half a mile (0.8 km) south of Paso Real, turn off the Inter-American Highway and span the wide Río Terraba via a bridge that replaced the ferry, taking the fun out of the crossing. The wiry bare-chested ferrymen who operated the motor looked, thought local ecologist Gail Hewson de Gómez, "as if they were born in the reeds with the crocodiles" (which once waited for scraps thrown from the ferry).

Highway 237, intermittently paved, runs east from here along the valley floor. The soaring peak of **Cerro Kamuk** (11,660 feet/3,554 m) reaches to the sky in the northeast, shadowing the valley, which is grazed by hardy humpbacked cattle. You will pass the sign indicating the turnoff for **Estación Tres Colinas ❷**, 17 miles (27 km) via dirt road. Nearby is Helechales, one of several ranger stations for Parque Internacional La Amistad (see pp. 188–189). At **Jabillo ❸**, 8 miles (13 km) farther along Highway 237, you pass the turnoff for the regional center of **Coto Brus** hunkering in the valley bottom. The road has now risen above the valley and sidles east along the ridge crest of the **Fila Guácimo,** giving you a grandstand view.

The local climate is favorable to coffee, and glossy green bushes brighten the hillsides, stippled in tree-shaded rows like endless folds of green silk—a delicate counterpoint to **Cerro Echandi** (10,374 feet/3,162 m), a hulking mass veiled in forest and cloud.

🅰 Also see area map p. 189
▶ Paso Real
↔ 63 miles (101 km)
🕐 3 hours (one way)
▶ Ciudad Neily

About 30 miles (48 km) southeast of Paso Real, the road coils steeply up toward the regional capital of **San Vito ❹** (see p. 202). Follow the main road—Highway 16—south as it snakes uphill past coffee farms including **Finca Cántaros ❺** (tel 2773-3760, closed Mon.–Fri. high season, by appt. low season, $), where you should stop for a nature walk along the trails that wind through the 15-acre (6 ha) reserve. Sit on a bench beside **Laguna Julia** and delight in the herons, grebes, and other waterfowl feeding on fish and frogs. It also has a splendid fine art gallery and an educational center for local children.

Four miles (6.4 km) south of San Vito you will pass **Las Cruces Biological Station ❻** (see p. 202) and shortly thereafter you will crest the mountain ridge. The world seems to drop away in front of you, as you stare down over the Valle de Coto Colorado, the Golfo Dulce, and the emerald forested carpet of the Península de Osa beyond. The view is truly awe-inspiring. Drive with utmost care as you descend the steep switchback that claws its way downhill—a drop of some 3,000 feet (915 m)—to the town of **Ciudad Neily,** the end of your scenic drive.

NOT TO BE MISSED:

Finca Cántaros • Las Cruces Biological Station

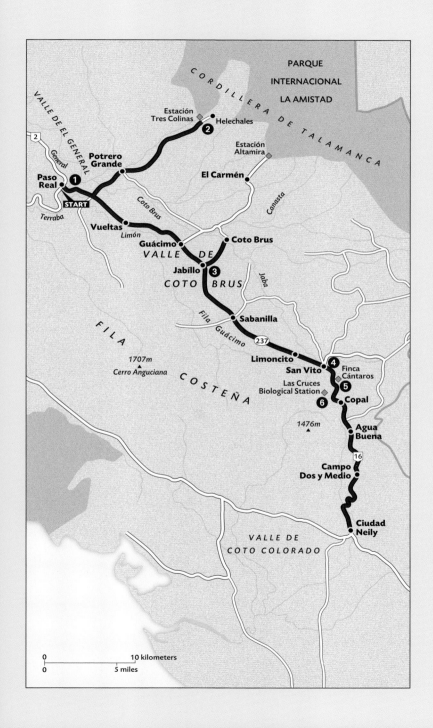

San Vito & Las Cruces Biological Station

The regional capital of San Vito is a jumping-off point for Las Cruces—one of the world's leading research centers for the study of tropical biota. A bonus is its cultivated botanical garden, which ranks among the most complete in the tropical world.

Las Cruces Biological Station & Wilson Botanical Garden

- Map p. 189
- 4 miles (6.4 km) S of San Vito
- 2773-4004 or 2524-0607
- Garden entrance: $$ Guided tours: from $$$$

www.ots.ac.cr

In the mid-19th century, Italian farmers founded the compact hill town of San Vito, at about 3,250 feet (990 m). Unlike most Costa Rican towns, San Vito lacks a main plaza. The *plazuela* at the southern end of the main street contains an intriguing verdigris-covered statue of two children who symbolize Italian–Costa Rican brotherhood. You may see Indian women in colorful traditional clothing.

Las Cruces Biological Station

Las Cruces, situated a mere 4 miles (6.4 km) south of San Vito, protects a 583-acre (236 ha) reserve of montane tropical rain forest on a ridge of the Fila Zapote range of mountains. It is owned and run by the Organization for Tropical Studies (see p. 112), with whom you can arrange educational stays.

The lush forest, which is often veiled with the mists that nourish a profusion of bromeliads, epiphytes, and other air plants, is a veritable Garden of Eden in a region that has suffered significant deforestation. Birding is especially rewarding— more than 330 species have been recorded. And anteaters,

armadillos, deer, kinkajous, monkeys, ocelots, sloths, and tayras are among the many large mammal species that visitors have a good chance of seeing while walking the miles of well-maintained trails.

The best time to visit is from mid-December through mid-April, when the persistent sopping rains diminish. The biological station offers a limited range of accommodations to nonscientific visitors by reservation (see p. 254).

Wilson Botanical Garden:

The real highlight of a visit to Las Cruces, however, is this 25-acre (10 ha) garden laid out in 1963 under the genius inspiration of Brazilian gardener Roberto Burle-Marx (1909–1994) using a theme of gardens within a garden. Some 6 miles (10 km) of trails dip and rise through lily beds, heliconia groves, a fern grove, an orchid grotto, and the world's largest collection of palms. Make sure that you allow time to stop at the greenhouses, where you'll find spectacular assemblages of anthuriums, cactuses, ferns, and other tropical plants composing a veritable hothouse fantasia. ∎

Superb birding, fishing, and other adventures in a lush world of lagoons, rivers, and rain forest

Northern Lowlands

Eyespots on the underside of a butterfly wing contrast with its iridescent surface.

Northern Lowlands

Like a vast green sea, the *llanuras*—flatlands—span northern Costa Rica, sweeping across the nation from east to west. Silt-laden rivers wind lazily across the rolling plains, slicing sinuous paths through the dense carpet of emerald rain forest that grows more lush to the east. The sparkling streams and rivers that rush down from the vaulting mountains leave indelible impressions on those who venture into the Northern Lowlands.

The plains were formed over millions of years by alluvial sediments washing into Lago de Nicaragua and pushing its southern shore north. The llanuras form an elongated triangle with the Río San Juan—the Nicaraguan border—as its northern perimeter, the Caribbean Lowlands to the east as the right-angled side, and the central cordillera, or mountain range, as the hypotenuse. The volcano-studded cordillera rises from the grasslands

in tiers of receding jungle, adding drama to an otherwise monotonously level landscape. The plains are divided into the Llanuras de los Guatusos to the west and the Llanura de San Carlos to the east. Dozens of rivers cascade from the mountains and merge into the Río Frio, the Río San Carlos, and the Río Sarapiquí; the three rivers merge into the Río San Juan, which drains into the Caribbean Sea. In the west, rivers flow into a vast swamp that drains into Lago de Nicaragua.

Rivers served as arteries for colonization during the 16th and 17th centuries and gained

prominence two centuries ago during the early coffee boom, when a trail was cut from Heredia to today's Puerto Viejo de Sarapiquí, and the Río Sarapiquí became the major highway to the Caribbean Sea. Yet the region remained virtually unsettled until the mid-20th century, when the Costa Rican government encour-

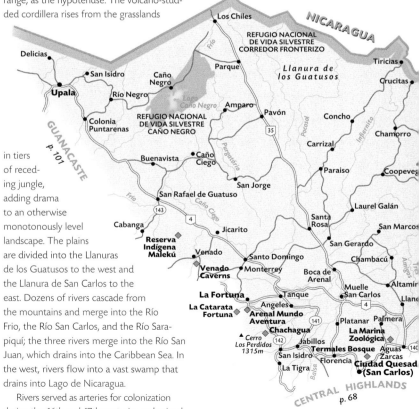

aged homesteading for cattle (subsidized by the World Bank). At the same time, large-scale banana plantations began to encroach from the east. Precious hardwoods continue to fall as homesteaders and loggers pick over the remnants of rain forests close to the Nicaraguan border. And much of the Llanuras de los Guatusos have been claimed in recent years for large-scale citrus operations.

The area remained isolated from mainstream Costa Rica until 1957, when Highway 126 linked Puerto Viejo to San José. Highway 4, which runs east-west along the base of the mountains and links lowland settlements, is a more recent development; from this road, minor roads wind

Costa Rica color-coded by region

NOT TO BE MISSED:

The Rara Avis private reserve's thundering waterfalls **206–207**

Touring the magnificent tropical garden at Heliconia Island **207–208**

The impressive cultural museum and canopy walkway at Centro Neotrópico SarapiquíS **208–209**

Spotting jungle wildlife in Selva Verde's dark forests **209**

A boat tour of the lakes and bayous of Refugio Nacional de Vida Silvestre Caño Negro **215**

among the volcanoes, tethering the lowlands to the highlands and to Guanacaste. A third highway runs north through the region's center to the border town of Los Chiles, site of cross-border subterfuge during the days of the Contra conflict. The regional capital and agricultural center of Ciudad Quesada is perched above the flatlands, on the northern flanks of Volcán Platanar. La Fortuna, gateway to Tabacón Hot Springs and Parque Nacional Arenal (see p. 116), is the main tourist center.

Despite their east-west expanse, climatically the Northern Lowlands lie fully within the aegis of the Caribbean. Be prepared for hot, humid weather and relatively ill-defined seasonal differences. Much of the region is prone to floods during the rainy season (May–Jan.), which draws migratory waterfowl in astonishing numbers. As elsewhere in Costa Rica, nature lovers can find their nirvanas here. Caño Negro is a vast wetland ecosystem and a prime choice for birding, viewing crocodiles, and sportfishing. Private reserves protect huge bands of montane rain forest on the cordilleras' lower slopes. Selva Verde is laced with boardwalks and well-maintained trails on the flatlands, while nearby Rara Avis offers a more rugged option with trails leading up the rain-soaked mountains. Several butterfly farms and a crocodile farm guarantee close-up encounters with wildlife. At Venado, you can explore caverns, soak in mineral hot springs, or enjoy therapeutic spa treatments. ■

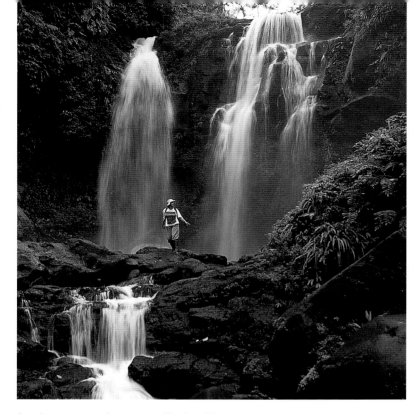

Cascades are commonplace at rain-sodden Rara Avis.

Llanura de San Carlos

This broad plain, drained by the Ríos San Carlos, Sucio, and Sarapiquí, is a patchwork of banana plantations and rain forests; the latter sweep down the northern flanks of Volcanes Barva and Cacho Negro and extend north in billowy green waves to the Río San Juan. The lush rain forests and riverbanks provide birding nonpareil—including a unique opportunity to spot the endangered green macaw (*Lapa verde buffon*).

Rara Avis
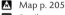 Map p. 205
✉ 9 miles (14.5 km) SW of Las Horquetas
☎ 2764-1111
💲 $$$$ (guided hikes including canopy tour)
www.rara-avis.com

One of the region's key attractions is **Rara Avis,** a private reserve that protects 3,163 acres (1,280 ha) of montane rain forest abutting Parque Nacional Braulio Carrillo (see p. 85), on Volcán Cacho Negro's eastern flank. As the rain forest is fed by 200 inches (500 cm) of rainfall annually, visitors are almost sure to be deluged. Rara Avis was created to explore ways to derive income from harvesting the rain forest ecosystem without felling trees—through sales of ornamental epiphytes and orchids, fruit seeds and saplings, and other valuable products. The complex includes a biological research station. Rara Avis is also famous as the site for Donald Perry's pioneering canopy research, described in his biographical *Life Above the Jungle Floor* (1986). The reserve's economic mainstay, however, is ecotourism.

Visitors can don waterproof boots to tramp the miles of trails, which range from easy to arduous. You can also explore a butterfly farm and an orchid garden. And treetop platforms put you at eye level with monkeys and other canopy species; one platform overlooks a thunderous waterfall—one of dozens that spill through the forest, forming invigorating swimming pools at their bases. Close-up sightings of monkeys, sloths, and toucans are virtually guaranteed, and the reserve is prowled by big cats such as jaguars, jaguarundis, and ocelots. That rustling in the undergrowth could be a brocket deer or a tapir foraging in the forest's deep recesses. Poison dart frogs are easy to spy in the leaf litter. Endangered green macaws and umbrella birds are among the 390-plus species of birds found here.

The reserve's remoteness and inaccessibility make day visits impossible. Rustic lodges provide accommodations (see sidebar below). Rara Avis is 9 miles (15 km) west of **Las Horquetas,** a tiny farming community beside Highway 4. It's reached by a challenging climb up steep slopes on a rutted dirt road.

Nearby, **Heliconia Island** is ablaze with heliconia and ginger blooming in riotous color.

Heliconia Island
Map p. 205
3 miles (4.8 km) N of Horquetas
2764-5220
$$$
www.heliconia island.com

EXPERIENCE: Wilderness Lodges to Sample

Costa Rica is blessed with dozens of wilderness lodges—its forte. They range from rustic heart-of-the-jungle facilities to deluxe safari-style tent camps where the sense of communion with the wildlife is enhanced by the knowledge that only a thin canvas separates you from the jungle cats. Compare a few lodges and decide what features are important to you before selecting your digs. There is a wide range of activities and features and some are a better value than others. Here are a few of the best.

La Amistad Ecolodge (tel 2289-7667, www.laamistad .com; see p. 129) sits on the edge of Parque Internacional La Amistad. Stay in simple rooms in the farmstead or at rustic high-mountain camps.
Laguna del Lagarto (tel 2289-8163, www.lagarto-lodge-costa-rica.com; see p. 216) Animals teems around this all-hardwood lodge with a wrap-around porch for easy wildlife viewing. Kayaks are available for exploring the rain forest lagoons.

Lapa Ríos (tel 2735-5130, www.laparios.com) offers deluxe lodging and gourmet fare. Thatched bungalows with screened glassless verandas are backed by dense rain forest abutting Parque Nacional Corcovado.
Rafiki Safari Lodge (tel 2777-2250, www.rafiki safari.com; see p. 170) is modeled on upscale African safari camps. Deluxe tents even have flush toilets. Dense rain forest backs the lodge, deep in Río Savegre Valley.

Rara Avis (tel 2764-1111, www.rara-avis.com), set within the montane rain forest on the eastern border of Parque Nacional Braulio Carrillo, is Costa Rica's original, and rustic, wilderness lodge.
Tortuga Lodge & Gardens (tel 2257-0766, www.costaricaexpeditions .com) is the most upscale of the wilderness lodges along Laguna Tortuguero and is acclaimed for its superb guides, cozy accommodations, and hearty family-style meals.

Puerto Viejo de Sarapiquí
⬛ Map p. 205

Visitor information

Cámara de Turismo de Sarapiquí
☎ 2761-1579

Centro Neotrópico SarapiquíS
⬛ Map p. 205
✉ 1 mile (1.6 km) N of La Virgen
☎ 2761-1004
💲 $$–$$$$

www.sarapiquis.org

Manicured to near perfection, this 5-acre (2 ha) garden—the creation of American naturalist Tim Ryan—displays more than 80 species of heliconia from around the world, as well as scores of bamboo, orchid, and other species. Birding is stupendous; the air thrums with the wings of hummingbirds. For an unusual experience, request a nighttime tour.

Freshwater Sharks?

For centuries, the sharks in Lake Nicaragua have baffled observers. Scientists once believed that the lake had begun as part of the ocean, and its sharks had adapted to fresh water; we now know, however, that it was formed by tectonic subsidence. The lake is linked to the Caribbean Sea by the 106-mile-long (170 km) Río San Juan. Electronic tagging has shown that sharks, a species able to tolerate both fresh and salt water, migrate between the lake and the sea via the river's rapids.

Puerto Viejo de Sarapiquí

Puerto Viejo, the region's only notable town, huddles at the confluence of the Río Puerto Viejo and Río Sarapiquí, at the foot of the Cordillera Central, whose eastern slopes bear the brunt of damp air masses moving in from the Caribbean. Puerto Viejo long ago relinquished its importance as the country's main shipping port for coffee brought down from the Meseta Central by mule.

Puerto Viejo now supports the banana plantations unfurling eastward for miles. It also caters to ecotourism. Several lodges highlight the superb nature viewing. **El Gavilán** (see p. 265), on the south bank of the Río Sarapiquí, offers guided hikes and horseback rides along trails amid its 450 acres (182 ha) of primary rain forest.

The stupendous variety of wildlife can also be seen on boat rides from the *muelle* (dock) at the eastern end of town. Water taxis ply the Ríos Sarapiquí and San Juan as far as Barra del Colorado; you can charter motorized canoes and canopied tour boats with **Oasis Nature Tours** *(tel 2766-6108, $$$ per hour per person)*. Expect to see caimans, monkeys, sloths, and even crocodiles as you cruise along the wide waterways. Bring binoculars and plenty of wet-weather clothing.

From San José, the quickest way to reach Puerto Viejo is Highway 4, which branches north from the Guápiles Highway (Highway 32) at **Santa Clara.** A more scenic route is Highway 126, which crawls down the western flanks of Volcán Barva to the lowland hamlet of **La Virgen.** Stop for refreshments at **Rancho Leona** (see p. 259), where North American transplant Ken Upcraft welcomes visitors to his stained-glass studio. Ken offers lodgings, plus white-water kayaking and hiking into Parque Nacional Braulio Carrillo.

Nearby, on the Río Sarapiquí, the fascinating attractions at the **Centro Neotrópico SarapiquíS** draw visitors. Among them is the state-of-the-art **Museo de Cultura Indígena,** celebrating the extant indigenous cultures of Costa Rica through an impressive collection

Suction-cup pads on its feet help the red-eyed tree frog hop to it.

of artifacts, masks, decorations, and shamanic objects, plus a documentary. An archaeological site features a pre-Columbian burial ground and a reconstruction of an Indian village. It's also an experimental farm with a fruit orchard and botanical garden displaying a vivid palette of native species. A contemporary hotel at its heart offers fine dining. Trails lead into 330-acre (133 ha) **Tirimbina Biological Reserve,** where a canopy walkway gets you close to monkeys.

La Selva Biological Station

This research center, immediately south of Puerto Viejo, abuts the northern edge of Parque Nacional Braulio Carrillo. It is owned by the Organization for Tropical Studies (see p. 112), an international body of 50 or so universities that share research facilities consisting of laboratories, an arboretum with more than one thousand tree species, and experimental lots surrounded by 3,700 acres (1,500 ha) of virgin premontane rain forest.

La Selva averages 160 inches (400 cm) of rainfall per year; rare is the day without rain. Boardwalks offer easy hikes by the educational center, but the 38 miles (61 km) of trails are mostly muddy going (Feb.–March is driest). Twice-daily guided hikes are offered by reservation only. More than 420 bird species have been recorded here, as have more than half of Costa Rica's butterfly species, two-thirds of its mammal species, and 55 of its 162 species of snakes.

Selva Verde

At Chilamate, 4 miles (6.4 km) west of Puerto Viejo, this private reserve protects 475 acres (192 ha) of lowland rain forest bordering Parque Nacional Braulio Carrillo's northwestern reaches. Trails and boardwalks penetrate the dark forests, where snakes and poison dart frogs abound. Blue-and-gold tanagers, jacamars, motmots, parrots, and toucans are numerous; they're most easily identified in the company of a trained naturalist guide. Noisy flocks of oropendolas sport daffodil yellow tails.

Selva Verde has a netted butterfly garden that visitors can enter to gain familiarity with the goings-on of lepidoptera. It also has canoe and horseback trips, plus nice accommodations. ∎

La Selva Biological Station

Map p. 205

2 miles (3.2 km) S of Puerto Viejo de Sarapiquí

2766-6565

Guided hikes from $$$$

www.ots.ac.cr

Selva Verde

Map p. 205

6 miles (9.7 km) W of Puerto Viejo de Sarapiquí

2766-6800

$$$ (guided hikes), $$ (butterfly garden)

www.selvaverde.com

Snakes

Snakes—*culebras* or *serpientes*—are a fact of life in Costa Rica, which is home to 162 species. The ubiquitous creatures, which are much maligned and little understood, are found in every one of the country's environments. The majority of serpientes are rarely seen, since they are nocturnal.

A huge head and exquisite markings are dead giveaways of the boa.

Many species are painted in magnificent colors and patterns, with a beauty that belies their fearsome reputations. In fact, only 22 species are venomous, of which 9 are potentially fatal to humans (except for the coral snakes, which produce a unique venom, the species all produce the same venom, which varies only in degree of toxicity). While most species are camouflaged in greens and browns the better to catch passing prey, many species—such as the coral snakes— boast gaudy colors meant to advertise their highly venomous nature.

Snakes range in size from diminutive species such as the foot-long (30 cm), pencil-thin bright green vine snake *(bejuquillo),* with its beaked nose, to the 10-foot (3 m) boa constrictor *(boa),* which coils around its prey and squeezes it to death. The boa, which gives

birth to live young, is normally benign and retiring, but will strike if you approach too closely; though they are non-venomous, their fangs can inflict a nasty bite.

Some species are highly localized, such as the *cascabel,* the sole tropical species of rattle-snake (a member of the viper family) found only in Guanacaste. It rarely uses its rattle and produces an unusually toxic venom. Vipers include the highly venomous eyelash or palm viper *(bocaracá).* This exotically colored Day-Glo green or yellow arboreal snake lies in sensuous coils on branches, where it can keep a keen eye for passing prey. The much-feared bushmaster *(matabuey)* is a giant among the poisonous snakes and highly aggressive—it has even been known to chase people. The bushmaster is restricted to densely forested mountain terrain. Its equally lethal cousin, the terrestrial fer-de-lance—colloquially called the *terciopelo* (velvet)—is far more ubiquitous and accounts for four-fifths of snake bites in Costa Rica, as well as most fatalities. Rather than slink away at the approach of humans, the fer-de-lance holds its ground and will strike with little provocation. Although found in every major life zone, it prefers wet habitats; it is prevalent in tall grassland and along riverbanks in drier regions. Amazingly, even the fer-de-lance has something to fear in Costa Rica: *Clelia clelia,* an arboreal snake that feeds on small reptiles, preys on juvenile fer-de-lances.

Vipers are mostly nocturnal. They hunt with the aid of a sensory device located in a pit, or depression, between the nostril and eye. The device detects infrared radiation and is so sensitive that it can sense a rise in temperature of five-hundredths of a degree Fahrenheit (three-hundredths C) per yard, which indicates the presence of warm-blooded prey. This serpentine infrared sensor can also tell the direction of a heat source in pitch darkness, allowing the pit viper to close in unseen until within striking range of its victim. Pit vipers are

Above: The highly venomous banded coral snake has a stunted head and stubby tail. Below: The fer-de-lance's dappled gray-brown skin is perfect camouflage for lying in wait amid decaying leaf litter.

INSIDER TIP:

Most snakebites happen when people step too close to hidden snakes; when walking, keep your eyes on the ground. Also, look carefully before reaching for a branch, as many snakes are arboreal.

—CHRISTOPHER P. BAKER
National Geographic author

the most evolved snake of all; like mammals, they nourish their unborn young through placental membranes. Uniquely, they even guard their young.

Costa Rica also has four species of coral snakes, identified by their bands of carmine red, white or yellow, and black. If threatened, they typically flatten their backs and perform a balletic dance meant to intimidate aggressors. One nonvenomous snake, the false coral snake, mimics these markings but is easily identified: Its rings are in the reverse order. Pelagic sea snakes—black-backed and yellow-bellied—are distant relatives of the coral snake; they are common off the Pacific shore, where they use their spatula-like tails to sidle through the warm water.

One commonly seen species is the chunk-headed snake, an extraordinarily slender snake that has evolved to forage for prey on thin branches (its I-beam shape is ideal for bridging gaps between branches). It hides in bromeliads, then ambushes lizards and frogs.

Around Ciudad Quesada

The capital of the region is not actually in the Northern Lowlands; instead, it perches loftily at 2,145 feet (654 m) on the slopes of the Cordillera Tilarán, while the *llanuras* (lowlands) unfurl majestically below. The town is a major transportation hub.

Ciudad Quesada
- Map p. 204

Visitor Information
- Juncture of Calle Central & Calle 1
- 2461-1112
- Closed Sun.

Termales del Bosque
- Aguas Zarcas
- 2474-4740
- $$. Canopy tour: $$$$$

La Marina Zoológica
- Map p. 204
- 8 miles (13 km) NE of Ciudad Quesada
- 2474-2202
- $
- www.zoocostarica .com

Muelle San Carlos
- Map p. 204

Reserva Biológica La Garza
- 2475-5222
- www.hotellagarza .com

Tapirs may be spotted drinking from lakes at dusk throughout Costa Rica.

The bustling market town of Ciudad Quesada, which slopes sharply northward and is known colloquially as San Carlos, is surrounded by emerald green pastures that are munched by brown Swiss cattle and black-and-white Holsteins. *Talabarterias* —saddle makers' shops—are a curiosity as you browse the town center, laid out in a grid around a tree-shaded square. If possible, time your visit for April, when a **Fería del Ganado** (Cattle Fair) is held. The main office for the region, the Cámara de Turismo de Zona Norte, is on Calle Central at the south end of town, but it has little literature.

From the main plaza, Highway 140 sidles down the northern flank of Volcán Platanar, from which gush forth thermal waters. At **Termales del Bosque** visitors can bathe in the mineral springs after hiking or riding horses through lush forest, or after joining monkeys and sloths in the treetops on a canopy tour. Spa treatments are offered at **Thermae Spa** *(Hotel El Tucano, tel 2460-6000),* which enjoys a splendid setting beside a ravine of steaming springs.

The road descends to **Aguas Zarcas,** setting for **La Marina Zoológica,** a private zoo caring for orphaned and confiscated birds and animals, including dozens of monkeys and such treasures as tapirs, jaguars, and a Bengal tiger. Farther west, at the crossroad town of **Muelle San Carlos,** the **Reserva Biológica La Garza** is a working cattle ranch with a rain forest and wetland preserve. It offers horseback rides, hiking trails, and charming hacienda-style accommodations. ∎

Around La Fortuna

The prosperous tourist center of La Fortuna de San Carlos nestles against the Cordillera de Tilarán in the lee of smoldering Volcán Arenal, which towers over the town to the west. La Fortuna is the main gateway to the volcano, enshrined within Parque Nacional Volcán Arenal (see p. 116), which is the primary draw for tourists. The attention has fostered a blossoming of local ecotour attractions.

The compact town of La Fortuna bustles with travelers hoping to see a volcano erupt, a feat that Volcán Arenal—4 miles (6.4 km) west of town—obligingly performs regularly. Pyrotechnics light up the inky night sky. A range of accommodations caters to the traffic. One rustic option, Albergue Ecoturística La Catarata, features the **Zoo Tepescuintle** (tel 2479-9522, $), named for the endangered brown-and-white-speckled rodents, also called agoutis. A farmers' cooperative raises agoutis for release in the wild. There is a small orchid garden, and a small butterfly garden allows visitors to wander freely within a netted enclosure.

Despite the tourists, La Fortuna still serves as a regional agricultural center and retains its strong ties to the local beef cattle economy. Sabaneros (cowboys) with lassoes and machetes are a local feature. Horseback riding is popular, and tour operators such as **Desafío Adventures** (see p. 265) offer rides as far as Monteverde, atop the Cordillera de Tilarán. The most popular ride is to the **Catarata La Fortuna** (tel 2479-8078), 1 mile (1.6 km) south of Highway 142, 3 miles (5 km) southeast of town. Here, you can follow a narrow trail and steep staircase downhill to a waterfall, which has pools good for

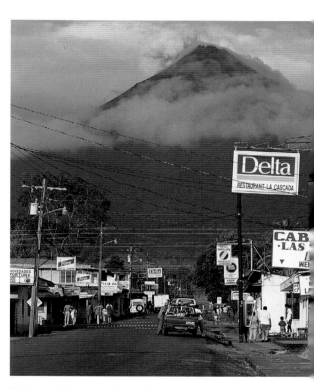

Volcán Arenal looms over the sign-happy town of La Fortuna.

swimming. However, swimming is unsafe in rainy weather due to flash floods. Intrepid travelers can also hike the steep, rain-soaked flanks of **Cerro Los Perdidos** (4,314 feet/1,315 m) and ascend into the Reserva Biológica del Bosque Nuboso de Monteverde (see p. 110) and the Bosque Eterno de los Niños (see p. 111).

La Fortuna
🔺 Map p. 204
Visitor Information
☎ 2479-9464

Arenal Mundo Aventura

🔺 Map p. 204
✉ 1.5 miles (2.4 km) S of La Fortuna
☎ 2479-9762
💲 $$–$$$$$
www.arenalmundo
aventura.com

Chachagua

🔺 Map p. 204
✉ Hwy. 142, 6 miles (9.7 km) E of Fortuna
☎ 2239-1164
💲 $$
www.chachaguarain
foresthotel.com

Tour operators offer a wealth of local adventure travels, from mountain biking, kayaking, and floating on the **Río Peñas Blancas,** fishing on **Laguna de Arenal** (see pp. 114–115), and spelunking at **Venado Caverns** (see p. 216) to bungee jumping from a bridge over the Río Peñas Blancas at San Isidro.

Highway 142 runs through town and continues toward the volcano and Tabacón Resort (see p. 116). En route you will pass **Baldi Hot Springs** (tel 2479-9651, $$$$), with soothing hot springs set in landscaped gardens; one has a swim-up bar, and there's a restaurant.

East of La Fortuna, **Arenal Mundo Aventura** has enough attractions to fill a day: rain forest hikes, riding horses, a zipline, or even rappelling down a waterfall. Tamer options here include snake and frog exhibits. A nocturnal guided walk in search of insects is a highlight.

Chachagua

This private reserve protects 124 acres (50 ha) of montane rain forest that melds into the Bosque Eterno de los Niños at the base of the Cordillera de Tilarán. Naturalist guides lead hikes in search of birds and wildlife, such as the large populations of poison dart frogs, ocelots, toucans, and howler and white-faced monkeys. The facility centers around a working cattle hacienda where visitors can watch cowboys ride bulls bareback. A stream bubbles through the property; guests are accommodated in rustic cabins at the forest's edge. It is best to use a four-wheel-drive vehicle to negotiate the dirt road that leads to the hacienda. ■

EXPERIENCE:
Appreciating the Indigenous Way of Life

The Spanish occupation proved devastating to indigenous cultures, which retreated to valleys where their descendants still live. Today, eight indigenous tribes live in scattered villages on 22 reserves under the jurisdiction of the National Commission for Indigenous Affairs.

Until recently, the reserves were off-limits to visitors, except by permit. Tourism is now being promoted as a way of fostering a renewed pride in traditional beliefs, crafts, and customs. Permits are no longer required to visit the reserves. The most accessible reserves can be reached by 4WD vehicles over trails. The **Museo de Cultura Indígena** (tel 2761-1004, www.sarapiquis.org), at La Virgen de Sarapiquí, is a superb museum profiling

Costa Rica's pre-Columbian and extant indigenous cultures. A visit will give you a sound appreciation as a prelude to visiting one or more reserves. Here are some that welcome visitors: **Reserva Indígena Boruca** (tel 2730-1673), in Puntarenas, is known for its Fiesta de los Diablitos, a three-day festival at the end of December. The community has a small museum. **Reserva Indígena Malekú** (tel 8888-4250 or 8839-

0540; see p.216), in the Northern Lowlands, has a small museum plus re-creations of traditional life, with performances of music and dance. **Reserva Indígena Yorkín** (tel 2248-9470, www .actuarcostarica.com), on the Panamanian border, is reached by boat and dug-out canoe. Lodging and facilities are basic. Visits are arranged through ACTUAR, which plans community-based rural tourism.

Refugio Nacional de Vida Silvestre Caño Negro

This 24,633-acre (9,968 ha) reserve is a watery world of swampy bayous. At its heart is a vast lake, which draws migratory waterfowl in such numbers that their rushing wings may be mistaken for the muffled roar of a distant jet aircraft. The waters also teem with plump, olive green crocodiles, grown fat on the local fish.

Lago Caño Negro floods with the onset of the rains, overflowing the reserve's borders.

The vast swamp occupies a large basin. **Lago Caño Negro,** at its heart, is filled by the **Río Frío** and other rivers that wash down from the Cordillera de Tilarán. In May the lake begins to swell, and vast lagoons form in the basin. Then, thousands of waterbirds flock here: anhingas, cormorants, ducks, egrets, grackles, and grebes, as well as ibises, wood storks, and roseate spoonbills ladling the black waters with their long, spatulate bills. In the relatively short dry season from February to April, many of the lagoons dry out; the lake shrinks, and much of the waterfowl departs for other climes.

Jaguars, ocelots, deer, tapirs, monkeys, sloths, and other large mammals inhabit the vast carpets of sedge and jolillo palm groves. Caimans are abundant, as are freshwater turtles. Pugnacious crocodiles the size of Peterbilt trucks can be seen sunning in saurian splendor on the banks of muddy sloughs.

Caño Negro is an angler's dream, with tarpon the ultimate prize during fishing season *(July– March, licenses required)*. Fishing trips and boat tours leave from the small border town of **Los Chiles,** about 60 miles (96 km) northwest of Ciudad Quesada, on the banks of the Río Frío. Canopied boats make the 16-mile (25 km) journey to Caño Negro. Boat trips also depart the hamlet of Caño Negro, on the western shore of the lake. ∎

Refugio Nacional de Vida Silvestre Caño Negro

- 🅰 Map p. 204
- ✉ Off Hwy. 35, 40 miles (64.4 km) NW of Ciudad Quesada
- ☎ 2471-1309
- 💲 $

www.sinaccr.net

More Places to Visit in the Northern Lowlands

The Venado Caverns near Venado were unknown until 1945, when a farmer fell into the entryway.

Hacienda Pozo Azul

Horseback rides are a specialty at this working cattle ranch, and so are white-water trips on the Río Sarapiquí, rappelling in the river canyon, and mountain biking. A zipline canopy tour will whisk you through the rain forest treetops. Guests can stay in a riverside tent camp, or at the Magsasay Lodge on the border of Parque Nacional Braulio Carrillo (see p. 85).
www.haciendapozoazul.com Map p. 205
✉ La Virgen de Sarapiquí ☎ 2761-1360
💲 $$$ (guided tours)

Laguna del Lagarto Lodge

This private reserve *(4WD access only)* protects 1,200 acres (485 ha) of virgin rain forest and crocodile-rich swamps near the confluence of the Ríos San Carlos and San Juan. The forests abound in wildlife, including a plentiful supply of poison dart frogs red as bright lipstick and blue as the morning sky. Visitors can see two-toed sloths, which spend most of their lives hanging upside down, and crocodiles. The nature lodge overlooks the Río San Carlos, which is good for exploring by canoe or on canopied boat trips.
www.lagarto-lodge-costa-rica.com
Map p. 205 ✉ 28 miles (45 km) NE of Aguas Zarcas ☎ 2289-8163 💲 $$ (guided tours)

Refugio Nacional de Vida Silvestre Corredor Fronterizo

Stretching the width of the country, the slender 230-square-mile (59,570 ha) wildlife refuge guards the forests along the Nicaraguan border. Much of the refuge fringes the broad Río San Juan, which can be explored by boat from the community of Boca San Carlos; at El Castillo, 25 miles (40.2 km) upstream, the **Fortaleza de la Immaculada Concepción** has been restored and has a museum on colonial history. Wildlife viewing along the banks is terrific.
✉ Bahía Salinas to Punta Castillo ☎ 2471-2191 💲 $$ (Nicaraguan border fee)

Reserva Indígena Malekú

Until recently, the Malekú indigenous culture was relatively unknown. Today the community of about 650 individuals, who speak their own language, promotes themselves to ecotourists, drawing visitors who want to learn about their cultural heritage and customs. **Rancho Típico Malekú Arara** *($$$$)*, on the northern slopes of Volcán Tenorio, offers traditional dance performances, and the nearby **Eco-Adventure Tafa Malekú** *(tel 2464-0443, $)* has a museum.
Map p. 205 ✉ 2 miles (3.2 km) E of San Rafael ☎ 8888-4250

Venado Caverns

These limestone caverns extend for almost 2 miles (3.2 km) beneath the foothills of the Cordillera de Tilarán. They are filled with underground streams, as well as stalactites and stalagmites in fascinating formations. Bats roost on the ceiling, transparent frogs hop about underfoot, and a blind species of fish swims in streams. Guides lead two-hour tours. Safety helmets and flashlights are provided. *(Bring waterproof footwear.)* The caverns are on the Solis family farm 1 mile (1.6 km) south of Venado, about 22 miles (35 km) northwest of La Fortuna.
Map p. 204 ✉ 5 miles (8 km) S of Jicarito on Hwy. 4 ☎ 2478-9081 💲 $$

Beaches washed by pounding waves, superb fishing and surfing, coral reefs, wildlife refuges, and unique local culture

The Caribbean

The Caribbean coast has a culture distinct from that of the rest of Costa Rica.

The Caribbean

Running for 125 miles (193 km) straight between the Nicaraguan and Panamanian borders, Costa Rica's palm-fringed, surf-pounded Caribbean coast is as wild as the nation's towering interior. Primeval rain forest spreads inland from the sandy littoral, melding into swampy lagoons to the north and rising into the spiraling, cloud-draped heights of the Talamancas to the south.

The entire coast varies little in its hot, humid climate. Rain cascades year-round but peaks from May to August and December to January, when storms bow the palms and turn dirt roads into quagmires. When the sun shines, surfers take to the waves, and the wildlife bursts into song and dance.

The Guápiles Highway (Highway 32) links San José with the former banana port of Puerto Limón, which lends its name to the province encompassing the Caribbean north to south. This funky terminus of the now defunct Atlantic Railroad idles with a languor typical of down-at-the-heels tropical ports, except during Carnival.

North of Limón, gray-sand beaches line the wave-washed shore. The rain-sodden hinterland (rains increase northward along the Caribbean) is backed by a broad alluvial plain—the Llanura de Tortuguero and Llanura de Santa Clara—that extends far inland, smothered in banana plantations and rain forest that culminate to the northeast

NOT TO BE MISSED:

in the wildlife-rich world of Parque Nacional Tortuguero and Refugio Nacional de Vida Silvestre Barra del Colorado, both reachable only by river or air. These two pristine environments form a haven of limpid lagoons fed by the murky waters of the Río San Juan and Río Colorado, providing anglers with world-class fishing for tarpon and snook. Numerous lodges cater to fishing enthusiasts and to nature lovers keen to spy the crocodiles, river otters, and manatees that inhabit the sloughs. The birding is equally fabulous. Motorboat tours give visitors the chance to glimpse a wealth of arboreal and terrestrial mammals.

South of Limón, the alluvial plain tapers sharply as the Talamancas crowd the shore. Year-round rains on the steep slopes nourish the virtually impenetrable montane rain forest. Reserva Biológica Hitoy-Cerere, albeit dauntingly rugged, is the most accessible of the reserves tucked into valleys deep in the mountains.

A coral reef is a highlight at Parque Nacional Cahuita, where snorkelers and scuba divers can mingle with reef fish streaming through aquamarine waters. Cahuita and Puerto Viejo draw surfers and other travelers who shun pretension. South of Puerto Viejo, the broad valley of the Río Sixaola opens inland, a portal to the indigenous reserves. This southern zone is known as Talamanca, a Native American word that refers to the slaughter of turtles. Marine turtles still nest up and down the coast: Tortuguero is the prime nesting site in the Caribbean for green turtles; and hawksbill and leatherback turtles nest here and at

Refugio Nacional de Vida Silvestre Gandoca-Manzanillo, which extends to the Panamanian border.

Hernán Cortés, who mapped the region in 1522, recorded trade between local Indians and Aztecs from Mexico. Cacao was an important export in the 18th century, shipped from the now defunct port of Matina. The inhospitable Caribbean coast was largely ignored by Spanish colonists; however, pirates and illicit traders filled the void. The region thus evolved apart from the rest of the nation. Its isolation ended in the 1880s, when the Atlantic Railroad was built and Puerto Limón became the chief coffee port. The era saw the arrival of Jamaican laborers, who stayed to work the burgeoning banana fields.

Today, about 50 percent of the culturally distinct Caribbean region's population is of West Indian extraction. The irresistible, syncopated beat of reggae and the highly spiced cuisine show how enduring their presence has been. While the area's economy is inextricably linked to the vicissitudes of the banana trade, tourism is now the economic mainstay. Accommodations from budget mountain retreats to chic beach cottages cater to this upsurge in popularity. ∎

Llanura de Santa Clara

These undulating alluvial plains extend eastward from the foot of Volcán Irazú, forming a vast green sea of banana plantations that meld into swamplands—which, in turn, push up to the ocean. The plains are walled to the south by the steep slopes of the Volcanes Irazú and Turrialba and, farther east, by the soaring Talamancas. Highway 32 runs along the base of this mountain chain, hopscotching scores of rivers that cascade from the high peaks above.

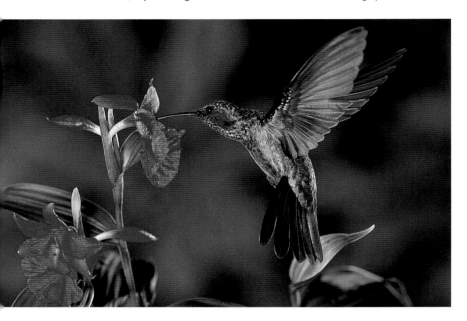

Hummingbirds sip nectar to meet their prodigious energy needs.

Bosque Lluvioso
🅰 Map p. 218
✉ 2 miles (3.2 km) S of Hwy. 32 from Km 56, 4 miles (6.4 km) W of Guápiles
☎ 2224-0819
💲 $$

www.bosque-u.com

Three main towns along Highway 32—**Guápiles, Guácimo,** and **Siquirres**—are service centers for the Río Frío banana region that dominates the western plains, accessed by a maze of dirt roads that extend to the border of Parque Nacional Tortuguero. The towns are rather dirty, disheveled affairs, but they offer notable attractions in their hinterlands. For example, 4 miles (6.4 km) west of Guápiles, one of Costa Rica's most acclaimed artists, North American Patricia Erickson, has a studio—**Gallery at Home** *(tel 2711-0823, by appt.),* in her house beside the Río Blanco. Her husband, Brian, makes and sells bamboo furniture.

From Highway 32, it's easy to access small private reserves that protect premontane rain forest on the flanks of Volcán Irazú and Volcán Turrialba. They share a wealth of wildlife—coatimundis, howler and white-faced monkeys, ocelots, sloths, snakes, and birds such as aracarias, hummingbirds, motmots, oropendolas, and toucans. Colorful

INSIDER TIP:

A tour of a banana plantation is fascinating, even if you are opposed to large-scale agriculture.

—JOHN LONGINO
National Geographic field researcher

poison dart frogs are easily spotted on the damp forest floor.

Half a mile (1 km) south of Gallery at Home at the **Casa Río Blanco Rain Forest Reserve** (see p. 256), charming cabins look directly over the forest canopy on the banks of the Río Blanco.

Bosque Lluvioso, a scientific research facility protecting 420 acres (170 ha) of virgin forest offers an even broader experience. You can see all the familiar species on self-guided hikes along manicured trails posted with educational boards (a booklet is also available). Trails lead to a lagoon and herbal and orchid gardens. Poison dart frogs are numerous here. A zipline gives a bird's-eye canopy experience, and there is a small zoo and exhibits on indigenous culture.

Jardín Botánico Las Cusingas, straddling the Río Santa Clara, also offers hikes and horseback rides into tropical montane rain forest, but it is better known for its botanical research and its vast gardens of ornamentals, raised for export. It has a visitor center, plus trails into the rain forest. Guided tours add a lot to the experience and enhance the chances of viewing wildlife.

Travelers with a keen interest in flowers should head north from Guácimo to **Costa Flores** (*tel 2716-7645*), claiming to be the largest flower farm in the world, with 300 acres (120 ha) of floral beds. Visitors are welcome at **EARTH,** a university dedicated to tropical agricultural sciences and preserving a 990-acre (400 ha) swath of lowland rain forest. ∎

Jardín Botánico Las Cusingas
- 🅰 Map p. 218
- ✉ 2.5 miles (4 km) S of Hwy. 32, 1 mile (1.6 km) E of Guápiles
- ☎ 2382-5805
- 💲 $$

EARTH
- 🅰 Map p. 218
- ✉ 800 yards (731.5 m) E of Guácimo
- ☎ 2713-0246
- 💲 $$$$$ (guided tours)

www.earth.ac.cr

Bananas' Cost

The Llanura de Santa Clara are awash with banana plantations. Costa Rica exported $603 million of bananas in 2006 (up from $473 million in 2005). Around 105,000 acres (42,500 ha) are planted, mostly in the Caribbean. U.S.-based Standard Fruit Company is the major producer. The resulting monoculture is blamed for many ecological ills, including the felling of rain forest for plantations. Fertilizer runoff has led reeds and water hyacinths to blossom, filling in habitats and channels, while silt washing out to sea has destroyed much of the coral reefs. Pesticides such as DBCP, banned in North America, have poisoned plantation workers. When plastic bags used to protect fruit stems end up in the ocean, marine turtles mistake them for jellyfish and choke. In a bid to secure an Eco-OK seal of approval, Costa Rica's banana industry is adopting more ecologically responsible methods.

Refugio Nacional de Vida Silvestre Barra del Colorado

Río San Juan forms the border with Nicaragua. Between it and Laguna de Tortuguero lie 225,365 acres (91,200 ha) of swampland and rain forest teeming with exotic wildlife. The labyrinthine lagoons and rivers boil with tarpon, snook, and antediluvian garfish, making the refuge the premier sportfishing center in Costa Rica.

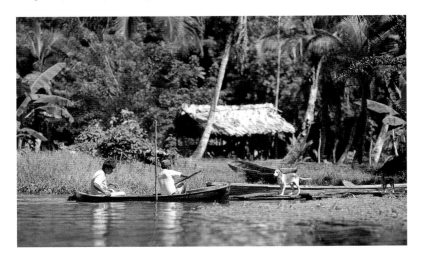

Plying the river in a traditional boat lets you meet the locals and get close-up views of wildlife.

Refugio Nacional de Vida Silvestre Barra del Colorado

 Map p. 218

 40 miles (64 km) N of Guápiles

☎ 2771-1201

$ $$

The rivers sluggish deposit vast amounts of silt that shift the watercourses yearly in a mosaic of deltas. Endless green rain forest fills the horizon; the forests are gnawed at by loggers, and banana plantations push up against the park's southern borders. The wet, hilly, lowlands are bordered to the west by 1,096-foot-high (334 m) hills, the **Lomas de Sierpe.**

Swampy sloughs meander from lagoon to lagoon. Most backwaters are inaccessible; here manatees breed in relative isolation. Jabiru storks, orpendolas, and green macaws are among the numerous intriguing bird species. Crocodiles bask on mud banks. And caimans, monkeys, sloths, river otters, and terrapins are sure-bet sightings.

The tumble-down village of **Barra del Colorado**—served by an airstrip—straddles the **Río Colorado,** a branch of the Río San Juan. Anglers set out from sportfishing lodges for colossal fights with record-setting tarpon and snook. The **Caño de Penitencia,** clogged by silt and water hyacinths, links Barra to Tortuguero (see pp. 224–225).

All along the riverbanks are dilapidated shacks on stilts. The river is entirely within Nicaraguan territory; you will need a passport and be prepared to pay a fee. ■

Parque Nacional Tortuguero

This 47,000-acre (19,000 ha) park encompasses diverse wetlands penetrating inland for 9 miles (15 km), a 14-mile-long (23 km) section of shoreline that is the Caribbean's premier nesting site for green turtles, and ocean waters that stretch 18 miles (29 km) offshore. Tortuguero, which is deluged by up to 200 inches (500 cm) of rain a year, comprises coastal rain forest and several distinct wetland ecosystems that are astonishingly rich in wildlife.

This popular, but remote, park is pinned by the funky hamlet of **Tortuguero,** sprawling along a 4-mile-long (6.4 km) sandy peninsula between a lagoon and the sea. At the northern end of the promontory, aircraft swoop down to the grass strip, from where boats ferry travelers to lodges or to the isolated village, which offers budget accommodations, canoes and guides for hire. A trail leads north from **Tortuga Lodge** (see p. 256), a prominent nature and sportfishing lodge, 1 mile (1.6 km) from **Cerro Tortuguero,** a 360-foot (110 m) hummock with views over the park.

The park's maze of waterways guarantees superb wildlife viewing. You are not likely to spot jaguars, tapirs, or any of the other endangered mammal species that inhabit the park. But visitors can expect to see monkeys, giant iguanas, and sloths, while aracarias, oropendolas, parrots, and toucans are among the most commonly seen of Tortuguero's 300 bird species, which include rare green macaws. Caimans and river otters rarely prove elusive as you cruise the canals.

A well-timed visit may coincide with leatherback, hawksbill, or green turtles coming ashore to lay eggs *(Feb.–Oct.).* Tortuguero is the Caribbean's primary green turtle hatchery. Guides from a local

Not-So-Tiny Bubbles

Endangered manatees inhabit lagoons in the remote western parts of the park. This herbivorous, heavily wrinkled mammal resembles a tuskless walrus with a spatulate tail. It grows to 12 feet (3.7 m) in length and can weigh a ton (907 kg). It spends most of its time submerged, foraging on water hyacinths and other aquatic fodder that produce flatulence. Bubbles rising to the surface of the water are therefore a good indication that a healthy manatee is expressing itself below.

cooperative escort nocturnal hikes on the beach *($$$),* which is otherwise off-limits after 6 p.m. *(only 400 people permitted nightly).* Report any guides who illegally dig up nests to show you the eggs of hatchlings. To learn more, stop at the **John H. Phipps Biological Station,** north of the village, where a **Natural History Visitor Center** has exhibits. At the village's south end, the **Cuatro Esquinas Ranger Station** also has exhibits; a trail leads into the rain forest, but rubber boots *(available for rent)* are compulsory in the wet season. ∎

Parque Nacional Tortuguero
- Map p. 219
- 10 miles (16 km) NE of Zancudo
- 2710-2929 or 2709-8086
- $$

John H. Phipps Biological Station
- Map p. 219
- Tortuguero
- 2709-8125
- $

A Ride on the Canal de Tortuguero

Until the 1960s, travel along the Caribbean coast was nearly impossible. Rough waves and the lack of bays precluded safe passage and anchorage, while the swamps that extend far inland thwarted the construction of roads. During the Trejos Administration (1966–1970), a canal was dredged parallel to the shore, linking the remote hamlets of Barra del Colorado and Tortuguero with Puerto Limón and the port of Moín.

Today a journey along the Tortuguero Canal is one of Costa Rica's most rewarding journeys—thrilling, too, as your boatman canes your craft with the throttle wide open.

The narrow, 70-mile-long (113 km) Canal de Tortuguero links the various lagoons and major rivers along the northern Caribbean plains and runs a few hundred yards inland of the surf-pounded shore. The canal is a liquid highway of commerce and the throbbing of weary engines is its mantra. Most of the lodges at Tortuguero and Barra provide their own watercraft for guests opting for the slow, scenic route. Watch for *cayucos*—motorized dugout canoes carved from a single log and traditionally used for ferrying bananas and other agricultural produce—and public water taxis, usually fast-paced *lanchas*. These small riverboats are not built for comfort; a waterproof poncho is recommended. (Be aware that this boat ride can be done in either direction.)

It is a 3.5-hour trip from **Moín ❶**, 3 miles (4.8 km) north of Limón. Private boats leave from the JAPDEVA dock *(tel 2799-1167, $$$$ round-trip)*. Within minutes you are enveloped in the deepest verdure, with patches of rain forest towering over the river. Egrets and numerous other waders stalk the grassy banks in search of tasty tidbits while kingfishers skim over black waters.

Twelve miles (19 km) from Moín, the canal opens into the **Boca del Río Matina ❷**, a broad estuary whose sluggish river deposits silt from the mountains; the tides spin the silt into long, brown-sand beaches. Female green, hawksbill, and leatherback turtles favor these warm sands for their nests, as well as at Playa Barra de Matina, where 4 miles (6.4 km) of shoreline backing the

beach are protected within the **Pacuare Nature Reserve ❸** *(tel 2541-2677)*, where scientists conduct turtle research; trails run parallel to the beach and to an inland lagoon amid rain forest.

Tour company charter boats depart for Tortuguero from Caño Blanco marina, at **Barra del Matina Sur,** 2 miles (3 km) upriver.

In all these miles there are no settlements to speak of, although occasionally you will pass a ramshackle hut made of wood and bamboo, raised on stilts to guard against flooding and snakes. The *cimaronnes* (literally, "wild ones" in reference to people of mixed blood) who live along the riverbank subsist on fishing, the sale of bananas, and cattle that graze in clearings cut from the grasslands and sedge.

The canal opens into the wide estuary of the **Río Parismina ❹**, a popular sportfishing location, particularly during the spring run of tarpon, which can be hauled in from the surf; and for snook, notably mid-August through November. Three sportfishing lodges cater to anglers. The silt that the river brings often clogs the canal—do not be surprised if your boat grounds. Beyond the river, the canal penetrates **Parque Nacional Tortuguero** (see p. 223), indicated by a sign beside the **Jaloba ❺** Ranger Station. No fee is charged for passage via the canal.

Northward, the overriding sense is of swamp and jungle. In places the rain forest canopy merges overhead, forming dark glades that echo with the roar of howler monkeys. Great stands of bamboo rise in feathery clusters. Freshwater turtles and caimans sunning themselves on logs will plop into the waters as you pass. Toucans are noisy and numerous. With good luck, you might even spot an endangered green macaw.

After 49 miles (79 km) you will arrive at the village of **Tortuguero** ❻, facing a broad lagoon that opens northward to the azure waters of the Caribbean. Most passengers end their journey here.

South of the village, the canal cuts inland and zigzags through the wetlands of **Refugio Nacional de Vida Silvestre Barra del Colorado** ❼

(see p. 222). Playful river otters are often seen along this 21-mile-long (34 km) section that slices through the aquatic wilderness, where raffia palms hang over the waters. Farther north, water hyacinths clog the channel. Eventually you come to a broad reach near the mouth of the **Río Colorado,** where crocodiles bask on the mudflats.

Three and a half hours from Moín, the village of **Barra del Colorado** ❽ marks the end of your journey.

NOT TO BE MISSED:

**Parque Nacional Tortuguero
• Refugio Nacional de Vida Silvestre Barra del Colorado**

🅐	Also see area map pp. 218–219
▶	Moín
⬌	70 miles (112 km)
🕒	3.5 hours (2 hours in opposite direction)
▶	Barra del Colorado

Barra del Colorado

REFUGIO NACIONAL
DE VIDA SILVESTRE
BARRA DEL COLORADO

❼

Suerte

Tortuguero

Tortuguero ❻

PARQUE
NACIONAL
TORTUGUERO

❺ **Jaloba**

Parismina   **Parismina**
❹ *Boca del Río Parismina*

Reventazón

Aguas Zarcas

Pacuare   *Boca del Río Pacuare*
San Rafael   **RESERVA FORESTAL
MATINA-PACUARE**

❸ Pacuare Nature
Reserve

Barra de
Matina Norte   ❷ *Boca del Río Matina*
Barra de Matina Sur/
Caño Blanco Marina

● **Boca del Pantano**

● **Nueve Millas**
● **Cocal**
Moín ❶   ● **PUERTO
LIMÓN**

32

START

= = = **Canal route**

0   10 kilometers
0   5 miles

Puerto Limón

Puerto Limón is a sultry town that is more a place to pass through than linger in. The only town along the Caribbean coast, Limón is the main service center for the eponymous region and is the country's main commercial port; it is also the gateway to both Tortuguero and Cahuita National Parks (see pp. 223 & 230), both of which are sea turtle nesting grounds. Puerto Limón hosts the country's main cruise dock and bursts to life during the annual Carnival. A brief visit reveals some minor attractions, including lovely beaches on the outskirts of town.

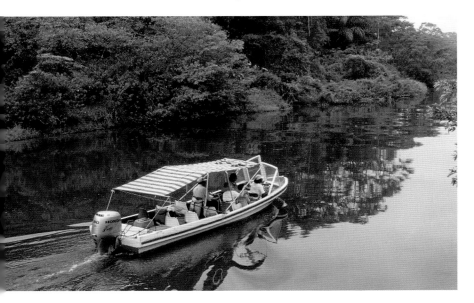

Tour boats ply the waterways near Puerto Limón.

Puerto Limón
🅼 Map p. 219
Visitor Information
☎ 2758-1906

The port evolved as a center for exporting hardwoods and, during the early colonial era, cacao, but soon fell beyond the pale of Spanish authority. It emerged as a refuge for buccaneers. Puerto Limón blossomed in the late 19th century, when the Atlantic Railroad was built and the banana trade followed. When blights scythed through the plantations from the 1930s on, the port suffered a decline from which it has only recently begun to recover. City leaders have

pulled the city up by its bootstraps in recent years: Streets are well paved, and cruise ships now arrive at the new port facility.

Despite its somewhat forlorn aspect, the city boasts some fine clapboard colonial buildings adorned with filigreed ironwork balconies. The town's oldest building, the **Black Star Line** (Ave. 5 & Calle 6), is of architectural and historic interest. Avenues are lined with tall palms and mango trees that cast great pools of shade. The most appealing building is the **town hall,** or *alcadia,* on the north side of the town plaza, **Parque Vargas,** which lies at the east end of Avenida 1. At its heart is a small bandstand surrounded by promenades shaded by tousled palms and by vine-draped strangler fig trees. Note the bronze busts of Columbus and his son Fernando on the northeast corner. They were dedicated in 1992 in celebration of the 500th anniversary of the Genoese explorer's landing in Mesoamerica. Facing it is an exquisite mural paying homage to

INSIDER TIP:

Some of the greatest rewards in travel come from what you give rather than receive. Volunteering to protect marine turtle nesting sites is a perfect example, and it is easily arranged through entities such as the Caribbean Conservation Corporation.

—CHRISTOPHER P. BAKER
National Geographic author

Columbus, pre-Columbian Indians, and the immigrant workers who put down roots locally.

An uninspired seafront boulevard overlooks a coral reef thrust from the sea on April 22, 1991, by an earthquake that razed several buildings and compounded the city's ill fortunes. The small isle of **La Uvita** lies 800 yards (730 m)

Carnival

When Día de las Culturas (Carnival) comes around in mid-October, Limón explodes in a bacchanal in which the Limoneses let down their hair and succumb to a promiscuous delirium. Rum, beer, and *guaro* (local grog of fermented sugarcane) flow freely. As many as 100,000 Ticos come to witness (and participate in) costume parades, beauty contests, and general revelry.

---

offshore. On September 18, 1502, Christopher Columbus anchored here and became the first European to set foot on the land he called La Huerta–The Garden.

The enclosed central market is worth a peek for the colorful stalls tucked into narrow alleys. Many restaurants and other businesses are run by Chinese, the offspring of indentured laborers who helped build the railroad, then stayed on and incorporated their culture into the city's fabric. The community has its own cemetery—**La Colonita China**—on Highway 32 west of town.

North of town, surfers ride the waves off **Playa Bonita,** a handsome beach that is excellent for sunning with occasional breaks for ceviche and grilled fish (washed down, of course, by homemade cashew wine) from thatch-roofed *ranchitas* where you can eat with your feet almost in the water. The **Original Canopy Tour Limón,** at Liverpool, lets you whiz through the treetops on a zipline. ∎

Caribbean Conservation Corporation
(See p. 144)

Original Canopy Tour Limón
- 🅰 Map p. 219
- ✉ In Liverpool off Hwy. 32
- ☎ 2291-4465
- 💲 $$$$$ (student & child discounts available)

www.canopytour .com/limon.html

Valle de la Estrella & the Talamancas

Shaded by coconut palms, a string of beaches leads the eye south from Limón. Highway 26 hugs the shore and makes brief forays inland, seeking narrow necks by which to cross the wide rivers—the Ríos Bananao, Bananito, and Estrella—that flood down from the Talamancas and seasonally inundate the narrow coastal plain and broad valleys.

Reserva Biológica Hitoy-Cerere

 Map p. 219

✉ Off Hwy. 36, 15 miles (24 km) W of Penshurst

☎ 2798-3170

$ $

www.sinac.go.cr

Selva Bananito

🅰 Map p. 219

✉ 9 miles (14.5 km) W of Bananito

☎ 2253-8118

$ $

www.selvabananito.com

Twelve miles (19 km) south of Limón, the road meets the mouth of the wide **Río Estrella,** where lagoons and channels abound with wildlife, including flocks of cattle egrets. The wetlands extend south along the shore to the **Aviarios del Caribe Sloth & Wildlife Refuge,** *(open to cruise ship groups only),* which serves as a refuge and research center for orphaned and confiscated sloths.

Half a mile (0.8 km) south of the river, at **Penshurst,** a side road snakes inland into the Valle de la Estrella. **Orquídeas Mundo** *(tel 2750-0789, $),* 600 yards (550 m) inland, raises hundreds of species of orchid. Guided hikes go into the nearby forest. Upriver, the valley opens into a wide basin carpeted with banana plantations and crisscrossed with dirt roads serving processing plants.

The Talamancas soar westward, clad in some of the densest montane rain forest in the isthmus. Some 22,363 acres (9,050 ha) is protected within **Reserva Biológica Hitoy-Cerere,** an undeveloped reserve accessed by four-wheel drive. Trails from the ranger station follow the valley of the Río Hitoy-Cerere to small waterfalls, and across the mountains into Valle de El General.

To the north of Hitoy-Cerere is **Selva Bananito,** a 2,350-acre (950 ha) cattle ranch and reserve with rustic cabins and a nature lodge in premontane rain forest, accessed by horseback or hiking trails. Expect to see sublime wildlife here, from monkeys to toucans. Tree climbing and rappelling tours, including rappels down a waterfall, are specialties. To reach it by road, you will need a four-wheel drive vehicle. ■

EXPERIENCE: Horseback Riding

Horseback riding is available nationwide. Here are some of the best places to saddle up (also see listings by region, pp. 260-265):
Rancho San Miguel *(La Guácima, Central Highlands, tel 2438-0849, see p. 75)*
Hotel Hacienda Guachipelín *(Curubandé, Guana-*

caste, tel 2666-8075, www.guachipelin.com)
Sabine's Smiling Horses *(Monteverde, Guanacaste, tel 2645- 6804, www.smiling horses.com)*
Finca Los Caballos *(Montezuma, Nicoya, tel 2642-0124, www.naturelodge.net)*
Marlboro Stables *(Manuel*

Antonio, Central Pacific, tel 2777-1108)
Bella Vista Lodge *(Escaleras, Central Pacific, tel 2787-8069, www.bellavista lodge.com)*
Seahorse Stables *(Punta Cocles, The Caribbean, tel 2750-0468, www. horseback ridingincostarica.com)*

Cahuita

Colorful Cahuita—named from *cawi*, the Native American word for the mahogany used to make dugout canoes—offers a taste of zesty culture and a laid-back lifestyle that draws a hip, unpretentious crowd keen to let down its hair. The rustic hamlet, gateway to Parque Nacional Cahuita (see p. 230), offers fine beaches, simple accommodations, some of the country's best regional cuisine, and activities that range from horseback riding to scuba diving to glass-bottom boat tours.

A horseback ride along Playa Negra is an exciting way to explore Cahuita.

The southern Caribbean was once a neglected regional backwater shunned by the national government. This area survived by fishing and by growing cacao, but the latter industry was destroyed by the *Monilia* fungus two decades ago, about the same time Highway 36 linked it to the rest of the country. Today, lively, colorful Cahuita boasts an unabashedly earthy charm.

The main village has no central plaza, merely two dirt roads paralleling the coast, with four dirt roads in between. The main street ends eastward at **Kelly Creek** and the entrance to Parque Nacional Cahuita, with a coral-colored beach curling into the hazy beyond. North of the village, dozens of simple accommodations and eateries line a black-sand beach—**Playa Negra**—sweeping north in a palm-shaded scimitar. (Be cautious when swimming, due to riptides.) Contact **Cahuita Tours** for horseback riding and other local activities.

Cahuita's spicy regional cuisine, dialect, and musical influences reflect longstanding links with Jamaica. Rastafarians are numerous, dressed in their trademark clothing of red, yellow, black, and green. Reggae riffs mingle with the sound of the surf, while pungent *ganja* (marijuana) hangs in the salt air. Locals pick up the beat each October, when a five-day Carnival prompts the Caribbeans to whirl and gyrate in the dusty streets.

Cahuita has earned a negative reputation, combated recently by heightened community policing. ■

Cahuita
- Map p. 219

Cahuita Tours
- 2755-0000

Parque Nacional Cahuita

This 2,711-acre (1,097 ha) park envelops a promontory—Punta Cahuita—clad with rain forests, where beaches curl away north and south around topaz blue bays. A coral reef covers 600 acres (242 ha) and extends around Punta Cahuita to Punta Vargas.

Parque Nacional Cahuita

- Map p. 219
- S of Cahuita village
- 2755-0461
- Donation (Kelly Creek); $$ (Punta Vargas)

The distinctive scarlet macaw

A 4-mile-long (6.4 km) trail traces the shoreline and links the **Kelly Creek Ranger Station** with the **Punta Vargas Ranger Station** about 1 mile (1.6 km) south of Punta Vargas and midway down the park. Be prepared to wade the shallow **Río Perozoso,** just west of Punta Cahuita. Much of the wildlife that inhabits the jungle green shore can be experienced without leaving the beach. Bands of inquisitive white-faced Capuchin monkeys often scamper in the treetops; coatis, iguanas, and raccoons poke their noses onto the sands; and the barking of howler monkeys echoes from within the dark forests. Agoutis, anteaters, and armadillos are among the other species to be seen while hiking—watch for snakes underfoot, and for harm-

less caimans cooling off in the lagoons and watercourses. Birdlife is also prolific, including green ibises, herons, toucans, garrulous parrots, and scarlet macaws, magnificent in their imperial cloaks of blue, red, and yellow, which flock here seasonally (Dec.–March).

Green, hawksbill, and leatherbacks marine turtles nest on the sweeping beach south of Punta Vargas, where waves help bring

INSIDER TIP:

Capuchin monkeys have learned to beg for food. Don't feed them! Human foodstuffs are unhealthy for monkeys, which have also been known to bite the hand that feeds them.

—CHRISTOPHER P. BAKER
National Geographic author

them in at high tide and the tidal pools are good on the ebb.

More than 125 species of fish, including blue parrot fish, gambol amid the hard and soft corals. The wreck of a slave ship with cannon and manacles in 20 feet (6 m) of water is an added highlight. Water clarity and reef ecology suffer from silt washing down from the banana plantations *(Feb.–April best for viewing reef).* ∎

Puerto Viejo

Puerto Viejo, the Caribbean coast's surfing capital, emits a centripetal pull on counterculture vacationers; it is Costa Rica's mecca of the offbeat. The legendary Salsa Brava wave pumps ashore in front of restaurants that bear an international imprimatur, and discos come alive at night. It all results in a hamlet spiced with a cosmopolitanism that belies its otherwise funky flavor.

A surfer gets a taste of La Salsa Brava, Puerto Viejo's renowned waves.

Vultures hop on the unpaved streets of the village, 2 miles (3.2 km) east of Highway 36 and 8 miles (13 km) south of Cahuita at the southern end of Playa Negra, which ends at **Punta Pirikiki.** Native American culture is strong here; guided trips into adjacent indigenous reserves are popular. The **Asociación Talamanca de Ecoturismo y Conservación** (ATEC; see p. 265) acts as the local information bureau and arranges visits to the Bribrí, Cabecar, and KeKöLdi reserves. Snorkeling, diving, and dolphin viewing are offered by **Reef Runner Divers** *(tel 2750-0480);* **Seahorse Stables** *(tel 2750-0468),* 3 miles (4.8 km) south of the village, offers horseback trips.

Puerto Viejo's lone attraction is the **Finca la Isla Botanical Garden,** which spans 12 acres (5 ha) of rain forest and gardens where spices, exotic fruits, and ornamental plants are grown. A self-guided booklet explains the trails, where monkeys, sloths, and snakes abound. Poison dart frogs live among the bromeliads, a tough-to-top photo op.

South of Punta Pirikiki, **Playa Cocles, Playa Chiquita,** and **Playa Manzanillo** extend 6 miles (9.6 km) south to Refugio Nacional de Vida Silvestre Gandoca-Manzanillo (see p. 232). About 60 hostelries, from funky to chic, line the road; most are run by North American transplants and other foreigners. At **Chocoart** *(tel 2750-0075, $$),* a Swiss couple produce delicious chocolate from their farm's organic cocoa. ∎

Finca la Isla Botanical Garden

🅰 Map p. 219

✉ 800 yards (732 m) W of Puerto Viejo

☎ 2750-0046

🕐 Closed weekends

💲 $ (guided tour)

Refugio Nacional de Vida Silvestre Gandoca-Manzanillo

This remote jewel extends from Punta Uva, 3 miles (4.8 km) south of Puerto Viejo, to the Río Sixaola, forming the border with Panama. The refuge (a prime turtle sanctuary) combines lush lowland rain forest with a coral reef and an amalgam of wetland habitats where visitors may spot manatees, crocodiles, and even an endemic species of freshwater dolphin. With more than 360 bird species on hand, don't rule out a sighting of the rare harpy eagle.

Refugio Nacional de Vida Silvestre Gandoca-Manzanillo

- 🅜 Map p. 219
- ✉ 12 miles (19.3 km) E of Puerto Viejo
- ☎ 2754-2133
- 🅢 $

Punta Mona Center for Sustainable Living & Education

- 🅜 Map p. 219
- ✉ 4 miles (6.4 km) S of Manzanillo
- ☎ 2614-5735
- 🕒 Visits by reservation only, minimum two people
- 🅢 $$$$$ (per person, includes lunch, kayak rental, and farm tour)

www.puntamona.org

The 23,348-acre (9,450 ha) refuge protects an invaluable mangrove system—the only one along Costa Rica's Caribbean coast—as well as the nation's only remaining orey swamp and two equally rare jolillo palm swamps where tapirs find safe haven. These labyrinthine mangroves extend along the estuary of the **Río Gandoca** and the **Laguna Gandoca,** where they provide a breeding place for sea life, including tarpon.

You might catch a glimpse of endangered manatees and rare pink-skinned estuarine dolphins—the *tucuxí*—as they come to the surface, snuffling and snorting, to breathe. The endemic tucuxí can also be seen swimming in the mouth of the **Río Sixaola;** these dolphins are found in coastal lagoons as far north as Nicaragua.

The wetlands back a beautiful palm-lined beach, **Playa Gandoca,** that four species of marine turtles consider a perfect place to deposit their precious eggs. To safeguard their nests, the sanctuary encompasses more than 10,961 acres (4,435 ha) of sea, which also protect a live coral reef. If you would like to lend a hand, the **Marine Turtle Conservation Project** (see p. 265) welcomes volunteers.

Access is from the hamlets of **Manzanillo** or **Gandoca** which are linked by a trail that skirts Laguna Gandoca inland and provides fantastic wildlife viewing along the way. Another trail follows the coast to **Punta Mona** (Monkey Point). Scuba diving and kayaking are available here.

Between Punta Uva and Manzanillo, the 8,765-acre (3,547 ha) **KéKöLdi Indian Reserve** meets the shore. Much of the reserve lies in the Gandoca-Manzanillo refuge; this safeguards the lands of the Bribrí and Cabecar tribes, who are exploring ecotourism and experimental income sources such as an iguana farm. Visits can be arranged in Puerto Viejo and Manzanillo through ATEC (see p. 265), as well as with ASACODE *(tel 2835-6819);* the latter is a *campesino* association that operates an ecotourism project at **San Miguel,** in the heart of the rain forest that smothers the hills inland. Here water buffalo have replaced tractors, while selective logging by community members has replaced clearing of entire stands of hardwoods. Counterculture types might enjoy a stay at **Punta Mona Center,** a community that practices and teaches about restorative agriculture. ∎

Travelwise

Costa Rica's roads can require nerves of steel.

TRAVELWISE

PLANNING YOUR TRIP
When to Go

Time your visit according to where you wish to go, as the country's climate varies by region. In general, the dry season (verano, or summer) is November to April, and the wet season (invierno, or winter) is May to October. The tourist board calls winter the "green season."

The Central Highlands enjoy a year-round springlike climate, with clear skies and warm weather. The wet season means clear mornings and afternoon showers, although prolonged rain is possible. Upper mountain slopes have alpine climates, with persistent fog and high winds.

Guanacaste sizzles during the dry season, when temperatures soar. Trees explode into bloom and stiff northwesterly winds whip the Pacific—fun for surfers but puts a damper on fishing.

Rainfall increases progressively southward in Nicoya and along the Pacific coast. Though Golfo Dulce and the Osa Peninsula have torrential rainfall throughout the year, clear skies are also frequent. Be prepared for stifling humidity. The same is true year-round of the Northern Highlands and Caribbean coast, where rainfall increases northward (almost 200 inches/ 500 cm annually in the Barra del Colorado and Tortuguero regions). January through April are the driest months, although heavy rain can fall at any time.

Most tourists visit in the dry season, when the more popular hotels may be booked solid. During green season, many hotels and car rental agencies lower their rates. This is a good time to visit, as many national parks and attractions are less crowded and the foliage is at its best.

What to Take

Costa Rica has a tropical climate, so dress accordingly. Expect hot days with warm evenings, except in mountain areas, where nights can be chilly. On higher slopes, cold winds bring fog and driving rain, so wind- and rainproof gear is essential. A sweater is useful, and a poncho works well against downpours in lowland areas. Loose-fitting cotton shorts and T-shirts are fine, as is clothing made of quick-drying, wicking fabrics. Avoid tight-fitting clothes (which promote fungal growth in the hot, humid climate), and bright colors (if you want to get close to wildlife). Informal wear is fine almost everywhere, but you might want an elegant outfit for smarter restaurants in San José.

You'll want a comfortable pair of shoes for hiking, but be prepared to get them wet. Pack a spare pair.

You will need insect repellent, particularly for wilderness excursions. Mosquitoes and other biting insects can be ferocious in Costa Rica, although they are not such a problem in the highlands.

Do not underestimate the tropical sun's strength. Sunglasses are important, and sunscreen is mandatory, even for brief periods outdoors. Wearing a hat or cap will keep you cooler and block the sun.

BEFORE YOU GO
Customs

Check with customs before bringing culture orchids and plants in sealed vials into the United States. For details contact the U.S. Customs Service, 1300 Pennsylvania Ave., NW, Washington, D.C. 20229, tel 202/354-1000, www.customs.gov.

Passports

A passport is mandatory for entry into Costa Rica. U.S. citizens do not need a visa to visit Costa Rica if they are traveling as tourists with a U.S. passport valid for at least 30 days, and if they will be staying for no more than 90 days.

If traveling with children under 18, remember that they become subject to local child welfare laws after 30 days, and you must request permission to take them out of the country. Contact the National Child Protection Agency (Patronato Nacional de Infancia), Calle 19 and Ave. 6, San José, tel 2523-0700.

HOW TO GET TO COSTA RICA
By Air

The majority of flights arrive at Juan Santamaría International Airport (tel 2437-2262) 11 miles (18 km) west of San José. An increasing number of flights arrive at Daniel Oduber International Airport (tel 2668-1032) 8 miles (13 km) west of Liberia, the provincial capital of Guanacaste.

The national carrier, Taca (tel 800/400-8222, www.taca.com) serves more than 25 destinations throughout the Americas, including several in North America.

The following U.S. airlines offer regular flights to Costa Rica: American Airlines (tel 800/433-7300, www.aa.com), Continental Airlines (tel 800/523-3273, www.continental .com), United Airlines (tel 800/864-8331, www.united.com), and Delta (tel 800/221-1212, www.delta.com).

Several charter airlines from major cities in the United States and Canada offer flights to and from Costa Rica.

By Car

The 2,000-mile (3,220 km) trip from the U.S.-Mexican border takes around two weeks. Preparation, and a four-wheel-drive vehicle, are essential. Arrange all documentation in advance and check your insurance. For advice, contact: **Sanborn's** *(tel 800/222-0158, www.sanbornsinsurance.com).*

Group Tours

Around one-third of travelers to Costa Rica choose a package tour. Most such tours are nature related, though sightseeing tours are also available. Contact the Institute of Costa Rican Tourism (ICT; see p. 239) for a list of recommended tour companies. Or try CANATUR (see p. 239).

GETTING AROUND
By Air

Major destinations are linked to each other, to Juan Santamaría International Airport, and to Tobias Bolaños domestic airport *(tel 2232-2820).*

Two domestic carriers serve regional airstrips with a network of scheduled flights. Both use 20- to 35-passenger aircraft. **SANSA** *(tel 2221-9414, www.flysansa.com)* is a government-subsidized airline that operates from Juan Santamaría International Airport. **NatureAir** *(tel 2299-6000 or 800/235-9272 in North America, www.natureair.com).* This airline operates from Tobias Bolaños Airport and offers a more flexible and reliable service.

Families and groups can charter small airplanes to airstrips throughout Costa Rica.

By Bus

There is no national bus network. Dozens of private companies offer fast *(directo)* and slower *(normal* or *corriente)* service. Trips should cost less than $10. Standards vary, with comfortable, modern buses on major routes. Rural areas are often served by retired U.S. school buses. Some lines sell tickets in advance; on others you pay when boarding. Be prepared for crowded condi-

tions, avoid travel on weekends, and guard against pickpockets and luggage theft.

Two shuttle bus services can take you almost anywhere in Costa Rica; fares start at around $21. **Interbus** *(tel 2283-5573, fax 2283-7655, www.interbusonline.com)* serves Cahuita, Fortuna, Manuel Antonio, Tamarindo, and other major destinations. **Grayline Fantasy Bus** *(tel 2220-2126, www.graylinecostarica.com).* transfers passenders between major tourist destinations.

Several bus companies also operate regular service from San José to destinations throughout Central America. Fares are cheap, but trips are time consuming.

San José's bus terminals are widely spread throughout the district called Coca Cola. It is a high-crime area; caution is advised. The bus lines in Costa Rica are privately operated by a myriad of companies, so determining route information can be difficult. There is no central information source.

Bus fares are extremely low—from around 75–200 colones (15–40 cents) to travel from the suburbs to central San José, to $3–$10 for cross-country trips.

Car Rental

To rent a car, you must be over 21, hold a passport, and a valid driver's license (a U.S. license is fine) that has been held for at least one year. You will also need a credit card and have to leave a hefty deposit (about $500). Beware additional charges that might appear on your bill when you return the car or get your credit card statement. Check that the rental includes unlimited mileage. Insurance is mandatory, and most rental companies, including U.S. franchises, refuse to honor insurance issued abroad. Rates vary from about $38 daily for the smallest vehicles, and $50 for mid-size cars, to between $60 and

$90 for four-wheel-drive vehicles (recommended, as the road network is in appalling shape). For off-road exploration, a rugged vehicle is essential.

In addition to Europcar, a reputable local company, most major international car rental companies are represented: **Avis,** tel 2293-2222, www.avis.com.cr **Budget,** tel 2255-4750, www.budget.co.cr **Dollar,** tel 2436-2000, www.dollarcostarica.com **Hertz,** tel 2221-1818, www.hertz.com **Europcar,** tel 2443-2950, www.europcar.co.cr

These agencies provide 24-hour breakdown assistance, but it can take hours to reach you in outlying areas.

Roads throughout the country are poor, with only 23 percent of the 18,000-mile (29,000 km) highway network paved. In the wet season many roads are quagmires, while Nicoya and Guanacaste are thick with dust during the dry season. Many Tico (Costa Rican) drivers are inconsiderate and reckless—there is a high auto fatality rate. Drive slowly and be on your guard. Stray cattle, pedestrians in the road, and potholes are additional hazards.

PRACTICAL ADVICE
Communications
Mail

It costs 115 colones (23 cents) to mail a postcard to North America and 145 colones (29 cents) to mail one to Europe. Postal rates for letters start at 155 colones (31 cents) to North America and 180 colones (36 cents) to Europe. Never mail anything of value, as theft is endemic within the postal service. Allow two weeks for air mail between Costa Rica and North America.

Most mail is delivered to shared postal boxes *(apartados,* abbreviated *Apdo.).* Most major settlements have a post office, usually open Monday to Friday, 7 a.m. to 6 p.m., and Saturday 7 a.m. to noon. In smaller towns, the Correo may close as early as 4:30, and not be open on Saturdays. Many gift stores and hotels sell postage stamps.

Faster, more reliable service is offered by private express mail services, such as DHL *(tel 2209-6000, www.dhl.co.cr)* and Federal Express *(tel 2239-0576, www.fedex.com/cr)*.

Telephones
In remote areas public phones are usually located at the local *pulpería* (grocery store and bar). Service is generally efficient. Have a stack of coins ready: They do not accept credit cards or foreign calling cards. Calls to the U.S. start at 65 cents per minute. Prepaid phone cards—look for the Viajera Internacional *199* symbol—are sold nationwide in increments of $10 and $20 for international direct-dial calls. Insert the card into the phone, and the cost of your call is deducted. USA-Direct phones link you to an AT&T operator. You can also dial direct to U.S., Canada, and U.K. operators:
AT&T, tel 164 or 0800/011-4114
MCI, tel 162 or 0800/012-2222
Sprint, tel 163 or 0800/013-0123
Canada, tel 161 or 0800/015-0161.
U.K., tel 167 or 0800/044-1044.
Hotels often charge a high fee for calls from in-room phones.

For direct-dial international calls, dial 00, then the country code and area code, then the number. For information, dial 113. Dial 116 for assistance in placing international calls, or to call collect.

Calling from the U.S., dial 011 plus Costa Rica's country code, 506. There are no area codes. In 2008, Costa Rica adopted an eight-digit system; all noncellular numbers now begin with 2, while cellular numbers now begin with 8.

Email
Internet cafés are available throughout Costa Rica. Rates vary from about 350–1500 colones (70 cents–$3) per hour, depending on the venue.

Conversions
Costa Rica uses the metric system of measurement. Useful conversions are:

1 mile = 1.61 kilometers
1 kilometer = 0.62 mile
1 meter = 39.37 inches
1 liter = 0.277 U.S. gallon
10 liters = 2.8 U.S. gallons
1 U.S. gallon = 3.61 liters
1 kilogram = 2.2 pounds
1 pound = 0.45 kilogram

Weather reports use Celsius. To convert quickly (but roughly) from Fahrenheit to Celsius, subtract 30 and divide by two. From Celsius to Fahrenheit, multiply by two and add 30.

0°C	=	32°F
10°C	=	50°F
30°C	=	86°F
100°C	=	212°F

Etiquette & Customs
Costa Rican society is more formal than most. Ticos rarely address individuals by their first names without an invitation to do so. They are class conscious, with *campesinos* (peasant farmers) and the urban working classes deferring to people considered of a higher status. Black visitors may experience some aloofness.

Costa Ricans use the formal *usted* for you, while the informal *"tu"* is reserved for intimates. You may also hear the term *vos* used instead of *tu*. They respect professional titles and use them when addressing title holders, such as engineers (e.g., Ingeniero Rodríguez) and architects (Arquitecto García).

Adults are addressed as Señor

(Mr.), Señora (Mrs.), or Señorita (Miss). The terms Don (for men) and Doña (for women) are used for high-ranking or respected individuals and senior citizens.

Behavior is dictated by *quedar bien*–a desire to leave a good impression. Ticos are courteous and easily offended. They prefer to use hidden cues rather than state forthright opinions that might disappoint. Thus they will often conceal the truth to create an immediate good impression as, for example, when visitors ask directions. Society operates on "Tico time;" punctuality is not a national trait. Verbal commitments are not necessarily meant to be taken at face value. Costa Ricans tend to be fatalistic about events. Si Díos quiere– God willing–is a standard refrain for life's ups and downs.

Bathing suits are frowned on away from the beach. Carry a coverup or shorts and T-shirt to change into after swimming.

Life revolves around the family. Personal contacts are the key to success, particularly in business and politics. Individualism is frowned upon; team spirit and cooperation take precedence. Costa Ricans tend to be guarded about their family life and rarely extend invitations to their homes.

Outside the main tourist areas you may not be understood in English, so it is advisable to learn a few Spanish phrases. Most restaurants in tourist areas have menus in English; you may have to ask for them.

Health
The national service, Seguro Social (also known as the "Caja"), offers medical treatment for tourists for minimal fees. However, the service is not up to North American standards and visitors are advised to seek treatment at private facilities, such as **Clínica Biblica** *(tel 2257-5252)* in San José, or **Hospital CIMA** *(tel 2231-*

2781) in Escazú. Most towns have private physicians and clinics.

Take out full travel insurance, which should cover all medical costs—hospitalization, nursing services, doctors' fees, etc. A medical evacuation clause is also important in case sufficient care is not available and you need to return home.

If you require medical help, consult your hotel. Most maintain a list of doctors and medical centers, which can save time. Otherwise, consult the Yellow Pages of the telephone book. Keep any receipts or paperwork for insurance claims. Make a note of the generic name of any prescription medications you take before you leave home. They may be sold by a different trade name in Costa Rica.

The main health hazards relate to Costa Rica's tropical climate, where bacteria and germs breed profusely. Wash all cuts and scrapes with warm water and rubbing alcohol. Although most water is potable, it is wise to regard it as suspect: Drink and brush your teeth with bottled water. Boil water when camping to eliminate giardia, a parasite that thrives in warm water. Avoid uncooked seafood and vegetables, unwashed salads, and unpeeled fruits.

Be liberal with the application of sunscreens and build up your tan gradually, as the tropical sun is intense and severe sunburn or sunstroke can effectively ruin a vacation. Drink plenty of water to guard against dehydration.

Biting insects are common, particularly in the humid lowlands. Malaria is present in the southern Caribbean zone and is spread by mosquitoes: Consult your physician for a suitable malaria prophylaxis. Dengue fever is also spread by mosquitoes and occasional outbreaks are reported in the Caribbean and Pacific Lowlands. There is no preventative medication, so it is wise to try to avoid being bitten.

Use insect repellents liberally, and wear earth-colored clothing with long sleeves and full-length pants. Be aware that no-see-ums, tiny biting fleas, strike on the beaches at dawn and dusk.

Wear long pants when hiking in grasslands, particularly in Guanacaste, to guard against chiggers *(coloradillos)* and ticks *(garrapatas)*.

Hunting & Fishing

Hunting is prohibited for foreign visitors and firearms cannot be brought into the country. Fishing is also regulated and visitors must obtain a nonresident permit. This is usually arranged by specialist sportfishing outfitters and lodges. Permits for mountain fishing can be obtained from the Ministry of Agriculture *(Antigüo Colegio La Salle, Sabana Sur, San José, tel 2231-2344, www.mag.go.cr).*

Media
Newspapers

Costa Rica has three national newspapers (each of which offers a conservative view), published in Spanish: *La Nación, La República,* and *La Prensa Libre,* available at newsstands throughout the country. The English-language weekly *Tico Times* is available in hotel lobbies and gift stores, and offers a well-rounded and often critical perspective of the nation.

A number of other English-language publications also circulate, including the monthly magazines *Costa Rica Traveler* and *Costa Rica Outdoors.* Major U.S. daily newspapers, such as the *New York Times* and *USA Today,* and weekly magazines, such as *Time* and *Newsweek,* are usually available at leading hotel gift shops and at select newsstands in major towns and beach resorts.

Television & Radio

Television reaches almost everyone, although service is intermittent in remote areas.

There are 16 local stations, plus numerous cable channels. Most upscale hotels offer cable TV with U.S. programs.

Costa Rica has about 120 radio stations. All but a few broadcast local and Latin music. The BBC World Service and Voice of America offer English-language news. The granddaddy of English-language stations is Radio 2 (99.5 FM), which plays hits from the 1960s on, as does SuperRadio (102.3 FM).

Money Matters
Currency

The national currency is the *colón.* U.S. currency is widely accepted (and welcomed, due to the colón's daily devaluation) throughout the country. Most stores, shops, restaurants, and tour companies will accept them, including those in smaller towns. Elsewhere you'll need *colones.* Exchange rates are notoriously fickle, so check the rate before leaving for your trip.

Bills come in denominations of 1,000 *(rojo),* 2,000 *(dos rojos),* and 5,000 *(tucán),* and 10,000 *(jaguar)* colones. Coins are issued in denominations of 5, 10, 25, 50, and 100 colones.

Banks in larger towns usually have foreign exchange counters. Most hotels exchange currency, as do foreign exchange bureaus *(cambios)* in the major towns and tourist centers. Check for high commission fees. In remote areas, expect long lines at banks. Limit the amount of U.S. currency you exchange, as only $50 worth of colones can be exchanged for dollars on leaving.

Visitors may experience trouble cashing traveler's checks anywhere but banks, due to widespread fraud. Many shops will simply refuse to accept them.

Automated Teller Machines

Many banks now have 24-hour automated teller machines (ATMs) for cash advances using credit cards or withdrawals from your account using a bank card. This means your own bank does the exchange. There is usually a small charge for using the ATM.

You will need your personal identification number, or PIN, to withdraw cash. Before leaving home, it is wise to check how much you can withdraw at one time or on any one day. Using ATMs during regular banking hours is advisable, in case of problems (e.g., machines not returning cards).

Credit Cards

Credit cards (tarjetas de crédito) are widely accepted. Visa is the most commonly accepted credit card, followed by MasterCard and American Express.

National Holidays

In addition to Christmas, New Year's Day, and Easter, the following national holidays are observed:

March 19, St. Joseph's Day
April 11, Juan Santamaría Day
May 1, Labor Day
July 25, Guanacaste Day
August 2, Feast of the Virgin of Los Angeles
August 15, Feast of the Assumption
October 12, Columbus Day
December 8, Feast of the Immaculate Conception

Most tourist sites and services, and many stores, stay open for these holidays, but banks and government offices close. Except for tourist services, the country closes down for Easter week (Wed.–Sun.), when fiestas and religious processions occur nationwide; Few buses operate on Holy Thursday and Good Friday.

Opening Times

Most stores in Costa Rica are open from 8 a.m. to 6 p.m., Monday through Saturday, with a one- or two-hour lunch break. Malls, supermarkets, and souvenir stores tend to have longer hours, and are also open on Sunday.

Bank hours vary, with most opening around 8:15 to 9 a.m. and closing between 3 and 3:45 p.m. Some banks have Saturday morning hours. Most businesses and government offices are open Monday to Friday, 8 a.m. to 5 p.m., often with a two-hour lunch break. Some are open on Saturdays from 9 a.m. to noon.

Most restaurants and other tourist-oriented businesses do not close for lunch.

Places of Worship

Every community has at least one Roman Catholic church, and often a Protestant church as well. Local tourist information offices and leading hotels can usually supply a list of places of worship.

Smoking

Many Costa Ricans smoke. Smoking is banned on public transportation and in taxis, and is restricted in public places, including bars. However, many restaurants lack nonsmoking facilities, and many bars choose to disregard the law.

Taxes

A minimal sales tax is applied to many, but not all, purchases. Only full-service restaurants add taxes to your bill, not sodas or snack bars. There is a 23 percent sales tax at restaurants and for most service industries. Hotels levy a 16.39 percent tourist tax. Be prepared to pay an exit tax of $26 (payable in colones or U.S. dollars) when leaving the country via air.

Time Zones

Costa Rican time is the same as U.S. Central Standard Time (CST), one hour behind Eastern Standard Time (EST), and 6 hours behind Greenwich Mean Time (GMT). Costa Rica does not observe daylight savings time, during which the country is 2 hours behind EST, and 7 hours behind British Summer Time.

Tipping

Tipping is not a fact of life in Costa Rica, except in tourist areas, where many people in service jobs depend on tips to make ends meet. However, a tip is an acknowledgment of good service: If the service is not satisfactory, do not tip.

Although a 10 to 15 percent service charge is often added onto restaurant bills, an additional tip should be given for good service. Tour guides should be tipped about $2 per person per day for group tours, and more for personalized services and private tours.

Hotel porters should be given 50 cents per bag, and room service staff 10 percent of the bill before taxes. Taxi drivers do not expect tips, although those serving the airport generally expect $1 or so.

Travelers with Disabilities

Costa Rica does not display great sensitivity to the needs of visitors with disabilities, although this situation is changing. Few buildings have wheelchair access or provide accessible toilets. Buses are not adapted for wheelchairs, and curb cuts are rare. In fact, most sidewalks are major obstacle courses, with deep fissures, open gutters, and so forth.

Some modern, upscale hotels have wheelchair access and a few provide specially equipped suites. However, older accommodations and restaurants may present some difficulties. Fortunately, new compliance codes are coming into effect. Outside San José, there are few handicapped-accessible services. New codes are not widely enforced yet.

The following agencies provide information on tour operators, special guides, and other aspects of traveling abroad for visitors with disabilities:
Vaya Con Sillas de Ruedas, (Go with Wheelchairs), tel/fax 2454-2810, www.gowithwheelchairs.com, offers transfers and tours for wheelchair-bound travelers.
Information Center for Individuals with Disabilities, P.O. Box 750119, Arlington Heights, MA 02475, fax 781/860-0673, www.disability.net
Society for Accessible Travel & Hospitality, 347 Fifth Ave., Ste. 610, New York, NY 10016, tel 212/447-7284, www.sath.org
Flying Wheels Travel, 143 W. Bridge St., Owatanna, MN 55060, tel 507/451-5005, www.flyingwheelstravel.com

Visitor Information
The Costa Rican government's **Instituto de Costa Rican Tourism** (ICT, *tel 866/COSTA-RICA, www.visitcostarica.com*) has several regional tourism bureaus, including the main information bureau situated beneath the Plaza de la Cultura in San José *(tel 2222-1090)* and in San José's main post office, *(tel 2258-8762)*. The **Costa Rican National Chamber of Tourism,** (CANATUR, *tel 2234-6222, fax 2253-8101, www.canatur.org*) represents the private tourism sector and publishes brochures and tourist information.

The following locations all have chambers of tourism:
Alajuela, tel 2441-8118
Caribe Sur, tel 2750-0151
Cartago, tel 2551-0396
Cahuita, tel 2755-0017
Costa Bellena, tel 2787-0025
Dominical, tel 2787-0087

Golfito, tel 2775-1179
Guanacaste, tel 2654-5355
Heredia, tel 2237-2620
Liberia, tel 2378-1972
Limón, tel 2758-1906
Manuel Antonio, tel 2777-2222
Monteverde, tel 2645-5926
Nicoya, tel 2685-5417
Osa, tel 2786-6534
Pacífico del Sur, tel 2787-0087
Playas del Coco, tel 2667-0125
Puerto Jiménez, tel 2735-5440
Puntarenas, tel 2661-2980
Sarchí, tel 2454-1633
Sarapiquí, tel 2761-1579
Talamanca, tel 2751-0026
Tortuguero, tel 2257-3887
Zona Norte, tel 2460-2020

Individual tour operators have websites. Costa Rican travel agencies and tour operators are represented by the **Asociación Costarricense de Agencias de Viajes** *(tel 2257-3285, www.acav.or.cr).*

The following conservation groups can provide information on environmental issues:
Fundación Neotrópica, tel 2253-2130, www.neotropica.org
Monteverde Conservation League, tel 2645-5003, www.acmcr.org
Organization for Tropical Studies, tel 2524-0607, www.ots.ac.cr
Rainforest Alliance, tel 212/677-1900, www.rainforestalliance.org.

EMERGENCIES
Crime & Police
Crime in Costa Rica is on the increase. Burglary and petty theft are more prevalent than in most North American cities. Caution should be exercised at all times. In major towns, avoid parks, back streets, and unlit areas after dark. In towns there is a danger of pickpockets, so be wary in crowded areas. Highway robbers target tourists. If you get a flat tire, keep driving to a public place to change the tire.

Never leave anything in cars, especially at surfing beaches,

where car break-ins are endemic. Don't carry lots of cash or wear expensive-looking jewelry, and keep passports and credit cards out of sight. If anything is stolen, report it immediately to the police and/or your hotel.

For police, fire, and ambulance, call 911. In most areas you can also call 127 for police, or 117 for traffic police; call 128 for the Red Cross, and 118 for the fire department.

The ICT (see this page) maintains a 24-hour emergency hotline *(tel 800/012-3456).*

Report crimes to the Judicial Police (OIJ) at Calle 17, Ave. 16/18, San José, tel 2295-3271. Visitors from the U.S. can request a representative of the U.S. Embassy be present.

The traffic police patrol the highways, and a new professionalism belies their reputation for corruption. However, dishonest officials still exist. Never pay a policeman; report any attempts at extortion to the OIJ *(tel 2295-3272).*

Embassies
U.S. Embassy, in front of Centro Comercial, road to Pavas, Rohrmoser, San José, tel 2519-2000, www.usembassy.or.cr
Canadian Embassy, Oficentro Ejecutivo La Sabana, Edificio 5, Tercer Piso, Sabana Sur, San José, tel 2242-4400, fax 2242-4410, www.dfait-maeci.gc.ca/sanjose
British Embassy, Centro Colón, Paseo Colón, Calles 38/40, San José, tel 2258-2025, fax 2233-9938, www.britishembassycr.com

Snake Bites
If a venomous snake bites you, get immediate medical help. Give snakes a wide berth and wear ankle-high shoes when hiking.

Hotels & Restaurants

Accommodations in Costa Rica are varied and reasonably priced, although standards vary widely. There are great differences between the types of facilities available, and it will help you to understand these differences when deciding where to stay. Remember that large areas of the country are remote, so the available or more desirable accommodations may fill quickly during the busy winter months, particularly during Christmas and Easter holidays.

Eating out can be a great pleasure in San José, which offers a wide variety of possibilities. Elsewhere menus are typically restricted to traditional fare and seafood, with more cosmopolitan options in tourist destinations and upscale hotels.

Accommodations

There are several types of accommodations. While these terms are sometimes used interchangeably, *albergues* (hostels), *hospedajes* (boardinghouses), and *cabinas* (cheap hotels) are among the budget options. Mid-range hotels are widely available, offering minimal service and no frills; standards vary. Top-of-the-range city and resort hotels offer international standards. These range from small, family-run boutique hotels, often in superb settings, that combine intimacy with charm, to large beachside resorts and city hotels owned by international chains. Some of these chains have toll-free numbers:
Best Western International, tel 800/780-7234, www.bestwestern.com
Choice Hotels International, tel 877/424-6423, www.choicehotels.com
Marriott Hotels & Resorts, tel 888/236-2427, www.marriott.com
Radisson Hotels & Resorts, tel 800/333-3333, www.radisson.com
　　Six superb boutique hotels compose the Small Distinctive Hotels of Costa Rica *(tel 2258-0150, www.distinctivehotels.com).*
　　Principally for nature lovers, hikers, and anglers, wilderness

lodges range from tent camps and no-frills wooden lodges with basic family-style meals to more sophisticated options with fine dining, spa pools, and saunas.
　　Avoid "motels," usually used for short-term sexual trysts. *Apartotels* are self-catering units, popular in San José.
　　In budget hotels, sink plugs may be missing, and showers are often cold. Warm (tepid) water may be provided by an electric element above the shower. Electric elements (aka "suicide showers") are common throughout the country; unless the wiring is damaged, electrocution is no worry. Ensure windows and doors are secure.
　　Bed-and-breakfast homestays are increasingly popular. Look for advertisements in the *Tico Times,* or try agencies such as:
Bells' Home Hospitality, Dept. 1432, P.O. Box 025216, Miami, FL 33102, tel 2225-4752, www .homestay.thebells.org.
　　The ICT rating system for hotels uses a Sustainable Tourism ranking, taking into account factors such as the retention of natural ecosystems, the use of recyclables, and the application of energy-saving devices. A 13 percent sales tax and 3.9 percent ICT tax are added to most bills.
　　Unless otherwise stated:
1. All hotels have dining rooms and private bathrooms.
2. Hotels are open year-round.
3. All numbers over eight digits are dialed direct from the U.S.

Restaurants

The vast majority of Costa Rican restaurants serve *comida típica*

(see p. 20), and are open from 11 a.m. to 2 p.m., and 6 p.m. to 11 p.m. Make reservations for the more expensive restaurants, particularly on weekends. Service is slow; you may have to ask for your bill.
　　A selection of good quality restaurants is given below. These are both individual and typical, with notable local associations wherever possible.

Credit Cards

Giving a card number is often the only way to reserve rooms in upscale hotels. Many hotels add a fee of up to 6 percent for credit card payments, however.

Making Reservations

Although we have tried to give comprehensive information, please check details before making reservations. This applies particularly to the availability of facilities for disabled guests or nonsmoking rooms, acceptance of credit cards, and rates. Do not rely on booking by mail: Fax or email your reservation. **Please note that 800 numbers listed do not work within Costa Rica.**

■ SAN JOSÉ

Hotels

AUROLA HOLIDAY INN
$$$$
AVE. 5, CALLE 5
TEL 2232-2424 OR 800/465-4329
FAX 2255-1171
www.aurolahotels.com
High-rise elegance overlooking Parque Morazán. Full complement of services

🏨 Hotel　🍴 Restaurant　ⓘ No. of Bedrooms　🪑 No. of Seats　🅿 Parking　🕐 Closed　🛗 Elevator including a casino, bars, and 17th-floor restaurant with great views.

ⓘ 201 🔲 🔲 🔲 🔲
🔲 All major cards

BARCELÓ SAN JOSÉ PALACIO
$$$$
AUTOPISTA GENERAL CAÑAS, 1 MILE (1.6 KM) NW OF PARQUE SABANA
TEL 2220-2034   FAX 2220-2036
www.barcelo.com
Elegant, modern high-rise with full services. The upscale casino, sports facilities, and spa are highlights, but the location is unappealing.

ⓘ 254 🅿 🔲 🔲 🔲 🔲
🔲 All major cards

COSTA RICA MARRIOTT
$$$$
1 MILE (1.6 KM) NW OF CIUDAD CARIARI, 800 YARDS (732 M) W OF SAN ANTONIO DE BELÉN
TEL 2298-0000 OR 800/228-9290
FAX 2298-0011
www.marriott.com
A rural location on a coffee farm with views to distant mountains. The hacienda-style building has elegant decor, shops, ballroom, golf practice range, and restaurants.

ⓘ 252 🅿 🔲 🔲 🔲 🔲 🔲
🔲 🔲 All major cards

DOUBLETREE CARIARI
$$$$
CIUDAD CARIARI, 5 MILES (8 KM) NW OF SAN JOSÉ
TEL 2239-0022   FAX 2239-2803
www.doubletree.com
A full-service resort with modern decor and in-room services, midway between the city and the airport. Popular with groups. Tennis courts, two swimming pools, golf course, casino, lively bar, and choice of restaurants. Wireless and high-speed Internet. Children's activities.

ⓘ 220 🅿 🔲 🔲 🔲
🔲 All major cards

RAMADA PLAZA HERRADURA
$$$$
CIUDAD CARIARI, 5 MILES (8 KM) NW OF SAN JOSÉ
TEL 2209-9841   FAX 2293-2713
www.ramadaherradura.com
Several very good restaurants (including Mediterranean and Japanese; see p. 243), a casino, spa, and golf and country club complement the large conference center.

ⓘ 232 🔲 🔲 🔲
🔲 All major cards

BARCELÓ PALMA REAL
$$$
2 BLOCKS N OF THE I.C.E. BLDG.
TEL 2290-5060   FAX 2290-4160
www.hotelpalmareal.com
This stylish business hotel west of downtown has amenities such as wireless and high-speed Internet, business center, conference rooms, fitness room, a bar, and two restaurants. There are king-size beds and spa pools in suites.

ⓘ 65 🅿 🔲 🔲 🔲 🔲 🔲 🔲 AE, MC, V

BRITANNIA
$$$
CALLE 3 & AVE. 11
TEL 2223-6667 OR 800/263-2618
FAX 2223-6411
www.hotelbritanniacosta rica.com
This turn-of-the-20th-century mansion is complete with antiques, colonial tilework, and stained-glass. King-size beds are a new addition. The dining room is located in an old wine cellar.

ⓘ 24 🔲 🔲 AE, MC, V

CLARION AMÓN PLAZA
$$$
AVE. 11 & CALLE 3 BIS
TEL 2523-4600 OR 800/575-1253
FAX 2523-4614
www.hotelamonplaza.com
A modern interpretation of a colonial period style in the historic Barrio Amón district,

a 15-minute uphill walk to the city center. Business center, casino, and elegant restaurant.

ⓘ 87 🔲 🔲 🔲
🔲 All major cards

SOMETHING SPECIAL

GRANO DE ORO
$$$
CALLE 30, AVES. 2/4
TEL 2255-3322   FAX 2221-2782
www.hotelgranadeoro.com
A Canadian-run hotel off Paseo Colón in a leafy district a 20-minute walk from downtown. Charming decor includes bathrooms adorned with hand-painted tiles. Peruvian artwork abounds and soothing music wafts through the narrow skylit corridors. Impeccable service highlights the top-notch restaurant, enhanced in 2007, where Costa Rican fusion cuisine is served. Elegant wood paneling. Reservations recommended.

ⓘ 32 rooms, 3 suites 🅿 🔲
🔲 AE, D, MC, V

HOTEL CITY ONE
$$$
AVE. 9, CALLES CENTRAL/2
TEL 2248-1580
www.hotelcityone.com
Chicly contemporary newcomer with a hip blazing white, chocolate, and orange color scheme and minimalist furnishings. Fine restaurant.

ⓘ 50 🔲 🔲 All major cards

TRYP COROBICÍ
$$$
CALLE 42, 50 YARDS (46 M) N OF BULEVAR LAS AMÉRICAS
TEL 2232-8122   FAX 2231-5834
www.solmelia.com
This high-rise hotel stands on the northeast corner of Parque Sabana. Arranged around a steepled atrium, it has modern facilities including a casino, a nightclub, and spa.

ⓘ 202 🅿 🔲 🔲 🔲 🔲 🔲
🔲 🔲 AE, MC, V

🔲 Nonsmoking 🔲 Air-conditioning 🔲 Indoor Pool 🔲 Outdoor Pool 🔲 Health Club 🔲 Credit Cards

🏨 BALMORAL
🍴 $$
AVE. CENTRAL, CALLES 7/9
TEL 2222-5022 OR 800/691-4865
www.balmoral.co.cr
Modern decor, an in-house casino, and on-site car rental and tour desk highlight this modest hotel. Rooms are small and rather noisy, but the location is good for exploring the city core. The restaurant is undistinguished.

ℹ️ 112 ⇄ 🅂 🍸
🄰 All major cards

🏨 DON CARLOS
🍴 $$
CALLE 9, AVE. 9
TEL 2221-6707   FAX 2255-0828
www.doncarloshotel.com
A rambling converted colonial mansion with a homey ambience, in the heart of Barrio Amón. Stained glass, sculptures, and pre-Columbian treasures abound in public areas. Small restaurant.

ℹ️ 36 🄰 All major cards

🏨 GRAN HOTEL
🍴 $$
AVE. 2, CALLES 1/3
TEL 2221-4000   FAX 2221-3501
www.granhotelcr.com
This recently renovated hotel, a historical and architectural landmark, has a superb location on Plaza de la Cultura, and a lively outdoor café. Has a 24-hour casino, and several dining options.

ℹ️ 110 🅿️ ⇄ 🄰 AE, MC, V

🏨 HOTEL FLEUR DE LYS
🍴 $$
CALLE 13, AVES. 2/6
TEL 2223-1206   FAX 2257-3637
www.hotelfleurdelys.com
This Swiss-owned hotel is situated in a restored Victorian mansion. Rooms feature wicker and wrought-iron beds and pastel walls. Rates include tropical breakfast. French restaurant on-site.

ℹ️ 31 🄰 AE, MC, V

🏨 HOTEL 1492 JADE Y ORO
$$
AVE. 1, CALLES 31/33
TEL 2225-3752
www.hotel1492.com
A quaint hotel in a charming colonial home in quiet Barrio Escalante. The decor features tile mosaics. Evening wine and cheese on a garden patio.

ℹ️ 10 🅿️ 🅂 🄰 MC, V

🏨 HOTEL OCCIDENTAL
🍴 TORREMOLINOS
$$
AVE. 5, CALLE 40
TEL 2222-5266   FAX 2255-3167
www.occidental-hoteles.com
This well-appointed hotel with Egyptian-themed decor is situated near Parque Sabana. Courtesy bus to city center. Italian restaurant.

ℹ️ 92 🅿️ 🅂 📶 🄰 AE, MC, V

🏨 HOTEL PRESIDENTE
🍴 $$
AVE. CENTRAL, CALLES 7/9
TEL 2222-3022   FAX 2221-1205
www.hotel-presidente.com
Modern amenities in this heart-of-downtown hotel complement comfortable rooms. Appealing restaurant. Casino.

ℹ️ 110 🅿️ ⇄ 🅂
🄰 All major cards

🏨 HOTEL VILLA TOURNON
$$
N BANK OF RÍO TORRES, 200 YARDS (183 M) E OF CALLE 3
TEL 2233-6622   FAX 2222-5211
www.costarica-hotelvilla tournon.com
This modern hotel near the El Pueblo complex has contemporary art, and pools in the garden. Fireside dining.

ℹ️ 80 🅂 ⇄ 📶 🄰 AE, MC, V

🏨 LE BERGERAC
🍴 $$
CALLE 35, 50 YARDS (46 M) S OF AVE. CENTRAL, LOS YOSES
TEL 2234-7850   FAX 2225-9103
www.bergerachotel.com

French provincial style pervades this family-run charmer set in a quiet eastern suburb. Antique furnishings and modern art, plus business facilities and gourmet dining on a terrace.

ℹ️ 19 🅿️ 🄰 AE, MC, V

🏨 SANTO TOMÁS
🍴 $$
AVE. 7, CALLES 3/5
TEL 2255-0448   FAX 2222-3950
www.hotelsantotomas.com
A small bed-and-breakfast in a centenarian home between Barrio Amón and downtown. North American owner maintains high standards.

ℹ️ 20 🅂 📶 🄰 MC, V

🏨 KAP'S PLACE
$
CALLE 19, AVE. 11/12
TEL 2221-1169   FAX 2256-4850
www.kapsplace.com
A colorful, well-kept, and secure budget option, run to high standards. Guests get kitchen privileges in this rambling former home.

ℹ️ 22 🅿️ 🅂 🄰 AE, MC, V

🏨 Hotel 🍴 Restaurant ℹ️ No. of Bedrooms 🔼 No. of Seats 🅿️ Parking 🕑 Closed ⇄ Elevator

Restaurants

🍴 BAKÉA
$$$$
CALLE 7, AVE. 11
TEL 2221-1051
Contemporary decor and creative nouvelle cuisine draw the culinary cognoscenti to this small restaurant with theme rooms. The best of fine dining, though both the menu and the portions are small.
🕐 Closed Sun. & Sat. L 🔲 🔷 AE, MC, V

🍴 CARIBBEAN LOFT
$$$
AVE. 9, CALLES CENTRAL/2
TEL 2248-1580
Caribbean-themed restaurant in the Hotel City One. All-white minimalist chic.
🕐 Closed Sun. D 🔲 🔷 All major cards

🍴 JÜRGEN'S
$$
CALLE 41, 219 YARDS (200 M) N OF AVE. CENTRAL, SAN PEDRO
TEL 2283-2239
Hip comes to San José in this upscale, contemporary eatery with a bold aesthetic and splendid nouvelle cuisine. Finish your fine dining experience with a nightcap at the cigar bar.
🕐 Closed Sun. 🔲 🔷 AE, MC, V

🍴 LA BASTILLE
$$
PASEO COLÓN AT CALLE 22
TEL 2255-4994
This French restaurant is popular with San José's social elite. Elegant ambience and dependable food.
🅿 🕐 Closed Sun. 🔲 🔷 MC, V

🍴 LA ESQUINA DE BUENOS AIRES
$$
CALLE 11, AVE. 4
TEL 2223-1909
An Argentinian restaurant with warm bohemian decor, plus superbly executed nouvelle Latin cuisine. Excellent wine list and gourmet beers.
🔲 🔷 All major cards

🍴 LE CHANDELIER
$$
100 YARDS (91 M) W & 100 YARDS (91 M) S OF I.C.E. BLDG., SAN PEDRO
TEL 2225-3980
Choose from ten dining areas in this colonial mansion. The nouvelle Costa Rican cuisine is inspired by French classics. Superb artwork decorates the walls.
🅿 🕐 Closed Sun. 🔲 🔷 MC, V

🍴 LOS ANTOJITOS
$$
600 YARDS (549 M) W OF PARQUE SABANA
TEL 2225-9525
Classic Mexican staples, such as grilled tenderloin. Mariachis sometimes entertain.
🅿 🔲 🔲 🔷 AE, MC, V

🍴 LUBNAN
$$
PASEO COLÓN, CALLES 22/24
TEL 2257-6071
Lebanese specialties such as kafta naie (marinated ground beef), kabobs, and falafel. Elegant decor, modest prices.
🅿 🕐 Closed Sun. 🔲 🔷 MC, V

🍴 TIN JO
$$
CALLE 11, AVE 6/8
TEL 2221-7605
Unpretentious ambience and filling meals at fair prices for Asian fare from sushi and Szechuan to Indian and Thai.
🔲 🔲 🔷 MC, V

🍴 BALCÓN DE EUROPA
$
CALLE 9, AVES. CENTRAL/1
TEL 2221-4841
This classic Italian restaurant has served traditional pastas, steaks, and seafood since 1909. After longtime chef Franco Piatti's death, French chef Jean Pierre took ownership in 2005; he's said to be shifting the menu toward French dishes.
🕐 Closed Sat. 🔲 🔷 MC, V

🍴 COCINA DE LEÑA
$
EL PUEBLO COMMERCIAL CENTER
TEL 2256-5353
The best of traditional campesino-style fare such as olla de carne soup and tamales wrapped in a plantain leaf.
🅿 🔲 🔷 MC, V

🍴 FLOR DE LOTO
$
CALLE LOISA, 50 YARDS (46 M) E OF I.C.E. BLDG., SABANA NORTE
TEL 2232-4652
This restaurant serves up a selection of spicy Hunan and Szechuan fare.
🅿 🔲 🔷 MC, V

🍴 KING'S GARDEN
$
CENTRO COMERCIAL YOAHAN, AUTOPISTA GENERAL CAÑAS
TEL 2255-3838
A popular, elegant restaurant that specializes in Cantonese and Szechuan dishes. The set lunches for two are a bargain.
🅿 🔲 🔲 🔷 AE, MC, V

🍴 MACHU PICHU
$
CALLE 23, AVES. 1/3
TEL 2222-7384
Peruvian seafood such as garlic octopus, picante de mariscos (spicy seafood casserole), and ceviches. For drinks, try the house Pisco sour.
🅿 🕐 Closed Sun. 🔲 🔷 AE, MC, V

🍴 RESTAURANTE VISHNU
$
AVE. 1, CALLES 1/3
TEL 2256-6063
This popular vegetarian restaurant with several outlets

---

serves salads, veggie burgers, and fruit juices.

🕐 Closed Sun. L 🟦 🟩 🟫 V

🍴 SPOON
$

AVE. CENTRAL, CALLES 5/7
TEL 2224-0328
A bargain with various outlets. Salads, submarine sandwiches, plus delicious baked goods.
🟦 🟩 🟫 None

■ CENTRAL HIGHLANDS

ALAJUELA

SOMETHING SPECIAL

🏨 XANDARI RESORT & SPA VILLAGE
$$$$

TACACORI, 3 MILES (4.8 KM) N OF ALAJUELA
TEL 2443-2020 OR 800/686-7879
FAX 2442-4847
www.xandari.com
Contemporary boutique hotel with villas and an innovative tropical spa complex sits atop a ridge overlooking coffee fields and the Central Valley. Stunning architecture and stylish furnishings. Trails lead to waterfalls. TV/video lounge. Macrobiotic nouvelle Costa Rican meals served on the dining terrace. The spa complex includes five hot tubs, treatment rooms, yoga, and physical fitness room.
🛈 22 villas, 1 studio 🅿 🚲
🟥 🟫 AE, MC, V

🏨 PURA VIDA BED & BREAKFAST
$$$

TUETAL NORTE, 3 MILES (4.8 KM) N OF ALAJUELA
TEL/FAX 2430-2929
www.puravidahotel.com
Surrounded by lush gardens, this intimate inn has individually themed cottages. Run by a nice North American couple, who serve gourmet meals.
🛈 7 🅿 🟩 🚲 🟫 MC, V

🏨 ORQUÍDEAS INN
$$

1 MILE (1.6 KM) W OF SAN JOSÉ DE ALAJUELA
TEL 2433-9346   FAX 2433-9740
www.orquideasinn.com
Set on lush grounds with mountain vistas, this charming, boutique hotel has an eclectic choice of rooms, suites, and a skylit geodesic dome. Lively Marilyn Monroe bar.
🛈 27 🅿 🟩 🚲 🟫 AE, MC, V

🍴 JAULARES
$

4 MILES (6.4 KM) N OF ALAJUELA
TEL/FAX 2482-2155
Experience a traditional country atmosphere in an alpine setting. Hearty *campesino* fare is prepared on an open wood-burning stove, and *refrescos* are created from fresh locally grown fruits.
🅿 🟫 None

ATENAS

🍴 MIRADOR DEL CAFETAL
$$

4 MILES (6.4 KM) W OF ATENAS
TEL 2446-7361
Colorful roadside restaurant splendidly situated over coffee fields with views toward Nicoya. Creative menu offers Central American dishes.
🅿 🕐 Closed D 🟦
🟫 MC, V

ESCAZÚ

🏨 THE ALTA HOTEL
🍴 $$$$$

ALTO LAS PALOMAS, 2 MILES (3.2 KM) W OF SAN RAFAEL DE ESCAZÚ
TEL 2282-4160 OR 888/388-2582
FAX 2282-4162
www.thealtahotel.com
A tasteful Mediterranean-style hotel with views . La Luz Restaurant serves stylish continental/Costa Rican cuisine.
🛈 23 🅿 🟦 🔄 🟩 🚲 🟥
🟫 AE, MC, V

🏨 WHITE HOUSE RESTAURANT CASINO & SPA
🍴 $$$$$

SAN ANTONIO DE ESCAZÚ
TEL 2288-6362   FAX 2288-6365
www.whitehousecostarica.com
This Southern-style plantation above the Central Valley boasts cavernous rooms and gracious two-bedroom villas. The Capital Grill restaurant offers spectacular views. Cigar bar. Helicopter tours.
🛈 15 rooms 🅿 🚲 🟥
🟫 MC, V

🏨 REAL INTERCONTINENTAL
🍴 $$$$

AUTOPISTA PROSPERO FERNÁNDEZ, 2 MILES (3.2 KM) NW OF SAN RAFAEL DE ESCAZÚ
TEL 2208-2100   FAX 2208-2101
www.ichotelsgroup.com
Deluxe hotel with huge rooms and warm, charming decor. Executive floor, business center, travel agency, and upscale shops. The Restaurant Mirage serves French cuisine.
🛈 261 🅿 🟦 🔄 🟩 🚲 🟥
🟫 AE, MC, V

🏨 CASA DE LAS TÍAS
$$

SAN RAFAEL DE ESCAZÚ
TEL 2289-5517   FAX 2289-7353
www.hotels.co.cr/casatias.html
Endearing and colorful family-run bed-and-breakfast in a wood-paneled, plantation-style home close to central Escazú. Breakfast is served on patio.
🛈 5 🅿 🟫 All major cards

🍴 SAGA
$$$$

400 YARDS (366 M) N. OF PLAZA DE LA PACO, ESCAZÚ
TEL 2289-6615
Sophisticated restaurant with minimalist decor and garden surrounds. Chef Evelyn Leff is renowned for her fusion cuisine and desserts. Pastry shop.
🅿 🟦 🟫 All major cards

🏨 Hotel 🍴 Restaurant 🛈 No. of Bedrooms 🪑 No. of Seats 🅿 Parking 🕐 Closed 🔄 Elevator

LA GARITA

🏨 MARTINO RESORT & SPA
$$$$
TEL 2433-8382   FAX 2433-9052
www.hotelmartino.com
Vast grounds with tennis and squash courts, a gym and jogging track surround a Romanesque villa boasting huge rooms, a casino, bars, a spa, and gourmet Italian food.
🛏 42 🅿 🕲 🌊 🏋
🕲 AE, MC, V

🍴 DELICIAS DEL MAÍZ
$
TEL 2433-7206
Traditional corn-based dishes, such as tamales and *chorreadas* (corn fritters) from the open grill, are served in atmospheric surroundings based on a traditional theme.
🅿 🕲 None

LOS ANGELES CLOUD FOREST RESERVE

🏨 VILLABLANCA CLOUD 🍴 FOREST HOTEL & SPA
$$$$
6 MILES (9.7 KM) NE OF LOS ANGELES NORTE
TEL 2461-0300   FAX 2461-0302
www.villablanca-costarica.com
An enchanting eco-lodge on the Continental Divide, at the edge of a cloud forest. Graciously appointed cottages have fireplaces. Wedding chapel and spa; nature activities include horseback riding and guided hikes.
🛏 35 cottages 🅿 🕲
🕲 All major cards

MONTE DE LA CRUZ

🏨 HOTEL CHALET TIROL 🍴
$$
TEL 2267-6222   FAX 2267-6229
www.tirolcr.com
Accessed only by horse or by guided hike is a cozy Tyrolean lodge situated on the edge of cloud forest. Choose from modern rooms or rustic cabins. The French restaurant serves dishes such as shrimp in a fennel Pernod sauce.
🛏 36 rooms, 10 chalets 🅿
🌊 🏋 🕲 AE, MC, V

🍴 BAALBEK BAR & GRILL
$
LOS ANGELES DE SAN RAFAEL
TEL 2267-6482
Lebanese restaurant with hookahs, belly dancing, and genuine Levantine fare. Tremendous views.
🅿 🕲 🕲 All major cards

PIEDADES

🏨 POSADA CANAL GRANDE
$$
TEL 2282-4089   FAX 2282-5733
www.hotelcanalgrande.com
A luxurious place, with parquet floors in the guest rooms, antiques, leather sofas, and flowers in the lounge. The hotel is surrounded by coffee fields and has an Italian restaurant. Breakfast included.
🛏 12 🅿 🌊 🕲 AE, MC, V

POÁS

SOMETHING SPECIAL

🏨 PEACE LODGE
$$$$$
MONTAÑA AZUL, 3 MILES (4.8 KM) N OF VARA BLANCA
TEL 2225-0643   FAX 2225-1082
www.waterfallgardens.com
Stunning, one-of-a-kind decor combines sensually rustic elements with luxury in cavernous rooms on the edge of Braulio Carrillo National Park. Natural stone hot tubs and cave-like bathrooms evoke the Flintstones, but the effect is quite romantic enhanced by canopy beds. The amenities and activities of La Paz Waterfall Gardens are at hand.
🛏 17 🅿 🕲 🕲 AE, MC, V

🏨 POÁS VOLCANO LODGE
$$
VARA BLANCA DE HEREDIA
TEL 2482-2194   FAX 2482-2513
www.poasvolcanolodge.com
Set in a superb location between Barva and Poás volcanoes, this mountain lodge on a cattle farm offers cozy charm, with a log fire in the timber-beamed lounge. Basic meals; rates include farmhouse breakfast. Some shared baths. Trail network leads through cloud forest.
🛏 11 🅿 🕲 AE, MC, V

🍴 RESTAURANT COLBERT
$$$
VARA BLANCA DE HEREDIA
TEL 2482-2776
Straddling the Continental Divide, with fine views, this airy modern restaurant-bakery serves croissants, pastries, etc., plus nouvelle Costa Rican fare with a French twist. Try the local cheeses.
🅿 🕲 🕲 MC, V

ROSARIO

SOMETHING SPECIAL

🏨 VISTA DEL VALLE PLANTATION INN
$$$$
ROSARIO, 2 MILES (3.2 KM) W OF INTER-AMERICAN HWY.
TEL/FAX 2451-1165 OR 2450-0900
www.vistadelvalle.com
Hints of Frank Lloyd Wright in a timber-beamed lodge with plate glass all around, situated at the heart of a citrus and coffee farm overlooking the Río Grande Canyon Preserve. The landscaped grounds feature a stable, and guided hikes are offered. Cottages are tastefully ascetic in Japanese style. Inspired nouvelle dishes based on fresh local produce are served on an outdoor terrace. Free wireless Internet.
🛏 7 cottages, 1 room 🅿
🌊 🕲 V

🕲 Nonsmoking 🕲 Air-conditioning 🌊 Indoor Pool 🌊 Outdoor Pool 🏋 Health Club 🕲 Credit Cards

SALISPUEDES

🏨 ALBERGUE MIRADOR DE QUETZALES
$$

PAN-AM HWY. KM 70
TEL 2381-8456
Ideal for spotting quetzals—birding is a specialty—this rustic lodge with cabins sits on the edge of a cloud forest. Simple meals and fabulous views.

🛏 11 cabins 🅿 🚭 None

SAN GERARDO DE DOTA

🏨 DANTICA CLOUD FOREST LODGE
$$

2 MILES (3.2 KM) E OF SAN GERARDO DE DOTA
TEL 2740-1067   FAX 2740-1061
www.dantica.com
IKEA furnishings and walls of glass in charming two-bedroom cottages on a magnificent hillside. Lovely restaurant/café. First-rate gallery of indigenous art.

🛏 5 cottages 🅿 🚭 AE, MC, V

🏨 TROGON LODGE
$$

TEL 2293-8181   FAX 2239-7657
www.grupomawamba.com
Nestled in a deep mountain valley, this gracious lodge provides a perfect base for both birding and trout fishing. Rustic hardwood cabins sit over a brook and trout pond. Simple meals are provided.

🛏 10 🅿 🚭 DC, MC, V

SAN RAMÓN

🏨 INN AT COYOTE 🍽 MOUNTAIN
$$$–$$$$$

TEL 2383-0544
www.cerrocoyote.com
This boutique mountain eco-lodge has views of the Pacific amid forest and coffee fields. Spanish hacienda-style lodge with courtyard. Rooms have handmade hardwood

furniture and custom baths. Fine restaurant offers 3-day culinary programs.

🛏 4 🅿 🚭 AE, MC, V

SANTA ANA

🍽 BACCHUS
$$$

200 YARDS (183 M) E & 100 (91 M) YARDS N OF PLAZA SANTA ANA
TEL 2282-5441
Converted colonial home with tasteful contemporary touches. Gourmet Mediterranean nouvelle dishes such as baked mushroom-and-polenta ragout draw the monied cognoscenti.

🅿 🕐 Closed Mon. 🚭 🚭 All major cards

🍽 LE MONASTÈRE
$$$

IN THE HILLS ABOVE SANTA ANA
TEL 2289-4404
www.monastere-restaurant.com
The waiters dress as monks in this converted chapel offering French-inspired cuisine such as grilled lamb chops, together with a big wine list. Enjoy the fine views over the valley.

🅿 🕐 Closed L & Sun. 🚭 🚭 All major cards

SANTA BARBARA DE HEREDIA

SOMETHING SPECIAL

🏨 FINCA ROSA BLANCA 🍽 COUNTRY INN
$$$$

0.75 MILE (1.2 KM) NE OF SANTA BARBARA DE HEREDIA
TEL 2269-9392   FAX 2269-9555
www.fincarosablanca.com
Designed as a private home and inspired by Gaudí and the Santa Fe style, this exquisite boutique hotel offers eclectic decor. Set on a working coffee farm, it has spectacular views over the valley and its own stable. The inventive gourmet cuisine uses local ingredients. Reservations required. Full

breakfast included.

🛏 9 suites, 6 cottages 🅿 🚭 🚭 AE, MC, V

SANTO DOMINGO DE HEREDIA

🏨 BOUGAINVILLEA 🍽
$$

0.6 MILE (1 KM) E OF SANTO DOMINGO
TEL 2244-1414   FAX 2244-1313
www.bougainvillea.co.cr
On landscaped grounds containing tennis courts, this modern hotel boasts engaging modern art. Elegant restaurant serves popular Sunday brunch.

🛏 80 🅿 🚭 🚭 🚭 AE, MC, V

TURRIALBA

🏨 CASA TURIRE
$$$

8 MILES (13 KM) SE OF TURRIALBA
TEL 2531-1111   FAX 2531-1075
www.hotelcasaturire.com
Large comfortable rooms in an award-winning modern hotel with classical hints. Situated on a working plantation, it offers horseback riding, biking, and rafting. Edwardian bar. Excellent cuisine served on the patio.

🛏 16 🅿 🚭 🚭 🚭 AE, MC, V

▪ GUANACASTE

CAÑAS

🍽 RESTAURANTE RINCÓN COROBICÍ
$

INTER-AMERICAN HWY., 4.5 MILES (7 KM) N OF CAÑAS
TEL 2669-6262
Diners can watch rafters far below floating on the Río Corobicí. Seafood specialties include *corvina ajillo* (sea bass in garlic), and *comida típica* is also served. Renowned for its refreshing lemonades.

🅿 🚭 🚭 None

LAGUNA DE ARENAL

SOMETHING SPECIAL

ARENAL KIORO
$$$$$
12 MILES (19.3 KM) W OF LA FORTUNA
TEL 2461-1700   FAX 2461-1710
www.hotelarenalkioro.com
This deluxe newcomer sets a new standard for the area. Unnervingly close to the lava flows, it offers stupendous ringside views through walls of glass in expansive suites, all with hot tubs by the verandas. The restaurant is first-rate, and there's a full-service spa, modern gym, and two thermal swimming pools, plus hot springs nearby.
🛈 53 suites 🅿 ⚒ 🎽 🃏 All major cards

ARENAL LODGE
$$$$
13 MILES (21 KM) W OF FORTUNA
TEL 2460-1881   FAX 2460-6119
www.arenallodge.com
Atmospheric mountain lodge with volcano views. Large lounge bar with stone hearth offers the most impressive vistas. Library, TV lounge, and pool table. Sportfishing is offered, as are tours. Rates include buffet breakfast, plus use of mountain bikes, hot tub, and trails.
🛈 50 🅿 🃏 AE, MC, V

HOTEL LA MANSION INN
$$$$
5 MILES (8 KM) N OF NUEVO ARENAL
TEL 2692-8018   FAX 2692-8019
www.lamansionarenal.com
A magnificent hillside setting overlooking the lake plus exquisite decor in 16 *cabinas*. The inn has a horizon swimming pool, and a charming, bar / restaurant. Offers horseback riding; rowboats and canoes are available for boating.
🛈 16 🅿 🃏 ⚒ 🃏 MC, V

ARENAL OBSERVATORY LODGE
$$
1.5 MILES (2.4 KM) SE OF VOLCÁN ARENAL
TEL 2692-2070 OR 2290-7011
FAX 2692-2074
www.arenal-observatory.com
Mountainside lodge offers up-close views of Volcán Arenal. Accommodations vary from cozy volcano-view rooms to spacious and elegant suites, plus a farmhouse villa. Some rooms are handicapped accessible. Horseback riding, free volcano tour, pool and hot tub, and trails. Family-style meals.
🛈 37 🅿 ⚒ 🃏 AE, MC, V

CHALET NICHOLAS
$$
HWY. 142, 1.5 MILES (2.4 KM) W OF NUEVO ARENAL
TEL 2694-4041
www.chaletnicholas.com
This charming, cozy guest house is run by North American hosts. Rooms boast a winning combination of orthopedic mattresses and volcano views, and the upstairs bedroom is reached via a spiral staircase. Hiking and horseback rides are offered. Healthy meals are a treat.
🛈 3 🅿 🃏 🃏 None

VILLA DECARY
$$
HWY. 142, 1.5 MILES (2.4 KM) E OF NUEVO ARENAL
TEL/FAX 2694-4330
www.villadecary.com
Charming country inn backed by rain forest accessed by trails. Large guest rooms have Guatemalan covers, balconies, and lake views. Gracious North American hosts serve breakfasts, included in rates.
🛈 5 rooms, 3 bungalows 🅿 🃏 🃏 None

RESTAURANT WILLY'S CABALLO NEGRO
$$
1 MILE W OF NUEVO ARENAL

TEL 2694-4515
This German-run bakery and restaurant sits over a pond. Its European menu runs from sausages and schnitzel to veal, plus some vegetarian options.
🅿 🃏 🃏 None

TOAD HALL
$
HWY. 142, 3 MILES (4.8 KM) E OF NUEVO ARENAL
TEL 2692-8020
Delicatessen, gift store, and café perched above the lake. Views can be enjoyed from a terrace with granola and banana pancake breakfasts, and "California lunches" such as grilled sesame chicken salad. Awesome desserts.
🅿 🃏 None

LIBERIA

RESTAURANTE PASO REAL
$$
AVE. CENTRAL, CALLES CENTRAL/2
TEL 2666-3455
This clean, spacious modern restaurant-sports bar has a huge seafood menu of well-prepared dishes, plus *casados* (set meals). Balcony overlooks plaza. Large-screen TV.
🃏 🃏 🃏 V

MONTEVERDE

MONTEVERDE LODGE
$$$
TEL 2257-0766, 2645-5057
FAX 2257-1665, 2645-5129
www.costaricaexpeditions.com
An eccentric modern design maximizes light in this upscale brick-and-timber nature lodge. The mezzanine bar, which has a fireplace and a view of the glass-enclosed spa pool, is a lively social center. Spacious guest rooms offer fine vistas. Birds abound on the landscaped grounds. Rates include meals.
🛈 27 🅿 🃏 AE, MC, V

EL SAPO DORADO
$$$
TEL 2645-5010   FAX 2645-5180
www.sapodorado.com
Awesome views from stone-
and-timber cabins amid
landscaped grounds. Units
with fireplaces are preferred.
Massages offered. Forest trail.
Health food restaurant.
30 P AE, MC, V

BELMAR
$$
TEL 2645-5201   FAX 2645-5135
www.hotelbelmar.net
This alpine lodge set on a hillside has clean, wood-paneled
rooms with wide balconies
providing superb sunset views.
Dine in or out at the popular
continental restaurant.
34 P V

HELICONIA
$$
TEL 2645-5109   FAX 2645-5007
www.hotelheliconia.com
This lodge has modern fixtures
in modestly furnished rooms
with balconies. Spa pool.
Trails into a private reserve.
Continental and local favorites
in the restaurant.
33 P V

RINCÓN DE LA VIEJA

HOTEL BORINQUEN
MOUNTAIN RESORT
THERMAE & SPA
$$$$
8 MILES (13 KM) NE OF CAÑAS
DULCES
TEL 2690-1900   FAX 2690-1903
www.borinquenresort.com
Mountain resort with
cavernous rooms furnished in
neocolonial style. A spa offers
mud and thermal treatments,
plus plunge pools. Horseback
rides, ATV safaris, and hikes
lead into surrounding forest.
Decent restaurant.
30 P MC, V

RINCÓN DE LA VIEJA
MOUNTAIN LODGE
$$$
OFF INTER-AMERICAN HWY.,
NEAR NATIONAL PARK
TEL/FAX 2200-0238
FAX 2666-2441
www.rincondelaviejalodge.net
Perfect for exploring, this
remote lodge on the western
flank of Rincón has basic
furnishings, a serpentarium,
dairy, butterfly collection, and
canopy tour. Four-wheel-drive
access. Rates include meals.
50 P AE, MC, V

AROMAS DE CAMPO
$$
CURRUBANDÉ, 8 MILES (13 KM)
NE OF LIBERIA
TEL 2665-0008   FAX 2665-0011
Homey, Mexican-style bed-
and-breakfast with colorful
rooms simply appointed and
glazed concrete floors. Family-
style meals on the airy patio.
Animals abound.
4 P None

BUENA VISTA LODGE
$
8 MILES (13 KM) NE OF CAÑAS
DULCES
TEL 2690-1414
FAX 2690-1406
www.buenavistalodgecr.com
A real mountain hideaway on
the slopes of Rincón. Stone-
and-timber cabins amid lawns,
with horseback rides, hikes, a
canopy tour, thermal steam
bath, and rustic restaurant.
77 P None

NICOYA

BAHÍA CULEBRA

OCCIDENTAL ALLEGRO
PAPAGAYO
$$$$
PLAYA MANZANILLO
TEL 2690-9900 OR 800/858-2258
FAX 2690-9910
www.occidental-hoteles.com
Casually elegant cliffside resort

with stylishly furnished rooms.
Suites are worth the premium.
Diving, golf, and tennis.
308 P
All major cards

SOMETHING SPECIAL

FOUR SEASONS RESORT
AT PAPAGAYO
PENINSULA
$$$$$
PUNTA MALA
TEL 2696-0000   FAX 2696-0500
www.fourseasons.com/
costarica
This large-scale deluxe hotel
enjoys a dramatic location
with spectacular coastline
views. Sumptuous tropical-
themed decor graces public
areas and spacious rooms with
balcony views. A championship golf course is a major
draw, as is the posh spa. Four
restaurants and a lounge offer
a range of dining experiences.
145 P
All major cards

MONTEZUMA

HOTEL HORIZONTES DE
MONTEZUMA
$$$
1 MILE (1.6 KM) N OF
MONTEZUMA
TEL/FAX 2642-0534
www.horizontes-montezuma
.com
Clinical whites bathe this
well-run hilltop, plantation-
style hotel with hammocks
on broad verandas around an
atrium court. Intensive Spanish
classes begin on Mondays.
Meals are served on the patio.
7 P MC, V

NATURE LODGE FINCA
LOS CABALLOS
$$$
1 MILE (1.6 KM) N OF
MONTEZUMA
TEL/FAX 2642-0124
www.naturelodge.net
Tasteful rooms show flair at
this hillside lodge with views

from cantilevered decks. Excellent meals served outdoors, plus massage and other spa treatments. Horseback riding, trails, and ocean views.

[i] 12 [P] 🏊 🏦 MC, V

🏨 YLANG YLANG BEACH RESORT
$$
0.5 MILE (0.8 KM) E OF MONTEZUMA
TEL/FAX 2642-0068
www.elbanano.com
Enjoying a secluded beachfront location, this eclectic place has bungalows and three-story units set amid landscaped foliage.

[i] 14 ❄️ 🏊

NOSARA

🏨 LAGARTA LODGE
$$
TEL 2682-0035   FAX 2682-0135
www.lagarta.com
German-run hilltop lodge with views north over the wetlands and along Ostional beach. Relaxed, no-frills ambience. Several trails lead to the estuary, with maps and tree lists available for self-guided tours.

[i] 7 [P] 🏊 🏦 V

🍴 MARLIN BILL'S
$
TEL 2682-0458
This unpretentious hillside eatery serves international favorites, from French onion soup to New York strip steak.

[P] 🏦 None

PLAYA COCO

🏨 RANCHO ARMADILLO
$$$
TEL 2670-0108   FAX 2670-0441
www.ranchoarmadillo.com
Gracious Texan-run colonial hacienda with timber-beamed bungalows. Meals prepared on request by a former culinary arts instructor.

[i] 6 [P] ❄️ 🛗 🏊 🏦 MC, V

🏨 PUERTA DEL SOL
$
TEL 2670-0195   FAX 2670-0650
A small, simple option with fashionably contemporary decor. Inventive cuisine in an open-air restaurant/café.

[i] 10 [P] ❄️ 🏊 🍸
🏦 AE, MC, V

PLAYA CONCHAL

🏨 🍴 PARADISUS PLAYA CONCHAL BEACH & GOLF RESORT
$$$$
TEL 2654-4123 OR 800/336-3542
FAX 2654-4181
www.solmelia.com
Huge upscale resort backing a white-sand beach. Spacious rooms with marble baths. Watersports, entertainment, tour services, restaurants, and casino are on-site, and two great golf courses are nearby.

[i] 310 [P] ❄️ 🏊 🍸 🏦 All major cards

PLAYA FLAMINGO

🏨 FLAMINGO BEACH RESORT
$$$$
TEL 2654-4444   FAX 2654-4060
www.resortflamingobeach.com
This recently upgraded full-service resort is centered around a vast swimming pool. Car rental and tour services.

[i] 91 [P] ❄️ 🛗 🏊 🍸
🏦 AE, MC, V

PLAYA GRANDE

🏨 🍴 HOTEL BULA BULA
$$$
TEL 2653-0975   FAX 2653-0978
www.hotelbulabula.com
Trendily yet simply furnished, this boutique hotel nestles between the beach and estero. Gourmet fusion cuisine served at the Great Waltini restaurant.

[i] 10 [P] 🏊
🏦 All major cards

PLAYA HERMOSA

🏨 HOTEL PLAYA HERMOSA
$$$
TEL/FAX 2672-0046
www.hotelplayahermosa.com
A tasteful remodel by new owners has metamorphosed this once-ugly beachfront hotel into a snazzy option, despite dowdy decor. Bi-level suites centered around a magnificent pool.

[i] 38 [P] ❄️ 🏊 🏦 MC, V

🏨 LA FINISTERRA
$$
TEL/FAX 2670-0227
www.finisterra.net
A small contemporary property with live-in owners. The hilltop setting catches the breezes, and rooms open onto a terrace inset with a pool. The restaurant is renown for its cuisine.

[i] 10 [P] ❄️ 🏊 🏦 AE, MC, V

PLAYA OCOTAL

🏨 OCOTAL BEACH RESORT
$$$
TEL 2670-0321   FAX 2670-0083
www.ocotalresort.com
Spacious rooms in a hilltop setting with ocean vistas. A scuba-diving and sportfishing resort with horseback riding, tour services, tennis courts, and a choice of restaurants.

[i] 71 [P] ❄️ 🏊
🏦 All major cards

🏨 VILLA CASA BLANCA
$$
TEL 2670-0518   FAX 2670-0448
http://boutiquehotelsguana-caste.typepad.com
This deluxe bed-and-breakfast boasts four-poster beds and stenciled murals in the bedrooms. Gleaming bathrooms have wall-to-wall mirrors. The garden has sheltered gazebos where buffets are served.

[i] 14 [P] ❄️ 🏊
🏦 All major cards

🏦 Nonsmoking ❄️ Air-conditioning 🏊 Indoor Pool 🏊 Outdoor Pool 🍸 Health Club 🏦 Credit Cards

🍴 **FATHER ROOSTER RESTAURANT**

$

TEL 2670-1246

This rustic shorefront eatery serves seafood, burgers, and similar dishes. It has an appealing, offbeat ambience, and its beach volleyball court gets lively.

🅿 🚭 None

PLAYA TAMBOR

🏨 **TANGO MAR**

$$$$

HWY. 160, 3 MILES (4.8 KM) SW OF TAMBOR

TEL 2683-0001   FAX 2683-0003

www.tangomar.com

Set splendidly on the water, Tango Mar boasts stilt-legged hardwood cabins, spacious rooms, or villas. There's a nine-hole golf course. Kundalini, Hatha, and Kripalu yoga and breathing workshops are taught on-site.

ⓘ 37 🅿 🛗 🏊 🚭 All major cards

PUNTA ISLITA

🏨 🍴 **HOTEL PUNTA ISLITA**

$$$$

TEL 2290-4259   FAX 2232-2183

www.hotelpuntaislita.com

Santa Fe–style architecture and luxurious furnishings in individual casitas, which have a commanding hilltop setting. Cliff-face pool, activities, and restaurant serving nouvelle Costa Rican dishes. More than 30 spa treatments available.

ⓘ 20 bungalows, 9 suites, 5 villas 🅿 🛗 🏊 🍸 🚭 All major cards

SAMARÁ

🏨 **SÁMARA TREEHOUSE INN**

$$

TEL 2886-6137

www.samaratreehouse.com

For a touch of Polynesia, reserve one of these delightful beachfront cabins on stilts. Shaded patios with hammocks. Secure parking.

ⓘ 4 🅿 🏊 🚭 None

SAN FRANCISCO DE COYOTE

🏨 **CASA CALETAS BOUTIQUE HOTEL**

$$$

5 MILES (8 KM) W OF SAN FRANCISCO DE COYOTE

TEL 2655-1271   FAX 2655-1270

www.casacaletas.com

This difficult-to-reach hotel has a spectacular location at the mouth of the Río Jabillo. Deluxe lodgings with tasteful contemporary furnishings. It doubles as a working cattle ranch.

ⓘ 8 🅿 🏊 🚭 V

SANTA TERESA

SOMETHING SPECIAL

🏨 🍴 **HOTEL FLOR BLANCA**

$$$$$

3 MILES (4.8 KM) N OF MALPAÍS

TEL 2640-0232   FAX 2640-0226

www.florblanca.com

Infused with a Balinese motif, this calming resort sprawls over 7 acres (2.8 ha) of beachfront. Spacious, romantic villas feature outdoor showers and sumptuous furnishings. The gourmet outdoor Nectar Bar & Restaurant serves Pacific fusion cuisine. Large-screen TV lounge is good for rainy days. A spa has been added; yoga is offered in an open-air dojo.

ⓘ 10 🅿 🛗 🏊 🚭 All major cards

TAMARINDO

🏨 🍴 **CAPITÁN SUIZO**

$$$$

TEL 2653-0075   FAX 2653-0292

www.captainsuizo.com

An elegant resort with rooms and bungalows set around a pool. Howler monkeys live in the treetops. The restaurant serves nouvelle creations.

ⓘ 22 rooms, 8 bungalows 🅿 🛗 🏊 🚭 AE, MC, V

🏨 🍴 **JARDÍN DEL EDÉN**

$$$$

TEL 2653-0137   FAX 2653-0111

www.jardindeleden.com

Stylish, European-run hotel with landscaped gardens studded with artistic pools and a floodlit spa pool. Seafood specialties are served in a thatched-roof restaurant.

ⓘ 20 🅿 🛗 🏊 🍸 🚭 AE, MC

🏨 **VILLA ALEGRE BED & BREAKFAST**

$$$

TEL 2653-0270   FAX 2653-0287

www.villaalegrecostarica.com

This beachside villa is a charming hotel run with style by gregarious North American expats who specialize in arranging and hosting honeymoons. Individually decorated rooms play an international calliope. Pool, honor bar.

ⓘ 4 🅿 🛗 🛗 🏊 🚭 MC, V

DRAGONFLY BAR & GRILL
$$$
TEL 2653-1506
www.dragonflybarandgrill.com
Some of the finest dining.
Chef Tish Thalman's fusion
cuisine makes the most of
local ingredients, such as Thai-
style crispy fish cake with cur-
ried sweet corn. An airy and
romantic setting. Hip music.
Closed L & Sun. & Oct. P
None

STELLA'S FINE DINING
$$$
TEL 2653-0127
www.stella-cr.com
Aptly named, this thatched
restaurant serves gourmet
nouvelle cuisine.
P S MC, V

▪ CENTRAL PACIFIC

BRUNCA COAST

VILLAS GAIA
$$
PLAYA TORTUGA
TEL 2786-5044   FAX 2786-5009
www.villasgaia.com
Wooden bungalows feature
attractive contemporary decor.
Trails lead to rain forest and
mangroves. Kayaking, snorkel-
ing, and scuba-diving trips,
fishing, and hiking.
12 bungalows P
AE, MC, V

DOMINICAL

THE VILLAS AT DOMINICAL
$$$$
PLAYA DOMINICAL
TEL 2258-0150   FAX 2787-4006
www.kiana-dominical.com
New in 2008, this collection
of sumptuous villas has a
first-class beachfront spa, airy
thatched public lounges, and a
gourmet restaurant.
26 villas P S
All major cards

HACIENDA BARÚ NATIONAL WILDLIFE REFUGE & ECOLODGE
$$
1.2 MILES (2 KM) N OF RÍO BARÚ
BRIDGE, COASTAL HWY.
TEL 2787-0003   FAX 2787-0057
www.haciendabaru.com
Renowned for its nature
reserve, this hacienda is
ideal for wildlife viewing.
Choose between the simple
two-bedroom cabins or house
rental. The restaurant serves
Italian and local fare. A variety
of tours can be arranged.
6 P AE, MC, V

JACÓ

BEST WESTERN JACÓ BEACH RESORT
$$$
AVE. PASTOR DIAZ
TEL 2643-1000 OR 800/780-7234
FAX 2643-3833
www.bestwestern.com
Large rooms with modern
furnishings are situated on the
edge of the beach. Full range
of services and activities, and
adequate fare is served in El
Muelle restaurant.
130 P S
All major cards

PACIFIC BISTRO
$$$
CALLE LAS PALMERAS & AVE.
PASTOR DÍAZ
TEL 2643-3771
Mouthwatering Asia-Pacific
dishes from a U.S. chef make
a visit to this tiny spot more
than worthwhile.
Closed Mon.–Tues. S S
None

LIGHTHOUSE POINT STEAK & SEAFOOD HOUSE
$$
COAST HWY. AT JCT. FOR JACÓ
TEL 2643-3083
This lively spot boasts a splen-
did ambience and a menu
spanning the spectrum from

hearty American breakfasts to
crocodile nuggets. The eclectic
decor is straight from a '60s
surfing movie. Open 24 hours.
P MC, V

MANUEL ANTONIO

ARENAS DEL MAR
$$$$$
1 MILE (1.6 KM) W OF LA
MARIPOSA
TEL 2777-2777
www.arenasdelmar.com
This deluxe, eco-sensitive
hotel opened in 2008 and
upped the ante with an
exclusive beachfront locale.
Gorgeous villa-suites and
apartments rise over treetops
and boast stylish contem-
porary decor. Two gourmet
restaurants incorporate local
ingredients in their menus;
room service available.
38 P S
All major cards

LA MARIPOSA
$$$$
2.5 MILES (4 KM) S OF QUEPOS
TEL 2777-0355   FAX 2777-0050
www.hotelmariposa.com
Unsurpassed coastal vistas.
Accommodations range from
cottages that hug the cliff's
face to junior suites with
spa pools, plus contempo-
rary suites and penthouses.
Creative French cuisine is
served. Swim-up bar. Free
park shuttle available.
60 P S MC, V

MAKANDA BY THE SEA
$$$$
3.5 MILES (5.6 KM) S OF QUEPOS
TEL 2777-0442   FAX 2777-1032
www.makanda.com
Japanese-inspired studios and
villas tucked into Japanese
gardens. Cliffside pool. The
nouvelle cuisine is said to be
region's best. Extensive wine
list. Reservations required.
6 villas, 4 studios
AE, MC, V

S Nonsmoking S Air-conditioning Indoor Pool Outdoor Pool Health Club Credit Cards

🏨 SI COMO NO
🍴 $$$$

2 MILES (3.2 KM) S OF QUEPOS
TEL 2777-0777   FAX 2777-1093
www.sicomono.com
Avant-garde design and decor, with split-level, all-suite villas around a dramatic pool and cascade. Theater shows first-run movies and camp classics. Shops, a conference center, and two acclaimed eateries.

🛏 70 🅿 📶 🏊 ❄ AE, MC, V

🏨 TULEMAR BUNGALOWS
$$$$

2.5 MILES (4 KM) S OF QUEPOS
TEL 2777-0580   FAX 2777-1579
www.tulemar.com
A villa, deluxe rooms, and octagonal bungalows with picture windows and modern furnishings in a secluded setting with trails. Breakfast and snacks only, but restaurants are close by.

🛏 14 bungalows, 1 villa 🅿
🏊 ❄ AE, MC, V

OJOCHAL

🍴 EXÓTICA CAFÉ
$$

2 MILES (3.2 KM) E OF PLAYA TORTUGA
TEL 2786-5050
Tiny, open-air eatery serving surprisingly accomplished and exotic tropical nouvelle cuisine.

🕐 Closed Sun. ❄ None

PARRITA

🏨 TIMARAI BAMBOO RESORT
$$$

ISLA PLAYA SECO
TEL 2770-8355   FAX 2779-9426
www.timaraibambooresort.net
Set amid palms, this beach-front resort, constructed of bamboo and hardwood, specializes in adventures. Spacious rooms feature TVs and other modern conveniences. Activities include paragliding, kitesurfing, and kayaking.

🛏 22 🅿 📶 ❄ MC, V

PLAYA ESTERILLOS

SOMETHING SPECIAL

🏨 XANDARI BY THE
🍴 PACIFIC
$$$$

PLAYA ESTERILLOS ESTE
TEL 2778-7070   FAX 2778-7878
www.xandari.com
A twin to Xandari Resort & Spa Village (see p. 243), this contemporary stunner offers colorful villas adorned with the owners' art and every conceivable convenience. Private gardens and full-service spa. Serves health-conscious gourmet cuisine.

🛏 15 villas 🅿 📶 🏊 ❄
🃏 All major cards

PLAYA HERMOSA

🏨 TERRAZA DEL PACIFICO
$$

HWY. 34, 1 MILE (1.6 KM) S OF JACÓ
TEL 2643-3222   FAX 2643-3424
www.terrazadelpacifico.com
This specialized surf hotel and restaurant is tucked beneath cliffs, with miles of black-sand beach to the south. It offers genteel decor combined with a modicum of facilities, including a small casino. Surfing lessons and horseback riding available. Two swimming pools.

🛏 43 🅿 📶 🏊 ❄ AE, MC, V

PLAYA HERRADURA

🏨 LOS SUEÑOS MARRIOTT
🍴 OCEAN & GOLF RESORT
$$$$$

TEL 2637-8886   FAX 2637-8895
www.lossuenosresort.com
This deluxe beachfront resort provides access to an 18-hole golf course, a spa, tennis courts, watersports, a 250-slip marina, and a choice of restaurants, bars, and lounges.

🛏 201 🅿 🔄 📶 📶 🏊 ❄
🃏 All major cards

SOMETHING SPECIAL

🏨 VILLA CALETAS &
🍴 ZEPHYR PALACE
$$$$–$$$$$

HWY. 34, 3 MILES (4.8 KM) N OF JACÓ
TEL 2637-0606   FAX 2637-0404
www.villacaletas.com
Lavishly furnished rooms and hillside villas in a stunning clifftop setting. The two restaurants serve Costa Rican fare with a French twist. Horizon pool and classical amphitheater for concerts. Poolside bar. For the ultimate luxury, check into Zephyr Palace, with seven mammoth suites inspired by Imperial Rome.

🛏 25 rooms, 11 villas 🅿 📶
🏊 🃏 AE, MC, V

QUEPOS

🍴 EL GRAN ESCAPE
RESTAURANT &
FISHHEAD BAR
$

TEL 2777-0395
www.elgranescape.net
Burgers, tuna melts, surf-and-turf, and local seafood dishes in this open-air restaurant. Sushi offered upstairs.

🕐 Closed Tues. 🃏 None

SAVEGRE

🏨 RAFIKI SAFARI LODGE
$$$

20 MILES (32.2 KM) SE OF QUEPOS
TEL 2777-2250
www.rafikisafari.com
African-style lodge specializing in nature activities and white-water adventures, set amid 842 acres (341 ha) of jungle. Accommodation is in fully furnished tents with ensuite bathrooms and porches with rocking chairs. Rafiki, which is South African–run, has a traditional *braai* (barbecue) in the Lecker Bar.

🛏 9 🅿 🏊 🃏 MC, V

🏨 Hotel 🍴 Restaurant 🛏 No. of Bedrooms 🍴 No. of Seats 🅿 Parking 🕐 Closed 🔄 Elevator

■ ZONA SUR

BAHÍA DRAKE

🏨 AGUILA DE OSA INN
$$$$$
MOUTH OF RÍO AGUJITAS, 0.5
MILE (0.8 KM) S OF AGUJITAS
TEL 2296-2190 OR 2291-0318
FAX 2322-7722
www.aguiladeosainn.com
An upscale nature lodge decorated with a native theme,
tucked in a canyon. Good for
scuba diving and sportfishing.
Rates include inventive meals
with free-flowing wine.
🛈 13 ◈ AE, MC, V

🏨 VILLAS LA PALOMA LODGE
$$
0.5 MILES (0.8 KM) S OF AGUJITAS
TEL 2239-2801   FAX 2239-0954
www.lapalomalodge.com
Cozy hardwood cabins and
spacious villas in landscaped
grounds facing the Pacific.
Family-style meals in an airy
restaurant. Tours and activities
are offered.
🛈 12 ⚊ ◈ MC, V

CORCOVADO

🏨 LAPA RÍOS
🍴 $$$$$
CABO MATOPALO
TEL 2735-5130   FAX 2735-5179
www.laparios.com
A deluxe nature lodge backed
by rain forest. Spacious, airy
ranchos sleep up to six people.
Offers nature tours, horseback
riding, and kayaking. Rates
include meals, served in a
thatched restaurant with
spiraling mirador.
🛈 14 bungalows ⚊ ◈ AE,
MC, V

🏨 BOSQUE DEL CABO
$$$$
CABO MATOPALO
TEL/FAX 2735-5206
www.bosquedelcabo.com
The Casa Blanca, a clifftop
villa on this serene oceanfront

property, is the epitome of
luxury. Simple meals in a
thatched restaurant.
🛈 8 bungalows, 1 house 🅿
⚊ ◈ V

🏨 CASA CORCOVADO JUNGLE LODGE
$$$$
N BORDER OF CORCOVADO
NATIONAL PARK
TEL 2256-3181 OR 888/896-6097
FAX 2256-7409
www.casacorcovado.com
This former cacao plantation
provides accommodation in
graciously appointed thatched
cabins. Watersports, guided
hikes, and horseback riding
are offered. There is a bar and
family-style dining. Two-night
minimum stay.
🛈 10 bungalows ⚊ ◈ AE,
MC, V

🏨 CORCOVADO LODGE TENT CAMP
$$$$
S BORDER OF CORCOVADO
NATIONAL PARK
TEL 2257-0766   FAX 2257-1665
www.costaricaexpeditions.com
These unusual tentlike accommodations on wooden plat-
forms appeal to the adventurous traveler. Family-style meals
are served in a lofty thatched
restaurant. A wide range of
adventure activities is offered;
canopy platform over 100 feet
(30 m) high is popular.
🛈 20 ◈ AE, MC, V

🏨 LUNA LODGE
$$$$
CARATE
TEL 2380-5036 OR 888/409-8448
www.lunalodge.com
A dramatic hillside setting
and tastefully conceived and
decorated thatched cabins that
have views into the rain forest.
Safari-style tents are also
available. A dojo is used for
yoga. Can only be reached by
four-wheel-drive vehicles.
🛈 8 cabins, 7 tents 🅿 ⚊
◈ MC, V

GOLFITO

🏨 BANANA BAY MARINA
$$$
TEL 2775-0838
FAX 2775-0735
www.bananabaymarina.com
This small hotel and sportfishing resort adjoins its namesake
marina. Contemporary rooms.
American and nouvelle cuisine
served in the Bilge Bar & Grill.
🛈 4 🅿 ◈ ⚊ ◈ MC, V

PAVONES

🏨 CASA SIEMPRE DOMIN-GO BED & BREAKFAST
$$$$$
TEL/FAX 8820-4709
www.casa-domingo.com
This is a deluxe Western-style
lodge with a cathedral ceiling.
It is set amid landscaped lawns
with ocean views to the front
and rain forest behind.
🛈 4 🅿 ◈ None

🏨 TISKITA LODGE
$$
TEL 2298-8125   FAX 2296-8133
www.tiskita-lodge.co.cr
Surrounded by rain forest and
fruit orchards, this property
centers on an old farmhouse
where meals are served family style. Accommodation is in
wooden cabins with private
alfresco showers and toilets.
Horseback riding, nature
tours, and birding trips.
🛈 16 🅿 ◈ ⚊ ◈ AE, MC, V

PIEDRAS BLANCAS

🏨 ESQUINAS RAIN FOREST LODGE
$$$
LAS GAMBAS
TEL/FAX 2775-0901
www.esquinaslodge.com
A comfortable, simply appointed nature lodge on the edge
of Piedras Blancas National
Park. Locals lead nature treks,
among other activities. Part
of a model project combining
research, conservation, and

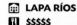

community development.

(i) 14 **P** ⛴ 🏄 AE, MC, V

🏨 PLAYA NICUESA RAIN FOREST LODGE
$$$

PLAYA NICUESA, 9 MILES (14.5 KM) NW OF GOLFITO
TEL 2258-8250 OR 866/504-8116
www.nicuesalodge.com

This rain forest lodge enjoys a beachfront location, with trails into a private reserve. Simply furnished accommodations have delightful open-air bathrooms. Hammocks abound on broad balconies. Kayaking and windsurfing.

(i) 4 cabins, 4 rooms 🏄 None

PUERTO JIMÉNEZ

🏨 IGUANA LODGE & PEARL OF THE OSA
$$$

PLAYA PLATANARES
TEL/FAX 8829-5865
www.iguanalodge.com

A jungly beachside setting adds allure to this reclusive no-frills lodge with four thatched stilt cabins. The adjoining Pearl of the Osa lodge has 8 airy budget rooms with private bathrooms. Two open-air restaurants offer snacks to gourmet meals.

(i) 4 cabins, 8 rooms **P** 🏄 None

🍴 RESTAURANT JADE LUNA
$$$

1 MILE (1.6 KM) E OF PUERTO JIMÉNEZ
TEL 2735-5739

Remarkable for its middle-of-nowhere location, this open-air restaurant serves truly gourmet fare prepared by chef/owner Barbara Burckhardt. The changing menu might include coconut-and-macadamia fried shrimp with orange chilpotle marmalade. Romantic and chic candlelit ambience.

🕐 Closed Sun. **P** 🏄 None

🍴 JUANITA'S MEXICAN BAR & GRILL
$$

TEL 2735-5056

A lively Mexican cantina serving quality chimichangas, burritos, and other staples, including killer margaritas. The tremendous ambience is enlivened by crab races, Hula Hoop contests, and other fun events.

🏄 MC, V

SIERPE

🏨 VERAGUA RIVER HOUSE
$$

RÍO ESTERO AZUL
TEL 2788-8111   FAX 2786-7460

An exquisite riverside guesthouse surrounded by swampy grasslands good for birding. Charming Italian decor in a choice of rooms, cabins, or a beachfront house.

(i) 8 🏄 None

ZANCUDO

🏨 CABINAS SOL Y MAR
🍴 **$$**

TEL 2776-0014   FAX 2776-0015
www.zancudo.com

This beachfront property has attractive cabins with skylit bathrooms. The outdoor bar and grill serves dishes such as tuna with capers and burgers.

(i) 5 cabins, 1 house **P** 🏄 None

■ SOUTH CENTRAL

PARQUE INTERNA-CIONAL LA AMISTAD

🏨 LA AMISTAD LODGE
$$

LAS MELLIZAS
TEL 2289-7667   FAX 2289-7858
www.laamistad.com

This mountain lodge on the edge of the park has rooms and cabins. Horseback riding, hiking, and camping available. Organic meals served family-

style. Four-wheel-drive access. Rate includes entrance to reserve and a tour.

(i) 10 **P** 🏄 None

SAN GERARDO DE RIVAS

🏨 RÍO CHIRRIPÓ MOUNTAIN RETREAT
$$

CANAAN
TEL 2742-5109   FAX 2771-2003
www.riochirripo.com

Inspired by the Santa Fe style, this handsome lodge has homey yet tastefully decorated cabins with balconies overhanging the gorge. Roofed platforms accommodate campers. Airy rancho dining area.

(i) 8 **P** ⛴ 🏄 MC, V

🏨 TALAMANCA RESERVE
$$

0.5 MILE (0.8 KM) N OF SAN GERARDO DE RIVAS
TEL 2742-5080
www.talamancareserve.com

Modestly furnished cabins, plus a sunlit two-story café-restaurant with 21st-century styling. Hiking and ATV trails. Perfectly positioned close to both the village and the Cerro Chirripó trailhead.

(i) 10 cabins **P** 🏄 MC, V

SAN VITO

🏨 LAS CRUCES BIOLOGICAL STATION
$$

HWY. 16, 4 MILES (6.4 KM) S OF SAN VITO
TEL 2773-4004   FAX 2773-4109
www.ots.ac.cr

Attractive contemporary rooms boast verandas, picture windows, and modern amenities in the heart of a forest reserve. The station is set amid the Wilson Botanical Garden, a collection more than 1,000 genera in 212 plants families, considered the most important Central American plant collection.

(i) 12 **P** 🅿 🏄 AE, MC, V

■ NORTHERN LOWLANDS

CHACHAGUA

🏠 CHACHAGUA RAIN FOREST LODGE
$$

1 MILE (1.6 KM) W OF CHACHA-GUA

TEL 2239-6464   FAX 2290-6506
www.chachaguarainforest
lodge.com

A working cattle and fruit farm with a private nature reserve at the foot of the Cordillera de Tilarán is the setting for this rustic wilderness lodge. The cabins overlook a pond.

🛏 23 ᴾ 🌊 ᐧ AE, MC, V

LA VIRGEN

🏠 CENTRO NEOTRÓPICO
🍴 SARAPIQUÍS ECOLODGE
$$$$

1 MILE (1.6 KM) S OF LA VIRGEN

TEL 2761-1004   FAX 2761-1415
www.sarapiquis.org

This upscale stunner nestles in the heart of an ecotourism project adjacent to a rain forest reserve. Architecture and decor blend contemporary and pre-Columbian styles, with stone floors and tropical pastel colors. The elegant restaurant offers à la carte and buffet options, plus forest views over the canopy. Botanical garden, archaeological site, and museum nearby.

🛏 36 ᴾ 🌊 ᐧ MC, V

LAS HORQUETAS

🏠 RARA AVIS
$$

9 MILES (14.5 KM) SW OF LAS HORQUETAS, SARAPIQUI

TEL 2764-1111   FAX 2764-1114
www.rara-avis.com

A remote wilderness lodge located on a private reserve with swimming holes, canopy platforms, butterfly and orchid houses, naturalist guides, hiking trails, and horseback riding. Two-night minimum stay;

reservations required. Simple food; rates include meals.

🛏 5 cabins, 10 rooms ᴾ
ᐧ AE, MC, V

MUELLE

🏠 TILAJARI RESORT
🍴 HOTEL
$$$

1 MILE (1.6 KM) W OF MUELLE CROSSROADS

TEL 2469-9091   FAX 2469-9095
www.tilajari.com

Spacious, modestly furnished rooms on the banks of the Río San Carlos. Adequate meals in a large restaurant. Wildlife abounds, including crocodiles on the riverbanks. Butterfly garden, squash courts, disco, sauna, and sports facilities. Tours offered.

🛏 76 ᴾ 🌊
ᐧ All major cards

PUERTO VIEJO

🏠 SELVA VERDE
$$$

CHILAMATE DE SARAPIQUÍ, 6 MILES (9.7 KM) W OF PUERTO VIEJO

TEL 2766-6800   FAX 2766-6011
www.selvaverde.com

This lodge is set on the edge of rain forest. Choose between rustic rooms, upscale cabins, or bungalows. There is a library, lecture room, and communal dining room. Guided hikes and canoe trips can be arranged.

🛏 40 rooms, 5 bungalows ᴾ
ᐧ MC, V

TABACÓN

🏠 TABACÓN HOT
SPRINGS RESORT & SPA
$$$

TABACÓN, 8 MILES (13 KM) W OF LA FORTUNA

TEL 2519-1999 OR 877/277-8291
FAX 2519-1940
www.tabacon.com

This modern lodge with views of Volcán Arenal offers guests direct access to the adjacent

spa. Rooms are tastefully furnished. A choice of restaurants includes an atmospheric eatery situated directly above the thermal pools.

🛏 106 ᴾ 🌊 🍴 ᐧ DC, MC, V

■ THE CARIBBEAN

BARRA DEL COLORADO

🏠 RÍO COLORADO LODGE
$$$

BARRA DEL COLORADO SUR

TEL 2710-6879   FAX 2231-5987
www.riocoloradolodge.com

This sportfishing lodge boasts a large fleet plus a tackle shop. Simple rooms with modern necessities. Small zoo. Seafood and local dishes are served in the dining room or on the riverside deck.

🛏 18 🌊 ᐧ AE, MC, V

🏠 SILVER KING LODGE
$$$

BARRA DEL COLORADO SUR

TEL 800/847-3474
FAX 2381-0849
www.silverkinglodge.net

Well-furnished wooden cabins linked by catwalks on the banks of the river from which a fleet of sportfishing boats put out. Tackle shop, TV and video room, indoor spa pool, bar, and restaurant.

🛏 20 🌊 ᐧ AE, MC, V

CAHUITA

🏠 LA DIOSA
🍴 $$

PLAYA NEGRA, 2 MILES (3.2 KM) N OF CAHUITA

TEL 2755-0055   FAX 2755-0321
www.hotelladiosa.net

Squatting on its own little beach, this quaint hotel has charming cabins featuring riverstone walls and batik spreads. Delightful gardens with yoga dojo and Oriental adornments.

🛏 6 rooms, 2 cabins ᴾ 🌊
ᐧ None

ᐧ Nonsmoking 🌊 Air-conditioning 🏊 Indoor Pool 🌊 Outdoor Pool 🍴 Health Club ᐧ Credit Cards

🍴 MISS EDITH'S
$$

PLAYA NEGRA, 2 MILES (3.2 KM)
N OF CAHUITA
TEL 2755-0248
The place to try authentic
Caribbean cuisine such as
"run-down" and curried lobster
in coconut milk. Family-run,
laid-back, and open-air.

🅿 🚫None

ESTRELLA

🏨 SELVA BANANITO LODGE
$$

9 MILES (14.5 KM) W OF
BANANITO
TEL 2253-8118   FAX 2280-0820
www.selvabananito.com
A simple, atmospheric lodge
on the edge of the rain forest.
Stilt-legged cabins with solar-
heated water. No electricity.
Hiking, horseback rides, and
family-style dining. Four-
wheel-drive access.

ⓘ 11 🅿 🚫None

GUÁPILES

🏨 CASA RÍO BLANCO ECOLODGE
$$

RIO BLANCO, 3 MILES (4.8 KM) W
OF GUÁPILES
TEL/FAX 2710-4124
www.casarioblanco.com
Charming Dutch-run hotel
with wooden cabins. Balconies
overlook a river on the edge of
rain forest. Delightful, simple
decor. Has a small educational
center on-site. Trails lead past
waterfalls and bat cave.

ⓘ 4 cabins, 2 rooms 🅿
🚫MC, V

🏨 RÍO DANTA
🍴 RESTAURANT & PRIVATE RESERVE
$

3 MILES (4.8 KM) W OF GUÁPILES
TEL 2710-2626
www.grupomawamba.com
Local cuisine served in airy

eatery decorated with regional
icons. Trails lead to rain forest
with hopping poison dart frogs.

🅿 🕐Closed D 🚫AE, MC, V

PUERTO VIEJO

🏨 SHAWANDHA LODGE
$$$

PLAYA CHIQUITA, 4 MILES (6.4
KM) SE OF PUERTO VIEJO
TEL 2750-0018   FAX 2750-0037
www.shawandhalodge.com
Splendid setting for cabins close
to the beach. Tasteful furnish-
ings include four-poster beds.
The open-air lounge offers
similarly contemporary grace.
Rates include breakfast.

ⓘ 12 🅿 🚫AE, MC, V

🏨 ALMONDS & CORALS LODGE TENT CAMP
$$

PUNTA MANZANILLO, 5 MILES (8
KM) SE OF PUERTO VIEJO
TEL 2271-3000   FAX 2759-9056
www.almondsandcorals.com
A minimalist, eco-sensitive
wilderness lodge with tents
on roofed wooden platforms,
situated in shore-front jungle.
Private bathrooms nearby.
Communal restaurant. Tours
and outdoor activities.

ⓘ 24 🅿 🚫AE, DC, MC

🏨 COCO LOCO
$

400 YARDS (366 M) SW OF
PUERTO VIEJO
TEL 2750-0281
www.cocolocolodge.com
Simplicity is the watchword
at this back-to-basics retreat
set amid lawns surrounded
by forest. Small Tahitian-style
cabins offer few frills but plenty
of charm. Mosquito nets over
beds. No restaurant.

ⓘ 4 cottages, 1 four-person
bungalow 🅿 🚫None

🍴 LA PECORA NERA
$$$

PLAYA COCLES
TEL 2750-0490
Delicious Italian fare of

world-class standard at this
unpretentious, thatched open-
air restaurant. Staples such as
calzones, gnocchi, and pizzas
are supplemented by superlative daily specials.

🅿 🕐Closed Mon. 🚫
🚫AE, MC, V

TORTUGUERO

🏨 TORTUGA LODGE & GARDENS
$$$

2 MILES (3.2 KM) N OF TORTU-
GUERO
TEL 2257-0766   FAX 2257-1665
www.costaricaexpeditions.com
This comfortable nature lodge
on the banks of Tortuguero
Lagoon is close to the airstrip.
You can eat in the airy dining
room or on the riverside
terrace. Guided boat tours of
Parque Nacional Tortuguero,
plus hikes and sportfishing.
At night, rockers on verandas
prove handy for watching bats
scoop fish from the lagoon.

ⓘ 24 🅿 🏊 🚫AE, MC, V

🏨 CASA MARBELLA B&B
$

TORTUGUERO VILLAGE
TEL 8833-0827 OR 2709-8011
FAX 2709-8094
http://casamarbella.tripod
.com
A simple, colorful, and
charming Canadian-run bed-
and-breakfast in the heart of
Tortuguero. The owner is a
font of local knowledge.
Community kitchen.

ⓘ 5 🚫None

🍴 MISS JUNIE'S
$

TEL 2711-0683
Down-home cooking by a
village elder. Fish platter special
comes with beans and rice
simmered in coconut milk.
Homemade ginger cookies,
and *pan bon*, bread laced with
caramelized sugar, prove to be
extremely tempting desserts.

🚫None

Shopping in Costa Rica

The tourist boom has spawned an outpouring of quality crafts, from beautiful pottery, wooden bowls, and carvings to exquisite gold jewelry and colorful wooden *carretas* (traditional oxcarts). San José is filled with crafts stores and art galleries; the latter reflects an explosion of energy in the art world.

Many crafts use hardwoods, such as lignum vitae, purpleheart, rosewood, satinwood, and tigerwood. Larger items include carved headboards, lathe-turned rockers with leather seats, and decorative mini-carretas for use as liquor bars or garden ornaments which can be shipped home with relative ease.

Costa Rica's renowned coffee is available nationwide. Buy prepackaged, premium export-grade coffee; domestic coffee is notably inferior. Juan Santamaría International Airport has several quality gift stores, including those of Café Britt where you can buy coffee. Most upscale hotels have stores selling arts and crafts, as does the airport, which also has duty-free stores.

Opening Times
See p. 238.

■ SAN JOSÉ
West of Avenida 2, between Calles 4 and 9 are art and craft stores. Centro Comercial El Pueblo to the northeast of the city center, has alleys lined with galleries, stores, and restaurants. The suburb of Moravia (San Vincente) is known for art, crafts, jewelry, local leatherwork and wicker furniture.

Arts & Antiques
Andrómeda Gallery *(Calle 9, Ave. 9, tel 2223-3529)*. Paintings by Costa Rican and Central American artists, including top local names. Works cost as much as $10,000.
Galería de Arte Amir *(Ave. 5, Calle 5, tel 2221-9128)*. Broad representation of works by leading artists, including deceased masters.
Galería Valanti *(Avenida 11, Calles 33/35, tel 2253-1659)*. This compact gallery specializes in works from throughout the Americas, with a focus on local artists of note.

Kadinsky *(Centro Comercial, Calle Real, San Pedro, tel 2234-0478)* stocks artwork by Costa Rica's preeminent artists.

Books & Maps
7th Street Books *(Calle 7, Aves. Central/1, tel 2256-9251)*. English-language store stocks novels, nature books, travel guides, and international magazines.
Instituto Geográfica Nacional *(Ave. 20, Calles 9/11, tel 2257-7798 ext. 2630)*. Detailed topographic and city maps of the whole country.
Librería Internacional *(Ave. Central, Calles 3/5, www.libreria internacional.com)*. Costa Rica's preeminent book chain has six outlets in San José.

Clothes & Accessories
Mercado Central *(Ave. 1, Calles 6/8)*. Local clothing, including *guayaberas*, cowboy boots, leather belts, and embroidered blouses.
Artesanías Malety *(Ave. 1, Calles 1/3, tel 2221-1670)*. Pick up a pair of stylish cowboy boots, including alligator skin.
Choza Folclórica *(Ave. 3 & Calle 1)*. Frilly white cotton dresses with colored sashes are Guanacaste's traditional dress.

Crafts & Jewelry
Boutique Annemarie *(Hotel Don Carlos, see p. 242)*. Arts and crafts, from carved walking sticks to balsawood masks.
La Casona *(Calle Central, Aves. Central/1, tel 2222-7999)*. Christmas crèches and ornaments, textiles.
Esmeraldas & Diseños *(Sabana Norte, tel 2231-4808)*. Jewelry includes pre-Columbian-style gold.
Galería Namú *(Ave. 7, Calles 5/7, tel 2256-3412, www.galerianamu. com)*. High-quality indigenous arts

and crafts and paintings from Costa Rica and Panama.
Museo de Oro Precolumbino *(see p. 58)*. Contemporary gold and silver, precious stones. Superb pre-Columbian reproductions.
Plaza Esmeralda *(Carretera Sabana-Escazú, tel 2296-0312)*. A vast range of jewelry, from pre-Columbian motifs to chic contemporary settings.

Gifts
Casa del Habano *(Calle 4, Ave. 1, San Pedro, tel 2280-7931)* has the best selection of cigars in Costa Rica, including premium Cubans.
Guitarras Guzmán, Ltd. *(Tibas, tel 2235-1603)* sells classical guitars carved from precious woods.
Habanos de Costa Rica *(Calle 7, Ave. 7/9, tel 2383-6835)*, operated by Cuba's Habanos S.A., offers genuine Cubans.
Orquídeas del Bosque *(Rohrmoser, tel 2232-1466, www.costaricaorchids .com)* sells more than 75 species of orchids for export.

Malls
San Pedro Mall *(Ave. Central Circunvalación, tel 2283-7540)*. The city's largest mall, with dozens of upscale stores. Everything from jewelry and fashion to leathers and books. Also a bank, movie theater, and two-story food court.

Markets
Mercado Borbón *(Calle 8, Aves. 3/5)*. Farmer's market on the west side of Plaza Víquez. A great place to buy fresh produce and flowers. Saturday mornings.
Mercado Central *(Bet. Calles 6/8 and Aves. Central/Calle 1)*. A maze of tight alleyways where street stalls and shops sell everything from medicinal herbs and flowers to cowboy

boots and guayabero shirts. Closed Sundays. Beware of pickpockets.
Mercado de Artesanía Las Garzas *(Moravia, tel 2236-0037).* Around 30 craft stores under a single roof.
Mercado de Artesanías Nacionales *(Calle 11, Aves. 4/6, tel 2223-0122).* An eclectic daily craft market offering T-shirts, leather goods, rugs, Guatemalan jackets, and hammocks. Closed Sun.

■ CENTRAL HIGHLANDS

Santa Ana is famous for ceramics. Sarchí is the nation's undisputed center of crafts, with furniture workshops, and fine leatherworkers. It also is the sole remaining production center in the country for *carretas* (traditional oxcarts). Workshops and craft stores line the main street.

Crafts & Jewelry

Biesanz Woodworks *(Biesanz, see p. 70),* Costa Rica's premier wood-carver, oversees 20 master carvers in his workshop. Exquisite bowls, boxes, and humidors.
Casa El Soñador, see p. 86. Buy primitive-style pieces carved from coffee wood.
Cerámica Santa Ana *(Santa Ana, tel 2282-6024).* Earthenware bowls, vases, and urns, as well as smaller ceramic pieces are made on old-fashioned kick wheels and fired in an outdoor kiln.
Creaciones Santos *(Ave. 3, Calles 1/3, San Miguel de Escazú, tel 2228-6747).* Exotic stained glass made on-site.
Fábrica de Carretas Joaquín Chaverrí *(Sarchí Sur, tel 2454-4411).* A huge selection of arts and crafts from hardwood to kitchenware. In the family-run workshop, you can see miniature carretas being made.
Molas & Coffee Gift Shop *(Atenas, tel 2446-5155).* A fine array of native arts and crafts, plus jewelry. Indigenous craftspeople employed on-site.

Gifts

Café Britt, see p. 83. Offers premium prepackaged coffees at wholesale prices, plus handcrafted wooden kitchen utensils, bowls, and other gift items with Costa Rican themes. Café Britt outlets are also located in the José Santamaría International Airport.
Plaza de Artesanías *(Sarchí Sur, tel 2454-3430).* Over 30 stores ranging from leather goods to Guatemalan textiles to jewelry.

Malls

Centro Comercial Escazú *(San Rafael de Escazú).* Boutiques and specialty stores.
Multiplaza *(Autopista Prospero Fernández, Escazú, tel 2288-1178, www.multiplazamall.com).* Costa Rica's largest mall has specialty stores that range from books to fashion to jewelry.

Markets

Mercado Central *(Bet. Calle 4/6 and Aves. Central/1, Alajuela).* An entire block of stalls selling fresh farm produce, meats, fish, spices, leatherwork, and household goods. Be alert for pickpockets and thieves.
Mercado Central *(Bet. Calle 2/4 and Aves. 6/8, Heredia).* A tight warren of stores offering farm produce, crafts, and general wares. As with all markets, guard your valuables.

■ GUANACASTE

Monteverde has galleries and gift stores selling some of the most creative works in the country.

Crafts & Jewelry

Committee of Artisans of Santa Elena & Monteverde (CASEM) *(Monteverde, tel 2645-5190).* Works by over one hundred local artists, from paintings to ceramics. Sales benefit the local community.
Extasis Gallery *(Monteverde, tel 2645-5548).* Works by gifted local artist Marco Tulio Brenes include jewelry, paintings, and sculptures.

Hummingbird Gallery *(Monteverde, tel 2645-5030).* Wildlife posters and prints, Guatemalan textiles, and crafts from throughout the isthmus, including hand-painted wooden animal figurines. Prints and slides by local photographers Michael and Patricia Fogden.
Souvenirs La Gran Nicoya *(Hwy. 21, near Daniel Oduber Internacional Airport., tel 2667-0062, www .lagrannicoya-cr.com).* A vast range of souvenirs, including ceramics, beachwear, and cigars.
Toad Hall, see p. 247. Quality arts and crafts, books, postcards, and Cuban cigars.

Gifts

La Lechería, see p. 109. Various cheeses and ice creams made on site, plus meats.

Markets

Mercado Central *(Ave. 3, Calle 2, Puntarenas).* Waterfront market crammed with seafood and fresh produce stalls.

■ NICOYA

Guaitíl is the center of the Indian pottery tradition. Matriarchs work clay into bowls, plates, and vases painted in traditional animal motifs. Ask for a tour. A trademark three-legged vase in the form of a cow costs between $15 and $50.

Crafts & Jewelry

Cooperativa de Mujeres de Guaitíl *(Guaitíl).* Artisans sell their handmade pottery.
El Mundo de la Tortuga, see p. 141. Crafts and clothing on an environmental theme; marine turtles are most popular items.
Galeria de las Estrellas *(Tamarindo).* Stylish gold and silver jewelry, much of it reproductions of pre-Columbian styles.
Tamarindo Beach Cigar Lounge *(Tamarindo, tel 2653-0862).* Hand-rolled cigars produced on site, including coffee-flavored cigars sold in miniature *carretas.*

CENTRAL PACIFIC

Quepos has numerous souvenir stores and art galleries, and Manuel Antonio has beachfront stalls; several hotels have excellent gift stores. Boruca produces Indian crafts. The men make balsawood masks and decorate gourds.

Clothes & Accessories

Guacamole (Jacó, tel 2643-1120). Indonesian-inspired batik beachwear produced at this small clothing store. Also has an outlet in Plaza Il Galeone (tel 2643-3297).

Crafts & Jewelry

Boutique Mot Mot (Quepos, tel 2777-3559, www.motmotcr.com). Good selection of local crafts. Purchases support Fundación Neotrópica.
Buena Nota (Manuel Antonio, tel 2777-1002). Resortwear, handicrafts, and souvenirs, plus books, magazines, and maps.
Galería Arte la Heliconia (Jacó, tel 2643-3613). Pottery and artwork, as well as souvenirs.
L'Aventura Multiboutique (Ave. Central, Calle 2, Quepos. tel 2777-1019). Great choice of crafts, batiks, jewelry, and leather goods.
Regalame (Si Como No Hotel, Manuel Antonio, see p. 252). First-class paintings, sculptures, and handicrafts by local artisans.
Villa Caletas, see p. 252. Only juried gold items and quality crafts are sold here.

Gifts

House of Cuban Cigars (Quepos, tel 2777-2208). A Cuban exile rolls quality smokes on-site. Closed Sun.
Lighthouse Point (Jacó, tel 2643-3083) has a huge stock of souvenirs, T-shirts, and cigars.

ZONA SUR

Golfito draws Costa Ricans from afar to its duty-free Depósito Libre zone, although there are few items of interest for tourists. Puerto Jiménez has several souvenir shops; many hotel gift shops sell local crafts, including balsawood masks.

Crafts & Jewelry

Reserva Indígena Boruca. Marina Lázaro Morales runs the local cooperative; members make colorful animal masks and figures, plus hammocks and woven goods.

SOUTH CENTRAL

Shopping is not this region's strong suit. However, San Isidro and San Vito have many shops selling cowboy boots and other leather goods. The indigenous communities of the Talamancas produce crafts, including colorful molas.

Crafts & Jewelry

Finca Cántaros (Hwy. 16 at Linda Vista, 2 miles S of San Vito, tel 2773-3760). Quality arts and crafts, including ceramics, jewelry, and clothing. Closed Mon.–Fri.

NORTHERN LOWLANDS

Ciudad Quesada has several talabarterías (saddle shops) selling cowboy boots, decorated saddles, and other leather goods. Fortuna has souvenir shops selling crafts from throughout the nation.

Crafts & Jewelry

Coco Loco Art Gallery & Café (Chachagua, tel 2468-0990). Fabulous selection of quality arts and crafts includes indigenous masks and contemporary ceramics.
Rancho Leona (La Virgen, tel 2761-1019). Masterful stained-glass works made to order or bought on spec for $80–$125 per square foot. Part of the proceeds helps buy endangered forest.
Reserva Indígena Malekú (2 miles E of San Rafael de Guatuso). Naïve native crafts, including masks.

Gifts

MUSA (El Tigre, tel 2710-3815). Women's cooperative selling herbal teas and balms, medicinal herbs, aphrodisiacs, and toiletries.

Markets

Mercado Central (Calle 2, Ave. Central, Ciudad Quesada). Bustling hive offering produce, plus arts and crafts from the local artisans' cooperative.

THE CARIBBEAN

Puerto Viejo's entrepreneurial expatriate population produces and sells a wide selection of jewelry, batiks, and tourist trinkets.

Art & Antiques

Gallery at Home (Río Blanco, tel 2711-0823). Studio of acclaimed North American artist Patricia Erickson. Call for appointment.

Clothes & Accessories

Boutique Bombata (Cahuita). A small, well-stocked shop specializing in resortwear, including batik wraps, as well as jewelry and crafts. **Color Caribe** (Puerto Viejo, tel 2750-0075). One of the country's best-stocked souvenir stores offers jewelry, plus hand-painted and silk-screened T-shirts and other clothing.

Crafts & Jewelry

LuluBelu (Puerto Viejo, tel 2750-0394). Splendid range of souvenirs, including hammocks, jewelry, embroidered Guatemalan vests, and sandals.
Paraíso Tropical (Tortuguero, tel 2709-8095). Diverse array of arts and crafts, plus hammocks, swimwear, and more. Donates 10 percent of proceeds to the local school.

Markets

Mercado Central (Bet. Calles 3/4 and Aves. 2/3, Limón). A small, intriguing, crowded market replete with stalls that sell everything from household goods and crafts to fresh meats and fish. Be on guard for thieves.

Entertainment & Activities

San José has everything from classical concerts to discos. Casinos are here and in a few resort hotels; though most are small, classier ones have opened recently. The *Tico Times* and the "Viva" section of *La Nación* list festivals and events. The entertainment scene is supplemented by activities highlighting Costa Rica's natural diversity. The companies listed may cover additional activities and other areas.

Activities

Cheeseman's Ecology Safaris, tel 408/741-5330 or 800/527-5330, fax 408/741-0358, www .cheesemans.com

Costa Rica Expeditions, tel 2257-0766, fax 2257-1665, www .costaricaexpeditions.com

Costa Rica Temptations, tel 2508-5000, fax 2508-5134, www .crtinfo.com

Holbrook Travel, tel 800/451-7111, fax 352/371-3710, www .holbrooktravel.com

Horizontes Nature Tours, tel 2222-2022, fax 2255-4513, www .horizontes.com

Canoeing & Kayaking

Costa Rica's rivers offer a range of experiences. Contact:
Canoe Costa Rica, tel/fax 2282-3579 or 732/736-6586, www .canoecostarica.com

Desafío Adventure Company, tel 2479-9464, www.desafiocosta rica.com

Canopy Touring

Get close-up views of wildlife from narrow walkways between trees or ziplines that whisk through the treetops. See regional entries.

Fishing

See feature pp. 164–165 for details on the types of fishing available. Boat charters for up to four people cost $250–$400 for a half day and $350–$650 for a full day:
JP Sportfishing Tours, tel 2244-6361 or 866/620-4188, www. jpsportfishing.com

Papagayo Excursions, tel 2653-0254, fax 2653-0227, www .papagayoexcursions.com

Rain Goddess, tel 2231-4299, fax 2231-3816, www.bluwing.com

Golfing

The Central Highlands and Pacific Northwest have six premier golf courses. See regional entries.

Horseback Riding

Horseback riding is available nationwide; in Guanacaste, working cattle farms cater to visitors.
Cross Country International, tel 845/635-2200 or 800/828-8768, fax 845/635-3300, www .equestrianvacations.com

Equitour USA, tel 307/455-3363, 800/545-0019 or fax 307/455-2354, www.ridingtours.com

Motorcycling

Costa Rica's back roads are ideal for motorcycle touring for those who know how to ride.
María Alexandra Tours, tel 2289-5552, fax 2289-5551, www.mariaalexander.com

Moto-Discovery, tel 830/438-7744 or 800/233-0564, fax 830/438-7745, www.motodiscovery.com

Mountain Biking

Many hotels rent bikes. Most tours are one or two days; a van carries luggage and equipment.
Backroads, tel 510/527-1555 or 800/462-2848, fax 510/527-1444, www.backroads.com

Coast to Coast Adventures, tel 2280-8054, fax 2225-6055, www.ctocadventures.com

Experience Plus! Specialty Tours, tel 800/685-4565, fax 970/493-0377, www.experience plus.com

Nature Cruising

Travel at night; spend days at wilderness sights. Guides lead hikes. May offer diving and snorkeling.
Cruise West, 2401 Fourth Ave., Ste. 700, Seattle, WA 98121, tel 888/851-8133, fax 206/441-4757, www.cruisewest.com

Windstar Cruises, 2401 Fourth Ave., Ste. 1150, Seattle, WA 98121, tel 206/292-9606 or 877-827-7245, fax 206/340-0975, www .windstarcruises.com

Rafting

The industry (see feature pp. 196–197) is not regulated by the government, so book only with a reputable company. Large operators include: **Costa Rica Expeditions** (see Activities above)

Costa Sol Rafting, tel 2431-1183, fax 2431-1185, www.costasol rafting.com

Ríos Tropicales, tel 2233-6455, fax 2255-4354, www.riostropicales.com

Scuba Diving

On the Pacific coast, see groupers, manta rays, and sharks. Catalinas, Isla del Coco, and Islas Murciélagos (Bat Islands) are popular trips. Caribbean diving focuses on coral reefs, best Feb.–April. Visibility is poor by international standards. Temperatures are above 75°F (24°C) year-round. See regional entries.

Surfing

The Pacific coast has some of the world's longest rides. Rent boards at surf camps such as Tamarindo in Nicoya. **Costa Rican Surf Report** *(tel 2233-7386, www.crsurf .com)*, and **Surf Costa Rica** *(tel 888-751-0135, www.surf-costarica .com)* give local information.

Windsurfing

Laguna de Arenal (see pp. 114–115) and Bahía Salinas (see p. 128) are the two major sites. Contact:
Sun Tours and Fun, tel 8826-5221, www.suntoursandfun.com

■ SAN JOSÉ
The Arts
Little Theater Group *(Centro Cultural Eugene O'Neill, tel 2355-1623)*. English-language theater.
National Lyric Opera Company *(Teatro Melico Salazar (see p. 60), tel 2222-8571)*. Performances June–Aug.
North American Cultural Center *(San Pedro, tel 2225-9433, www.cccncr.com)*. Movies, lectures and more for North American expatriates.
National Symphony Orchestra *(Teatro Nacional, see pp. 58–59, tel 2221-9417)*. Weekly, April–Dec.

Festivals
Festival de la Carretas, Nov., Paseo Colón & Parque Central. Parade with oxcarts *(carretas)* and traditional dress. Musicians play the *cimarronas*.
Festival de la Luz, Christmas. A nocturnal parade of dozens of floats decorated with lights, from Parque Sabana straight to downtown.

Nightlife
Discoteque Infinito *(Centro Comercial, El Pueblo, tel 2223-2195)*. Three disco areas under one roof.
El Cuartel de la Boca del Monte *(Ave. 1, Calles 21/23, tel 2221-0327)*. Live music and dancing.
Fantasía Folclórica *(Teatro Popular Melico Salazar, see p. 60)*. Traditional music and dance. Tues. only.
Jazz Café *(Ave. Central, Los Yoses, tel 2253-8933)*. The best spot for live jazz and blues.
Key Largo *(Calle 7, Ave. 1/3, tel 2221-0277)*. Raffish bar and dance club in colonial mansion.
Río *(Ave. Central, San Pedro, tel 2225-8371)*. Packs in chic hipsters; live music and music videos.
Shakespeare Bar *(Ave. 2, Calle 28, tel 2257-1288)*. Piano bar with occasionally live jazz.
Tobogán, Calle Blancos, tel 2223-8920. Popular disco beneath thatch. Occasional live bands.

Other Activities
Bowling
Boliche, Calle 37, San Pedro, tel 2253-5745

Casinos
Casino Club Colonial, Ave. 1, Calles 9/11, tel 2258-2807
Horseshoe Casino, Ave. 1, Calle 9, tel 2233-4383

Dance Lessons
Merecumbé, S. Pedro, tel 2224-3531
Prodanza, tel 2290-2293, www.prodanza.com

Golf
Cariari Country Club *(tel 2293-3211, www.clubcariari.com)* has an 18-hole championship course.

■ CENTRAL HIGHLANDS
Festivals
Easter Procession, Easter Sunday, San Isidro de Heredia. Solemn religious festival, a celebratory theme.
International Music Festival, July–Aug., Hotel Chalet Tirol and other venues (see p. 245).
Juan Santamaría Day, April 11, Alajuela. Week of festivities honoring the boy hero (see p. 27). Music, parades, and street fairs all week.
La Negrita Pilgrimage, Aug. 2, see p. 87.
Día de Boyeros, 2nd Sun. in March, San Rafael de Escazú. Oxcart drivers' *(boyeros)* parade, music, dancing, and folk tales.

Nightlife
Casino Real at the Real Intercontinental, see p. 244.
The Martini Bar *(Centro Comercial, Escazú, tel 2288-8572)* Is a chic bar serving iced martinis.

Other Activities
Auto Racing
La Guácima Race Track *(San Antonio de Belen, tel 2293-6359, www.laguacima.com)*. Formula 3, go-kart, and motorcycle racing.

Bungee Jumping
Tropical Bungee, Rosario, tel 2248-2212, www.bungee.co.cr

Casinos
Fiesta Casino, Garden Court Hotel, Río Segundo de Alajuela, tel 2431-1455

Fishing
Trout farms offer fishing from pools. Bring your own tackle.
Albergue de Montaña Savegre, San Gerardo de Dota, tel 2771-1028

Golf
Parque Valle del Sol *(Santa Ana, tel 2282-9222, www.vallesol.com)*. 18-hole course.

Horseback Riding
Club Hípico la Caraña *(Santa Ana, tel 2282-6754, www.la carana.com)*. Lessons and tours
Hacienda el Rodeo, Ciudad Colón, tel 2249-1013
Rancho San Miguel, La Guácima, see p. 75.

Mountain Biking
Hotel Casa Turire, tel 2531-1111, www.hotelcasaturire.com

Polo
Los Reyes Country Club, La Guácima, tel 2438-0004

Rafting
One- or three-day runs with Class III or IV rapids.
Costa Rica Expeditions, San Jose, see p. 260
Ríos Tropicales, San José, see p. 260

Swimming
Waterland *(Ciudad Cariari, tel 2293-2891, www.waterlandcr.com)*. Aquatic park. Closed Mon.

■ GUANACASTE
The Arts
Fiesta Brava *(Hacienda La Chácara, Liberia, tel 2350-1627, www .haciendalachacara.com)*. Cowboys, rodeo, marimba, traditional food, music. Wed. & Sat.

Festivals

Día de Guanacaste, July 25, Liberia. Marimba and mariachi music, parades, and rodeos.
Día del Sabanero, Nov., Liberia. Cowboys whoop it up with *topes* and rodeos.
Fiesta Cívica, May, Cañas. Traditional music and dance, rodeos, and *topes.*
Virgin of the Sea Festival, July, Puntarenas. Gaily decorated boats, including a dragon boat representing the Chinese community, honor Carmen, the Virgin of the Sea.

Nightlife

Moon Shiva Café, Bromelias Art Gallery, Monteverde, tel 2645-6270. Live music.
La Cascada, tel 2645-5186. Full-blown disco, with hot tubs.

Other Activities

Birding
Costa Rican Trails, tel 888/803-3344, www.costaricantrails.com

Canopy Tours
The Original Canopy Tour, Mahogany Park (see p. 103) or Santa Elena, tel 2291-4465, www.canopytour.com
Rincón de la Vieja Lodge, see p. 248.
Selvatura, see p. 111
Sky Walk, Santa Elena, tel 2645-5238, www.skywalk.co.cr

Diving
See p. 263 for operators to the Islas Murciélagos.

Driving
Tamarindo Adventures *(Tamarindo, tel/fax 2653-0108, www.tamarindoadventures.net).* All terrain four-wheel-drive vehicles.

Fishing
Rain Goddess, see p. 260

Guided Hikes
Heliconias Lodge, tel 2290-8646, www.turismoruralcr.com

Horseback Riding

Buena Vista Mountain Lodge & Adventure Center, 8 miles NE of Cañas Dulces, tel 2690-1414, www.buenavistalodgecr.com
Hotel Hacienda Guachipelín, Curubandé, tel 2666-8075, www.guachipelin.com
Sabine's Smiling Horses, Monteverde, tel 2645-6804, www.smilinghorses.com

Mountain Biking

Hotel Hacienda Guachipelín (see Horseback Riding above)

Rafting

Río Corobicí is a calm float, with short rapids, and water all year.
Safaris Corobicí, Hwy. 1, 3 miles (4.8 km) N of Cañas, tel 2669-6191, www.nicoya.com

Surfing

From Witch's Rock you can ride to Playa Naranjo. Try Playa Portrero Grande (featured in *Endless Summer II)* and Playa Blanca.
Wavehunters Surf Travel, tel 760/494-7391, www.wavehunters.com

Windsurfing

Winds peak at Laguna de Arenal November to April. Bahía Salinas has high winds November to May.
Kitesurfing Center & School, Bahía Salinas, tel 2826-5221, www.suntoursandfun.com
Tico Wind Surf Center, Hwy. 142, Laguna de Arenal, tel/fax 2692-2002, www.ticowind.com
Tilawa Viento Surf Center, Hwy. 142, Laguna de Arenal, tel 2695-5050, www.windsurfcostarica.com

▪ NICOYA

Festivals

Festival of the Virgén de Guadalupe, December 12, Nicoya. This colorful and often very lively festival combines Catholic and Chorotega traditions with the legend of the Virgin of Guadalupe, or La Yequita (Little Mare). Streets are thronged with crowds who throw fireworks *(bombas),* drink *chicha,* and play traditional music.
Fiesta Cívica, late January, Playas del Coco. Beauty pageants, rodeos, and street parties.
Fiesta Cívica, January 15 & July 25, Santa Cruz. Firecrackers, marimba music, dancing, rodeos.

Nightlife

Disco Coco Mar *(Playas del Coco, tel 2670-0358).* Pumped-up Latin beat.
El Sano Banano *(Montezuma, tel 2642-0636).* Health-food café with movies nightly.
Father Rooster *(Playa Ocotal, tel 2670-1246).* Atmospheric beach bar. Theme parties.
Rey Sol Disco Bar, Tamarindo. Late night disco. Ladies night Thurs.
Zouk Santana *(Playas del Coco, tel 2670-0191, www.zouksantana .com).* Upscale disco with dining and theme parties.

Other Activities

For a variety of outdoor activities contact:
Brasilito Excursions, Playa Brasilito, tel 2654-4237, www.brasilito.com
Costa Rica Temptations, see p. 260.
Montezuma Expeditions, Montezuma, tel 2440-8078, www.montezumaexpeditions.com
Papagayo Excursions, see p. 260.

Canopy Tours
Congo Trail Canopy Tour, 5.6 miles (9 km) W of Sardinal, tel 2666-4422
Montezuma Canopy Tour, Montezuma, tel 2642-0808, www.montezumatraveladventures.com
Witch's Rock Canopy Tour, Bahía Culebra, tel 2667-0661
Wingnuts, Playa Sámara, tel 2656-0153

Golf
Four Seasons Golf Club, Bahía Culebra, tel 2696-0000, www.fourseasons.com
Hacienda Pinilla, Playa Avenallas,

tel 2680-7060, www.haciendapinilla
.com
Los Delfines Golf & Country Club,
Playa Tambor, tel 2683-0303, fax
2683-0612, www.delfines.com
**Paradisus Playa Conchal Beach &
Golf Resort,** see p. 249.
Tango Mar, see p. 250.

Cruises
Bay Island Cruises, tel 2258-
3536, www.bayislandcruises.co
Calypso Cruises *(tel 2256-2727
or 800/887-1969, fax 2256-6767,
www.calypsocruises.com).* State-of-
the-art catamaran.

Horseback Riding
Capitán Suizo Stables, Tamarindo, tel 2653-0075
Finca Los Caballos, Montezuma,
tel 2642-0124, www.nature
lodge.net

Scuba Diving
See eagle rays at Punta Gorda, or
visit the Islas Murciélagos.
Bill Beard's Costa Rica, tel
954/453-5044, www.billbeard
costarica.com
El Ocotal Diving Safaris,
Playa Ocotal, tel 2670-0321, www
.ocotaldiving.com
Resort Divers de Costa Rica, Playa
del Coco, tel 2670-0421, www
.resortdivers-cr.com
Rich Coast Diving, Playa del Coco,
tel/fax 2670-0176, www.richcoast
diving.com

Sea Kayaking
Kayaking grants close-up views of
bird colonies and mangroves.
Gulf Islands Kayaking, S-24 C-34,
Galiano Island BC, VON 1PO,
Canada, tel/fax 250/539-2442,
www.seakayak.ca

Spelunking
Barra Honda's caves are open
November to April. Experienced
spelunkers can enter without a
guide (by permit only).
**Asociación de Guías Ecologistas
de Barra Honda,** tel 2569-1716.
Guided descents.
National Park Service, tel 2659-1551

Sportfishing
The Gulf of Papagayo delivers
record sailfish and blue marlin.
Asociación de las Pangueros,
Playas del Coco, tel 2670-0228
Flamingo Bay Pacific Charters,
tel 2253-6713 or 800/836-7133,
www.fishincostarica.com
Grandslam Fishing Tours, Playa
Carrillo, tel 877-441-3474, www
.grandslamfishingtours.com
Tamarindo Sportfishing, Playa
Tamarindo, tel/fax 2653-0090,
www.tamarindosportfishing.com

Surfing
Check out Playa Tamarindo, Santa
Teresa, and Malpaís.
Iguana Surf Shop, Playa Tama-
rindo, tel/fax 2653-0148, www
.iguanasurf.net
Malpaís Surf Camp & Resort,
Malpaís, tel 2640-0031, www
.malpaisurfcamp.com

Ultralight
Flying Crocodile Flying Center,
Sámara, tel 2656-8048, www
.flying-crocodile.com

Yoga
Nosara Retreat, Nosara, tel/fax
2682-0071, www.nosarayoga.com.

■ CENTRAL PACIFIC
Festivals
International Music Festival,
July–Aug., Villa Caletas, see
pp. 170 & 252. Local and international performers play in a small
amphitheater.

Nightlife
Casino Kamuk *(Hotel Best Western
Kamuk, Quepos, tel 2777-0811, www
.kamuk.co.cr).* Small, unpretentious
casino.
El Caballo Rey *(Quebrado Ganado
de Jacó, tel 2824-3360).* Andulusian
horse show with dinner, Thurs.
& Sat.
El Gran Escape *(Quepos, tel 2777-
0395).* Lively bar with large-screen
TVs and occasional live music.
Hotel Amapola *(Playa Jacó,
tel 2643-2255, www.hotelamapola
.com).* Small casino and disco.

Oz Sport Bar *(Jacó, tel 2643-2162,
www.barandhoteloz.com).* Huge sports
bar with pool tables.
San Clemente Bar & Grill *(Dominical, tel 2787-0055).* Disco, live bands,
sports TV, and foosball.
Si Como No Movie Theater, Si
Como No Hotel, see p. 251.
Thrusters, Dominical. A young
crowd fills this atmospheric bar.

Other Activities
Local tours offer cruises, horseback riding, and visits to palm oil
plantations.
Lynch Travel, Quepos, tel 2777-1170,
fax 2777-1571, www.lynchtravel.com

ATV Tours
**Paradise Adventure Travel &
ATV Tours,** Jáco, tel 2278-6598,
www.paraisocostarica.com.

Canopy Tours
Hacienda Barú, see p. 251.
Pacific Rain forest Aerial Tram,
Playa Jacó, tel 2257-5961, www
.rainforesttram.com
Rainmaker Conservation Project,
see p. 170.

Crocodile Safaris
Crocodiles are prolific.
Jungle Crocodile Safari, Tárcoles,
tel 2637-0338, www.jungle
crocodilesafari.com

Diving
Villas Gaia, see p. 251. PADI
certification and snorkeling.

Dolphin Safari
Planet Dolphin, Quepos, tel 2777-
1647, www.planetdolphin.com

Golf
**Los Sueños Marriott Ocean &
Golf Resort,** see p. 252.

Horseback Riding
Bella Vista Lodge, Escaleras,
tel 2787-8069, www
.bellavistalodge.com
Del Pacifico Horseback Riding,
Esterillos, tel 2778-7080
Marlboro Stables, Manuel Anto-
nio, tel 2777-1108
**Refugio Nacional de Vida Silvestre
Rancho la Merced,** Uvita, see p. 168.

Kayaking

Explore the mangroves of Pacific river mouths silently by kayak to get close to the critters.
Dolphin Tour, Uvita, tel 2743-8013, email: dolfintours@yahoo.com

Rafting

Ríos Naranjo and Savegre.
Adventures Manuel Antonio, Manuel Antonio, tel 2777-1084, www.adventuremanuelantonio.com
Ríos Tropicales, Quepos, tel 2777-4092

Sailing & Cruises

Sunset Sails Tours, Quepos, tel 2777-1306

Sportfishing

Quepos is one of three key centers on the Pacific coast.
Bluefin Sportfishing, Quepos, tel 2777-0000, www.bluefinsportfishing.com
Costa Rica Dreams, Los Sueños Marina, Playa Herradura, tel 2637-8942, www.costaricadreams.com

Surfing

Surfboards and other surfing equipment are available for rent at Playa Jacó and Playa Hermosa. Playas Esterillos, Oeste, Este, Dominical, and Manuel Antonio are also popular.

Ultralight

Skyline, Uvita, tel 743-8037, www.flyultralight.com

▪ ZONA SUR

Nightlife

Cabinas Iguana Iguana *(Puerto Jiménez, tel 2735-5158).* Popular outdoor bar with pool and darts.
Centro Turístico Samoa *(Golfito, tel 2775-0233).* Open-air bar with pool, foosball, and darts competitions.
Juanita's Mexican Bar & Grill, Puerto Jiménez, see p. 254

Other Activities

Land-Sea Tours, Golfito, tel/fax 2775-1614, www.golfitocostarica.com

The Canopy Tours

Original Canopy Tour, Drake Bay, tel 2291-4465, www.canopytour.com

Diving

Aguila de Osa Inn, Drake Bay, see p. 253
Aventuras Maritimas Okeanos, tel 2257-0191 or 866/OKEANOS, www.okeanoscocoisland.com

Hiking

Reserva Biólogica Campanario, see p. 175. Treks, ecology courses.

Nature Tours

Aldea del Río Sportfishing *(Sierpe, tel 2788-1157, www.aldeadelrio.com).* Tours of the Terraba-Sierpe delta, Corcovado, etc., plus nighttime crocodile tour.
The "Bug Lady" Tour *(Agujitas, tel 8382-1619, www.thenighttour.com).* Fascinating nocturnal insect tour.
Tour Gaviotas de Osa *(Sierpe, tel 2788-1212, www.tgaviotas.com).* Tours of the Terraba-Sierpe delta and Osa.

Panning for gold

Asociación de Productores Villa Nueva, Dos Brazos de Río Tigre, tel 2775-1422, fax 2775-5045
CoopeUnorio *(Valle del Río Rincón, tel 2225-8966, fax 2735-5073).* Ex-miners cooperative.

Sea Kayaking

Kayaking provides a silent entrée into mangrove swamps.
Escondido Trex, Puerto Jiménez, tel 2735-5210, www.escondidotrex.com
Zancudo Boat Tours, Playa Zancudo, tel/fax 2776-0012, www.loscocos.com/boattours.htm

Sportfishing

Crocodile Bay Lodge, Puerto Jiménez, tel 800/733-1115, www.crocodilebay.com
Banana Bay Marina, Golfito, tel 2775-0838, www.bananabaymarina.com
Roy's Zancudo Lodge, Zancudo, tel 2776-0008 or 877/529-6980, fax 2776-0011, www.royszancudolodge.com. Closed Oct.

Whale-watching

Aldea del Río Sportfishing, see Nature Tours, this page.
Delfin Amor Marine Education Center, Drake Bay, tel 831/345-8484, www.divinedolphin.com

▪ SOUTH CENTRAL

Festivals

Día del Boyeros, May 15, San Isidro de El General. Traditional oxcarts, rodeos and more.
Festival de los Diablitos, Dec. 30, Boruca. Masked men disguised as animals and devils rush through the village creating harmless mayhem, aided by copious amounts of alcohol. The colorful Native American celebration lasts three days, and has an allegorical happy ending.

Other Activities

Durika Biological Reserve *(Buenos Aires, tel 2730-0657, www.durika.org).* Run as a commune.

Hiking up Chirripó

Two-day hike can be done solo (see feature pp. 192–193) or with a guide.
Costa Rica Trekking Adventures, San Isidro, tel 2771-4582, www.chirripo.com

Rafting

Ríos General and Chirripó are Class III or IV experiences.
Costa Rica Expeditions, see p. 262.
Explornatura, tel 2556-2070 or 66/571-2443, www.explornatura.com
Ríos Tropicales, see p. 260

▪ NORTHERN LOWLANDS

Festivals

Fería del Ganado, April, Ciudad Quesada. Costa Rica's largest cattle fair, with a parade *(tope),* rodeos, and festivities.

Nightlife

Volcán Look Disco, Fortuna, tel 2479-9690. The deafeningly loud music and whirling lights on display draw patrons from miles around. Dance classes offered.

Other Activities

Ballooning
Serendipity Adventures, Turrialba, tel 2558-1000, 877/507-1358, www.serendipity adventures.com

Canoe Trips
Laguna del Lagarto, Lagarto, tel 2289-8163, www.lagarto-lodge-costa-rica.com
Rancho Leona, see p. 259.
Selva Verde, see p. 255.
Tilajari Resort Hotel, see p. 255.

Canopy Tours
Costa Rica Arenal Canopy Tour, La Fortuna, tel 2479-9769, www.crarenalcanopy.com
SkyTrek, Arenal, tel 2479-9944, www.skytrek.com
Termales del Bosque, see p. 212.

Spelunking
Explore the Venado Caverns.
Aventuras Arenal, Fortuna, tel 2479-9133, www.arenal adventures.com

Fishing
Inland fishing at Caño Negro lagoon or Laguna de Arenal.
Caño Negro Natural Lodge, village of Caño Negro, tel 2265-3302, www.canonegrolodge.com
Hotel de Campo Caño Negro, village of Caño Negro, tel 2471-1012, www.canonegro.com

Horseback Riding
Desafio Adventure Company, La Fortuna, see p. 260.
El Gavilán Lodge, Puerto Viejo de Sarapiquí, tel 2766-6743, www.gavilanlodge.com
Hotel La Garza, Muelle, tel 2475-5222,www.hotellagarza.com
Tilajari Resort Hotel, see p. 255.

Rafting
Ríos Peñas Blancas and Sarapiquí both offer Class II and III trips.
Aguas Bravas, Puerto Viejo de Sarapiquí, tel 2292-2072, www.aguas-bravas.co.cr
Desafio Adventures, see p. 260.

Rain Forest Hiking
Chachagua Rainforest Lodge, see p. 254.
Selva Verde, see p. 255.

▪ THE CARIBBEAN

Festivals
Carnival, Oct. 12, Puerto Limón. Traditional Caribbean carnival with beauty pageants, parades, and music. Revelers flood the town to celebrate to the beat of calypso and reggae.

Nightlife
Johnny's Place *(Puerto Viejo, tel 2750-0445).* The liveliest hip-hop and reggae scene in the Caribbean.
Maxi *(Manzanillo, tel 2759-9086).* Unpretentious bar, with dancing.
Ricky's Bar *(Cahuita, tel 2755-0228).* Colorful restaurant/bar with live music, tropical cocktails, and a beer garden.

Other Activities
Puerto Viejo Tours, Puerto Viejo, tel/fax 2750-0306, www.ptoviejotours.com

Canoeing
Rent dugout canoes *(cayucas)* and motorized *pangas* to explore Tortuguero. Rent kayaks to visit Río Estrella's wetlands and Gandoca-Manzanillo.

Diving
Cahuita's small coral reef includes the remains of a small wreck. Gandoca-Manzanillo also has a coral reef.
Aquamor, Manzanillo, tel 2759-9012, email: aquamorel@racsa.co.cr
Reef Runner Divers, Puerto Viejo, tel/fax 2750-0480, www.reef runnerdivers.net

Dolphin Safaris
Talamanca Dolphin Foundation, Manzanillo, tel 2759-9115, www.dolphinlink.org

Fishing
Caribbean Expedition Lodge, Parismina, tel 888/341-5525, www.costaricasportfishing.com

Costa Rica Outdoors, tel 800/308-3394, www.costaricaout-doors.com. Offers fishing trips in Costa Rica's lakes, rivers, sea, and ocean.
Río Colorado Lodge, see p. 255.
Río Parismina Lodge, Parismina, tel 210/824-4442, www.riop.com
Silver King Lodge, see p. 255.
Tortuga Lodge & Gardens, see p. 256.

Hiking
You can hike alone in many places, but a guide is always recommended.
ATEC, (Asociación Talamanca de Ecoturismo y Conservación) Puerto Viejo, tel/fax 2750-0191, www.greencoast.com/atec.htm
Puerto Viejo Tours, see this page.

Horseback Riding
Cahuita Tours, Cahuita, tel 2755-0000, email: cahuitatours@yahoo.com
Seahorse Stables, Punta Cocles, tel 2750-0468, www.horseback ridingincostarica.com

Surfing
Puerto Viejo's legendary Salsa Brava wave kicks up during storm season. Boards can be rented, and there are specialized accommodations. Lesser spots include Playas Bonita and Portrete, north of Puerto Limón.

Turtle Research
Sign up as a volunteer, and help guard hatcheries against poaching and predation.
Caribbean Conservation Corps, Tortuguero, tel 224-9215 or 800/678-7853, www.cccturtle.org
Marine Turtle Conservation Project, c/o ATEC (see Hiking above).
Pacuare Nature Reserve, Pacuare, see p. 224.

INDEX

ILLUSTRATIONS CREDITS

Abbreviations for terms appearing below: (t) top; (b) bottom;(c) center; (l) left; (r) right:

Cover, Marco Saborio;

2-3, Michael Melford; 4, Mark Newman; 8, Mike & Corinna Blum/Collection of the pre-Colombian Gold Museum, Museums of the Central Bank of Costa Rica; 10, Imagestate; 12, Michael & Patricia Fogden; 13, Mike & Corinna Blum/Collection of the pre-Colombian Gold Museum, Museums of the Central Bank of Costa Rica; 14-15, Alex Webb/Magnum Photos; 17, Nicholas de Vore III/National Geographic Image Collection; 18, Danny Lehman/CORBIS; 20-21, Clive Sawyer/AA Photo Library; 22-23, T. John Skiffington; 25, William Thompson/National Geographic Image Collection; 27, Hulton Archive/Getty Images; 29, Getty Images; 31, William Thompson/National Geographic Image Collection; 32, Miguel Alvarez/AFP/Getty Images; 35, Sylvain Grandadam/age fotostock; 37, Michael Melford/National Geographic Image Collection; 38-39, Art Directors & TRIP Photo Library; 40, Bill Curtsinger/National Geographic Image Collection; 43, Imagestate; 45, Tom Blagden/Larry Ulrich Stock; 47, Tom Blagden/Larry Ulrich Stock; 48, Luiz Claudio Marigo; 53, Robert Harding Picture Library; 55, Clive Sawyer/AA Photo Library; 58, Ian Cumming/Axiom Photographic Agency Ltd.; 60, Mike & Corinna Blum/Collection of the pre-Colombian Gold Museum, Museums of the Central Bank of Costa Rica; 61, Superstock/zefa; 63, Isabel Cutler; 64, Isabel Cutler; 67, Mark Newman; 70, Barry Biesanz; 72, Waina Cheng Ward; 73 (up), Stephen J. Krasemann; 73 (low), Michael & Patricia Fogden; 74-80 (all), Clive Sawyer/AA Photo Library; 82, Christopher P. Baker; 84, Christer Fredriksson/Alamy; 86, Tom Till/drr.net; 88, Guido Cozzi/Atlantide Phototravel; 90, Lode Greven; 92, Tom Blagden/Larry Ulrich Stock; 97, Michael & Patricia Fogden; 99, Jon Arnold Images/Alamy; 102, Tony Morrison/South American Pictures; 106, Ian Cumming/Axiom Photographic Agency Ltd.; 108, Michael & Patricia Fogden; 110, Lode Greven; 112, Uwe Walz; 113, Doug Wechsler/naturepl.com; 114, Clive Sawyer/AA Photo Library; 116, Nik Wheeler; 117, Robert Francis/Robert Harding Picture Library; 118-119 (art), courtesy AA Photo Library; 119 (up), Kevin Schafer/CORBIS; 119 (low), Nik Wheeler; 120, Kevin Schafer/CORBIS; 121, André Rousseau/Travelvacation.com; 122, Tony Arruza; 123, Kevin Schafer/CORBIS; 126, Günter Ziesler; 129, Buddy Mays; 132, Marie Read; 133, Corey Wise/Alamy; 134-135, AA/Ann Winterbottom; 136, Nik Wheeler; 138, Eye Ubiquitous; 141, Philip van den Berg/HPH Publishing; 142, Doug Wechsler/naturepl.com; 143, AA/Ann Winterbottom; 144, Doug Wechsler/naturepl.com; 145, Macduff Everton/Image Bank/Getty Images; 146, Larry Ulrich; 150, D. Maybury/Art Directors & TRIP Photo Library; 152, Robert Francis/South American Pictures; 153, Lode Greven; 156, Dietermar Nill/naturepl.com; 158, Perry Mastrovito/Creatas/Jupiterimages; 159, Isabel Cutler; 160, Nik Wheeler; 162, Christer Fredriksson/Alamy; 164, Tony Arruza; 165, T. John Skiffington; 166, Clive Sawyer/AA Photo Library; 168, Clive Sawyer/AA Photo Library; 171, Lynn M. Stone/www.bciusa.com; 174, Steve Watkins/AA Photo Library; 179, Rod Williams/www.bciusa.com; 180-181, AA/Ann Winterbottom; 182, Stuart Westmorland/Getty Images; 184, Clive Sawyer/AA Photo Library; 186, Jim Clare/Oxford Scientific; 187, Michael & Patricia Fogden; 190, Michael & Patricia Fogden; 192, Clive Sawyer/AA Photo Library; 194, Michael & Patricia Fogden; 196, Steve Watkins/AA Photo Library; 198, Tom Blagden/Larry Ulrich Stock; 203, Phil Savoie/naturepl.com; 206, Michael & Patricia Fogden; 209, Tom Blagden/Larry Ulrich Stock; 210, Michael & Patricia Fogden; 211 (up), Michael & Patricia Fogden; 211 (low), Michael Fogden/Oxford Scientific; 212, Michael & Patricia Fogden; 213, Gary Braasch; 215, Ian Cumming/Axiom Photographic Agency Ltd.; 216, Steve Watkins/AA Photo Library; 217, Christer Fredriksson/Lonely Planet Images; 220, Michael & Patricia Fogden/naturepl.com; 222, Clive Sawyer/AA Photo Library; 226, Danny Lehman/CORBIS; 229, Christopher P. Baker; 230, Ian Cumming/Axiom Photographic Agency Ltd.; 231, Buddy Mays; 233, Michael Melford.

National Geographic
TRAVELER
Costa Rica

**National Geographic Traveler: Costa Rica
(Third Edition)
ISBN: 978-1-4262-0387-9**

The Library of Congress catalogued the first edition as follows:
Library of Congress Cataloging-in- Publication Data
Baker, Christopher
        National Geographic Traveler. Costa Rica
            p   cm
        Includes index.
        ISBN 0-7922-7946-8 (alk. paper)
            1. Costa Rica–Guidebooks. 1. National Geographic Society
    (U.S.)
    11. Title: Costa Rica
    DC16.N37 2000
    914.404'839—dc21   98-54974

    CIP

Printed in China

NATIONAL GEOGRAPHIC
TRAVELER

- **Alaska** (2nd Edition)
- **Amsterdam**
- **Arizona** (3rd Edition)
- **Austra**
- **Barcel**
- **Beijing**
- **Berlin**
- **Boston**
- **Califor**
- **Ca**
- **T**
- **C**
- **C**
- **C**

- **Los Angeles**
- **Madrid** (2nd Edition)
- **Mexico** (2nd Edition)

ion)

id Edition)

-
-
-
-
-
-
-
-
-
-
-
-
-
-
-
-
-
-

AVAILABLE WHEREVER BOOKS ARE SOLD